The two were left

c

JANUA LINGUARUM

STUDIA MEMORIAE
NICOLAI VAN WIJK DEDICATA

edenda curat

C. H. VAN SCHOONEVELD

Indiana University

Series Didactica, 19

THE TWO-WORD VERB

*A Dictionary of the Verb-Preposition Phrases
in American English*

by

GEORGE A. MEYER

1975

MOUTON

THE HAGUE · PARIS

ISBN 90 279 3323 5

Printed in The Netherlands

CONTENTS

Introduction

INTRODUCTION

1. WHY A DICTIONARY OF THE TWO-WORD VERB

The two-word verb has been for a century or more, and is today, the most active and creative pattern of word formation in the American language. New forms are being created constantly to express new concepts in many fields such as science, technology, social developments, art, sport, warfare, human relations, and mass communications. While new terminology in the sciences continues to be developed by using Greek and Latin word elements to describe events, processes, and relationships, the folk mentality takes more readily to the creation of the new vocabulary through the use of Anglo-Saxon and Early English elements to meet the need for new vocabulary in new fields of knowledge and activity.

The two-word verb pattern is at hand to furnish verb, noun and adjective elements needed for communication in our present day, rapidly evolving society.

Examples   *to dröp óut, a dróp öut*
            to bläst óff, the blást öff
            to wĭnd úp, the wínd ŭp, all wöund úp
            to sĭt ín, a sít ĭn (a teách ĭn, etc.)
            to drĭve ín, a drĭve ĭn

This type of verb and noun formation appears to be especially congenial to the American mind, although the production of new forms based on the pattern is not exclusively a feature of English as spoken and written in the United States.

American English seems destined to be for a century or more the dominant form of English in the world community. This dictionary is designed to help non-native speakers to understand and communicate more easily with other users of American English.

Millions of people all over the globe are learning English as a second language. The dictionaries and text books being used by many of them often pay little attention to the two-word verb. Our huge unabridged dictionaries are only partially successful in presenting and defining the terms. They are often done in fine print and are hard to find.

This dictionary will make available to teachers of English throughout the world and to advanced students a fairly compact, complete, and up-to-date presentation of the vocabulary, verbal, nominal, and adjectival, which the two-word verb has produced.

Foreigners in the United States, whether diplomats, business and professional men, students, or immigrants, will find it of great value in learning how to use these forms, which are generally thought of as "idioms" and for which textbooks give no satisfactory explanation.

Americans who use the forms so easily and so frequently, but who are unaware of the special problems of non-native speakers in learning to use them effectively, will gain a greater appreciation of this pattern of word usage in their own ever-growing vocabulary.

2. WHAT IS A TWO-WORD VERB?

The two-word verb consists of two elements: (1) a verb, and (2) a second element which, combining closely with the verb, produces a verbal concept that the verb alone does not have. The meaning of the two elements combined is a *plus* over the meaning of the verb by itself.

Using the verb **to shoot,** we can produce a great variety of differing verbal concepts by changing the second element. For example — **shoot up, shoot off, shoot out, shoot by.** The "plus" value is given by the second element in somewhat the same manner as the prefixes *con-, e-, in-,* and *pro-* change the aspect of the Latin verb *ducere* 'to lead'. But the two-word verb has much more flexibility and subtlety than the Latin verb with its prefixes. A native speaker of English will be able to use the concept **shoot up** in a great variety of situations. The expression can be either transitive or intransitive.

Examples   *The rocket shot up. They shot up an Atlas (rocket). The bandits shot up the town* Then take **shoot off.** *The rocket shot off into space. They shot a rocket off into space. He shot off his gun. William Tell shot the apple off. He is always shooting off his mouth.*

These concepts are complicated for the non-native student of English, but the subtleties of meaning, word order, and intonation are all second nature to the native speaker, and they follow definite patterns.

The meaning which the second element adds to form the total concept may be one of the primitive, literal meanings of the element, as in **mount up, lead out, ride through,** but much of the time it is an extended meaning that has developed during the thousand year period since the element came into common use, as in **shut up** 'be quiet', **fall out** 'break friendship', **get through** 'finish'.

The most productive second elements used to form two-word verbs are seventeen in number: *about, across, along, around, aside, away, back, by, down, in, off, on, out, over, through, under, up.* (See below p. 17, for the different meanings of these second elements, when used to form two-word verbs.)

3. ORIGIN AND DEVELOPMENT

The two-word verb pattern developed from two sources.

1. Old Anglo-Saxon intransitive verbs of motion such as *go, come, ride, walk, fly.* Verbs of this type could have certain elements as prefixes which showed the direction of movement in space made by the subject of the verb. In the 9th and 10th centuries the elements *in, off, on, out, through,* and *up* were commonly used in this way.

2. Old Anglo-Saxon transitive verbs denoting actions that involved movement in space such as *strike, cut, dig, send, bring, bear.* They could be prefixed with the same elements that were used on the intransitive verbs of motion.

The prefixes added to intransitive verbs indicated originally the position in space of the subject of the verb while moving or after having moved. Added to transitive verbs, they indicated the position in space of the object of the verb which the action of the verb aimed to bring about.

By the 11th century these prefixes began to be shifted to a position of loose suffixation after the verb, so that you did not say *He has outgone,* but *He has gone out.* You did not say, *He updug the roots,* but *He dug up the roots.*

This change came about as English gradually developed what we call logical word order, for narrative and expository prose. That order was to become in brief: (1) Subject; (2) Verb; (3) Predicate. The prefixed elements denoting the direction in space of the action were felt to be secondary in importance to the action itself, and therefore were placed after the verb. In the same way predicate nouns and adjectives came to follow intransitive verbs, while adverbs and noun objects came generally to follow transitive verbs.

This word order was well established in English by the time of Chaucer, the English language versions of the Bible, and Shakespeare, and by this time the two-word verb was a fixed pattern for the creation of new verbal concepts.

From the 9th to the 16th century various other words came to be used as second elements in forming two-word verbs. The dating of the appearance of seventeen of the elements can be established by checking through the Oxford English Dictionary.

9th century . . . . *in, on, out, up*
10th century . . . . *away, by, off*
11th century . . . . *over, through*

12th century	. . . .	*down, under, about*
13th century	. . . .	*along, aside*
15th century	. . . .	*back*
16th century	. . . .	*across, around*

This development sets English apart from the other Indo-European languages. Sanskrit, Greek, Latin, Russian, and other major languages that share a common origin with the Germanic tongues had and still maintain in their modern descendants a liking for prefixation as a means of giving semantic variation to verbal root words. But English took a different turn. It developed a flexible and very productive pattern of loose suffixation.

This pattern grew gradually, from the 9th century to the 16th, while the older pattern of prefixation weakened. The early language had numerous verbal prefixes, some of which finally disappeared and are now found only in isolated and often archaic words. The once very common unstressed prefixes *a-*, *be-*, and *for-* ceased being creative, and survive only in such fossils as *arise, awaken, bedeck, bedew, forfend, forget*. Their functions were taken over by the new two-word verb pattern. We now say **rise up, wake up, deck out, moisten over** or **up, black out.**

Even some of the old stressed prefixes are no longer productive. *Aet-, bi-, fore-, forth-, full-, of-* as prefixes have been abandoned. *Aetberan* becomes **bear** or **take away;** *bistanden* becomes **stand around** or **stand by;** *forestanden* becomes **stand out;** *forthcumen* becomes **come out;** *fullgrowan* is not **grow up;** *ofgiefan* is now **give up.**

The once so common intensive prefix *to-* has left no mark in present day English. Its functions are taken over by the second elements up, down, off, out, through, etc.

Examples	*to-beatan* > **beat up, beat down, beat out**
	to-blawan > **blow off, blow down, blow out**
	to-brecan > **break up, break down, break through**

4. NEW MEANINGS FOR THE SECOND ELEMENTS

Used with intransitive verbs of motion, the meanings of the second elements remained close to the early or primitive sense — that of the direction of movement in space.

However, as these second elements came to be used more and more with transitive verbs, the nature of the action denoted by the verb allowed for numerous variations in the sense of the second elements.

For example, *up* in its earliest documented use (9th century) meant 'up from the surface of the earth'. In the 11th century, it could mean 'up from below the earth's surface'. You could dig (delve) things up. Later you could say, *We dug up the field and broke up the soil.* Still later you could *break up a riot or a meeting.* One could then say, *The meeting broke up*, and *We were all broken up about it.*

It is this gradual acquisition of new meanings for the second elements that has made the two-word verb so much of a problem for non-native users of English. Even native speakers have trouble in explaining many of our commonest everyday expressions using two-word verbs to non-native speakers.

They may *throw up their hands* and *give up* when asked to do so. They may say *I guess it's just idiomatic* and remain as much confused as the questioner.

5. A BRIEF HISTORY OF THE SECOND ELEMENT *UP*

Up is the most frequently used second element in present day American English. It has acquired many new meanings in the course of a thousand years, from the 9th century to the 20th century. There is no reason to believe that it will not acquire additional meanings as need arises.

1. In the 9th century, *up* was prefixed to simple verbs. Ex. *up-hebben* 'lift up', *up-wenden* 'go up'. It signified up from the surface of the earth.

2. In the 11th century and after, *up* follows the verb. It can signify up from below the earth's surface, or up without reference to the earth's surface. Water comes up, out of the ground. Food comes up from the stomach.

3. In the 13th century, *up* can mean 'from a lower to a higher status', socially or spiritually. One can **rise up, mount up, come up** to some condition or ideal.

4. In the 14th century, *up* can mean 'into a state of higher activity'. One can **stir up, rouse up, speed up, work up** energies.

5. In the 15th century, *up* can mean 'to or towards a greater maturity or completeness'. One can **grow up, end up, add up.**

6. In the 16th century, *up* can mean 'so as to separate into many parts or pieces'. One can **break up** a surface, or other solid objects. One can **cut up, slice up, carve up** meats and other softer materials.

These developments took place without the influence of American English. In America *up* became a very active element. In popular speech it came to express, in its use with many verbs, a busy, energetic activity, with some purpose behind it. Many objections have been made to this development, by purists and traditonalists, who say that the simple verb adequately expresses the idea to be conveyed, but most Americans find that the added element is important for the full sense of what they want to say.

In present day American English *up* may express the following notions:

1. To a good or better state or condition.
   Ex. **polish up, clean up, paint up, tidy up.**
2. For a purpose or end, generally a good one.
   Ex. **cook up, fix up, get up** (a party or game), **make up** (after a quarrel).

    3. In preparation for something to follow.
        Ex. **study up, bone up, dress up, tune up.**
    4. To a closer or more compact state.
        Ex. **bundle up, cuddle up, squeeze up, tie up.**

In many instances the speaker may have in mind more than one of the accepted meanings of *up* as listed above. This situation in which he uses the expression, and the awareness on the part of his listeners, determine for both the speaker and the listener the full sense of the expression.

6. THE TWO-WORD VERB IN COLLOQUIAL ENGLISH

About forty percent of the English vocabulary is of Germanic origin. Common everyday spoken English is largely made up of words and expressions drawn from this source which we will call the folk vocabulary. About sixty percent of the English vocabulary comes from Latin sources, through French, and by direct borrowing from Latin. This part of the vocabulary was gradually added to the basic Germanic stock of words, first through the influence of the Church, later by the Norman Conquest, and still later by the Renaissance, and the development of literature, philosophy, and science. This portion of the word stock we will call the learned-literary vocabulary. In time, many of those words found their way into common everyday speech so that one finds a great number of doublets in colloquial English. This is especially true of verbs. The verb *enter* is learned-literary. It has a folk equivalent **come in, go in.** *Exit* is learned-literary. Its folk equivalent is **go out, come out.**

    The formal written language will often choose the learned-literary form, but informal conversational English usually chooses the folk form. It is important, therefore, that people who wish to communicate easily and naturally in English should spend a great deal of time becoming familiar with the two-word verb and how to use it.

    The following is a list of 26 learned-literary verbs with their equivalent in the folk vocabulary.

Learned-Literary	*Folk*
abandon	give up
accelerate	speed up, hurry up, rev up
advance	move on, move up, go on, keep on
arrive	come in, get in, get back
continue	go on, keep on, keep up, stay on
defer	put off, give in (to)
depart	take off, be off, go away, get away
deposit	put down, set down, get down

descend	go down, come down, get down
enter	go in, come in, walk in, get in
excavate	dig up, dig out
exit	go out, come out, walk out, get out
explode	blow up, set off
imagine	think up, figure out
inflate	blow up, puff up
invent	make up, find out
masticate	chew up
mount	go up, come up, get up
penetrate	go in, get in, go through
prepare	make up, set up, fix up, get up
proceed	go on, keep on, carry on, get on (with)
remove	take away, take off, take out
return	go back, come back, get back, be back
revert	go back, turn back
surrender	give up, give in
traverse	cross over, go over, go across

7. TWO-WORD VERBS IN THE SPOKEN LANGUAGE HOW TO STRESS THE VERB, NOUN, AND ADJECTIVE FORMS

When using two-word verbs, or the nouns and adjectival forms derived from them, in speaking English, certain definite patterns of stress and pitch must be observed. The pattern varies according to the use of the form in a sentence.

In American speech much use is made of stress and pitch to give the full meaning of what is said. The "most important" word in a group of words (a thought group) is spoken with more force (stress) and a higher tone (pitch) than the other words. This greater stress and higher pitch will be indicated by a long acute accent over the stressed vowel of the word.

Examples   *begín, énter, come dówn.*

"Less important" words are spoken with less force and a lower tone. These will be indicated by the sign .. placed over the stressed vowel.

Examples   *for a lóng tïme, täke them óut, he cäme ïn yésterday.*

The words without stress marks are said quickly, with less stress and lower pitch than the "important" and "less important" words.

Non-native speakers of English should practice the following exercises in order to become familiar with the stress and pitch patterns.

I.   With intransitive verbs of motion.
    a. The verb as a vocabulary item
        cöme abóut, -acróss, -alóng, -aróund, -asíde, -awáy, -báck, -bý, -dówn, -ín, -óff, -ón, -óut, -óver, -throúgh, -únder, -úp.
        Repeat the exercise using the verbs *get, go, walk, put, ride*, etc.
    b. Use the same series of second elements in a short sentence in which the second element is the final word.

Examples   *I want to wälk abóut, -acróss, etc.*

    c. Use the same series in the simple past tense.

Examples   *He rän abóut, -acróss*, etc.

    d. Use the same series in the future tense.

Examples   *They will hürry abóut, -acróss*, etc.

II. With transitive verbs
    a. When the direct object is a pronoun, the pronoun comes between the first and second elements, and the same stress pattern is used as for intransitive verbs of motion.

Examples   *I want to möve it abóut, täke them acróss, brïng her alóng, türn it aróund, püt them asíde, thröw it awaý, sënd him báck, drïve it bý, knöck them dówn, püsh it ín, täke them óff, hëlp you ón, püt him óut, röll them óver, türn it únder, lëad us thróugh, brëak it úp.*

    b. When the direct object is a noun, the noun may come either between the two elements or after the second element. Normally the noun is the "most important" word in the sentence and it therefore will receive the primary stress in the group. The two elements of the two-word verb will receive secondary stress.

Examples   *She püt her hánd öut.*
               or, *She püt öut her hánd.*

    c. Practice the following exercise, reading in succession the two sentences in the left hand column followed by the sentence in the right hand column.

With noun object | *With pronoun object*

1. They bröught aboüt a chánge.
   They bröught a chánge aboüt.
   They bröught it abóut.

2. He göt acröss his méssage.
   He göt his méssage acröss.
   He göt it acróss.

3. She toök alöng her drésses.
   She toök her drésses alöng.
   She toök them alóng.

4. We sënt aroünd a nótice.
   We sënt a nótice aroünd.
   We sënt it aroúnd.

5. She püt asïde her sávings.
   She püt her sávings asïde.
   She püt them asíde.

6. Let's täke awäy their háts.
   Let's täke their háts awäy.
   Let's täke them awáy.

7. Be sure to gïve bäck the móney.
   Be sure to gïve the móney bäck.
   Be sure to gïve it báck.

8. He püt bÿ ten döllars a wéek.
   He püt ten döllars a wéek bÿ.
   He püt them bý.

9. Cäll döwn the chíldren.
   Cäll the chíldren döwn.
   Cäll them dówn.

10. She lët ïn the cát.
    She lët the cát ïn.
    She lët it ín.

11. Please türn öff the wáter.
    Please türn the wáter öff.
    Please türn it óff.

12. He will türn ön the rádio
    He will türn the rádio ön.
    He will türn it ón

13. They will drïve öut the énemy.
    They will drïve the énemy öut.
    They will drïve them óut.

14. I'll sënd över the létters.
    I'll sënd the létters över.
    I'll sënd them óver.

15. He püt thröugh our télegram.
    He püt our télegram thröugh.
    He püt it thróugh.

16. They türned ünder the sód.
    They türned the sód ünder.
    They türned it únder.

17. He wröte üp his nótes.
    He wröte his nótes üp.
    He wröte them úp.

III. The present participle used as a noun, or as an adjective has the primary stress on the second element.

   a. As a noun, *He received a drëssing dówn, a beäting úp, a goïng óver, a bäwling óut, a cälling dówn.*

   b. As an adjective. *Her parents gave her a cöming óut pärty, a göing awáy pärty. This is our türning óff pläce. She is taking a slïmming dówn trëatment, a fättening úp dïet. A fïnishing óff, a cleäning úp pröcess. Sëtting úp ëxercises.*

IV. The past participle used as an adjective has primary stress on the second element.

Examples　　*His shoes were wörn óut.*
　　　　　　　The ice was bröken úp.
　　　　　　　His mind was mäde úp.
　　　　　　　The car was bröken dówn.
　　　　　　　The clothes were püt awáy.

V. The noun formed directly on the two-word verb is made simply by reversing the stress pattern. The first element receives primary stress and the second element receives secondary stress.

Exercise: Read across from the left hand column to the right hand column.

Verb	*Noun*
bäck dówn	a báck-döwn
blöw úp	a blów-üp
breäk thróugh	a bréak-thröugh
cöme ón	a cóme-ön
coünt dówn	a coúnt-döwn
cöver úp	a cóver-üp
drïve ín	a dríve-ïn
feëd báck	a feédbäck
goöf óff	a góof-öff
hoök úp	a hoóküp
loök óut	a loókoüt
shöw óff	a shów-öff
sït ín	a sít-in
täke óver	a tákeöver

Note: Two-word nouns that have been in use for a long time are written as one word, cf. **lookout, takeover.** More recent forms have a hyphen between the two elements, cf. **drive-ïn, sit-in.** Some can be found written as two separate words, cf.**love in.**

VI. The noun form can also be used as an adjective, and will keep the noun form stress pattern.

Examples　　*A cóme-ön sïgnal, a dríve-ïn theäter, a féedbäck devïce, a lóokout töwer, a sít-döwn strïke, a sít-ïn demonsträtion, a túrn-döwn cöllar, a túrn-öff välve.*

8. PREPOSITIONS NOT USED TO FORM TWO-WORD VERBS

At, for, from, into, to (with exceptions noted below), and *with* do not form two-word verbs. They serve as prepositions after verbs, to govern noun objects. They are not stressed, but are reduced in sound. This fact proves that they are not second elements of a two-word verb, which must always be stressed. They are often found at the end of a thought group, or a sentence. They are then called dangling prepositions.

Examples

Regular formation	*Dangling preposition*
We want to look at that picture.	That's the picture we looked at.
They'll call for a taxi.	Here's the taxi you called for.
He comes from Texas.	Where does he come from?
She drove into the park.	What park did she drive into?
We often think of them.	Who are you thinking of?
He'll talk with some students.	Who will he talk with?

Thirteen of the second elements used to form two-word verbs can be used also as prepositions. It is easy to determine that they are being used as prepositions, because a noun or pronoun object will always follow. The object can *not* be placed *between* the verb and the second element, which position is normal in two-word verbs.

Examples

With noun object	*With pronoun object*
He walked about the garden.	He walked about it.
She came across the room.	She came across it.
They drove along the river.	They drove along it.
She looked around the corner.	She looked around it.
I sat by my friend.	I sat by him.
They marched down the street.	They marched down it.
He sat in the chair.	He sat in it.
Johnny fell off the chair.	He fell off it.
They wrote on the wall.	They wrote on it.
He looked out (of) the window	He looked out (of) it.
They rode over the bridge.	They rode over it.
She peeked through the curtain.	She peeked through it.
He climbed up the tree.	He climbed up it.

9. *TO* AS A SECOND ELEMENT

To is no longer employed in forming two-word verbs. Following is a list of older formations using this element, with sample sentences showing their use.

bring tó   'to cause to regain consciousness'.
Ex. They brought him tó by throwing cold water on his head.

come tó   'to regain consciousness; to come back to reality'.

Ex. She fainted at the sight of blood, but came tó after a few minutes. His mind was wandering during the long, tiresome speech, but he came tó with a start when the music began.

fall tó   'to begin vigorously some activity'.

Ex. They fell tó at their leader's command. [Started doing what he ordered.]
When the food was placed on the table the workers fell tó with a will. [Began to eat hungrily.]

lay tó   'to fight vigorously, especially in person to person combat'.
See **fall tó.**

set tó   'to begin vigorously some activity'.
See **fall tó.**

Three nautical terms

heave tó   'to bring a ship close to another, or to a dock'.

lay tó   '(of a ship) bring to a stop, heading into the wind'.

lie tó   '(of a ship) be at rest against the dock or in a safe place'.

To is also found with verbs used to show the *complete* closing of a door.

Examples   The door came tó.
He banged the door tó.
He pulled the door tó.
He pushed the door tó.
He shoved the door tó.
He slammed the door tó.

10. EXTENDED TWO-WORD VERBS

Two of the second elements that form two-word verbs are often used with other second elements to form what could be called three-word verbs. These elements are *back* when it means 'in a reverse direction', and *on* when it means 'forward', in continuing motion.

This combination makes it possible to express in very economical fashion an action that has two "aspects", or special meanings attached to the verb. The combination can be made with transitive or intransitive verbs.

Examples   with *back*, and intransitive *get*.

He went up on the roof but got back down when he heard the telephone.

They got out of the car to pick some flowers, then got back in.

Johnny climbed onto the top of the table, but got back off when his mother called to him.

When his mother left the room, he got back on again [on the table].

He squeezed into the narrow opening, then got back out, for fear of being trapped.

He crossed the river at one o'clock, and got back over before two.

He had entered the garden by a hole in the fence, then got back through when he saw the gardener.

He went away from the tree, but got back under when the rain started.

She had fallen down from the chair, but got back up immediately.

Examples   with *back* and transitive *put*.

He picked up the book, then put it back down in a hurry.

She took the pen out of the drawer, signed the check, and put it back in [in the drawer].

She took off her hat, and after a moment put it back on.

The person who let the cat in had better put it back out.

Whoever took the cover off the piano should put it back over. [Over the piano.]

Those presents are supposed to be left under the tree. Now put them back under. [Under the Christmas tree.]

If the dishes fall off the shelf, just put them back up. [Up on the shelf.]

Examples   with *on* and intransitive verbs. It has the feeling of urging someone to do something.

It's dangerous up on that ladder. Come on down!

We're glad to see you. Come on in! [Into our house.]

Come on out! We're going to play a game. [Children urging their friends to come out of the house.]

We're having a party at our house. Come on over!

We decided to come on through without stopping for dinner. [Finish our trip.]

Come on up! We're expecting you. [Said to people who are downstairs.]

Sometimes there can be three second elements which then show three different "aspects" to the action.

Examples   with *on* and *back* plus one of the other second elements. *On* will have the meaning 'without stopping' as well as one of urgency. *Back* will mean reversing the action.

Come on back in! I have something to tell you [You have gone out. Come back inside. Don't stop.]

Go on back out! I told you to stay outside for a while. [A mother speaking sharply to a child who came back into the house.]

I don't want the children downstairs now. Take them on back up!

These combinations are common in folk speech, where the two-word verb is most at home. In small-town Ohio at the turn of the century it was possible to hear even more elaborate forms.

Examples   Now, Tommy, you come right back on down out of there. [To a boy who has climbed into a tree or the hay mow.]

11. HOW TO USE THE DICTIONARY

All verbs are entered in alphabetical order.

A definition of each verb follows. If the verb is of the type that has different meanings when used as a two-word verb, the verb will be entered separately for each meaning, e.g. **Turn I, Turn II, Turn III.**

The two-word verbs derived from the simple verb follow in the alphabetical order of their second elements.

After each two-word verb will be found the abbreviation T if the verb is transitive; the abbreviation I if the verb is intransitive.

In parentheses following the abbreviations T or I will be one or more numbers which refer to the meaning or meanings of the second element in this particular situation. Check these numbers on the chart of Different Meanings of the Second Elements (p. 17).

After the parentheses will be a sentence illustrating the use of the form.

In brackets following the sentence will be a phrase or sentence in simple language showing the meaning of the expression used.

Examples   add up T (4) When you have added up that column of figures, give
me the total. [Completed the addition.]

             I (2,4) The budget figures add up to over three billion dollars.
[Amount to.]

A series of exercises for practice in the use of two-word verbs will be found beginning
with page (9).

To get a good introduction to the use of the second elements in conversational
and informal English, a student of the language should begin by a close study of the
sentences used to illustrate the different meanings produced by them when used
with the verbs *be, come, cut, get, go, put, run, set, strike, take, throw, turn,* and *walk.*

12. THE DIFFERENT MEANINGS OF THE SECOND ELEMENTS

In the following chart are listed alphabetically the seventeen second elements which
are most often used to form two-word verbs. They are all words which in their
earliest history indicated *location* or *direction* in *space.* Number 1 gives the early
meaning, and the succeeding numbers show the gradual development for extended
meanings that were acquired in the course of a thousand years of growth of the
English language. As was demonstrated in the above history of the element *up,* the
new meanings develop from the use of the element with certain types of transitive
verbs which could permit extended meanings. For example, to *dig up roots* (bring
them above the surface of the earth) leads easily to the idea of *dig up the soil.*

The exact history of each element would be hard to determine since that history
could be found mainly in folk speech, which the written language has not fully
recorded.

As far as was possible, the meanings given in the chart are listed in chronological
order, with the most modern developments in final position.

Each form listed in the dictionary will have a number referring back to this chart,
so that a person can check back and compare the dictionary item with the meaning
of the element as listed.

About   1. To or in the vicinity; near.
              2. Here and there, without regular plan or system.
              3. In or into a circle; making a turn.
              4. Into effect.

Across   1. From one side to or toward the other.
              2. On the other side.

Along   1. In a progressive manner, forward.
              2. As a companion or colleague; with someone or something.
              3. In a continuous manner; for an indefinite time.

Around	1. To or in the vicinity; near.
	2. Here and there, without plan or system.
	3. Into or making a circle; into an improved condition.
	4. Into agreement.
	5. In a companionable way; socially involved.
Aside	1. To or toward the side.
	2. Out of the way; away.
Away	1. To or toward another place or condition; onward.
	2. From a place.
	3. From contact or close association.
	4. From an earlier state or condition.
	5. In or into a special or secret place.
	6. In a continuous manner; for an indefinite time.
Back	1. To, toward or at the rear.
	2. In a rearward position; behind.
	3. At, in or to a place of original departure.
	4. To or toward a former state or condition.
	5. To or toward an original source or speaker.
By	1. To or in the vicinity; near.
	2. Pausing in passing; going past; past.
	3. Aside; apart; in a special place.
	4. Through difficulties or hardship.
Down	[In general the opposite of *up*.]
	1. Toward or in a lower position; to or toward the ground.
	2. To a lower level or degree; to a worse condition; from a past time.
	3. To or for a lower price; to the highest bidder.
	4. To a halt; so as to overtake or find; to completion or death.
	5. In a vigorous or threatening manner; so as to test.
	6. To a reduced size, strength or quality; into pieces.
	7. Into writing; on paper or record.
In	[In general the opposite of *out*.]
	1. To or on the inside from someplace outside; into.
	2. Into the surface; so as to penetrate; as an outline.
	3. So as to enclose or bar passage to.
	4. Into an organization or group activity; into office.
	5. Into a mixture or total; into a system or structure.
	6. Into a disciplined or usable condition.
	7. To or at a point of exhaustion; to a stop; to death.
	8. Into so as to challenge; bearing ill will; fraudulently.
	9. In a positive or enthusiastic way; observantly.
Off	[In general, the opposite of *on*, when *on* means in contact with a surface.]

1. Away from a surface; to or at a distance.
2. Away from a place or position; away from a group.
3. So as to divide or separate; bar passage.
4. Out of duty or service; in a canceled or non-functioning state.
5. To or in a discontinued or exhausted state; to a decision; to death.
6. From a list or record; to a lower level; as a deduction.
7. So as to free from excess, obstruction or pollution.
8. In or into action or execution; into possession.
9. In a regrettable, loud, or hurried way.
10. To a complete or satisfying degree; in a congenial way.

On [There are two distinct meanings of *on*.]

I. In contact with the surface of something.
  1. On top of; on the surface of; inside.
  2. In or into figurative contact with.
  3. In position for use or operation.
  4. United with or at the end of.

II. With verbs of motion, indicating onward, continuing movement.
  1. Forward in space or time; progressing.
  2. In a continuous manner.
  3. In direction toward something.
  4. Into a functioning state. The opposite of Off 4.
  5. In an excessive or disgraceful manner; as an adversary.

Out [In general, the opposite of *in*, or *into* a place. Usually followed by *of* when the place is named.]

1. Away from the inside or center.
2. In or into the open air; in public; socially.
3. From a hidden or complex source.
4. From a group; from a competition, organization or group activity; from operation.
5. Beyond possession or control.
6. From an original position; into a state of detachment or disagreement.
7. In a detailed manner; to a logical conclusion.
8. To a state of discomfort, exhaustion or extinction; to an end or finish.
9. To the fullest degree; energetically; totally.
10. In an extended manner; continuously.
11. So as to gain substance or put on flesh.

Over [Usually the opposite of *under*.]

1. Above; in a higher place; overhead.
2. Covering the surface in every place or part.
3. From one side or place to another; from inside to outside.

4. As a remainder or surplus; in excess.
5. From or as if from the perpendicular; down or upside down.
6. From beginning to end.
7. A second time; repeating the action; temporarily.
8. To or at an end or stop; completely.

Through
1. From one end or side to the other; through in a spatial sense.
2. Over the whole distance to a destination, without stopping.
3. From beginning to end of a project or activity.
4. To a successful finish or completion.
5. To an unhappy or unsuccessful end.

Under
[In space relations, the opposite of *over*.]
1. In or through a place beneath; below.
2. Directly underneath; in contact with the lower surface of.
3. Below the surface of; covered or hidden by.
4. In or to a lower position or state.
5. To a lower amount or total.

Up
[In general, the opposite of *down*.

Up is the most frequently used of the 17 second elements. The speaker may, with some verbs, have more than one of the following meanings in his mind.]
1. To or toward a higher or previous position in space.
2. To an increased level or degree; to an improved condition; to maturity.
3. To or into a confined state; closely.
4. To a full degree or extent; completely.
5. In a determined or lively way; as a matter of endurance.
6. In a regrettable way; badly.
7. Into existence or operation; under consideration.
8. In or to a finished state; over.
9. Before an official body; in public.
10. In, into or as a group; into military service.
11. In preparation; taking place.
12. In or into a capable or informed state (for).
13. So as to arrive or approach; to a stop.
14. Over the telephone.
15. Resembling in external appearance.
16. As the last step in a sequence; as a consequence.
17. So as to find or recognize.

THE DICTIONARY

A

Act   To behave or conduct oneself in a particular fashion; do the work of an actor.

    act out   T (7)   The man who had confessed his crime, acted out the scene for the police. [He performed it as would an actor.]

    act over   T (8)   He acted the scene over, at the request of the jury. [A second time.]

    act through   T (3)   He acted the scene through. [From beginning to end.]

    act up   **1.** I (2,6)   The children acted up shamefully after their parents left. [They behaved very badly.)   **2.** I (2,6)   My car acted up last night. [It behaved badly. There was some mechanical difficulty.] See **kick up 2.**

Add   To unite or join so as to increase the number.

    add in   **1.** T (1,5)   By adding in a teaspoon of salt you will improve the flavor. [Into the food being prepared.]   **2.** T (5)   You should add in the taxi fare when you make out your expense account. [In with the other items.]

    add on   T (I,4)   They added on an extra coach when the train reached Ogden, because of the heavy traffic. [Attached it to the other coaches.]

    add over   T (8)   Those figures are not correct. You'll have to add them over. [Repeat the action.]

    add up   **1.** T (4)   When you have added up that column of figures, give me the total. [Completed the addition.]   **2.** I (2,4)   The budget figures add up to over three billion dollars. [Amount to.]   **3.** I (4)   It (all) adds up. [It is logical. The result or conclusion is what we think is correct.] See **count up.**

Air   To expose to the air, ventilate.

    air out   **1.** T (1)   Let's open the windows and air out the room. It has needed a good airing out for a long time. [Replace bad air with good.]   **2.** T (3)   The committee's job is to air out the rumors of graft and favoritism. [Bring them into the open.]

Amount   To form a total, add up.

    amount up   I (2)   When you think of the cost of a college education — the books, the travel expenses, the clothing, the medical fees — it (all) amounts up. [The cost is high.]

Analyze   To separate into constituent parts or elements.

    analyze out   T (4)   Extract one substance from a complex of substances, by chemical analysis.

Answer   To reply, respond to.

    answer back   I (3,5)   When father accused our son of telling a lie, he answered back that there was no proof of it. [He spoke angrily.] See **talk back, throw back (at).**

answer up I (5,9) If they ask you whether you need some help, you must answer up. [Speak frankly and openly.] See **speak up.**

Anger To make angry.

anger up T (2) She was all angered up at the suggestion that she must leave. [Very angry.]

Ante Poker. To put one's initial stake into the pot.

ante in I (5) Poker. You'll have to ante in if you wish to join (or continue) the game. [Put a chip or coin in the pot, or pool.]

ante up 1. I (4,10) Poker. Ante up, old timer, if you want to play in this round. [Put your coin or chip in the pot.] **2.** I (4,10) We all anted up to help pay for the refreshments. [We paid our share.] See **chip in.**

Argue To present reasons for or against a thing.

argue away I (6) The two men argued away for an hour or more, without reaching agreement. [The argument was long and energetic.]

argue down T (1,4,5) He wanted to postpone the meeting but we argued him down. [His idea was defeated.]

argue on I (II 2) He argued on (and on) till we all wished he would sit down. [He refused to stop.]

argue out T (7) They argued the matter out, and finally reached agreement. [Talked of all the possibilities.]

Arm To provide with arms, weapons.

arm up **1.** I (2,10) The guerillas are arming up for an attack on the government. [Increasing the supply of arms.] **2.** T (2,10) The government armed up the militia to combat the guerillas. See **arm up 1.**

Ascend To move, climb or go upward.

ascend up I (1) The disciples saw Jesus ascending up into Heaven. [Rising from the earth.]

Ask To invite guests.

ask With the meaning of "invite to come".

ask back T (3) We asked him back. [Back to our house.]

ask down T (1) We asked him down. [To our apartment from one above us.]

ask in T (1) We asked him in. [Into our house, etc.]

ask over T (3) We asked him over. [To our house from across the street, or elsewhere.]

ask up **1.** T (1) We asked him up. [Upstairs to our apartment.] **2.** I (5,9) You'll have to ask up, if you want them to listen to your request. [Be persistent in asking.] See **speak up.**

Assist To give help.

assist up T (1) He ran to the old woman who had fallen down, and assisted her up. [Helped her to get up.] See **help up.**

Auction To sell by auction.

auction off T (1) He needs cash. He's going to auction off his library [Sell his books at public auction.]

Average To have or show an average.

average out I (8) The bank averaged out on its stock transactions. [It finished the business without loss, or at a profit.]

average up **1.** T (4) If you average up your daily travel expenses, they will be around $20.00. [Make a careful counting and comparison.] **2.** I (4,10) Young people of today average up very well in comparison with those of twenty years ago. [Are equal or better.]

B

Baby To treat a person or thing as a baby.

baby along T (1) Sport. He babied the puck along, until he found an opening for a shot. [Hockey. Move forward with the puck, handling it gently as one would a baby.] v. nurse along.

baby up T (2) You can win her affection by babying her up. [Treating her as you would a baby.]

Back I To move backward, to the rear.

back away **1.** I (2) He backed away from the fire because it was too hot. [Stepped backwards.] **2.** I (4) He backed away from the idea of using force. [He was not willing to use force.]

back down **1.** I (1) Johnny started up the ladder, but backed down when his mother called to him. [Down the ladder.] **2.** I (4) He insisted that he would do as he planned, but we made him back down. [Change his mind.]

back in **1.** I (1) He opened the garage door and backed in. [Drove his car in, in reverse.] **2.** T (1) He backed the car in without any trouble.

back off **1.** I (1) Noticing that he had driven onto the neighbor's lawn he backed off quickly. [Off the lawn.] **2.** T (1) You've driven your car right onto my flower bed. Please back it off. [Off the fiower bed.] **3.** I (1) The two men had been arguing heatedly, when one of them backed off and swung at the other. [Stepped back in order to strike.]

back out **1.** I (1) He put the car in low gear and backed out slowly. [Out of the garage.] **2.** T (1) He backed the car out slowly. [Out of the garage.] **3.** I (6) We thought we had reached an agreement, but three of the people backed out. [They changed their minds.] See **bug out, drop out.**

back up **1.** I (13) If you back up a little the hose will reach. [Up closer to the gasoline pump.] **2.** T (13) You'll have to back your car up a little. The hose won't reach. [Up to the pump.]

Back II To give help or support. Originally to stand behind a person, supporting him from the rear.

back up **1.** T (5,9,10) Don't be afraid to fight for your rights. We'll back you up. [Give physical or moral support.] **2.** T (4,5) He has some strange ideas, but he can always back them up with statistics. [Support them.] **3.** *backup* N.A. Each astronaut has a backup (man) in case of emergency. [A person who is prepared to take the place of another, in some activity.]

Bag To put into bags.

bag up T (3) It took several hours to bag up all the potatoes. [Put into bags.] See **bale up, box up, do up, package up, sack up, tie up, wrap up.**

Bail I To dip water (or other liquid) out of a container, especially a boat.

bail out T (1) Water kept leaking into the boat. We had to keep bailing it (either the water or the boat) out. [Remove the water with a small container.]

Bail II To grant or obtain the liberty of a person under arrest, by giving security.

bail out: **1.** T (5) After he was arrested for robbery, his brothers bailed him out. [They gave security, probably money, to have him freed from jail.] **2.** T (5) No matter how often John got into trouble, his friend Jim would always bail him out. [Help him out of trouble.] **3.** I (1) When his plane caught fire, the pilot had to bail out. [Use his parachute to escape from the plane.]

Bake To cook in an oven.

bake in T (5) Bake nuts in a cake. [Instead of adding them to the icing.] *baked-in* A. (1,5) Baked-in goodness. [Advertiser's cliché.]

bake on T (1) The final step in making pottery is to bake on the glaze. [Fix it by firing.] *baked-on* A. (1) Baked-on enamel. [United to the surface by baking.]

bake out T (1) He used a heat lamp to bake out the soreness. [Out of his body.]

bake through T (1,4) This cake (meat, pie crust, etc.) isn't baked through. Leave it in the oven a while longer. [It is not thoroughly cooked.]

bake up T (7.11) The grandchildren are coming tomorrow. I'll have to bake up a batch of cookies for them. [Prepare.]

Balance To add up the two sides of an account and determine the difference.

balance up T (4) We balance up our accounts at the end of each month. [Make an accurate accounting of credits and debits.]

Bale To make or form into bales.

bale up T (3) To transport cotton, hay and other such products you should first bale it up. [Make a closely pressed package. Usually a large one.] See **bag up, crate up.**

Ball To make or form into a ball or balls.

ball up **1.** I (6) When the wire John was unwinding slipped from his hand it balled up. [It coiled into a confused ball shape.] **2.** T (6) Informal. He balled up the works. [He brought confusion to everything.] **3.** *(all) balled up* A. (6) You're all balled up. [You are very confused.] See **foul up.**

Bang To make a noise while striking; to damage by striking.

bang about/around   T (2)   Johnny found a tin can in the street and began banging it around with his stick. [Making much noise while hitting it.]

bang away   I (6)   She sat down at the piano and began banging away at a great rate. [Without stopping.]

bang out   T (1,9)   Informal. The pianist banged out three or four popular tunes for us. [Out of the piano.]

bang up   **1.** T (2,6)   The children played so roughly that they banged up some of the furniture. [Damaged it with marks and scratches.]   **2.** *(all) banged up* A. (2,6)   I'm all banged up from that ride in the back of the truck. [I have bruises and scratches on me.]   **3.** *bang-up* A.   (1,2)   Informal. He did a bang-up job as president. [An excellent job.]

Bar   To put up bars at doors, gates, windows, and other openings.

bar out   T (1)   To bar out all intruders we must put guards at all the openings. [Use men in place of bars.]

bar up   T (3,5)   Bar up the doors and windows. We may be attacked at any moment. [Place bars across the openings.]

Bark I   To remove the bark from a tree.

bark up   T (2,6)   He barked up his shins while trying to jump over the fence. [Had skin scraped from his shins.]

Bark II   To speak in the way a dog barks.

bark out   T (2,9)   The officer barked out a command and his company came to a halt. [Spoke sharply.]

Bat   Baseball. To strike with a bat.

bat around   **1.** I (1,2)   To keep in condition the players batted around for a while. [Practiced with bats.]   **2.** I   Slang. Those chaps spend most of their time batting around. [Acting like playboys.] See **fool around, play around.**

bat out   **1.** T (1)   The next player batted out a fly into left field. [Outside the diamond.]   **2.** I (4)   Johnson batted out in the second inning. [He lost his turn at bat because of failure to hit the ball.]

bat up   I (9,10)   It was Bob's turn to bat up. [Be at bat.]

Batch   To mix a specified amount of concrete.

batch-out N.   T (1)   The ready-mix truck returned just in time for the next batch-out.

Batter   To beat persistently or hard.

batter down   T (1,2)   The police battered down the door, which had been locked. [Caused it to fall down.]

batter in   T (1)   Artillery was brought up to batter in the walls of the fort. [Cause them to fall inward.]

batter up   (6)   His poor old car was badly battered up in the accident. [It was badly damaged.]

Battle   To fight as in a war.

battle out   T (8)   We'll battle this thing out if it takes all summer. [We will fight to the end for what we believe.]

battle through   T (4)   The sponsors of the bill battled it through to a final vote. [They continued to fight for it, until it was voted on.]

Bawl   To shout loudly.

bawl out   **1.** T (9)   Informal. The captain bawled out an order and the soldiers came to attention. [He gave the order in a loud voice.]   **2.** T (9)   Informal. The captain bawled the soldiers out for not keeping their rifles clean. [Reprimanded them in a loud voice.]   **3.** *bawling out* N. (9)   Informal. He gave them a good bawling out. See **bawl out 2.**

Be   To be found in a place, position, or state as a result of having moved to that place, position, or state, or having remained in it; to be found in such a place, position, or state as the result of some act performed previously on the subject of the sentence.

All of the second elements are used after the verb "to be". They usually have one of their primitive meanings, as is the case with intransitive verbs of motion. When so used they are like predicate adjectives, which show the position or state of the subject after some action has been performed. The use of the second elements as adjectives, in English, developed from their use with two-word-verbs.

Ex. He is away – because he went away.
He is out – because he went out, or because he struck out (baseball).
He is over – because he walked, rode or jumped over (something).
The water is on – because someone turned it on.

This use of the second elements as predicate adjectives is a late development. It started in Middle English and came into common use by the time of Shakespeare, as a short, concise way of expressing the state or condition of the subject as the result of some action denoted by a two-word-verb.

be about   **1.** (1,2)   Where's your mother? She's about somewhere. (She is not far away.]   **2.** (1,2)   Father was in bed ill for two weeks, but he's up and about now. [He is able to walk around, in and near the house.]   **3.** *be about (to)* (1)   We were about to leave. [We were near the time to leave.]

be along   **1.** (2)   How many people were along? [How many people went with you?]   **2.** (4)   Our friends will be along soon. [They will join us soon.]

be around   **1.** (1)   Where's your brother? He's around somewhere. [He's not far away (see be about).]   **2.** (1,2)   Mother has been in bed ill for a few days, but she's up and around now. [She is able to walk about, in and near the house.]

be away   **1.** (2)   Is your wife at home? No, she's away today. [She has gone away from the house for some reason.]   **2.** (1)   They're away! [The horses, the runners have left the starting line.] See **get off.**

be back   **1.** (2)   Are our seats in front? No, they're back. [To the rear.]   **2.** (3)

He'll be back in a few minutes. [He will return soon to the place he started from.] **3.** (5) Has John returned our lawn-mower? Yes, it's back. [In the hands of the giver or lender.] **4.** *back (of)* (2) Where is the phone? It's back of the door. [Behind.]

be by **1.** (2) Will the Smiths stop to see us before they leave town? Yes, they'll be by in half an hour. [They will come to our house for a short while.] **2.** (2) They're by! [They have gone past some spot or some obstacle.]

be down **1.** (1) Is Mary still upstairs? No, she's down. [She has come downstairs.] **2.** (1) He's down! [He has fallen, or been struck down.] **3.** (2) Yesterday Henry was in good spirits but today he's down again. [His spirits have fallen.] **4.** (6) Stock prices are down, due to the war scare. [They are lower.] **5.** (1,4,6) He's down and out. [He has lost all his money. He has been defeated. He is in a bad state of mind and body.] **6.** *down (for)* (7) How much am I down for? [How much did I, according to the record?] See **put down**. **7.** *down (on)* (5) They're down on me, and I don't know why. [They are angry with me. They dislike me.] **8.** *down (to)* (6) We're down to our last penny. [We have little or no money.] **9.** (5) We were down to business in very short order. [We began working at once.] **10.** *down (with)* (1,2) Mary is down with a cold. [She is in bed. She came down with a cold.]

be in **1.** (1) Did you put the car in the garage? Yes, it's in. [Inside the garage.] **2.** (1) The harvest is in. [It has been completed and is now in storage.] **3.** (1,4) He's in! [He has succeeded in entering some place, arriving at a destination, winning an election.] **4.** (6) They're "in" [They belong to an exclusive group.] **5.** *be all in* (7) I was all in after running so hard. [I was ready to collapse from fatigue.] See **give in, do in 2, wear out 5.** **6.** *be in (for)* (8) We're in for a bad storm, a hard fight, a difficult time [We're in a bad situation.] **7.** *be in (on)* (4) They're not in on the secret. [They do not have information about it.] **8.** *be in (with)* (4) He's in with his uncle. [He is in business, or has close relations with him.] **9.** *be-in* N. (4) A Hippie meeting where each person is to "be" his true self.

be off **1.** (2) They're off. [They are no longer on some place, or surface.] **2.** (2) Be off (with you)! [Leave this place immediately!] **3.** (2) They're off! [The horses, or runners have left the starting line.] See **get off**. **4.** (4) The electric power (the light, the gas, the radio, the T.V., the water, the steam) is off. [It has been turned off, cut off, or shut off. It is not functioning.] **5.** (4) The meeting (the lecture, the performance) is off. [It will not be held.] **6.** (4) We'll be off at five o'clock. [We will stop working then.] See **get off**. **7.** (1) Are the mountains close to the town? No, they're way off. [They are very far from the town.] **8.** (1) You're way off! [Your reasoning or your information is bad. You are far from the truth.] **9.** *be off (for)* (2) They're off for New York. [They have just left for New York.] **10.** *be off (of)* (1) I'm off of him for life! [I'll never be a close friend of him again.]

be on　**1.** (1)　He's on. [He has just gotten on the train, the plane, the boat, the stage, the platform, etc.]　**2.** (3)　You're on in a few minutes. [It will be your turn to perform on the stage, the program, the radio, the T.V., etc.]　**3.** (4) The electric power, the light, the gas, the radio, the T.V., the steam, etc., is on. [It has been turned on. It is functioning.] See **be off.**　**4.** *on (to)*　(2)　He's on to it. [He has understood. He knows what is happening.] See **catch on.**

be out　**1.** (1)　It's out! [The tooth has been extracted. Something is no longer in some place.]　**2.** (1,2)　Are your parents at home? No, they're out. [They have left home for a while.]　**3.** (2)　His new novel (the news, the statement, the decree) will be out soon. [It will be published.]　**4.** (4)　Baseball. He's out! [He has been temporarily eliminated from the game.] See **foul out. 5.** (9) The light (the candle, the fire, the lamp, the spark) is out. [It is no longer giving off light.]　**6.** (8)　He was out like a light. [He lost consciousness.]　**7.** (6,9)　He's way out. [He is ultra liberal or radical in his thinking.]　**8.** *out (for)*　(1,9)　He's out for senator. [He wants to be elected senator.] He's out for money. [He wants to get a lot of money.]　**9.** *out (of)*　(9)　We're out of sugar (coffee, tea, butter, money, etc.). [We have no more of it.]　**10.** *out (to)* (9)　He's out to get you. [He wants to do you some harm.]

be over　**1.** (3)　They're over! [They have walked, run, jumped, swum, etc., over some obstacle.]　**2.** (1)　It's over. [It has been put or placed over something.]　**3.** (1)　It's over. [It is more than it was before, or than we expected.] **4.** (2)　It's all over. [It is everywhere.]　**5.** (8)　It's all over now. [It has been completed, finished. There is nothing more to do about it.]　**6.** *over (with)* (8)　It's over with. [Some difficult or unpleasant situation or happening is no longer present.]

be through　**1.** (1)　They're through! [They have succeeded in passing through some obstacle or difficult situation.]　**2.** (3,4,5)　I'm through! [The work is finished. I have done everything I can do. I haven't the energy or will to do more.] **3.** (5)　You're through! [You are discharged, fired. You will not be allowed to continue in your job.]　**4.** *be through (with)*　(3)　You may have my pencil now. I'm through with it. [I no longer need it.]

be under　**1.** (3)　He walked into the water, and with a few steps he was under. [He was below the surface.]　**2.** (2)　Did you put the pillow under the patient's head? Yes, it's under. [His head is resting on it.]

be up　**1.** (1)　He's up. [He's out of bed. He was lying down, but he has gotten up.]　**2.** (2)　Stocks, prices are up. [They have gone higher.]　**3.** (7,10)　He's up. [It is his turn to act, to play, to perform, to appear in some situation.]　**4.** (8)　Time's up. Your hour is up. [The amount of time allowed for a person to do something is ended.]　**5.** (7,9)　What's up? [What is happening or is going to happen soon?]　**6.** (8)　The jig is up. Slang. [You have been discovered by the police or some authority. Your scheme or plot has failed.] **7.** *be up (for)*　(7,9)　He's up for re-election. [He is up before the public, the voters.] **8.** (6,9) He's up for robbery. [He is accused of robbery. Up before the judge, the court.] **9.** *be up (on)* (2,12) He's up on American History. [He has a good knowledge of the subject.] **10.** *be up (to)* (12) I'm not up to going to that party. [I am not prepared, or in good condition to go.] See **I keep up 1.** **11.** (10) What are the children up to? [What mischief are they doing, or preparing to do? **12.** *be up (with)* (8) It's all up with him. [He is finished, through. There is no hope for him.]

Bear I To put pressure on, move toward threateningly.

    bear down **1.** I (1,5) With his full weight he bore down heavily and succeeded in closing the lid of the trunk. [Used great pressure.] **2.** *bear down (on)* I (5) You should bear down on your students the week before examinations. [Put pressure on them to work harder.] **3.** I(5) If you bear down on mathematics in the next week or so I'm sure you can pass the test. [Study hard.] **4.** I (1,5) We looked up and saw a big trailer-truck bearing down on us. [Approaching in a way to cause fear.] **5.** I (5) The big battleships bore down on the enemy fleet, and opened fire. [They approached the fleet threateningly.] **6.** I (5) Informal. At the reception who should come bearing down on us but my mother-in-law? [Said jokingly of not seriously threatening approaches.]

Bear II Carry, support, hold up, encourage.

    bear off T (2) The bandits seized all the weapons and supplies and bore them off to their hideout. [Carried them away.]

    bear out T (7) The facts do not bear out your theory. Your theory is not borne out by the facts. [Your theory is not completely a true one.]

    bear up **1.** I (12) That bridge was old and not very strong. It couldn't bear up under heavy traffic. [It would break down.] **2.** I (5) His wife bore up well under the strain of two operations. [She endured.] See **put up 16.** **3.** I (2) They were borne up by the help and sympathy of their friends. [They were encouraged by their support.]

Beat I To strike vigorously.

    beat back T (1,3) The enemy made a surprise attack, but our troops beat them back. [Forced them to retreat.]

    beat down **1.** T (1) If the dogs start jumping on you, beat them down. [Down to the ground.] **2.** T (2) With united consumer action we can beat food prices down. [Force them to be lower.] **3.** T (2,3) I asked $800 for the horse and Mr. Smith tried to beat me down. [Force me to reduce the price.] **4.** I (1,5) The sky was clear, and the sun beat down unmercifully. [It was very hot.]

    beat up **1.** T (6) The thugs knocked the old man down and beat him up very badly. [Hurt him by beating him.] **2.** *beat up (on)* I (6) A gang of boys in the neighborhood threatened to beat up on the newcomer. [Give him a beating.] **3.** *beat-up* A. (6) He was driving a beat-up old jalopy. [A very much damaged old car.]

Beat II To defeat in a race or competition.

beat back   T (3)   The boys ran to get their guns from the house and Jim beat Charles back. [Reached the place they started from.]

beat down   T (1)   The children hurried to come to breakfast. The boys beat the girls down. [Arrived downstairs first.]

beat in   T (1)   John stood on the edge of the pool. "I'll beat you in", he said to the others. [Into the water.]

beat out   T (2)   They ran to the door to see which could beat the other out. [Out into the open].

beat over   T (3)   The girls all ran across the street. Mary beat them over. [She arrived first.]

beat through: **1.** T (4)   I'll beat you through! [Challenge of one boy to another to get through a fence.]   **2.** T (4)   Each student tried to beat the other through. [Finish his homework first.]

beat up   T (1)   They all ran to the top of the hill. Jim beat the others up. [He got there first.]

Bed   To put to bed.

bed down   **1.** I (1)   They pitched their tents and bedded down for the night. [Prepared their beds, and got in them.]   **2.** T (1)   We'll bed down the horses before we have dinner. [Prepare beds for them.]

Beef   Give new or more strength to.

beef up   **1.** T (2,10)   Informal. The mayor says that we need to beef up the police force to meet the crime wave. [Add more men to the force.]   **2.** *beef up* T (2,10)   Our football team could do with some beefing up. [It is weak.]

Beg   Request.

beg off   I (2)   They asked us to come to their party, but we begged off since my wife had a headache. [We asked to be excused.]

Bell   To expand in the shape of a bell.

bell out   I (10)   When he jumped from the plane the pilot's parachute belled out after he pulled the rip cord. [Opened out like a bell.]

Belt   Slang. To sing a song loudly.

belt out   T (2,9)   No young actress can belt out a song as effectively as Ethel Merman. See **shout out.**

Bend   To incline the body.

bend over   **1.** T (5)   The draftsman bent over his board. [Leaned forward over it as he worked.]   **2.** *bend over (backward)* I (5)   Informal. Her teacher bent over backward to help her pupils. [She made a great effort, tried very hard.] See **lean over (backward).**

Bet   Make a wager.

bet up   I (4,10)   Gambling. Bet up, if you want in on this round. [Make your bet.]

Bid   Make a money offer at an auction, make a declaration in bridge.

bid in   T (1)   When the auctioneer brought out the jewelry Mr. Jones had put up for auction, Mr. Jones bid it in. [Purchased it for himself.]

bid up   **1.** T (2)   When the Rembrandt went on the block (on sale) the buyers bid it up to over a million dollars.   **2.** T (2,6,10)   Bridge. He nearly fainted when his partner bid him up to six spades. [Increased the bid.]

Bind   To fasten or secure with a band or bond.

  bind out   T (5)   The young man was bound out as an apprentice to the local carpenter. [He made a bond, or agreement to work as an apprentice.]

  bind up   **1.** T (3,10)   The harvesters bind up the rice into bundles, and it is then put into piles. [Put a band around it.]   **2.** T (3)   The nurse bound up the soldier's wounds, after washing them with antiseptic. [Put bandages on them.]   **3.** *bound up* A.   (4,6)   Their problems are all bound up with the war situation. [They are closely related.]

Bite   To bring the teeth together (on something).

  bite down (on)   I (1,5)   He bit down hard on the pencil, and broke the point. [Illogical way of saying he brought his teeth together on the pencil.]

  bite off   **1.** T (2)   The shark bit off the hand of the swimmer he had attacked. [Severed it from the body.]   **2.** T (1)   He has bitten off more than he can chew. [Figurative for "He has planned or proposed to do more than he can do."]   **3.** T (2)   She's angry enough to bite your head off. [Do something violent to you.]

Black   To make black

  black out   **1.** T (9)   Military. The general gave the command to black out all news of the battle. [Conceal, cover up.]   **2.** *black out* N.   (9)   Military. The order was given for a black out over the whole area. [All lights were to be extinguished.] See **dim-out.**   **3.** I (9)   He blacked out when trying to recall the details of the crime. [He was unable to recall anything.]   **4.** T (9)   Athletic games on T.V. are often blacked out to people who live near the scene of the game being played. [They are not shown on the local T.V.]

  black up   **1.** T (2,10)   The actors in the old Minstrel Shows blacked up before the performance. [They colored their faces with lamp-black.]   **2.** *black-up* N. (2,10)   The actors wore black-up. See **make up.**

Blast   To use explosive force to move or remove some object; to make a loud explosive sound at the time of moving.

  blast away   **1.** T (2,3)   The engineers had to use fifty pounds of dynamite to blast away the face of the granite cliff. [Remove it by blasting.]   **2.** I (6)   The troops kept blasting away at the enemy for hours. [Continued to shoot with their firearms.]

  blast off   **1.** T (1)   The last charge of dynamite blasted off a huge portion of the cliff. [Off the cliff.]   **2.** T (1)   At Cape Kennedy today they blasted off a Titan rocket. [Off the launching pad.]   **3.** I (1)   The count down went smoothly and the rocket blasted off on schedule. [Left the launching pad.]   **4.** *blast-off* N.A.   (1)   The blast-off occurred at 9:30 sharp.

Blaze   To burn brightly

blaze away   **1.** I (6)   The forest fire blazed away for ten hours. [Continued to blaze.]   **2.** I (6)   The duck hunters kept blazing away as long as there was a duck in sight. [Continued to fire their shotguns.]

blaze up   **1.** I (2,5)   The log in the fireplace blazed up cheerfully. [Burned more brightly.]   **2.** I (2)   Fig. She blazed up in anger on hearing those words. [She was suddenly very angry.]

Bleach   To make white in color.

bleach out   **1.** T (9)   You can bleach those ugly stains (those spots) out with Clorox. [Remove them from the cloth by soaking them in Clorox.]   **2.** *bleached out* (9)   Her face was all bleached out from being away from the sunlight so long. [It had become completely white.]

Blend   Mix smoothly together, slowly.

blend in   T (5)   When preparing cookie dough, start with the proper amount of flour, then blend in some milk. [Mix it in without beating.]

Block   To use wood or some other material to achieve a purpose.

block in   T (2)   The artist blocked in some original designs for a tapestry. [She used wooden blocks, or drew lines on the paper.]

block off   T (4)   The police blocked the street off from traffic during the parade. [Put up barriers.] See **shut off.**

block out   T (7)   The architect blocked out the plans for the use of floor space. [Used lines on the paper to determine the spaces.]

block up   T (4,6)   Don't block up the hallways. You must leave room for people to pass. [Don't make it impossible for people to circulate.] See **stop up.**

Bloody   To stain or smear with blood.

bloody up   (2,6)   The bully bloodied up his face during the fight. [Covered it with blood.]

Blot   To cover something so that it cannot be seen; to destroy completely.

blot out   **1.** T (9)   The signature on this letter has been blotted out. [It has been covered with ink or some other opaque substance.]   **2.** T (9)   The heavy clouds blotted out the sun. [It was impossible to see the sun.]   **3.** T (8)   That city was completely blotted out by the bombing raid. [It was completely destroyed.]

Blow   a. To move with, or as a current of air.   b. To drive with a current of air.

blow away   **1.** I (2,3)   The storm blew away. [It left this area.]   **2.** T (2,3)   The electric fan blew the smoke away. [Away from us.]

blow down   **1.** T (1)   The hurricane blew many houses down. [Down to the ground.]

blow in   **1.** T (1)   The force of the explosion blew the walls in. [They collapsed inwardly.]   **2.** I (1)   Informal. John blew in just in time for dinner. [He came in suddenly, unexpectedly.]

blow off   **1.** I (1,2)   The roof of his house blew off during the hurricane. [It was carried away by the strong wind.]   **2.** T (2)   The exploding hand grenade

blew off one soldier's foot. [Separated it from his body.] See **cut off, break off.**
3. I (1) The safety valve blew off a great cloud of steam. [Out and away from the engine.] **4.** T (9) Informal. The children are getting very noisy. They have to blow off steam now and then. [Release some energy.] **5.** I (9) Informal. John's a great talker. He's always blowing off. [He is boasting, talking big.] **6.** *blow-off* N. (9) John is a great blow-off. [One who boasts a lot.] See **blow off 5.**

blow out **1.** T (8) Please blow out the candle. [Extinguish it.] **2.** T (8) The storm blew itself out. [It moved out of our area.] **3.** T (2) The explosion blew the windows out. [Out of the house.] **4.** T (4) We blew out a tire when we were nearly home. [Our tire exploded, lost its air.] **5.** I (4) The left front tire blew out. **6.** *blow-out* N. (4) a. The blow-out came at a very bad time. b. Informal. Bob is having a blow-out at his apartment tonight. (A lively and noisy party.]

blow over **1.** T (5) The storm blew over two trees in the park. [Toppled them from a standing position.] **2.** I (3,8) Let's stay inside the house till the storm blows over. [Goes away.] **3.** I (3,8) Fig. She will not appear in public till the scandal about her blows over. [Passes as a storm always passes.] See **blow over 2.**

blow up **1.** I (7,11) There is a storm blowing up. It's blowing up a storm [The storm will soon be here.] **2.** I (1,6) The battleship blew up when it was hit by a torpedo. [It was destroyed by the explosion.] **3.** T (1,6) The guerillas succeeded in blowing up an ammunition dump. [Caused it to explode.] **4.** I (5,6) Fig. My father blew up when I asked him for more money. [He talked loud and angrily.] **5.** T (2,4) Ask your uncle to show the children how to blow up their toy balloons. [Force air into them to make them larger.] **6.** T (2) He's going to blow up those photographs, so as to see the details better. [Make them larger.] **7.** *blow-up* N a. (6) An explosion. [There was a big blow-up at the factory today.] b. (5,6) A violent quarrel. [There was a big blow-up between father and son, after the boy's dismissal from school.] c. (2) An enlarged picture. [On examining the blow-up he had made of the snapshot, he could see a fourth man in the background.]

Bluff To deceive by pretending to have special knowledge or strength.
bluff out T (1,5) For a while it appeared that John would be held prisoner by the gangsters, but he bluffed his way out. [He deceived the gangsters as to his knowledge or strength, and he escaped.]

Board To use wooden boards for some purpose.
board up T (3,4) They boarded up the large hole in the wall, to keep the wind out. [Placed boards over the hole.)

Bob To appear unexpectedly, quickly.
bob up I (1) A familiar face bobbed up in the crowd. [It appeared in the way a float on a fishing line comes to the surface of the water after a "bite".

Bog To sink in, as into a bog or swamp.

  bog down **1.** I (1) The wheels of our car bogged down in the soft mud. [They sank into the mud.] **2.** I (5) Fig. We were completely bogged down with so much homework. [All our time and energy were taken by it.]

Boil a. To heat a liquid to the point that it gives off steam. b. To come to a boil.

  boil away I (2) Most of the water had boiled away when she looked in the kettle. [It had disappeared as steam.]

  boil down T (b) You make maple sugar by boiling down the sap from maple trees. [Remove the water by boiling.] I (6) The water in the kettle boiled down till there was only a cupful left. [It passed off as steam.] I (6) Fig. The question boils down to this. Do we go or stay? [This is the only question that remains.]

  boil off T (7) Textiles. It is necessary to boil off the sizing and impurities in processing silk fabrics. [Remove them by a boiling process.]

  boil over **1.** I (4) The kettle boiled over before she could turn off the heat. [Over the edge of the kettle and down.] **2.** I (4) Fig. Her husband simply boiled over when he received the bill for her fur coat. [He became very angry.]

  boil up **1.** I (1,5) The hot spring boiled up giving off clouds of steam. [Up from the ground, with increased intensity.] **2.** I (1,5) The anger of the mob boiled up when police dogs appeared. [Rose to a high degree.] See **mount up.**

Bolster To give support as with a bolster or pillow.

  bolster up T (2) Fig. The arrival of reinforcements bolstered up the spirits of the men in the trenches. [Gave them new courage.]

Bolt To eat hurriedly and hungrily.

  bolt down T (1,5) The workmen had only a few minutes to bolt down their lunch before the next load of building material arrived. [Eat it quickly.]

Bomb To attack with explosive bombs.

  bomb out 1. T (1,8) The enemy troops were dug in on the hillside. An air strike was ordered to bomb them out. [Out of their positions.] **2.** *bombed out* A. (8) Saw the bombed-out village where he had been born. [Out of existence; destroyed.]

Bone Informal. To study hard.

  bone up I (2,5,11) Informal. John and Mary are busy boning up for exams next week. [They are working very hard so as to get good grades.] [They are working themselves to the bone.]

Boo To say "boo" as an exclamation of contempt or displeasure.

  boo down T (1,4) When a man stood up in the meeting to criticize the speaker, the audience booed him down. [Made him sit down by shouting "boo".] See **shout down.**

  boo off T (1,9) The actor played his role so badly that the audience booed him off. [Off the stage.]

Book To register in advance, as for lodgings or a show; make reservations.

book back   T (3)   The ticket agent booked us out on the 13th, and back on the 20th. [He made reservations for us to leave on the 13th and return on the 20th.]

book through   T (2)   We were booked through to Paris, but had to spend the night in Gander. [Our reservations called for a continuous flight.]

Boost   To lift or raise by pushing from below.

boost up   **1.** T (1)   Jim couldn't reach the top shelf, so his father boosted him up. [Up to where he could reach the shelf.]   T (2,6)   Inflation will boost up the price of everything. [Make it higher.]

Boot   To drive by kicking.

boot out   T (4,9)   Slang. He made so much trouble for all the members of our group that we finally had to boot him out. [Expel him by force, or by our vote.] See **throw out.**

Botch   To spoil something by poor work.

botch up   **1.** T (6)   That inexperienced carpenter botched up the kitchen cupboards we ordered made. [Completely spoiled them.]   **2.** *botch up*   T (6)   Slang. Don't let John have anything to do with the plans. He'll botch up the whole works. [He will spoil everything.]

Bottle   To enclose, as if in a bottle.

bottle up   **1.** T (4,5,10)   Our fleet bottled up the enemy fleet in Manila Bay. [Closed the entrance to the bay, so that their ships could not escape.]   **2.** (T 4,6)   Traffic was bottled up in the tunnel due to an accident at the exit. [It could not move out.]   **3.** T (3,6)   Don't keep your emotions (your fears, your worries) bottled up inside. It's better to talk about them. [Let them come out.]

Bottom   Archeology; to reach the last layer in an excavation.

bottom out   I (8)   The archeological team expects to bottom out within a week. [They will finish their exploration of their "digs."]

Bounce   To spring back up, as a rubber ball.

bounce back   I (4)   Prices on the Stock Exchange fell on Monday, but bounced back at the opening on Tuesday. [Returned to their previous height.]

Bow   Bend the knee or body in reverence or respect.

bow down   I (1)   In the presence of the king the subjects were expected to bow down before him. [Bend toward the earth.]

bow in   T (1)   At formal parties there is a doorman to bow the guests in. [Make a reverence as he lets them come in.] See **ask in, usher in, show in, see in.**

bow out   **1.** T (2)   After a pleasant hour-long chat, our host bowed us out. [He politely took us to the door.]   **2.** I (6)   At first Mr. Jones was very much interested in our group, but he bowed out when we wanted him to be president. [He left the group, politely.]

Bowl   To roll, or to strike, as with a bowling ball.

bowl over   **1.** T (5)   As he was crossing the street he was bowled over by a car he hadn't seen coming. [He fell to the ground.]   **2.** T (5)   Fig. It simply bowled me over when I heard she had married my old friend. [I was emotionally upset.]

Box   To put into a box; to surround with walls or barriers.

box in   **1.** T (3)   Rows of tall trees boxed in the house on three sides. [They enclosed the area.]   **2.** T (3)   In the parking area we were boxed in by cars on every side. [We could not get out.]

box up   T (3)   We were busy in the orchard boxing up apples for market. [Preparing them for shipment.] See **bag up.**

Brace   To strengthen as with a brace, a support. See **bolster**.

brace up   **1.** T (1)   Some of those fence posts are falling down. We'd better brace them up with those cedar poles. [Give them support.]   **2.** I (1,5)   Brace up, old man, you haven't seen the worst yet. [Stiffen your will, your determination.]

Brag   To use boastful language.

brag up   T (5)   Mr. Smith is always bragging up his sons' athletic ability. [He brags a great deal about it.]

Brake   To use the brakes on a car or other vehicle.

brake down   T (2,6)   He braked his car down before making a left turn. [He reduced the motion by applying his brakes.] Opp. of **speed up.**

Break   a. To smash, split, divide into parts violently.   b. To become broken, separate into parts, especially suddenly and violently.

break away   **1.** I (3)   A huge mass of ice broke away from the face of the iceberg. [It became separated and fell into the sea.]   **2.** I (3)   Boxing. The two boxers broke away at the order of the referee. [They separated from close contact with each other. They came out of a clinch.]   **3.** *breakaway* N.   (3)   The boxers made a clean breakaway. [They did not try to hit each other.]

break down   **1.** T (1,2)   The intense artillery bombardment broke down the walls of the fortress. [Down to the ground.]   **2.** T (1,6)   Fig. Much constructive thinking and good will must be put forward to break down the barriers between the races. [cause the barriers to fall.]   **3.** I (1,2)   The wagon (the platform, the bridge, etc.) broke down under the heavy weight placed upon it. [It fell down.]   **4.** I (1,2)   Our car broke down when we were ten miles from home. [It could not run because of some mechanical difficulty.]   **5.** I (1,4)   Fig. The negotiations (the agreement, the plan, the treaty, etc.) broke down because of a disagreement on certain details. [It was impossible to continue with them.]   **6.** I (6)   Her health broke down a year after their marriage. [She was in very poor physical condition.]   **7.** I (2)   His unhappy wife broke down and cried when the doctor said she could have no more children. [She could not control her emotions.]   **8.** T (6)   In chemistry lab students learn to break down water into hydrogen and oxygen. [Analyze it into its elements.]   **9.** T (3,6)   He explained the national budget very clearly by breaking it down into six parts. [By analyzing it.]   **10.** *break-down* N. a. A failure to function.   (1,2)   [Our break-down occurred near Springfield.]   (1,4)   [The break-down of the treaty could not be avoided.] b.   (6)   A nervous collapse. [Her break-down came at a very bad time for her family.] c.   (3,6)   An analysis. [He gave us a break-down of the budget. **11.** *broken-down* A. a. (3,6) Damaged. [There was an old broken-down chair (bed or other piece of furniture) on the back porch. It was useless from being broken.] b. (3,6) Weak or infirm. [He was no longer a handsome and vigorous person, but a poor broken-down old man. He had lost his property, his good looks, his money.]

break in **1.** T (1) The police broke in the door, which had been locked on the inside. [Forced the door open.] **2.** I (1) Last night thieves broke in and stole all her jewelry. [Entered the house by breaking a window or door.] **3.** I (1) Fig. He was very rude. He broke in on our conversation, without apologizing. [He interrupted discourteously.] **4.** T (6) He had to spend three weeks breaking in the young colt he had bought. [Using force to break the spirits of the colt, in order to be able to put it in harness.] **5.** T (6) We were told to drive our new car at low speed for 400 miles in order to break in the motor. [To allow the parts to adjust to operation gradually.] **6.** T (6) His new shoes hurt his feet. It took him a long time to break them in. [Make them soft and pliable.] **7.** *break-in* N. (1) The thieves made their break-in through the back door. See **break in 2.**

break off **1.** T (1) The hungry boy broke off a piece of bread and began to eat. [Off the loaf.] **2.** I (2) A large limb broke off under the weight of snow, and fell with a crash. [It came away from the tree.] **3.** T (2,4) Fig. China has broken off relations with the U.S.A. [The relations are ended.] **4.** T (5) Fig. We had been chatting for two hours, but we broke off when the clock struck twelve. [We stopped talking.] **5.** I (1) Informal. We were all surprised when we heard that Phil and Mary had broken off. [Ended their friendship, their love affair, their association.]

break out **1.** I (1,5) Our regiment had been completely surrounded by enemy troops, but we succeeded in breaking out. [Out of the enclosed area.] **2.** I (1,5) Six of the prisoners broke out and escaped during the night. [Out of prison.] **3.** I (2,3) An epidemic of flu broke out last December. [Out in public.] **4.** I (1) The prisoner broke out in a cold sweat when his sentence was pronounced. [Sweat poured out of his skin.] **5.** I (1) Baby has broken out with a rash on his chest. [Reddish spots have appeared on the baby's skin.] **6.** T (1) Our host broke out a bottle of his best champagne to celebrate the victory. [Originally, out of a box or case.] **7.** *break-out* N. (1,5) A forcible escape from restraint. [The prison break-out occurred a little after midnight.] [The military break-out was achieved at a high cost in dead and wounded.] **8.** *breaking-out* N. (1) The mother noticed a breaking-out on her baby's chest when she bathed him. See **break out 5.**

break through **1.** I (1) The enemy lines put up a stiff resistance, but our men broke through and captured the town. [Through the enemy lines.] **2.** I (1) The sun was hidden behind a mass of dark clouds for a while but suddenly broke through. [Its light appeared.] **3.** *break-through* N. a. (1) An offensive thrust.

[After the break-through, our troops were able to advance rapidly toward Paris.]
b. (4) An abrupt, often unexpected, advance in knowledge or technique.
[The discovery of the Meson was an important break-through for atomic
physics.] [A break-through in the production of fresh water from sea water is
sure to come.]

break up **1.** T (2,11) To prepare the ground for planting the farmer breaks
up the soil with his plow and harrow. [He raises the soil and breaks it into small
pieces.] **2.** T (2,11) Those pieces of stone are too large for making a pathway.
You'll have to break them up. [Make smaller pieces.] **3.** I (2) The ice in
the river usually breaks up around the end of March. [It separates into smaller
pieces.] **4.** I (8) The meeting broke up at 10 p.m. [The people separated
and went home.] **5.** T (6,10) The police broke up the meeting (the assembly,
the demonstration, the mob) by using tear gas. [They forced the people to leave.]
6. T (6) Fig. Political rivalry broke up the long standing friendship of the two
men. [They were no longer friendly to each other.] **7.** T (6) Fig. That long
series of tragic events broke her up completely. [She was sad, heart broken.]
8. *break-up* N. a. (2) An act or instance of shattering. [The break-up of the
ice on the Mississippi came earlier this year.] b. (8) A rupture. [The break-up
of their long friendship was a sad thing.] **9.** *broken up* A. (6) Fig. She was all
broken up as a result of a series of tragic happenings.

Breathe To take air into the lungs and let it out.

breathe in **1.** I (1) Now breathe in slowly and hold your breath until I tell you
to let it out. [Take air into your lungs; inhale.] **2.** T (1) They stood in the
garden and breathed in the fragrance of the spring flowers. [Took it into their
lungs.]

breathe out **1.** I (1) He breathed out slowly as the doctor had told him to do.
[Let the air escape from his lungs. Exhaled.] **2.** T (1) The dying man
breathed out his last, while his wife stood near. [Let air escape from his lungs for
the last time. Died.]

Breed To procure by mating; propagate sexually.

breed back T (4) Some primitive species of horses and cattle have been produced
by breeding back. [Reversing the genetic inheritance.]

breed in T (1,5) Animal husbandry experts attempt to breed in the desirable
qualities of a species of animal. [Improve the descendants by selective breeding.]

breed out T (4) The same experts attempt to breed out undesirable qualities.
[Eliminate those qualities from their animals.]

Brew To make (beer, ale, etc.) by steeping, boiling, and fermenting processes.

brew up **1.** T (7) During prohibition days many men spent their week-ends
brewing up a batch of beer. [Preparing it for future use.] **2.** T (6,7) From the
looks of the clouds, it's brewing up a storm. I A storm is brewing up. [It is
approaching.]

Brick To use bricks for construction work.

brick over   T (2)   John was tired of raising flowers in his patio, so he decided to brick it over. [Use bricks to cover it completely.]

brick up   T (4)   The fireplace in the living room always smoked, and made the room drafty, so we bricked it up. [Filled the space with a brick wall.]

Bridge   To put a bridge across a barrier.

bridge over   T (2,3)   The open canal running by the house was dangerous for playing children so we bridged it over. [Built a bridge to cover the canal.]

Bring   To carry, or cause someone or something to come with or to, or toward the speaker.

bring about   **1.** T (3)   Nautical. The Captain brought his ship about, and steered for the harbor. [He turned the ship around to head in a different direction.] **2.** T (4)   The Civil Rights Movement brought about many changes in the laws of our nation. [It caused many changes.]

bring around   **1.** T (5)   We are anxious to meet your new boy friend. Bring him around sometime soon. [Invite him to visit us.]   **2.** T (4)   James didn't agree with our plan at first, but we finally brought him around to our point of view. [We persuaded him.] See **bring over, come around 3, talk around, win over.** **3.** T (3)   She fainted at the sight of blood, but the doctor brought her around after a minute or two. [Restored her to consciousness.] See **come around 4.**

bring back   **1.** T (3)   If you're going to the super-market, bring back a carton of Camels. [Back to this place.]   **2.** T (5)   Bring back my Bonnie to me. [To the original owner.]   **3.** T (4)   That war film brings back memories of Hitler and the Nazis.

bring down   **1.** T (1)   Go upstairs and bring down my glasses. They're on my dresser. [Bring them downstairs.]   **2.** T (1,4)   Hunting. Charles brought down a deer with his first shot. [He killed the deer. It fell to the ground.]   **3.** T (2)   The war scare brought stock prices down yesterday. [Made them lower.]   **4.** T (1)   Fig. The speaker brought down the house with the funny story he told. [He won great applause. The people laughed so hard they were almost rolling on the ground.]   **5.** T (1,5)   The sins of the children of Israel brought down the wrath of Jehovah on their heads. [Down from Heaven.]

bring in   **1.** T (1)   It's going to rain. We'll have to bring in the chairs. [Into the house.]   **2.** T (1)   The scouting patrol brought in six prisoners. [Into our camp, or headquarters.]   **3.** T (1)   The jury brought in a verdict of "not guilty". [Into the courtroom.]   **4.** T (1)   His stock investments will bring in $5,000 a year. [Into his banking account, into his pockets.]   **5.** T (6)   After drilling many dry wells, the oil company finally brought in a gusher. [They brought into production a very productive well.]

bring off   **1.** T (8)   The French brought off a victorious sweep in the Winter Olympics. [They won many firsts.]   **2.** T (8)   Senator Jones tried many times, without success, to get his bill passed. But today he brought it off without any difficulty. [Away from its static position.] See **carry off.**

bring on **1.** T (II 1) Bring on the food! We're starving! [Bring it to the table, so that we can start eating.] **2.** T (II 4) The invasion of South Korea by the North Koreans brought on the Korean War. [Caused it to start.] **3.** T (II 4) All that studying I did last night brought on a headache. [Caused it to start.]

bring out **1.** T (1,2) Please bring out the chairs. We're going to eat on the terrace. [Out of the house.] **2.** T (2) Ford is bringing out a new line of sports cars. [Out in public.] **3.** T (1) A good furniture polish will bring out the natural color of the wood. [Out onto the surface.] **4.** T (1,3) The speaker brought out some facts that helped us to make our decision. [He made them clear.] **5.** T (1,2) A hard political campaign can bring out the best or the worst qualities of a candidate. [Expose them to public view.] **6.** T (2) The publishers will bring out a new edition of Hemingway's works in the Fall. [They will publish it.] See **get out 5.**

bring over **1.** T (3) We can't get a baby-sitter. May we bring the children over? [Over to your house, for a visit.] **2.** T (3) We will need a lot of good arguments to bring John over. [Persuade him to join us.] See **bring around.**

bring through **1.** T (1) The door is too narrow to bring the piano through. [Through the door.] **2.** T (4) He had serious complications after his operation, but the doctor brought him through in fine shape. [Through the difficulties.)

bring up **1.** T (1) I left my book on the dining room table. Please bring it up when you come. [Upstairs.] **2.** T (7) At the meeting someone brought up the subject (the question, the problem) of teachers' salaries. [Proposed the subject for discussion.] **3.** T (1) When the sick man vomited he brought up a quantity of blood. [Up from his stomach.] **4.** T (2,12) To bring up children in our crowded cities is no easy matter. [Prepare them to be good adults.] See **raise up, train up.** **5.** I (13) The coachman brought up sharply at the entrance. [He stopped the horses by pulling on the reins. He brought the heads of the horses up.] **6.** I (13) The car brought up to the curb, to let some people out. [Stopped at the curb.] **7.** *bringing up* N. (2,12,10) Those children have had a wonderful bringing up. [They have been well trained.] See **bring up 4.**

broaden out **1.** I (1,11) From our hotel window the scene broadens out into wide fields. **2.** I (11) Fig. As he grew older his sympathies broadened out to include all mankind. [They spread very widely.]

Brown To become dark, somber, unhappy.

brown off **1.** I (4) Our football team browned off, after losing ten games in succession. [It was discouraged, unhappy, lifeless.] **2.** *browned off* A. (4) A fighter pilot often feels browned off after weeks of daily missions. [He feels gloomy, dissatisfied, lacking in energy.]

Bruise To injure the skin or the flesh by a fall or a blow, etc.

bruise up **1.** T (6) Those falls he took on the ice bruised him up badly. [Gave him many bruises.] **2.** *(all) bruised up* A. (6) His face was all bruised up from the pummeling he received. [It was covered with bruises.]

Bruit To spread a rumor.

bruit about T (2) After his death it was bruited about that it was a case of suicide. [People gossiped, and spread the rumor.]

Brush To make a gesture or movement, as with a brush.

brush aside T (2) We must brush aside all ideas of an early peace. [Keep those ideas out of our minds.]

brush away T (2,3) She smiled sadly and brushed away a tear. [Away from her eye or her cheek.]

brush off **1.** T (1) There's some lint on your jacket. Let me brush it off. [Remove it with a clothes brush.] **2.** T (7) Before he got off the train the porter brushed him off. [Used a brush to remove lint or other substances from his clothing.] **3.** T (1,9) A former friend came up to John and asked him for a loan, but John brushed him off. [Treated him a bit harshly and did not give him the money.] **4.** *brush-off* N. Slang. John gave him the brush-off.

brush up **1.** I (2) Informal. We just have time to brush up a bit before the guests arrive. [Quickly wash, comb our hair, and arrange our clothing.] **2.** *brush up (on)* I (2) I'm brushing up on Spanish, getting ready for our trip to South America. [Studying in preparation for further use of the language.]

Buck Of a horse, to leap up with arched back and stiff forelegs.

buck up **1.** T (2,5) Tom is discouraged about his job. Let's have a party to buck him up a bit. [Give him some hope and energy.] **2.** I (2,5) Buck up, old man. Things aren't as bad as they seem. [Show some energy, the way a bucking horse shows it.]

Buckle To fasten as with a buckle, make tight.

buckle down I (5) Informal. If you want to succeed in life, you'll have to buckle down. [Work hard and seriously.] See **bear down (on), knuckle down.**

buckle up I (5,12) Informal. Don't worry about not being good enough for your job. Just buckle up and go to it. [Get all your energies and intelligence under control, and start working confidently.]

Bud To come into bud, ready to bloom.

bud out I (1) The plum trees and peach trees are budding out. I hope the frost doesn't kill them. [The buds are ready to open.] See **leaf out.**

Bug To act in cowardly, purposeless manner.

bug out I (6) Slang. We counted on Jack to help us, but he bugged out. [He backed out, he did not keep his word.] See **back out.**

Build To construct, establish, increase.

build in T (1) Bob's wife asked him to build in bookcases on either side of the fireplace. [To put up shelves using the wall as the back of the bookcase.] *built-in* A. (1) a. Constructed as an integral part of the building. [All the newer apartments have built-in closets and bookcases.] b. Incorporated into a manufactured product. [Advertisers cliché — Margarine with "built-in" goodness. Face cream with "built-in" fragrance. Soap with "built-in" whitening power.]

build on T (I 4) As our family grew larger we had to build on two extra bedrooms. [Construct two bedrooms attached to the house.]

build up **1.** T (1) The soldiers built up a mound of earth around the gun position. [Up from the ground level.] **2.** T (2) Mr. Smith has built up a reputation as a successful businessman. [He has "made good".] **3.** T (2,7) To build up a business you must also build up a good bank account. [Increase savings in order to enlarge the business operations.] **4.** I (5) In mystery stories suspense builds up in the last two chapters. [It increases greatly.] **5.** T (2,4) Small states often spend too much of their resources building up their military forces. [Increasing them.] **6.** *build-up* N. Any increase in strength, force or potential, such as armament, industry, heat, electrical or atomic energy, tension, emotions, etc. **7.** *built-up* A. (4) Their new home is located in the built-up section south of town. [An area where there are already many houses.]

Bump To collide with, to strike.

bump off **1.** T (6) The airline bumped the salesman off the flight so the general could get to his meeting on time. [They gave his seat to the general.] **2.** T (5) Slang. The gang leader gave orders to bump off the leader of the rival gang. [To kill.] See **rub out**. **3.** *bump-off* N. (5) Slang. The orders were to give his rival the bump-off.

bump up (against) I (6) Informal. I'm sure that you're going to bump up against strong opposition to your plans. [Meet, encounter, find.]

Bunch Come together in a group, a cluster.

bunch up I (3,10) The demonstrators were bunching up into small groups. [Gathering together.]

Bundle Gather, or come together in a close unit.

bundle up **1.** T (3) Mother is going to bundle up all our old clothes and send them to the Relief Society. [Make bundles or packages.] See **wrap up, box up.** **2.** I (3,9) It's cold outside! You'd better bundle up. [Wrap yourselves in warm clothing.] **3.** *bundled up* A. (3,9) The children were all bundled up. [They had plenty of warm clothes on.)

Buoy To float, rise because of lightness.

buoy up **1.** T (1,5) Trained divers attached rubber rafts to the space capsule so as to buoy it up until the Naval vessel arrived.[Keep it afloat.] **2.** T (1,5) Fig. Even in the darkest hours of battle he was buoyed up by the knowledge that the war could not continue much longer. [His spirits were raised.]

Burden To load heavily.

burden down T (3) Grief and regret had burdened her down. [Her spirits were very low.]

Burn T. To set fire to, to consume as with fire. I. To undergo a burning process.

burn away: **1.** I (6) The forest fire burned away for six days before it could be controlled. [It continued to burn.] **2.** T (2,3) The workmen were burning away the dry grass and weeds along the highway. [Removing them by burning.]

burn down **1.** T (1) They burned down the old abandoned house to get rid of it. [Burned it to the ground.] **2.** I (1) The old house burned down after it was hit by lightning. [It burned to the ground.] **3.** I (2,6) The lamp (the lantern, the candle) slowly burned down and finally went out. [The light gradually became lower.]

burn in T (2) Photography. To expose one part of an image to more light, by masking the other parts, in preparing a print.

burn off **1.** T (1) We asked the Fire Department to burn off the dry grass and weeds in the vacant lot next to our house. [Remove them by burning.] **2.** T (1) Doctors sometimes use an electric needle to burn off warts and other skin defects. [Remove them by burning.]

burn on T (I 1,4) Welding. To weld lead with lead.

burn out **1.** T (8) The big fire last week burned out three blocks in the business district. [They were destroyed by fire.] **2.** I (8) The lamp (the lantern, the candle, the fire) burned out before morning. [Stopped burning for lack of fuel.] **3.** T (8) That eager son of yours is going to burn himself out if he doesn't learn to take it easy. [Lose his energy, his "fire".] **4.** *burned out* A. (9) A burned out light bulb (fuse, battery cell) is of no use. [One that can no longer give light or electric current.] **5.** (9) The city is planning a housing development in the burned out section of the business district.

burn over T (2) When the grain has been harvested from a field, it is sometimes a good idea to burn it over to destroy harmful weeds.

burn up **1.** T (4) Today I'm going to clean out my desk and burn up all the old useless papers and letters. [Destroy them completely by burning.] **2.** T (4) All his worldly possessions were burned up in the fire. [They were completely destroyed.] **3.** T (6) Slang. It burns me up to hear him say such mean things about people. [I become very angry.] **4.** *burned up* A. (6) Slang. I never saw anybody so burned up as she was. [So angry.] See **teed off.**

Burst Break open with sudden violence.

burst in I (1,4) The Smiths burst in with the exciting news of their son's safe return from the war. [They came in suddenly, interrupting us with loud talk.]

burst out I (1,9) Fig. Mary burst out laughing (crying, singing) when she heard the news. [She laughed, cried, sang, explosively.]

Bust Substandard and slang for burst.

bust out I (9) Title of a popular musical comedy song — "June is busting out all over". [It is exploding with vitality and beauty.]

bust up **1.** T (6) Slang. A group of young rowdies came along and busted up the party. [They spoiled it with noise and rough conduct.] See **break up 5.** **2.** I (4) Slang. Jim and Maggie busted up a year ago. [They separated.] See **break up 6.** **3.** *bust-up* N. (4,6) Slang. Jim and Maggie's bust-up came as no surprise to us. [Their separation.] See **break up 9. 4.** (9) Slang. That was a real bust-up we had at Johnny's last night. [A wild and noisy party.]

Butt   To strike or push with the head or horns.

butt in   1. I (4)   Slang. We were having a nice quiet party when Johnny came butting in. [He had not been invited. He came against our wishes.]   **2.** I (4) Slang. That chap is always butting in on our conversations. [He interrupts without being asked to speak.]   **3.** *buttinski* N.   (4)   He is a real buttinski. [Humorous nickname for a person who butts in.]

butt out   I (1,4)   Slang. You butted in without an invitation. Now just butt out, will you? [Leave us — stop talking.]

Butter   To spread butter (on bread); to flatter.

butter up   T (4)   Informal. Your father is not in a generous mood tonight. You'll have to butter him up a bit if you want the car. [Flatter him. Do something to please him.]

Button   To fasten with buttons.

button up   1. T (1,3,11)   It's very cold outside. Button up your overcoat. [Use all of the buttons so as to keep the cold out.]   **2.** T (3)   Teacher had to button him up. [He was too little to do it himself.] See **zip up. 3.** T (3)   Slang. Button up your lip. [Keep your mouth shut. Keep quiet.] See **shut up** (slang).

Buy   To purchase.

buy back   T (5)   The honest merchant bought back all the imperfect vacuum cleaners he had sold to his customers. [He refunded the money.]

buy in   1. I (1)   Grain merchants are buying in now to take advantage of the seasonal low prices. [They are increasing their stocks of grain.]   **2.** I (4)   There are still some shares available in the new company, if you want to buy in. [Into the company.]

buy off   T (2)   The owner of the gambling house tried to buy off the police, but without success. [Pay them not to raid his place.]

buy out   T (9)   The younger partner in the business firm bought out the older partner. [He bought everything, and the older partner was out of the business.]

buy up   1. T (4,11)   General Motors is buying up all the land in the neighborhood. They're going to build a big factory.   **2.** T (4)   The Atlas Corporation bought up all the outstanding shares of stock at a high price.

C

Cake   To form into a compact mass.

cake over   T (2)   His arms and legs were all caked over with thick black mud. [Covered with a thick coating of mud.]

cake up   I (4,6)   The lubricating grease caked up at twenty degrees below zero. [It became stiff and solid.]

Calculate   To make a mathematical computation.

calculate out   T (7)   He told his assistant to calculate the formula out to the smallest fraction. [Make a complete calculation.]

Call   To speak loudly; to call on the telephone.

call away   T (2)   Mr. Jones expected to be here tonight, but he was called away. [He received a message that forced him to leave.]

call back   **1.** T (3)   Bob started to return to his seat, but the teacher called him back. [Back to the teacher's desk.]   **2.** T (4)   Due to the war scare, many of the Air Force pilots were called back. [Back into active service.]   **3.** T (5) Telephone. As soon as my husband comes home I'll call you back. [I'll return your call.]

call down   **1.** I (1)   His wife, who was upstairs, called down to ask what the noise was about. [Downstairs.]   **2.** T (1,5)   The angry priest called down the wrath of God on the enemies of the church. [Prayed to God to punish them.] **3.** T (5)   Father called Johnny down for speaking rudely to his mother. [Spoke loudly and in a scolding manner.]   **4.** *calling down* N. (5)   Father gave Johnny a good calling down.

call in   **1.** T (1)   If you don't feel better in the morning, we'll have to call in the doctor. [Ask him to come to the house to see you.]   **2.** T (1)   The bank is calling in all outstanding notes. [They are asking for payment.]   **3.** I (1)   Telephone. Mr. Smith called in to say he can't keep his appointment.

call off   **1.** T (6)   At the meeting the secretary called off the names of the delegates to check the attendance. [He read them off a list.]   **2.** T (5)   I think we should call off the next regular meeting, because of the Holiday Season. [Postpone it.]   **3.** T (2)   Call off your dog! He'll kill that poor little thing!

call out   **1.** T (2)   The governor had to call out the National Guard to control the riot. [Out into service.]   **2.** T (2)   Dr. Brown was at the banquet, but was called out on an emergency. [He received a call to take care of a patient.]   **3.** T (4)   Baseball. The umpire called the runner out at third base. [He declared him to be put out.]   **4.** T (1,9)   Hard times always called out the best in him. [Caused his best qualities to show themselves.]   **5.** I (1,9)   As I was passing by his door he called out to me. [He spoke loudly, from inside his room.] **6.** *call-out* N.   (2)   The governor ordered a call-out of the National Guard. See **call out 1.**

call over   T (3)   He called his secretary over to take a dictation. [He called to her to come to his desk.]

call up   **1.** I (1)   She called up to tell us that breakfast was ready. [Upstairs.] **2.** T (14)   Telephone. She called (me, him, her, us, you, them) up to say goodbye. [Gave a call on the phone.]   **3.** T (10)   The President will probably call up the reserves, to meet the needs of the Armed Services. [Call them into service.]   **4.** T (5)   That movie calls up memories of World War I. [Brings them to our minds.]   **5.** *call-up* N. (10)   The call-up of the reserves will be part of the President's up-coming speech. See **call up 3.**

Calm To make or become calm.

    calm down **1.** I (2) She was terribly nervous on hearing of the accident, but calmed down when she learned that no one was seriously hurt. [Became calmer]. **2.** T (2) The doctor prescribed some sedatives to calm her down. [Reduce her tension.]

Camp To spend some time living in the open air, in tents.

    camp down I (1) We camped down for the night beside a rushing mountain stream. [We pitched our tent there.]

    camp out I (2) The children are camping out tonight. [They are sleeping in a tent, not in the house.]

    camp up T (2,6) Slang. In the second act the actors camped up the scene in the artist's studio. [They performed in an affected, ostentatious manner.] No relation to **camp down, camp out. See ham up.**

Cancel To eliminate, to cross out.

    cancel out **1.** T (4) When we arrived at the airport we found our reservations had been canceled out by mistake. [Our names had been dropped from the list.] **2.** I (10) Our debts and our credits cancel out. [They balance. There is no plus or minus.]

Carry To move while transporting; to continue an activity.

    carry around T (2) She's not at all well. She has been carrying around a virus infection for weeks. [The virus has stayed with her.]

    carry away **1.** T (2) Our son carried away the honors at the High School ceremony. [He won.] **2.** T (2,3) Their house beside the river was carried away by the Spring flood. [The water swept it down stream.] **3.** T (4) He was completely carried away by the enthusiasm of the crowd (the excellence of the performance, the eloquence of the speaker, etc.). [He was swept from his normal state of mind and feelings.]

    carry off **1.** T (1,2) He was too weak to leave the plane on his own. They had to carry him off. [Off the plane.] **2.** T (8) Our dog carried off first prize (a blue ribbon, a gold star, etc.) at the Kennel Show. [He won.] **3.** T (8) Our troops carried off a major victory in the final campaign of the year. [They won.] **4.** T (5) The Black plaque carried off hundreds of thousands of victims during the Middle Ages. [It killed them.]

    carry on **1.** T (I 1) He was too weak to get aboard the plane by himself. They had to carry him on. [Onto the plane.] **2.** T (II 1,2) Mr. Jones carried on a long conversation (correspondence, discussion, argument) with his friend, Judge Smith. [He continued it for a long time.] See **keep up. 3.** T (II 1,2) That family has carried on a hardware business for three generations. [It has been in that kind of business.] **4.** I (II 1,2) Carry on! [An officer speaks to soldiers off duty who have stopped what they were doing, in order to salute him. He wants them to go back to what they were doing.] **5.** I (II 2,5) When their parents left the house the children started carrying on something terrible. [They were noisy and behaved very badly.] **6.** I (II 2,5) Informal. After being scratched by the cat Mary carried on as though she had been hurt very seriously. [She cried in an exaggerated manner.] See **take on.** **7.** I (II 2,5) Informal I've heard that James has been carrying on in scandalous fashion with that girl down the street. [He has been acting shamefully, disgracefully.] **8.** *carryings-on* N. (II 1,2) I've never heard of such carryings on! [I am surprised and shocked by those actions.] See **carry on 5, 6, 7.**

carry out **1.** T (2) You'll have to carry out the garbage this morning. [Out of the house, to the street, for the garbage collection.] **2.** T (7) I hope we can carry out our plans for a picnic today. [Do as we had planned.] **3.** T (7) We'll carry out your plans (suggestion, command, request) if it is at all possible. [Do what you want us to do.] See **follow out.**

carry over **1.** T (3) They came to a river and carried the bundles over. [Over the river.] **2.** T (4) Bookkeeping — When you have found the balance for this month's accounts, carry it over to the next month. [Start the next month's account with that balance.] **3.** T (4) Commerce. After inventory they found they would have to carry over a large quantity of spring merchandise to the following year. [Keep it for sale the next year.]

carry through **1.** T (1) He opened the door and carried the T.V. set through. [Through the door.] **2.** T (4) We carried through our plans for the week. [We did what we planned to do.] See **carry out 2.** **3.** I (3,4) I've given you my idea about how to do this job. I expect you to carry through. [To do it completely and well.] **4.** I (2) The notion of the futility of human effort carries through all of his writings. [It is found in everything he has written.]

Cart To convey or carry, as in a cart or other vehicle.

cart away T (2) It took many hours for the street cleaners to cart away all the rubbish. [Remove it from the streets.]

cart off **1.** T (1,2) During the riot many looters were seen carting off pieces of furniture and cases of liquor. [Stealing them and taking them away.] **2.** T (1,2) The police arrested five looters and carted them off to jail. [Took them away in police wagons.]

Carve To cut with a sharp instrument, such as a knife, a sword, a chisel.

carve out **1.** T (1,7) A sculptor carves out his statues (busts, figures) by using a hammer and chisel. [He chips away pieces of stone or other material from a solid mass.] **2.** T (7) Fig. Einstein carved out a career for himself in atomic physics. [He worked hard and intensively as would a sculptor.]

carve up **1.** T (4) The cook carved up the roast so that it would serve twenty people. [He used a knife to cut it into twenty pieces.] **2.** T (6) Ext. As a result of the knife battle, two of the men had their faces badly carved up. [They had many knife wounds on their faces.]

Cash

cash in **1.** T (7) Gambling. He cashed in his chips, and withdrew from the game. [He received the money value of his chips.] **2.** T (7) He cashed in some bonds (stocks or other investments) and bought himself a new car. [He sold them for cash.] **3.** I (7) Slang. The old man finally cashed in (or cashed in his chips.). [He died.] See **kick in 3. 4.** *cash in (on)* T (1) You impressed the boss yesterday. Why not cash in on it, and ask for a raise? [Get some advantage in exchange.] See **cash in 1, 2.**

Cast To throw, hurl, fling, as with a line, or rope.

cast about I (2) He was casting about for a good answer (reason, excuse, explanation, etc.) to make, but nothing came to his mind. [He tried as a fisherman tries to find a fish by casting his line here and there.]

cast-away N.A. (3,5) On that small desert island were found two castaways (castaway sailors). [Their ship had been wrecked and they were "cast up" on the island.]

cast down 1. T (6) The refugee child cast her eyes down and refused to talk. [She looked sad.] **2.** *cast-down* A. (6) She had a cast-down look. [Sad and discouraged.]

cast off 1. I (1,2) Our boat cast off from the dock, and we were on our way. [The dock hands loosened the mooring line that held the boat close to the dock.] **2.** T (2) She was cast off by her family as a consequence of her scandalous love affair. [They refused to recognize her as part of the family.] **3.** *cast-off* N.A. (4) We give all our cast-offs (our cast-off clothing) to the Salvation Army. [The clothing that we no longer want or need.]

cast out T (9) Formal. We should cast out all evil thoughts from our hearts. [Remove them by strong action.]

cast up 1. T (1) Formal. The dying man cast his eyes up to Heaven, and uttered a prayer. [Raised them.] **2.** T (4) Mathematics. Now that you have all the correct figures, cast them up and give me the result. [Add them together.]

Catch To capture, to trap, to reach, to grasp with the mind.

catch on 1. I (1,2) Informal. That young man is new at the job, but he's catching on very quickly. [He is learning very fast.] **2.** I (1,2) I didn't catch on when she whispered to me something about our neighbor's wife. [I didn't understand well.] **3.** I (1,2) The Beatle's music caught on very quickly in most of the Western World. [It captured the public interest.] **4.** *catch on (to)* I (1,2) He tried to fool us with his arguments, but we caught on to him. [We could see what he was up to.]

catch out 1. T (2) Informal. Father says you must not leave the house tonight. If he catches you out, you'll suffer for it. [Out of the house.] **2.** T (4) Baseball. The batter was caught out by the right fielder. [Out of the game, for one inning.]

catch up 1. T (1,5) Little Marie ran to meet her father. He caught her up in his arms. [Up from the ground.] **2.** T (5,10) We were caught up in the excitement of the moment, and marched with the crowd to the White House. [Our emotions were captured.] **3.** I (2,10) You're way behind in your class work. You'll have to work hard to catch up. [Come up to where the other students are.] **4.** *catch up (on)* I (2,4) I've been staying up late for five nights. I'll have to catch up on my sleep. [Make up for lost sleep.] See **make up.** **5.** *catch (someone) up (on)* T (5,9) He made a statement that isn't true. I'm going to catch him up on it. [Expose the falsehood, catch him in a lie.] **6.** *catch up (with)* I (10) They're way ahead of us. We'll have to run to catch up with them. [Come to where they are.] **7.** *catch-up* N. (1,5) After a slow down in production last winter, our company is staging a catch-up. [An effort to reach the earlier rate of production] See **pull up.**

Cave   To fall, collapse toward the center.

  cave in   **1.** T (1)   Due to the rotting of the support beams the walls of the mine caved in. [Fell inwardly.]   **2.** T (1)   The collision caved in the hoods of both cars. [Bent them inward.] See **give in.**   **3.** *cave-in* N.   (3)   The cave-in of the trench walls buried five workmen. [The falling of the earth from the walls.]

Cement   To use cement for a purpose.

  cement over   T (3)   He was tired of trying to raise flowers in his patio so he cemented it over. [Covered it with cement.]

  cement up   T (2,3)   He cemented up the cracks that the earthquake made in his wall. [Used cement to repair it.]

Centrifuge   To remove solids from a liquid solution by centrifugal action.

  centrifuge out   T (1,10)   The chemist can remove certain solids from a solution by centrifuging them out.

Chain   To fasten by means of a chain.

  chain down   **1.** T (1)   The galley slaves were chained down to the deck of the ship to keep them in position. [Their ankles were attached to the deck by chains.]
  2. T (2,3)   We are often chained down by the customs of our ancestors. [We cannot move or act or think freely.]

  chain up   T (3)   That ferocious dog is a danger to the neighborhood. His owner should be required to chain him up. [Secure him with a chain.]

Chalk   To use chalk for a purpose.

  chalk in   T (2)   Before beginning to paint the artist usually chalks in an outline (a sketch, a design, a pattern). Makes a drawing with chalk.]

  chalk up   **1.** T (2,9)   Bowling. Harry chalked up three strikes and five spares during the match. [Used chalk to mark the score on the score board.]   **2.** T (2,9) Sport. Our team chalked up ten wins to five losses during the past season. [We won and lost that number of games.]

Change   To make or become different in form, nature content, condition, etc.

  change about (around)   T (1,2)   I don't like the way the furniture is arranged in this room. Let's change it about (around). [Move it into different positions.]

  change off   I (2)   When my wife and I take long trips in our car we change off every hundred miles. [We take turns driving.]

  change over   **1.** I (5)   Their company began by manufacturing wagons, but

changed over to making cars in 1905. [Began making a different product.]
2. *change-over* N. (5) The change-over required new buildings and new
capital. See **change over 1.**

Charge   To make an accounting.

charge off   T (5)   Accounting. The shop-keeper charged off all the unsold
winter overcoats. [He entered them as a loss.]

charge up   T (4,9)   When John lost the election, he charged it up to bad   publicity
(lack of experience, unfair tactics of his opponent). [He excused himself for
losing.]

Charm   To give pleasure or delight.

charm away   **1.** T (2,3)   The sweet music and the graceful movements of the
dancers charmed away her tears. [They made her tears stop, disappear, go away.]

Chat   To converse in an informal manner.

chat along/away   I (3)   When we came in we found them chatting along (away)
in very friendly manner. [Talking freely, easily and continuously.]

chat over   T (7)   Come in for a cup of tea, and we'll chat things over. [Have
a friendly talk about things.]

Check   To use a tag, ticket, or mark of some kind to keep account of persons or things.

check back   **1.** I (1,5)   If you check back through last month's accounts you
will find that bill has been paid. [Examine carefully.]   **2.** *check-back* N.   (1,5)
The check-back showed that the bill had been paid.

check in   **1.** I (1)   We checked in at the hotel (the convention, the factory,
the meeting, etc.) before noon. [We signed our names on a form or list.] See
check out 2. I (1)   Informal. We expected our guests to arrive at 8 p.m. but
they didn't check in till midnight. [They arrived late.]   **3.** T (1,5)   The athletes
checked in their uniforms at the end of the season. They were checked in by
the coach. [They returned them and the coach made a note of it.]   **4.** *check-in* N.
(1,5)   At the time of the check-in, three uniforms were missing.

check off   **1.** T (6)   As each prisoner entered the door the sergeant checked
him off. [Made a mark after his name on a list.]   **2.** *check-off* N. (6)   Labor
unions collect dues from their members by means of the check-off. [The dues
are deducted from the pay check by the employer, and given to the union.]
See **check off 1.**

check out   **1.** I (1)   We checked out of the hotel before 3 p.m. [Opposite of
check in 1. We paid our bill and left.]   **2.** *check-out* N.A. (1)   The check-out
(time) is usually 3 p.m.   **3.** I (7)   Upon close inspection, the various items
of the bill check out. [After a check is made, they are found to be correct.]
4. T (1)   As each worker came to get his tools, the boss checked them out.
[He made a note of the tools each man took.]   **5.** *check-out* N.A. (1)   After
the check-out the workmen were taken in trucks to the construction site. See
check out 4.   **6.** I (8)   Slang. The sick man wanted to have one more fling
before he checked out. [Have a gay, noisy party before he died.]   See **cash in 3.**

check up **1.** I (4) John told me that he thinks one of our horses is missing. I'll have to check up. [Make a count of our horses.] **2.** I (4) Check up and let me know how much time you have worked on that project. [Examine your records carefully.] **3.** *check-up* N.A. (4) She's not been feeling well. She should go to the doctor for a check-up. [A thorough physical examination.] **4.** (4) I left my car at the garage for a motor check-up. [A thorough examination of the motor.]

Cheer To become hopeful, glad; to encourage by words or actions.

cheer along T (1,3) As the bicycle racers sped down the highway, the bystanders cheered them along. [Encouraged them by shouts and applause.]

cheer off T (2) The departing soldiers climbed into the waiting trucks, and we cheered them off. [We waved to them and shouted words of encouragement.]

cheer up **1.** I (2,5) Cheer up, old man; things are not as bad as they seem. [Don't be sad. Have courage.] **2.** T (2,5) We gave him a drink and a good meal to cheer him up. [Make him feel happier.] See **humor up, jolly up.**

Chew To crush or grind with the teeth.

chew off T (1) The dog chewed off a large chunk of meat from the bone and swallowed it eagerly. [Used his teeth to bite it off.]

chew out **1.** T (9) Slang. Fig. His father chewed him out for wrecking the car. [He scolded him severely.] **2.** *chewing-out* N. (9) Slang. His father gave him a real chewing-out. [A severe scolding.]

chew over T (6) Informal. I'm not sure I can agree with you about that matter. We'll have to chew it over. [Discuss it at length.]

chew up **1.** T (2,11) Some animal parents chew up bits of food before giving it to their young. [Prepare it by chewing.] **2.** *chewed up* A T (6) Fig. Our front lawn was all chewed up when those boys drove their cars over it. [It gave the appearance of having been chewed.]

Chicken To act in cowardly fashion, be timid.

chicken out I (6) Slang. There were five boys in the gang that planned to rob the store. Two of them chickened out at the last moment. [They did not have the courage to do it.]

Chime To make harmonious sounds, as a bell.

chime in **1.** I (4) Marie sang the verses of the old song, and we all chimed in on the chorus. [We sang with her.] **2.** I (5) Informal. When we suggested going on a picnic, all of the children chimed in with cries of "Yes, yes". [They agreed with the idea.]

chime out I (2,9) On Christmas Day the church bells chime out, to celebrate the birth of Christ. [Out from the bell tower, to the public.]

Chink To fill cracks or chinks.

chink up T (2,3) The walls of the old house were full of cracks. We had to chink them up with putty and plaster. [Fill the cracks.]

Chip I To cut or break small pieces from a substance.

chip away   **1.** T (3)   The sculptor, with his chisel, chips away much of the marble in the block before the statue takes shape. [Removes it by chipping action.] **2.** T (6)   By chipping away day by day at the enemy forces, our army finally forced them to surrender. [Reducing their number by killing.]

chip off   T (1)   He chipped off a piece of ice and put it in the punch bowl. [Broke it off by chipping.]

chip up   T (6)   Women's spike heel shoes chip up the hardwood floors. [Break the surface of the floors.]

Chip II   To use chips or coins in gambling.

chip in   I (5)   Poker. You must chip in if you want to continue playing. [Put a chip or chips in the kitty.] **2.** I (5)   To make our community a better place to live we must all chip in and do our best. [Give contributions, energies, or money.]

Chirk   Make a shrill, chirping noise, usually cheerful.

chirk up   I (2,5)   Informal. He's been so solemn recently. I wish he would chirk up a bit. [Become more cheerful.] See **cheer up 1, perk up 1.**

Choke   To stop the breath, by squeezing or blocking the windpipe.

choke back   T (1,5)   She managed to choke back a sigh (her tears, her sobs) and show a little smile. [Stop them by conscious effort.]

choke off   T (5)   Fig. The presiding officer decided to choke off debate on the question. [Put an end to it.]

choke up   **1.** I (4,6)   She choked up, and could'nt say a word, when she heard that her son had been killed. [Her power of speech was lost.] **2.** T (4,6)   A thick wad of hair choked up the wash bowl drain pipe. [Made it impossible for the water to flow.] **3.** T (4,6)   Water hyacinth chokes up the channels of many streams in the South. [Blocks the flow of water.]

Choose   To select, make a choice.

choose up   T (10)   In many kinds of games the captains of opposing teams must choose up sides. [Choose the members they want to play on their side.]

Chop   To cut or sever with quick, heavy blows.

chop down   T (1)   The story is told that George Washington chopped down his father's favorite cherry tree. [Made it fall to the ground by cutting it with an axe.] See **cut down.**

chop off   T (1,4)   In olden days kings could order the executioner to chop off the heads of criminals. [Sever the head from the body with an axe.]

chop up   T (2,11)   To make almond cookies, first chop up a half pound of almonds. [Cut them into many small pieces.]

Clam   To close tightly as a clam closes its shell.

clam up   I (4)   Slang. The fellow who had been talking so noisily clammed up when the policemen entered. [Stopped talking.] See **shut up.**

Clamp   To fasten or fix with a clamp.

clamp down   **1.** I (1,5)   Informal. Too many motorists are exceeding the speed limit. The traffic cops will have to clamp down. [They will have to enforce the laws.] **2.** *clamp down (on)* I (1,5) College authorities are clamping down on the use of alcoholic liquors and marijuana on campus. [They are going to punish students who use these things.]

Clean To make clean, to remove dirt or other matter.

clean off T (7) Before applying new paint you should clean off the surface you are going to paint. [Remove dirt or old paint.]

clean out **1.** T (1) My wife is cleaning out the closets, getting ready for the arrival of our guests. [Removing dirt and other objects.] **2.** T (9) The newly elected Mayor promised to clean out the grafters from City Hall. [Remove them from office.] **3.** T (9) A sudden rush of customers cleaned out Mr. Black's stock of nylons. [The nylons were all sold.] **4.** T (9) In that poker game Jack was completely cleaned out. [He lost all his money.]

clean up **1.** I (2,11) Dinner's ready! It's time to clean up. [Wash hands and faces, and comb hair.] **2.** T (2,11) The room was so dirty it took us an hour to clean it up. [Put it in good condition.] **3.** T (2,4) Fig. The Republican candidate for President promises to clean up the mess in Washington. [Put an end to graft, corruption, bad government, etc.] **4.** I (5) John told us he cleaned up in Wall Street last week. [He made large profits buying and selling stocks.]

Clear To remove dirt or other objects; to become free of matter that is darkening. Closely related to clean.

clear away T (2,3) After the earthquake it took weeks to clear away the debris (the rubble, the wreckage, etc.). [Remove it from the streets, etc.]

clear off **1.** T (7) Mother asked Alice to help by clearing off the table. [Remove the dishes, etc.] **2.** I (1,2) It's clearing off. Maybe we can still have our picnic. [The clouds are moving away. There will be no rain.]

clear out **1.** T (1,9) I'll clear out the closet and the dresser drawers, so our guests will have a place to put things. [Remove what is in them.] See **rid out(up).** **2.** I (1,9) Informal. The neighbor boys were fighting with our boys in the back yard, but they cleared out when father appeared. [Ran.] See **take off.**

clear up **1.** I (2) It's clearing up! The sun will be shining before long. [The darkness is disappearing. The weather will be good.] **2.** I (2) Jim's skin infection is clearing up nicely. [The infection is disappearing.] **3.** T (2) The doctor gave him some antibiotic medication to clear it up. [To remove the infection.] See **clear up 2.** **4.** T (4) The teacher gave us some very helpful hints to clear up the problem in our minds. [Remove the difficulties we had in understanding.]

Clip To cut as with shears, with a quick motion.

clip away T (2,3) The hospital attendant clipped away the matted hair from the patient's wound. [Removed it by clipping.]

clip off   T (2)   She clipped off a branch of the lilac bush and placed it in a vase. [Removed it.]

clip out   T (6)   Here's an article from the Times I clipped out for you. [I made a "clipping".] See **cut out.**

Clock   To time, test, determine something by the use of a clock, often a stop-watch. Especially used for timing athletes, racing animals, etc.

clock around   T (3)   We clocked him around at 3 minutes 50 seconds. [We determined that it took him that amount of time to go around the race track.]

clock back   T (3)   We clocked him back at 4:15. [By our watch, that is when he returned.]

clock by   T (2)

clock down   T (1)

clock on   T (1)

clock off   T (1)

clock out   T (1,4)

clock over   T (3)

clock through   T (2,3)

clock up   T (1,4).

Clog   To hinder or obstruct with thick or sticky matter.

clog up   **1.** T (4,6)   A thick mass of grease and hair clogged up the drain pipe. [Made it impossible for water to flow through easily.]   **2.** T (4,6)   Fig. A long tradition of mutual hatred and distrust clogged up the channels of communication between the two nations. [Stopped the flow of diplomatic relations.]

Close   To shut.

close down   T (4,6)   The owners of the factory were losing money, so they closed it down. [They stopped operation.] See **shut down.**

close in   **1.** T (3)   To keep out dogs and strangers they closed their patio in. [Built a fence around it to protect it.] See **fence in.**   **2.** I (1)   The enemy closed in for the kill. [They came closer hoping to win by killing their opponents.]   **3.** *close in (on)*   I (1)   The bandit closed in on his victim, brandishing a knife. [Came closer.]

close off   T (3)   The living room was very large, so we closed off one corner of it to make a study. [Built a wall or partition, with a door.] See **curtain off.**

close out   **1.** T (9)   The Boston Department Store is closing out its stock of radios. [It will no longer sell them.]   **2.** *close-out* N.A. (9)   The store is having a close-out sale of radios. [It will sell all the radios it has in stock.]

close over   T (2)   There was danger of children falling into the open well, so we decided to close it over. [Put boards or a cement top on the well.]

close up   **1.** I (13)   We're going to close up. No more drinks served tonight. [A bartender speaking to the customers in the bar.]   **2.** *close up (shop)*   T (13)   All the groceries in town used to close up shop at 6:30 p.m. [Stop business at the end of the day.]   **3.** T (4,13)   After all these years as a druggist, Mr. X.

has decided to close up shop. [To go out of the drug business.] **4.** T (4,13) Our committee has done all that it could do about the problem. We might as well close up shop. [Resign our job as a committee.]

Cloud To grow cloudy.

cloud over I (3) The sky is clouding over. It may rain. [Becoming covered with clouds.] See **mist over.**

cloud up I (2,6) It's clouding up. I hope it won't rain. [Many clouds are appearing.]

Clutter To fill or litter in disorderly fashion.

clutter up **1.** T (4,6) The artist's studio was cluttered up with all kinds of strange materials. [It was full of odd things with no orderly arrangement.] **2.** T (6) Don't clutter up your mind with useless facts. [Don't fill it with things of no value.]

Coal To supply with coal.

coal up I (4,11) Locomotives always used to stop at Lafayette to coal up. [Take on a supply of coal for fuel.] See **gas up, tank up.**

Color To give color to, acquire color.

color over T (2) The artist first colored the canvas over with a pale blue shade. [Spread the color over the whole canvas.]

color up I (2,4) When she heard her name mentioned as one of the guilty people she colored up. [Her face became red. She blushed.]

Comb To arrange or process with a comb.

comb back T (1) She used to wear her hair down over her forehead, but now she combs it back. [Toward the back of her head.]

comb out **1.** T (10) When she combs out her hair it is so long it reaches to her waist. [Out to its full length.] **2.** T (1) The cotton gin combs the seeds and any impurities out of the cotton bolls. [It eliminates them.]

comb up T (1) She used to let her hair fall over her eyes, but now she combs it up. [Up above her forehead.]

Come To arrive at a place, position or state. The opposite of **go.**

come about **1.** I (4) How does it come about that you are not in school? [How does it happen?]

come across **1.** I (1) How did you get from New Jersey to New York? We came across on the ferry. [Across the Hudson River.] **2.** I (1) The gangster treatened his victim with a beating if he didn't come across. [Give some money or information.] **3.** *come across (with)* I (1) The gangster's victim came across with the money (the information) the gangster wanted. [He gave it to the gangster.]

come along **1.** I (1,2,3) The policeman took the suspect by the arm and said, "Come along now". [Come with me to the Police Station.] **2.** I (2) We're going on a picnic. Won't you come along? [Please come with us.] **3.** I (1,3) How is your business coming along? [Progressing.] **4.** I (1,3) Mother is coming along fine since her operation. [She is improving in health.] See **get along.** **5.** I (2) We have a better idea on how to handle this question. We hope your friends will come along. [Agree, and work with us.] See **go along, come around.**

come around **1.** I (1) Tell the children not to come around while I'm working. [Near to me.] **2.** I (3) I will be back of the house. Tell any visitors to come around if they want to see me. [Circle the house.] **3.** I (3,4) Do you think your mother will come around? See **go along.** [Will she agree with me?] **4.** I (3) He was knocked unconscious by the blow, but came around after half an hour. [Came back to consciousness.]

come aside **1.** I (1,2) Come aside a moment. I'd like to tell you something. [Come where other people can't hear us.]

come away **1.** I (2) Come away! It's too dangerous to stay so close to the fire. [Let's leave this place.] **2.** I (2) We came away without our hats. [We left them at the place where we were.] **3.** I (3) When he dug with his knife the bark came away from the tree trunk.

come back **1.** I (1) After the performance the President came back to congratulate the players. [To the rear of the stage.] **2.** I (3) After the performance we came back for a snack at my house. [To the place we left to go to the theater.] **3.** I (4) Winter weather has come back to our part of the country. [We are having cold weather again, after a warm period.] **4.** I (3) The cat came back. [We had given it away, but it returned to us.] **5.** I (3,4) She came back in a wonderful performance of *Traviata*. [She returned to the opera stage, after a long absence.] **6.** *comeback* N. (4) She made (staged) a wonderful comeback. See **come back 5.**

come by **1.** I (2) We'll come by and pick you up at 8 o'clock. [We will stop in our car to take you with us.]

come down **1.** I (1) Come down! I want to talk to you. [Downstairs, down from a tree, a ladder, the roof, etc.] **2.** I (1) The rain (the snow, the fog) came down and spoiled our plans. **3.** I (2) The price of milk is coming down. [It's getting lower.] **4.** I (2) The president of the corporation has come down in the world since the scandal. [His reputation has suffered.] **5.** *come down (with)* I (1) She came down with a cold (a fever, tonsilitis, any temporary illness). [Became ill and spent some time in bed.] **6.** *comedown* N. (2) It was a great comedown for him and his family. See **come down 4.**

come in **1.** I (1) a. Come in! b. Please come in. c. Won't you come in? [Invitations to enter a place.] I (6) Peaches (other fruits or vegetables) are coming in. [They are in season and appearing in market.] I (1) He came in second in the race (the competition). [He reached the goal in second place.]

come off **1.** I (2) As soon as the boat stopped the passengers came off. [Off the boat.] **2.** I (2) When he took hold of the door knob, it came off in his hand. [Off the door.] **3.** I (8) How did the experiment (the lecture, the class, the performance) come off? [Did it go well; was it effective?] **4.** (2) Slang. Aw, come off! [Abandon your silly pose! Stop talking or acting that way.]

come on **1.** I (I 1) He waved to the audience as he came on. [Onto the stage or platform.] **2.** I (I 3) After much pulling and tugging his boot came on. [He was able to get it on.] **3.** I (II 4) The lights (the power, the T.V., the radio) went off, but came on again in a few minutes. [Started to function.] **4.** I (II 1) I feel a cold coming on. [There are indications that I will have a cold.] **5.** I (II 1,2) The peaches are coming on nicely. [They are continuing to develop.] **6.** I (II 1) Don't wait any longer. We're leaving. Come on! [Join us to go somewhere.] **7.** I (II 4) Informal. Come on! Please sing something for us. [A friendly invitation to sing.] **8.** I (II 1) Informal. Ah (oh, aw) come on! I don't believe you. [Tell us the truth.] **9.** *come-on* N.A. (II 1) Slang. I think she's giving me the come-on (the come-on sign, the come-on look, the come-on nod, etc.). [She is inviting me to come near to her.]

come out **1.** I (1) I want to talk to her as soon as she comes out. [Out of a door, room, house, etc.] **2.** I (2) The new edition of his book is coming out next month. [It will be published.] **3.** I (2) Linda Martin will be coming out in June. [She will be formally introduced to polite society, at a coming out party.] **4.** *coming out* N.A. (2) The coming out of Linda Martin was preceded by a big coming out party, given by her parents. See **come out 3.** **5.** I (8) How did your experiment (your test, your trial, your marriage, your tennis game) come out? [What was the result?] **6.** I (2) It came out that she had been divorced twice, before her marriage to Albert. [It was revealed, made public.] **7.** I (2) Many Republican members of the House came out against the Medicare bill. [They spoke against the bill.] **8.** *come out with* I (2) They came out with a substitute bill. [They presented it.] See **come out 7.**

come over **1.** I (3) When we called to them, they came over. [From across the street, from some place at a distance.] **2.** I (5) We tried very hard to persuade him and he finally came over. See **go along.** [Came to our point of view.] **3.** I (3) The broadcast (on radio or T.V.) came over perfectly. [Over the air, or the wire.]

come through **1.** I (1) The gate was closed after we came through. [Through the gate.] **2.** I (2) That telegram you sent came through in less than an hour. **3.** I (4) The operation was successful. She came through without any bad side effects. **4.** I (3,4) No matter how difficult his enemies make it for him, he always comes through with flying colors. [He wins a victory.] **5.** *come through (with)* I (4) He came through with a plan that pleased everyone. [He worked until he found a plan.]

come under **1.** I (1) She told him to lift up the flap of the tent and come under. [Under the tent.] **2.** I (4) As a clerk, he comes under the supervisor. [He is lower in rank.]

come up **1.** I (1) It's time for bed. Come up and get undressed. [Upstairs.]

2. I (2) The child's temperature was down below normal, but it came up rapidly after he took the medicine. [Up on the thermometer.] **3.** I (2) Stocks have come up the past few days. [Up in price.] **4.** I (5,6,8) He wanted to come to the meeting tonight, but something came up that kept him away. [Something needed his attention.] **5.** I (8,9) What questions are coming up at the meeting tonight? [Up before the members.] **6.** I (6,8) There's a storm coming up. Let's go home! **7.** I (8,9) Mr. Thomas is coming up for re-election this month. [Up before the voters.] **8.** *come up (with)* I (5,12) Can't you come up with a better answer to our problem? [Find a better answer.] See **come through (with).**

Connect To join together.

   connect up **1.** T (4) It takes a skilled technician to connect up accurately all the wires in a telephone system. [Do a careful and accurate job of joining wire to wire.] **2.** I (4,10) We must hurry if we want connect up with the rest of the caravan. [Join the other cars that are leaving on a trip.]

Contract To enter into an agreement.

   contract out T (1) Large companies that have government orders, often contract out certain parts of the work to smaller companies. [They make agreements with the small companies to get the work done.]

Cook To prepare food, using heat.

   cook down T (6) To make jam and jellies you have to cook the ingredients down, to reduce the water content. [Reduce the volume by boiling off much of the water.] See **boil down.**

   cook out **1.** I (2) We're cooking out tonight. [On the patio, in the yard, in the open air.] **2.** *cook-out* N.A. (2) Our family loves a cook-out. See **cook out 1.**

   cook over T (7) That meat is too tough. You'll have to cook it over. [Repeat the cooking process.]

   cook up **1.** T (11) Our guests for dinner tonight are not big eaters, so don't cook up a lot of food. [Don't go to too much trouble to prepare for them.] **2.** T (7,11) Informal. Fig. Those two people have been talking very mysteriously. I wonder what they're cooking up. [What they are planning to do, perhaps to surprise us.] See **hatch up.**

Cool To reduce the heat of something or somebody.

   cool down I (2,6) They were having a very hot argument, but cooled down when we started to laugh at them. [Became more calm.] **2.** T (2,6) The coffee was too hot to drink so I cooled it down with a little cold water. [Reduced the heat.]

   cool off **1.** I (1) I'm hot! Let's go for a swim to cool off. [Remove the heat from the surface of out bodies.] **2.** T (7) A swim in the pool and a refreshing drunk cooled us off nicely. [Removed the heat from our bodies.] **3.** I (1) John and Mary were madly in love for months, but John began to cool off about Christmas time. [Lose his strong emotional attachment for Mary.]

Coop   To enclose in a pen or cage, as for chickens.

coop in   1. T (3)   This town coops me in. There's no place to go. Nothing to do. [I feel like a bird in a cage.] **2.** *cooped in* A.   I have a cooped in feeling.

coop up   1. T (3,5)   The neighbors are complaining about our chickens spoiling their garden and flower beds. We'll have to coop them up. [Put them in a pen.] **2.** *cooped-up* A. (3)   I don't want to spend all my time cooped up in this tiny apartment. [Like a chicken in a pen.]

Cop   Slang. To steal, take by stealth.

cop out   1. I (6)   Harry was one of our companions in the affair, but he copped out. [He did nothing to help. He goofed off.] **2.** *cop-out* N. (6)   He was just a cop-out. See **drop out, flake out, goof off.**

Copy   To make a copy.

copy down   T (1,7)   To make sure I could remember their names I copied them down in my address book. [Down on paper.]

copy off   T (6)   He showed me a list of the names of the members, and I copied them off. [Off the list.]

copy out   T (1)   There are many excellent passages in the book you loaned me. I want to copy them out. [Out of the book.]

Cough   To expel from the lungs suddenly, with a harsh noise.

cough out   1. T (1,9)   The dying man coughed out his last breath. [He expelled air suddenly as he died.] **2.** T (1,9)   Fig. The locomotive coughed out great clouds of black smoke. [Expelled them.]

cough up   1. T (1,6)   After a siege of bronchitis I always cough up great quantities of phlegm. [I expel it.] **2.** T (1,5)   Slang. If you want to be in on this party, you'll have to cough up 10 dollars. [Pay that much as your share.]

Count   To list numbers in their order, to reckon numerically.

count down   1. I (2)   Children learn to count down after they know how to count up. [Count from a higher number down to zero.] **2.** *count-down* N. (2)   Aero-Space. The blast-off comes at the end of the count-down. [When the count has gone from a higher number to zero.]

count in   T (4)   I'd like to join the group for the party (the game, the trip, the picnic). Please count me in. [Let me enter the group.]

count off   1. I (6)   Military. The officer lined the men up and gave the command to count off. [Starting from left to right, each man calls out his number in sequence, one, two, three, four, etc.] **2.** *count-off* N. (6)   The count-off showed that two men were missing. See **count off 1. 3.** T (6)   The officer counted off five men to send on special duty. [He chose them from the group of soldiers.]

count out   1. T (4)   Boxing. When a boxer is knocked down the referee begins counting to ten. If the boxer does not get up before the count of ten, the referee counts him out. [Out of the fight.] **2.** T (4,6)   I don't feel like going with you to the party. Just count me out. [Do not include me.] See **count in.** **3.** T (4,9) The officer counted out the numbers of men he needed for each special assignment. [He spoke loudly and clearly.]

count up **1.** I (2,4) My young son can already count up to fifty. [He knows his numbers to fifty.] **2.** I (2) When you have to pay taxes on income, food, property, entertainment, and travel it all counts up. [The total is high.] See **add up.**

Cover To place something over or upon, for protection or concealment.

cover over T (3) The killer placed the body of his victim in a shallow trench and covered it over with loose earth and dry branches. [Concealed it.]

cover up **1.** T (3) His mother put the cold and sleepy boy to bed and covered him up carefully. [Put warm blankets over him.] **2.** T (4) She tried to cover up her anxiety with a cheerful smile. [Hide her real feelings.] **3.** I (4) Boys usually will try to cover up for one of their play-mates who has done something bad. [They will not "tell on", give the name of the guilty one.] **4.** *cover-up* N.A. (4) He was the cover-up (man) for the gangsters. [His job was to prevent the authorities from identifying the gangsters.] See **cover up 3.**

Cozy To become close to, try to win the friendship of someone.

cozy up (to) I (3) Bob has been cozying up to Jack lately. He must want something. [Acting very friendly. Perhaps insincerely.] See **honey up.**

Crack I To break, without complete separation into parts.

crack off I (1) We'll have to have the house painted this summer. The old paint is cracking off. [It is developing cracks, peeling off.]

crack up **1.** I (6) The airplane cracked up on landing. [It was wrecked, but not completely broken into pieces.] **2.** T (6) John cracked up his car yesterday. [He had an accident that damaged his car.] **3.** I (6) He kept going through a long series of misfortunes, but cracked up when his wife died. [Had a mental and emotional break-down.] **4.** *crack-up* N.A. (6) a. Crash. [The crack-up was due to faulty landing gear.] b. Breakdown. [His crack-up was not much of a surprise to those who knew him well.] **5.** *cracked up (to be)* A. (4) This idiom comes from the use of the adjective "crack" with the meaning of "excellent", "first rate". Ex. a crack regiment [the very best regiment]; crack troops [first rate soldiers]. As a commanding officer, he's not all that he's cracked up to be. [He is not as capable as some people say he is.]

Crack II To make a sharp noise while striking, as with a whip. Ex. He cracked his whip. He cracked the boy on the head.

crack down **1.** T (1,5) The teacher had been very patient with the students who whispered in class, but finally had to crack down. [Be severe and order them to be quiet.] **2.** *crack down (on)* T (1,5) The mayor ordered the police to crack down on gambling and illegal sale of liquor. [Arrest and bring to trial the violators of the law.] **3.** *crack-down* N.A. (1,5) The crack-down came as a surprise to the underworld. See **crack down 2.**

Cram To fill something by force, with more than it can conveniently hold.

    cram down T (1,5) The boys hadn't eaten for two days. They crammed the food down like mad. [Down their throats.]

Crank To start an internal combustion motor by turning the crank shaft.

    crank up (5,11) The starter wasn't working so he had to get out and crank up. [Turn the crank shaft to start the motor.]

Crate To put into crates.

    crate up T (3) We spent the rest of the day crating up the lettuce (the vegetables, the fruit). [Putting them in crates for shipment.] See **bale up.**

Cripple To make lame.

    cripple up T (6) He was all crippled up with theumatism. [It was hard for him to move his limbs.]

Crisp To make or become crisp.

    crisp up **1.** I (2) Lettuce will crisp up when put in cold water. [Become more crisp.] **2.** T (2) Those crackers are a bit soggy. Put them in the oven for a while to crisp them up. [Make them more crisp.]

Crop To come to the surface of the ground.

    crop out **1.** I (2) A vein of gold was seen cropping out of the ore. [Appearing on the surface.] **2.** I (2) Fig. His true feelings crop out when he is tired and annoyed. [They show in his face and his speech.]

    crop up I (1,6) Fig. As each new problem crops up, we will deal with it [As it appears.]

Cross I To cancel by using the mark of a cross.

    cross off T (6) When I found that he had my name on his list, I asked him to cross me off. [Remove my name.]

    cross out T (4) One of the three answers to the printed question is correct. Cross out the two incorrect answers. [Use an X to eliminate them.] See **mark out 2.**

Cross II To go from one side to the other of a street, a river, etc.

    cross over I (3) We came to a river, but couldn't cross over because of the high water. [Get to the other side.]

Cross III To act unfavorably, contrarily, in a way to oppose.

    cross up **1.** T (6) I had expected to have his support in the election, but he crossed me up. [He did not support me, he was against me.] **2.** *crossed up* A. (6) I tried to read the directions in the printed pamphlet, but got crossed up. [The directions were not clear. I didn't understand them.]

Cry To utter or pronounce loudly; call out.

    cry down T (1,5) The critics of the President cry down his efforts to reform the tax laws. [They speak strongly against his program.]

    cry out T (2,9) The accused man cried out that he was not guilty. [Spoke loudly and with emotion.]

cry up   T (2,5)   The street vendors cry up their merchandise. [They speak loudly of the quality and value of it.]

Cuddle   To draw or hold close to someone or something in an affectionate manner; to lie close together for warmth or safety.

   cuddle down   I (1)   The kittens cuddled down against their mother and slept peacefully. [Lay close to her.]

   cuddle up   I (3)   The two tired children cuddled up on the sofa, and went to sleep. [Lay close together.]

Cue   To provide with a cue or suggestion as to the time for an action.

   cue in   T (6)   Theater. The stage director had a copy of the script on which the lighting effects were cued in. [Marked with a sign to indicate the timing.]

Cull   To choose, select, pick out.

   cull out   T (4)   The farmer culled out the imperfect vegetables before taking his produce to market. [Picked them out, separated them from the good ones.]

   cull over   T (3,6)   He culled over the potatoes to find the most perfect ones. [Looked carefully to find them.]

Cultivate   To use tools for taking care of crops.

   cultivate out   T (1,9)   A wise farmer will cultivate out all harmful weeds as soon as they germinate. [Remove them with a hoe or other tool.]

Cure   To make or become well in health.

   cure up   **1.** I (2,4)   The wound he had received in battle cured up quickly under the care of the doctor. [It was completely healed.]   **2.** T (2,4)   He had had a chest cold for three weeks, then antibiotics cured him up. [Made him completely well.]

Curse   To swear at.

   curse back   T (5)   The first taxi driver cursed the second one, and the second one cursed him back. [Returned the curse to the first one.]

   curse out   T (9)   He cursed out the taxi driver for taking him to the wrong address. [He cursed him loudly and thoroughly.]

Curtain   Use a curtain for some purpose.

   curtain off   T (3)   In a hospital ward it is the custom to curtain off the bed of a dying person. [Separate the bed from the others by a curtain.] See **partition off, close off.**

Cut I   To detach with, or as with, a sharp instrument.

   cut away   **1.** T (2,3)   The explorers had to cut away the brush (the trees, etc.) that hid the entrance to the cave. [Remove it by cutting.]   **2.** *cutaway* N.A. (2,3)   The professor was wearing an old-fashioned cutaway. [A coat having a skirt cut away from the waist in a curve or slope.]

   cut back   **1.** T (4)   The shrub had grown too tall for its place in the garden. Mr. Jones decided to cut it back. [Reduce it to an earlier height.]   **2.** T (4) Ford Motors has decided to cut back its production of heavy trucks. [Reduce the number produced.]   **3.** *cut back (on)*   T (4)   If peace is declared, the army will cut back on its troop requirements. [Reduce its request for more troops.]

cut down   **1.** T (1)   Young George Washington cut down his father's favorite cherry tree. See **chop down. 2.** T (2,6)   We'll have to eat less meat to cut down our living expenses. [Reduce them.]   **3.** T (4)   The escaping robber was cut down by a policeman's bullet. [He was shot, and fell down.]   **4.** T (4) He was cut down in the prime of life by an attack of pheumonia. [He was killed.]   **5.** *cut down (on)* I (2,6)   The doctor told me I should cut down on cigarettes (liquor, coffee, etc.). [Reduce the amount I used.]

cut in   **1.** I (4)   Fig. We were talking about money, when John cut in with a remark about the latest war news. [He interrupted our conversation.]   **2.** I (4) At the dance, Bob kept cutting in every time I danced with Harriet. [He came up to us, tapped me on the shoulder, and claimed Harriet as his partner. He interrupted our dancing.]   See **cut in 1. 3.** I (1)   The car behind us tried to pass us. We nearly had an accident when it cut in sharply in front of us to avoid an oncoming car. [Came quickly into our lane.]   **4.** T (4,6)   Informal. If you think there is money to be made in that business deal, please cut me in. [Let me have a share in the deal.]

cut off   **1.** T (1)   He cut off a slice of bread and began to eat hungrily. [Off the loaf.]   **2.** T (2)   In certain countries thieves are punished by cutting off their hands. [Off the arm.]   **3.** T (6)   Mr. Martin cut off his son without a penny. [In his will he left nothing to his son.]   **4.** T (5)   The chairman cut off all further discussion of the matter. [He stopped it.]   **5.** T (4)   The electricity (the gas, the power, the radio, etc.) was cut off during the blackout. [It did not function.]   **6.** T (5)   Because of the war all trade and communications were cut off between the two nations. [They were stopped.]   **7.** T (2)   Fig. He cut off his nose to spite his face. [What he did was more harmful to him than if he had done nothing.]   **8.** *cut-off* N.   (5)   a. A device for cutting off gas, electricity, steam, etc. b. The act of cutting off. See **cut off 5.**

cut over   **1.** T (2,3)   They cut over the land to start a housing development. [Removed the trees from it.]   **2.** *cut-over* A.   A cut-over tract of land.

cut out   **1.** T (1)   There's an article in today's Times I'd like to cut out. [Make a clipping of it.] See **clip out. 2.** T (1)   Before baking apples it is better to cut out the cores. [Remove them by cutting.]   **3.** T (9)   Slang. John was Mary's boyfriend for two years but Henry cut him out. [He took Mary away from John.]   **4.** T (9)   Slang. Cut that out! [Stop doing what you are doing. I don't like it!]   **5.** T (7)   William says he's not cut out to be a doctor. [That is not his style, his pattern, his type.]   **6.** T (7)   If you're going to go into politics you have your work cut out for you. [Your style, your pattern of life are determined.]   **7.** *cut-out* N.   (1)   a. Something that is cut out or off from something else. [The girls spent the evening making cut-outs. They cut pictures out of newspapers and magazines.] b. A device for permitting the noise from an internal combustion engine to by-pass the muffler.

cut up   **1.** T (2,11)   The women were cutting up old woolen garments to make braided rugs. [Cutting them into small strips.]   **2.** T (2,11)   We always cut the potatoes up small, so they will cook faster. [Cut them into small pieces.]   **3.** T (6)   He was badly cut up in the car accident. [He received many cuts.]   **4.** T (6)   She was terribly cut up when her fiance married another girl. [Deeply wounded in her emotions.]   **5.** I (6)   Slang. Johnny is always cutting up in class. [Acting like a clown, a rowdy.]   **6.** *cut-up* N. (6) Johnny is a regular cut-up. [He is a clown.]

Cut II   To move quickly toward some destination, by a shorter path than normal (by a "short cut").

cut across   I (1)   There was an open field on our left so we decided to cut across and not follow the road. [Take the short way to the house.]

cut back   I (1)   After crossing the field we cut back to the road through a little woods.

cut down   I (1)   We cut down over the hill and soon reached the river.

cut in   I (1)   We cut in toward the pasture, taking a little path.

cut out   I (1,9)   We cut out, on a run, toward the distant farm buildings.

cut over   I (3)   We cut over to the other side of the field.

cut through   I (1)   There was a thick woods on our right. We cut through and found ourselves on the highway.

D

Dam   To confine with a dam.

dam across   T (1)   A brook ran through their farm. They dammed it across to make a small pond. [From one bank to the other.]

dam up   T (2,3)   They used rock and earth fill to dam up the narrow gorge. [Provide a barrier for the water.] See **stop up.**

Darken   To become dark or obscure.

darken up   I (2,6)   It's darkening up. Maybe we're going to have a storm. [Becoming darker.] See **clear up.**

Dash   To move hurriedly; to write, draw, or paint hurriedly.

dash off   **1.** I (1,9)   I must dash off now. I have another engagement. [Leave at once.]   **2.** T (1,9)   He dashed off a letter (a sketch, a drawing, a report, etc.) before going out to dinner. [Finished it in a very short time.] See **whip off.**

Date   To belong to a certain period in time; to go out on dates with someone, usually boy with girl.

date back   I (4)   The development of agriculture dates back thousands of years. [It began that long ago.]

date up   **1.** T (11)   John dated up his girl friend three months before the dance. [He wanted to be sure he would have her for the dance.]   **2.** *dated up* A.   (4)

I asked her to go with me, but she was dated up. [She had another date.]

Deal To give to a person as his share.

deal in **1.** T (4) Poker. You can deal me in this round (this time, this hand). [I want to play.] **2.** T (4) Informal. Mr. Allen was organizing a new business venture. I asked him to deal me in. [Permit me to have a share.]

deal out T (6) Deal out the cards. [Distribute them equally.] See **measure out.**

deal up I (4,5) Cards. Deal up! We can't wait all evening! [Don't be so slow about dealing the cards.]

Deck To clothe or equip with ornamental clothing or furnishings.

deck out **1.** T (9) They decked the plaftorm out with flags and bunting. [They decorated it.] **2.** T (9) When I saw her she was all decked out in her bridal gown. [Clothed in her finest.]

Deed To convey or transfer by deed.

deed back T (5) She had received the property from her brother, but deeded it back to him when she married a rich man.

deed over T (3) Mr. Brown deeded his real estate holdings over to his wife. [Transferred them.]

Dent To make a hollow or depression in a surface, as from a blow.

dent in T (1,2) A glancing blow from the passing car dented in his left front fender. [Made a dent.]

dent up T (6) His fenders were all dented up from a series of little accidents.

Die To cease to live, to exist; to fade or stop activity gradually.

die away I (4,6) The roar of the airplane died away in the distance. [It became weaker and weaker.]

die back I (4) Some of my rose bushes are dying back. I wonder what the trouble is. [They are losing their foliage.]

die down **1.** I (2,6) The blaze in the fireplace died down to a flicker. [It no longer shone brightly.] **2.** I (2,6) The excitement in the crowd died down, as the news spread that the rumor was false. [It became less and less.]

die off **1.** I (5) All of our old acquaintances are dying off. [Dying one by one.] **2.** T (5) The trees and shrubs are dying off because of the drought. [They cannot survive.]

die out **1.** I (6,8) The blaze in the fireplace died out. [It gave no light at all.] **2.** I (6,8) The dinosaurs died out millions of years ago. [They became extinct.] **3.** I (6,8) Many ancient superstitions are dying out in this age of science. [They are no longer believed in.]

Dig To break up, turn over or remove earth, sand, etc. with a tool.

dig away **1.** T (2) If you dig away the top soil you will find an old abandoned well beneath. [Remove the top soil.] **2.** I (6) A fox terrier was digging away at a furious pace near tree in the back yard. [Fast and continuously.]

dig down **1.** I (2) On digging down the archeologists found evidence of six earlier civilizations at the same site. [Below the surface.] **2.** I (2) Slang.

They told me I'd have to dig down and cough up fifteen bucks (dollars) if I wanted in on the deal. [Dig into my pockets and produce the money.]

dig in　**1.** I (1,2)　The soldiers were given orders to dig in as soon as they had captured the hill. [Dig shelters for themselves.]　**2.** I (4)　Informal. We'll all have to dig in and help with the harvest. [Work energetically.]

dig off　**1.** T (1)　They'll need to dig off a thick layer of earth to reach the coal seam. [Remove it by digging.]　**2.** I (2,9)　Slang. As soon as the boys heard the policeman's whistle they dug off. [Escaped in a hurry]. See **take off 5.**

dig out　**1.** T (1)　The tree surgeons dug out the rotted wood from the tree and filled the hole with cement. [Removed it by digging.]　**2.** I (1,9)　Slang. We dug out across the field when we saw the farmer coming. [We ran away in a hurry.] See **dig off.**　**3.** *dug-out* N.A.　(1)　a. A shelter or trench. [The soldiers were well protected in their dug-out.] b. A boat made by hollowing out a log. (The natives used dug-out canoes.] c. Baseball. A place with a roof, enclosed on three sides, with the floor below ground level, facing the field. [When not on the field, the players usually sit in the dug-out.]

dig up　**1.** T (1)　It's time to dig up the potatoes (the beets, the carrots, etc.). [Remove them from the ground.]　**2.** T (4,11)　The police dug up the whole yard, looking for evidence of the crime. [They turned over all the soil.]　**3.** T (7,11)　Informal. I don't want to go to that party tonight. Can't we dig up an excuse? [Make an effort to find a reason for not going.]

Dike　To furnish with a dike.

dike back　T (1,2)　In Holland they have diked back the waters of the sea to gain large areas of cultivable land.

Dim　To make obscure by reducing the light.

dim down　T (2)　The hostess dimmed down the lights (the lamps) to give an atmosphere of romance. [Made them burn less brightly.]

dim out　**1.** T (8)　All cities on the coast and ships in the area were ordered to dim out. [To reduce their lights for fear of an air raid.]　**2.** *dim-out* N.A.　A state of partial darkness, not as complete as a black-out. [They immediately complied with the dim-out by drawing their curtains and turning out unnecessary lights.] See **black-out 2.**

Dine　To have dinner.

dine around　I (2)　When we are in San Francisco we like to dine around. [Go to different restaurants for dinner each day.]

dine in　I (1)　We're dining in tonight. It's too stormy to go out. [At home.]

dine out　I (2)　He and his wife always dine out on Saturdays. [Have dinner outside the home.]

Dish　To put into or serve in a dish.

dish out　**1.** T (1)　Today in the mess hall they dished out an unappetizing mess of stuff. [Served it to the soldiers.]　**2.** T (1,7,9)　Informal. He certainly can dish it out when he is in a bad humor. [Speak abusively, criticize harshly, say unpleasant things.] **3.** T (1,9) Informal. He dishes out money to his children as if it grew on trees. [Gives very generously.] See **hand out.**

    dish up   **1.** T (1)   The soldiers on kitchen duty take turns dishing up the food. [Serving it.]   **2.** T (2,9)   Slang. She's very good at dishing up the dirt. [She knows how to report scandal and unpleasant gossip.]

Dive   To plunge head first into the water or other element.

    dive down   **1.** I (1)   We watched the eagle dive down and seize its prey. [Down through the air.]   **2.** I (1)   The fighter pilot dove down, sprayed the convey with machine gun fire, then leveled off. [Down through the air.]

    dive in   **1.** I (2)   The men all ran to the end of the pier and dove (dived) in. [Into the water.]   **2.** I (2)   Informal. As soon as the food was put on the table they all dived in like starving men. [Began to eat eagerly.]   **3.** I (4)   After the holidays we'll all dive in and finish this project. [Begin to work hard.]   **4.** *dive-in* N. (2,4)   Last night some Civil Rights workers staged a dive-in at the municipal swimming pool. [Negroes and whites used a segregated swimming pool.]

    dive off   I (2)   The men all ran to the end of the pier and dove off. [Off the pier.] See **dive in 1.**

    dive through   I (1)   The circus dogs ran toward the hoop the trainer held up, and dove through. [Through the opening of the hoop.]

Divide   Separate into parts, groups, shares, etc.

    divide around   T (1)   If you want to help me, get the cookies from the kitchen and divide them around. [Give some to all persons sitting around the room.]

    divide up   **1.** T (4,11)   Go get the apples and divide them up into five piles, and give one pile to each person. [Make an accurate division.]   **2.** I (4,11)   After the opening ceremonies the audience divided up into small discussion groups.

Divvy   Informal and slang for divide, make a dividend.

    divvy up   **1.** I (4,11)   The robber gang divvied up the loot (the swag, the stolen money) after they reached their hideout. [They divided it into shares.]   **2.** T (4)   The business partners divvied up, in equal shares, the profits (the earnings, the winnings) the firm had made. [Each received his share.]

Do   To perform some act involving somebody or something.

    do away (with)   I (3)   I think we can do away with our garden tools. We won't need them living in an apartment. [Give them away, sell them, not take them with us.]

    do in   **1.** T (7)   The robbers threatened to do him in, if he tried to call the police. [Kill him.]   **2.** *done in* A. (7)   I'm all done in, I can't stay up any longer. [I am completely exhausted.] See **be all in.**

    do out (of)   T (9)   His business partner tried to do him out of his share of the profits. [Take them away by deceit or trickery.]

    do over   **1.** T (6,7)   Your composition (theme, thesis, story) is full of mistakes in spelling. You'll have to do it over. [Rewrite it making necessary corrections.]

2. T (7)   We want to do over our living room. It needs it very badly. [Redecorate it.]

do up   **1.** T (3,11)   We ought to do up our Christmas packages tonight. [Wrap them securely, tie them up, prepare them for mailing.] See **bag up.**   **2.** T (1,3,11) She did up her hair in curlers before going to bed. [Put it in curlers to keep it looking good.]   **3.** T (2,4)   Mary was doing up her room (her dresses, the dishes, etc.) when the phone rang. [Cleaning, putting in order, taking care of them.]   **4.** *done up* A.   (3,5)   Her sister was done up in her new spring dress. [Prettily dressed.] See **dress up.**   **5.** (6)   He was all done up after six hours of meetings. [Completely tired out.] See **wear out 5.**

Dole   To distribute to charity, give without receiving pay.

dole out   **1.** T (1,7)   The Red Cross was on the scene doling out food parcels and clothing to the victims of the flood. [Giving them freely.]   **2.** T (1,7)   The fresh water in the lifeboat was doled out to survivors. See **measure out.**

Doll   To make look pretty, as a doll.

doll up   **1.** I (5,11)   She dolled up in her very finest clothes. [Put on her best.] See **dress up, pretty up, primp up.**   **2.** *all dolled up* A.   (5,11)   She was all dolled up at the party. See **doll up 1.**

Dope I   Slang. To affect with dope, or drugs.

dope up   T (6)   He doped himself up by swallowing too many pills. [They made him dizzy, numb, unable to think clearly, etc.]

Dope II   Slang. To have the "dope", the information necessary.

dope out   **1.** T (3,7)   If you can dope out the solution to this problem, please let me know. [If you have the information necessary to solve it.]   **2.** T (3,7)   I can't dope that man out; can you? [I don't understand him or what he does.]

Dose   To administer medicine in doses.

dose up   I (2,4)   I have a terrible cold. I've been dosing up with aspirin and antibiotics but it doesn't seem to help. [Taking a great amount of them.]

Double I   To make double, or twice as great.

double up   T (10)   The two couples decided they could save 50 dollars a month by doubling up. [Living together in the same house.]

Double II   To turn back on a course.

double back   I (1)   The fox, when being chased, often doubles back on his tracks. [Goes back the same way he ran from the hunters.]

Double III   To bend or fold, with one part over the other.

double over   **1.** T (3)   He doubled the sheet of paper over and signed his name on the upper side. [He folded it over.]   **2.** *doubled over* A.   (5)   The poor man had suffered so much from rheumatism, he was all doubled over. [His body was bent forward and downward.]

double up   **1.** T (3,6)   He was doubled up with severe stomach pains. [He bent forward, holding his stomach to ease the pain.]   **2.** T (3,6)   The workers were doubled up under heavy bales they carried on their backs. [Their bodies were bent toward the ground.]

Doze   To fall into a light sleep unintentionally.

doze off   I (5,9)   Father dozed off during the long sermon. [He lost consciousness for a short while.]

Drag   To pull or draw along the ground or some other surface, usually with resistance and friction; to move slowly and painfully.

drag around   **1.** T (1,2)   The boys, playing in the back yard, were dragging their sister around on an old sled. [Here and there.]   **2.** T I (1,2)   Mother's not feeling well these days. She's barely able to drag (herself) around. [Move about with difficulty.]

drag away   **1.** I (2)   As I saw the branches off the tree, you can drag them away. [Remove them from under the tree.]   **2.** T (2)   Ext. The party was so much fun we couldn't drag ourselves away. [It was difficult to leave.]

drag by   I (2)   As the days dragged by we lost hope that our son would ever be found. [Passed slowly, and in sadness.]

drag in   T (4)   Ext. He doesn't seem to be interested in our project. We'll just have to drag him in. [Into our group or activity.]

drag on   I (II 2)   The meeting dragged on and on. It seemed it would never end. [Continued slowly and uninterestingly.] See **drag out, go on 3.**

drag out   **1.** T (1,2)   When the demonstrators staged a sit-in in the mayor's office, the police had to drag them out. [Out of the office.]   **2.** T (1,2)   Ext. When father scolded Johnny for being late to classes, Johnny dragged out all his familiar excuses. [Out in public.]   **3.** T (1)   The police questioned their prisoner for three hours but could drag nothing out of him. [Get him to give information.]   **4.** I (10)   The meeting dragged out till midnight. [It did not end till that hour.] See **drag on. 5.** *dragged out* A. (9)   I feel all dragged out this morning. I didn't sleep well. [Exhausted.] See **wear out 5.**

drag up   T (1)   The skindivers dragged up an ancient cannon from the sunken ship. [Pulled it to the surface with effort.]

Drain   To draw off a liquid gradually.

drain away   T (2,3)   Drainage ditches are needed to drain away excess water from marshy lands. [Remove water by draining.]

drain off   **1.** T (7)   A rubber tube was inserted in the wound to drain off pus and excess fluids. [Remove it from the wound.]   **2.** T (2,7)   High taxes were recommended to drain off the surplus spending power of the people. [Remove it from the economy.]

Draw I   To cause to move in a particular direction by a pulling force.

draw around   I (3)   When the candidate began to speak a large crowd drew around. [They formed a circle around him.]

draw aside   T (2)   Before he went into the meeting I drew him aside and gave him some advice. [Took him to where others could not hear what we said.]

draw away   I (3)   She drew away from his embrace, not wanting to be kissed. [Away from close contact.]

draw back   **1.** I (1)   On seeing the body of the murdered man lying on the floor she drew back in horror. [Took a step or steps backward.]   **2.** *draw back* I (1)   The two boxers were sparring face to face. Then one of them drew back and landed a "haymaker". [Took a step backward and gave a knockout blow.]   **3.** *draw-back* N. (1)   The biggest draw-back I can see in your plan (suggestion, project, organization, etc.) is the difficulty in finding money for it. [The reason for drawing back from it, not going ahead with it.]

draw down   T (3)   He draws down a big salary. [Receives it.] See **knock down, pull down.**

draw in   **1.** I (1)   The train drew in just as we reached the station. [Into the station.]   **2.** T (1)   He drew in his breath in short, painful gasps. [He had difficulty in inhaling.]   **3.** T (4)   The candidate's speeches about the war drew in large numbers of supporters (financial contributions, etc.). [Brought them to his side.]

draw off   **1.** T (1,7)   When the solid matter had settled to the bottom he drew off the liquid with a siphon. [Removed it from the container.]   **2.** I (1)   The two men were arguing angrily. Suddenly one of them drew off and hit the other with his fist. [Moved far enough away to be able to strike.]

draw out   **1.** T (1)   The dentist drew out two of my front teeth yesterday. [Extracted them.]   **2.** I (1)   The train drew out just as we reached the station. [Out of the station.]   **3.** T (7)   The reporter who interviewed the candidate tried to draw him out on the civil rights issue. [Persuade him to talk freely and at some length about it.]   **4.** *long-drawn-out* A. (10)   Last night we attended a long-drawn-out committee meeting (rally celebration). [It lasted for hours.]

draw up   **1.** T (3,10)   The officer drew up his men in front of the airport gate, as guard of honor for the President. [Had them line up in military fashion.]   **2.** I (13)   The coach drew up at the door of the inn. [The coachman drew the horses' heads up with the reins, and caused them to stop.]   **3.** I (13)   At his whistle, the taxi drew up to the curb. [It stopped there.]   **4.** T (4)   He drew himself up to his full height and gave a defiant answer to the charges made against him. [He stood tall, straight and proud, before his accusers.]

Draw II   To sketch something with lines or words.

draw in   T (2,3)   First draw in the general outline, then gradually work out the details. [Instructions of the art teacher to a beginner in design or painting.]

draw up   **1.** T (4,11)   I hired an architect to draw up plans for our new house. [Prepare on paper a design for building it.]   **2.** T (4,11)   Our committee is meeting tonight to draw up plans for the next year's activities (the United Fund Drive, the clean-up campaign, etc.). [Prepare to take action.]   **3.** T (4,7,11) The diplomats of the Big Powers have finally drawn up a treaty (an agreement) concerning the use of nuclear weapons. [Prepared it for submission to the nuclear powers.]

Dream   To form an idea or plan of action in the imagination.

   dream up   T (7)   My wife is very impractical. She is always dreaming up schemes for getting me elected to the Senate. [Using her imagination.]

Dredge   To clear out with a dredge; remove sand, mud or debris from a body of water.

   dredge out   T (1,9)   The engineers are busy dredging out a channel for the big steamers to come up the river to our city. [Removing materials blocking the channel.]

dredge up   **1**. T (1)   They have dredged up thousands of tons of silt and mud and deposited it on the river banks. [Up from the bottom of the river.]   **2**. T (7) Ext. The psychiatrist attempts to dredge up old fears and obsessions that lie in the sub-conscious mind of his patient. [Up to the realm of the conscious mind.]

Dress I   Military. To put into correct order or position.

   dress down   **1**. T (5)   The sergeant dressed the soldier down because he hadn't cleaned his rifle. [He scolded him severely for not doing so.]   **2**. *dressing down* N. (5)   Father gave Tom a good dressing down for taking the car without permission.

Dress II   To put clothes on.

   dress out   T (9)   The king dressed out his mistress in all the finery of a lady of the court. [He gave her all of the finest clothing.]

   dress up   **1**. I (4,11)   We always have to dress up for the opera. [Put on our best clothes, our dress clothes.]   **2**. *dress-up* A. (4,11)   Is this a dress-up party, or is it informal? [One at which we must wear formal clothes.]   **3**. *dressed up* A. (4,11)   Wearing one's best clothes, dressed for a party or other social engagement. See **doll up.**

   Ex.   The children were all dressed up in their Sunday best.

   Ex.   We're all dressed up and no place to go. [Said humorously by people who are wearing their party clothes, and trying to think of a good way to spend the evening.]

Drink   To take water or other liquid into the mouth and swallow it.

   drink down   **1**. T (1)   He poured himself a glass of brandy and drank it down at one gulp. [Swallowed it eagerly and hurriedly.]   **2**. T (1)   Here's to good old Yale, drink 'er down, drink 'er down. [College drinking song.] See **drink down 1.**

   drink up   **1**. T (4,11)   Children, drink up all your milk, or you can't have any dessert. [Finish all of it.]   **2**. I (5,8)   Drink up! We haven't much time before the taxi arrives. [Don't waste time talking. Finish your drink.]

Drive I   To send, expel or otherwise cause to move by force.

   drive away   **1**. T (2)   They use Flit to drive away the insects (the flies, the mosquitos). [Force them to go away.]   **2**. T (2)   Ext. We sing to drive away the blues (our fears, our unhappiness). [From our hearts and minds.]

   drive back   T (1)   Our troops succeeded in driving back the enemy, who had attacked in force. [Back to their previous position.]

drive in T (2) You will need a heavier hammer to drive those spikes in. [Into the board.]

drive off (2) A band of ferocious dogs was attacking the poor child, but some men drove them off with clubs and sticks. [Made them leave the child.]

drive out **1.** (1) It took two years to drive out the invading army. [Force them to leave the invaded territory.] **2.** T (4) Ext. Bad money drives out the good. [Economic axiom.]

Drive II To drive a car, or other vehicle. When this verb refers to driving a car there are three ways of using it.

1. Intransitive; with the meaning go or ride in a car.
2. Transitive; with the word car as the direct object.
3. Transitive; with the occupants of the car as the direct object.

Ex. 1. I. We drove around for a little while.
　　　2. T. We drove the car around for a little while.
　　　3. T. We drove our friends around for a little while.

In the following sentences the intransitive form is used. Good practice may be had in the use of the two-word verb, by repeating each sentence in the two possible transitive forms, as illustrated in the above example.

drive about I (2) We drove about (around) for the rest of the afternoon. [We drove for pleasure.] See **drive around**.

drive across I (1) When we came to the river, the bridge was out so we couldn't drive across. [Over the bridge or river.]

drive along I (3) We were driving along at slow speed for the sake of the view. [So that one could see everything that was to be seen.]

drive around See **drive about.**

drive away I (1,2,3) They drove away without saying goodbye. [From where we were.]

drive back I (1,2,3) They drove back after the rain stopped. [To the starting place.]

drive by I (2) She waved to us as she was driving by. [Past us, past our house.]

drive down I (1) When they are in Boston they will drive down for a visit. [Down to New York.]

drive in **1.** I (1) It was after midnight when they drove in. [Arrived by car at our place.] See **pull up.** **2.** *drive-in* N.A. (1) a. A restaurant where food is served to people in the cars. [We ate at a drive-in.] b. An open air movie, where people watch the screen from their cars. [We saw a good movie at the drive-in.] c. A teller's window opening to the outside, where the customer transacts business while seated in his car. [We deposited our check at the bank's drive-in.]

drive off I (1,2) They drove off without paying their bill. [From the store, the hotel, etc.]

drive on **1.** I (I 1) We reached the ferry just in time to drive on. [Onto the ferry.] **2.** I (II 1,3) He told us to drive on about a mile and a half. There we would see a sign. [Continue driving.]

drive out I (1,2) Our friends in the country wanted us to drive out. [Out of the city to their place.]

drive over I (3) When we were in New York we drove over to see our friends in New Jersey. [Over the Hudson River.]

drive through I (1,2) When we reached Camden we drove through without stopping. [In and out of the city.]

drive under I (1) The arch was high enough for us to drive under. [Below the arch.]

drive up **1.** I (1) When you come to Boston we'll drive up to see you. [Up north from New York.] **2.** I (13) When he drove up we were surprised to know he was in town. [Stopped his car in front of our house, or near to where we were.]

Drop I To fall or let fall from a higher position.

drop back **1.** I (1) Military. The advance guard dropped back after making contact with the enemy. [Moved backward, retreated.] **2.** I (1) Football. The quarterback dropped back to make a forward pass. [Took some steps backward.] See **fade back.**

drop down **1.** I (1) Great flakes of snow came dropping down. [Fell to the ground.] **2.** I (1) The faithful dropped down on their knees as the procession approached. [Down to the ground.]

drop off **1.** I (2) When we shook the tree large quantities of apples dropped off. [Fell from the tree.] **2.** I (6) Sales of spring clothing are dropping off this season, because of the cold weather. [They are becoming less.] **3.** T (2) We'll drop you off in front of the bank. [Let you get out of the car.] **4.** *drop-off* N. a. (6) A reduction. [The drop-off in sales will cause a big reduction in the amount of sales tax collected.] b. (1) A steep descending slope. [As we came down the mountain road we could see a drop-off of several hundred feet on our right.]

drop out **1.** I (4,9) Their oldest went to high school for two years, then dropped out to go to work. [Stopped going to school.] **2.** *drop-out* N. (4,9) a. A person who drops out of school or some other activity in which he was engaged. [A high school drop-out.] b. The act of dropping out.

drop over **1.** I (5) He was alive and well-looking, and in ten minutes he dropped over dead. [Suddenly fell dead.] **2.** I (5) Informal. I nearly dropped over dead when I heard she was going to marry that man. [Exaggerated way of saying "I was much surprised."]

Drop II Informal. To make an unexpected, unannounced social call on someone.

drop around I (5) We'll drop around for a highball one of these days. [We'll come for a drink but can't say just when.]

drop back I (3) We do hope you'll drop back before too long. [Make us another visit.]

drop by   T (2)   The Smiths dropped by to say hello this afternoon. [They were on their way to some other place, and only stayed a short time.]

drop down   I (1)   Won't you drop down for cocktails before you go out. [Down from your apartment on a higher floor.]

drop in   I (1)   Drop in sometime. I'd like to show you my art collection. [Pay me an informal visit.] See **happen in, look in, pop in, run in, stop in.**

drop out   I (1,2)   The Brown's want us to drop out to have a look at their new place in the country. [Make a short trip out of town to see them.]

drop over   I (3)   We're having a few friends in for cocktails. Won't you and John drop over. [Come from across the street, or cross town.]

Drum   To beat a drum in order to call attention to something or someone.

drum out   **1**. T (4,9)   Military. The officer who had disgraced his regiment was drummed out of the service. [A ceremony accompanied by the beating of drums.] **2**. T (4,9)   That man is a disgrace to our organization. He should be drummed out of office. [Forced to resign in disgrace.]

drum up   **1**. T (2)   In olden days merchants hired a drummer to drum up trade. (Beat his drum to attract buyers.] **2**. T (2,11)   Fig. What's John doing these days? Oh, he's out drumming up support (votes, enthusiasm, etc.) for Governor Wilson. [Speaking, going to meetings, stirring people up.]

Dry   To become or make dry, lose moisture.

dry away   T (3)   He kissed her to dry away her tears. [Make her stop crying.]

dry off   **1**. T (7)   When the children came out of the water, mother dried them off briskly with a big towel. [Removed the moisture from their bodies.] **2**. I (7) After a swim he lay in the hot sun and soon dried off. [The moisture left his skin.]

dry out   **1**. T (9)   They held their wet jackets in front of the fire to dry them out. [Get the moisture out of them.] **2**. I (9)   It took a half hour for them to dry out. [Lose the moisture.]

dry up   **1**. I (2,4)   After the rain it soon dried up. [The ground, the air became dry.] **2**. I (13)   Slang. Dry up, will you! [Stop talking. I don't want to listen to you.] See **shut up. 3**. *dried up*   A. (4)   He was a dried up old man with nothing to live for. [He had lost all the freshness of youth.]

E

Ear   To form ears, as with corn.

ear out   I (11)   The corn is beginning to ear out. [The ears are showing, developing.]

Ease   To move or be moved with great care. This verb may be followed by any of the second elements, showing the direction of the movement. v. push, shove, edge.

ease out   T (4,6)   He had been president of the company for many years but they eased him out and put in a younger man. [Took polite but firm action to replace him.]

ease up   **1.** I (2)   The doctor told him he should not work so hard. He ought to ease up a bit. [Take life more easy.]   **2.** *ease up (on)*   I (2)   One thing the doctor recommended was to ease up on cigarettes. [Smoke less.]

Eat   To have a meal.

eat out   I (1,2)   They often eat out on weekends. [Away from home. In restaurants or with friends.] See **go out.**

Edge I   To move edgewise, sidewise in some direction. This verb may be followed by any of the second elements. See **fight one's way.**

Edge II   To defeat or vanquish rivals or opponents by a narrow margin.

edge out   T (5)   John F. Kennedy edged out Richard Nixon for the presidency. [He won by a few thousand votes.]

Egg   To urge, encourage to do something. Not related to the noun egg, but to an old Scandinavian verb meaning to urge.

egg on   T (II3)   He didn't want to get into the fight, but we egged him on. [Said things to persuade him.]

Eke   To supply in some way something that is needed.

eke out   T (10)   The professor eked out a living by doing some writing for the newspapers. [He earned extra money for living expenses.]

Elbow   To use the elbows to help perform some act. Usually with "one's way" as the direct object. Can be used with all elements. See **fight one's way.**

elbow in   T (1)   There was a large group of reporters outside the door, but he elbowed his way in. [Pushed with his elbows to get inside.]

elbow out   T (1)   The crowd in the living room was so thick he had to elbow his way out. [Use his elbows to force his way out.]

elbow up   T (1)   So many people crowded around the platform he had to elbow his way up. See **elbow in, out.**

Empty   To make empty, discharge the contents of a container.

empty out   T (1,9)   Mother made Johnny empty out his pockets. [Take everything out.]

End   To come to an end.

end up   **1.** I (16)   If you're not careful you'll end up in prison. [You will finally be put in prison.]   **2.** I (16)   He ended up joining the army (losing his money, being made president, etc.). [That was the final result.] See **I wind up.**

Enter   To take part in some activity.

enter in   I (4)   At first he said he didn't feel like dancing (playing, singing, drinking, talking, etc.), but after a while he entered in enthusiastically. [Took part in the group activity.] See **join in.**

Even   To make even, to balance (accounts).

even up   T (4)   That check from the Martin Company will help us to even up our accounts for this month. [Make them balance.]

Eye   To look at intensively.

eye over (up and down)   T (2,3)   The customs inspector eyed me over (up and down) as though I were a smuggler. [Looked intently and suspiciously at me.]

Expect   To indicate or say that one wishes someone to come or be at a place.

expect back   T (3)   They're expecting us back by nine o'clock. [They hope we will return at that time.]

expect in   T (1)   Don't be out late. Father expects you in by midnight. [Wants you to be in the house.]

expect up   T (1)   We'll expect you up to meet our guests. [We want you to come up to our apartment.]

Explain   To give an explanation.

explain away   T (1,3)   Nothing you say can explain away the fact that the stolen goods were in your possession. [Remove the suspicion that you stole them.]

F

Face   To turn one's face toward something.

face down   T (1,4)   Two members of the group stood up to make serious charges against him, but he faced them down. [He answered their charges successfully.]

face off   **1.** I (8)   Ice hockey. Two players face off at the start of a game or period. [Vie for control of the puck.]   **2.** *face-off* N.   The act of facing the puck.

face out   T (9)   Our situation is dangerous and full of risks, but we'll have to face it out. [Act with courage until we have mastered it completely.]

face up (to)   I (4,5)   You must face up to the fact that you're not as young as you used to be. [Recognize your limitation, act with that in mind.]

Fade   To lose brightness of color or of sound.

fade away   **1.** I (2,6)   The light of the setting sun faded away in the distance. [Became less and less bright.]   **2.** I (4,6)   Fig. The opposition to the president's proposals faded away when it was learned that the opinion polls supported him.

fade back   I (1)   Football. The quarterback faded back to make a forward pass. [He disappeared from his normal position.] See **drop back**.

fade in   **1.** I (1,5)   Broadcasting. The music from a military band faded in as the candidate was ending his speech. [It began to be heard gradually.] The opposite of **fade out**.   **2.** I (1,5)   Cinema. Toward the end of the wedding ceremony, a scene showing the first meeting of the bride and groom faded in. [It began to be seen gradually.] The opposite of **fade out**.   **3.** *fade-in* N. (1,5)   a. Broadcasting. The act described in **fade in 1**. b. Cinema. The act described in **fade in 2**.

fade out   **1.** I (10)   The noise of the riot (the glow from the burning buildings) faded out, as we drove farther away from the scene. [They both diminished.]   **2.** I (10)   Broadcasting. The music from the military band faded out as the candidate began to speak. [It gradually disappeared.] The opposite of **fade in 1**.

3. I (10)   Cinema. The wedding scene faded out into a scene showing the first meeting of the couple. [It gradually disappeared.] See **fade in 2**.   **4.** *fade-out* N. (10)   Broadcasting, Cinema. The fade-out is a fairly recent technique that is very effective.

Fag   To tire by hard labor, exhaust.

fag out   **1.** T (8)   All that heavy lifting soon fagged us out. [We became completely exhausted.]   **2.** *fagged out* A.   (8)   We were all fagged out after a day of door-to-door campaigning. [Completely tired, exhausted.]

Faint   To lose consciousness.

faint away   I (4)   The poor girl hadn't eaten for two days. She was ready to faint away from hunger. [Lose consciousness.]

Fake   To practice a deception, to pretend.

fake up   **1.** T (7,11)   Father will be angry when we get home so late. We'll have to fake up an excuse. [Tell him a lie.] See **make up**.   **2.** *faked up* A.   (7,11) That's a faked up excuse if I ever heard one. [I am sure it isn't the truth.]

Fall   To descend under the force of gravity; to move from one position to another.

fall away   **1.** I (1)   A gentle slope fell away from the hilltop, ending in a field. [It extended downward.]   **2.** I (3)   Many of the candidate's supporters fell away after his unfortunate remark about "brain-washing". [They deserted him.]

fall back   **1.** I (1)   In the face of the fierce attack of the enemy, our troops had to fall back. [Retreat to the rear.]   **2.** *fall back (on)* I (5)   When their first baby came the young couple had to fall back on their parents to meet expenses. [Return to the parents for help.]   **3.** *fall-back* N.A.   (2)   Automotive. Some cars are equipped with a fall-back brake system. [A secondary system that can be used if the regular brakes fail.]

fall down   **1.** I (1)   Jack fell down and broke his crown. [Fell to the ground. Nursery rhyme.]   **2.** I (6)   She fell down on the job. [Did it poorly or not at all.]

fall in   **1.** I (1)   The child who had been playing on the canal bank fell in and was almost drowned. [Into the water of the canal.]   **2.** I (6)   Military. The officer gave his men the order to fall in. [To take their position in line.]   **3.** *fall in (with)* I (4)   When we were traveling in Europe, we fell in with a group of tourists from Australia. [We met and spent some time with them.]   **4.** I (4) Several of the people at the meeting fell in with our plan of raising money. [They liked our plan and agreed to help.] See **go along (with)**.

fall off   **1.** I (1,2)   When he was struck by the car his glasses fell off. [Off his head.]   **2.** I (6)   Business began to fall off after the Christmas holiday. [It was reduced from its former rate.]   **3.** *fall-off* N.   (5)   France has reported a considerable fall-off (or falling-off) in tourist trade. See **fall off 2**.

fall out   **1.** I (1,2)   Her dentures fell out when she tried to eat an apple. [Out of her mouth.]   **2.** I (6)   They used to be good friends but they fell out over an argument about money. [They were no longer close friends.]   **3.** I (3)   We thought they were just good friends but it fell out that they had been married two years. [It became known, it happened.] See **III turn out**. **4.** I (6)   Military. Fall out! [Command by an officer to have soldiers break a military formation.] Opposite of **fall in 2**.   **5.** I (2)   Military. The soldiers in their barracks fell out to line up for inspection. [They left the barracks.]   **6.** *fall-out* N. a.   (6) A quarrel. [They never spoke to each other after the fall-out (or falling-out).] b.   (2)   The falling of radioactive material to earth or the material that has fallen. [There is great danger to all the people of the world from the fall-out from atomic explosions.] c.   (2)   Fig. The political fall-out from the President's declaration that he would not accept renomination was enormous. [The effects of his declaration were very great.]

fall over   **1.** I (5)   The huge tree, uprooted by the hurricane, fell over with a crash. [Over and down to the ground.]   **2.** I (5)   She fell over in a faint on hearing of her son's death. [To the ground or the floor.]

fall through   **1.** I (1)   He stepped on a hidden trap door and fell through. [Through the opening.]   **2.** I (5)   Our plans (our scheme, our agreement, etc.) fell through because of the war. [They could not be carried out, carried through.]

Fan   To spread out like a fan.

fan out   I (1,10)   The troops (the searchers) fanned out over the countryside to hunt for the guerillas (the suspected criminals, the lost child, etc.). [They made a wide search.]

Farm   To let or lease (taxes, revenues, an enterprise) to another for a fixed sum or a percentage.

farm out   **1.** T (5)   The owners of the real estate development farmed out the collection of the rent. [Hired someone to collect the rent for a percentage.] **2.** T (5)   Baseball. The owners of the big league teams farm out new players to minor league teams for training. [They make financial arrangements.]

Fashion   To give a particular shape or form to; to make.

fashion out   T (7)   The sculptor took an old automobile fender and fashioned out a space symbol from it. [Changed its shape to make the symbol.]

Fasten   To attach firmly or securely in place.

fasten back   T (2)   He opened the swinging doors and fastened them back so the crowd could enter more easily. [Back toward the inner walls.]

fasten on   T (3,4)   The parachute jumpers were busily fastening on their parachutes. [Attaching them to their bodies.]

fasten up   T (3,11)   Fasten up your seat belts. We're ready to start. [Make them tight.]

Fatten   To make or become fat.

fatten out   I (11)   She has fattened out since I last saw her. [Become fatter.]

fatten up   T (2,11)   The farmers are fattening up their pigs for market. [Feeding them so they will have more weight.] See **feed up.**

Feather   To grow feathers.

feather out I (9) The young birds had feathered out, and were ready to leave the nest. [Their bodies were now covered with feathers.] See **fledge out.**

Feed To give food to, to provide with the necessary materials for development, maintenance, or operation.

feed back N. (1,3) The return of a part of an output of a device to the input.

feed up 1. T (2,11) Those calves are not heavy enough for market. We'll have to feed them up a bit. [Give them food to increase their weight.] See **fatten up.**
2. *fed up* A. (6) Fig. I won't listen to his arguments (his talk, his nonsense, etc.) any longer. I'm fed up. [My mind is so full now, I can't take in any more.]
3. *fed up (with)* A. (4,6) I'm fed up with him. I don't want to see or hear of him again. [I've had my fill of him.]

Feel I To perceive or examine by touch.

feel about (around) I (1,2) He felt about (around) under the bed, trying to find his other shoe. [Used his hand to try to touch the shoe.]

feel out T (3) Fig. I'm not sure he will agree with our plan. We'll have to feel him out on the matter. [Ask him some questions in an indirect manner.] See **sound out.**

Feel II To be aware of something.

feel up (to) I (12) He wants me to go on a trip with him, but I don't feel up to it. [I do not have the health or energy necessary.]

Fence To supply a fence for some purpose.

fence about (around): 1. T (3) To protect their garden from stray animals and children they fenced it about with a lilac hedge. [Planted a hedge around it.]
2. T (3) Fig. The right to use the public park was so fenced about with rules and regulations we decided not to hold our meeting there. [The rules and regulations were a barrier.]

fence in 1. T (3) Our neighbor fenced in a part of his yard to make a chicken run. [Enclosed it with a fence.] See **close in 1.** 2. T (3) Fig. Don't fence me in! [A popular song about a cowboy who doesn't like fences, either material or moral.]

fence off T (3) The farmer fenced off a part of his pasture and started a fruit orchard. [Enclosed it with a fence.]

fence out T (1) The farmer put barbed wire around his house lot to fence out the cattle. [Keep the cattle from the lot by means of a fence.]

Fend To ward off, keep something or some person from making contact.

fend off 1. T (1) The fallen man was trying to fend off the blows of the ruffian who had knocked him down. [Keep the blows from reaching him.]
2. T (2,3) The besieged troops succeeded in fending off the attackers until relief troops arrived. [Keeping them at a distance.]

Ferret To drive out as by the use of a ferret; to search for something in the same manner.

ferret out 1. T (3) The police ferreted out the agents who had been selling narcotics to the students. [Discovered them and had them prosecuted.] **2.** T (3) I'd like to ferret out all the information I can get on that subject. [Do the study and research necessary.] See **find out**.

Fetch To go, and bring back. (In current popular speech the word "back" is added as a second element.)

fetch back T (5) Take the lawn-mower over to Mr. Brown, then fetch it back as soon as he is through with it. [Bring it back.]

fetch up (at) I (13) Informal. We were out driving for an hour or so and fetched up at the Mountain Inn. [We stopped there for something to eat or drink.]

Fiddle Informal. To play the violin (called a fiddle in folk language).

fiddle around I (2) What's John doing with himself these days? Oh, he's just fiddling around, not doing much of anything. [He is lazy, not serious.]

fiddle away **1.** I (6) The old man was fiddling away, paying no attention to the people around him. [Playing his violin continuously.] **2.** T (6) On our vacation we didn't do anything exciting or interesting. We just fiddled the time (the hours, the days) away. [We were very much relaxed.]

Fight To contend in any manner, strive vigorously for or against something.

fight down T (1,6) Fig. Just before the battle he had to fight down his fear of being killed (a desire to flee, a feeling of despair, cowardice, etc.). [Keep them from rising within him.]

fight on I (II 2) They fought on through the night. [Continued to fight.]

fight off **1.** T (1) One battalion of our troops fought off a whole regiment of the enemy. [Kept them at a distance.] **2.** T (1) He was very tired after a full day of driving. He had to fight off sleep, as he drove on toward Boston. [Exert himself to stay awake.] **3.** T (1) I've been fighting off a cold for a week. [Taking medicine and doing what is necessary to avoid a bad cold.]

fight out **1.** T (8) We'll fight it out on this line if it takes all summer. [Continue to fight to the end.] **2.** T (7) After the bill was released by the committee its supporters fought it out on the floor of the House. [Made a good fight to have it passed.]

fight through T (3,4) The supporters of the bill fought it through to a 65 to 35 victory. [The bill was passed with that majority.]

Fight one's way To make one's way in some direction by struggling. See **elbow one's way, force one's way, make one's way, shoulder one's way, shove one's way, splash one's way, thread one's way, work one's way, worm one's way.**

These expressions may be used with all fifteen of the second elements to show the direction of the movement.

fight one's way about T (3) He managed to fight his way about, and start back to the house. [Turn back against some opposition, or obstacle.]

fight one's way across T (1) The troops fought their way across against heavy fire. [Across a bridge, a river, etc.]

fight one's way along T (1)   He fought his way along through the heavy underbrush. [Went forward through the obstacle.]

fight one's way around T (3)   They fought their way around, and continued to
advance. [They circled an obstacle.]

fight one's way back T (1,3)   He fought his way back, against heavy odds. [Back
to his unit.]

fight one's way by T (2)   There was a crowd on the sidewalk in front of the
doorway. He had to fight his way by. [Through the crowd past the door.]

fight one's way down T (1)   He had to fight his way down through a howling mob.
[Downstairs, or down the slope, etc.]

fight one's way in T (1)   There was such a crowd in the doorway he had to fight
his way in. [Into the house, the room, etc.]

fight one's way off T (1,2)   The passengers were all standing in the aisle (of the
plane, the train, the bus). He had to fight his way off. [Off the plane, etc.]

fight one's way on T (1)   So many people were crowded around the platform he
had to fight his way on. [Onto the platform.]

fight one's way out T (1,2,9)   The room was so crowded he had to fight his way
out. [Out of the room.]

fight one's way over T (3)   After the troops reached the bridge they fought their
way over, foot by foot. [Little by little across to the other side.]

fight one's way through T (1,2)   Our troops were opposed by a full regiment of
enemy infantry, but they fought their way through to the center of the town.
[Through the enemy troops.]

fight one's way up **1.** T (1)   Coming to a hill they fought their way up against
heavy fire. [Up the hill.] **2.** T (2)   He was born poor, but fought his way up to
wealth and honor. [Became rich and distinguished through his own efforts.]

Figure To calculate, compute.

figure in T (5)   When you start checking our expenses for the trip, don't forget
to figure in the bridge and highway tolls. [Add them to the total.]

figure out **1.** T (7)   I can't figure out why he was so unpleasant last night. [Find
the reason.] **2.** T (7)   My husband has figured out a way to save enough
money to buy a car. [Made calculations.] **3.** T (3)   He's such a strange person.
I can't figure him out. [Understand him, explain his actions.]

figure up T (4)   Just figure it up. There's no reason why we can't take our
vacation next month. [Do all the calculating necessary.]

File To arrange papers or records in convenient order for preservation or reference.

file away **1.** T (5)   The secretary took last year's records and filed them away in
the storage room. [Put them in a special filing place for possible future reference.]
2. T (5)   Fig. He filed away in his memory all the happenings of the last few
days. [Put them there for possible future use.]

Fill To make or become full.

fill in **1.** T (2,3)   There were many empty spaces in his back yard. He filled them in with shrubs and hardy plants. [Planted things to fill the spaces.] **2.** T (2,6) The clerk told him to fill in the lines on the application form that were marked with an X. [Put the correct information on those lines.] **3.** T (2,6) I told him that if he didn't know all the answers I would fill him in. [I would give him the information he lacked.] **4.** I (4) John was unable to go to the meeting, so I filled in for him. [I took his place at the meeting, doing what he would have done. I substituted for him.] **5.** *fill-in* N.A. (4) a. A substitute. [I acted as fill-in for John.] b. A detailed account. [I gave John a fill-in on what happened at the meeting. I told him all about it.]

fill out   **1.** T (9)   The clerk told him to fill out the application form and sign his name to it. [Put in all the information requested.] **2.** I (11)   As a little girl she was very thin, but she has begun to fill out as a teen-ager. [Grow bigger, heavier.]

fill up   **1.** T (4,11)   Fill up your glass. Let's drink a toast to the King, [Fill it to the top.] **2.** I (2,4)   The auditorium began to fill up an hour before the lecture. [Become full.] **3.** I (2,4)   The reservoir (the pond, the river, etc.) filled up after the heavy rain. [Became full.] **4.** *filled up* A. (4,6)   The bus driver said "We're all filled up", and closed the door of the bus. [All the seats were taken.]

Filter   To remove by the action of a filter.

filter off   T (2)   In the laboratory the students filtered off the solid matter in the mixture. [Removed what remained on the filter.]

filter out   T (7)   They filtered out the liquid. [Drained it off with a filter.]

Find   To learn, obtain by search or effort.

find out   **1.** T (3)   They couldn't find out the reason for his absence (his bad humor). [Discover it.] **2.** T (3)   He tried to hide the fact that he stole the watch, but he was found out. [The truth was learned.] See **ferret out.**

Finish   To bring to an end, or completion.

finish off   **1.** T (10)   It was a delicious roast. The guests finished it off with gusto. [They ate all of it eagerly.] **2.** I (10)   It was a five course dinner. We finished off with cognac. [After the dinner the host served cognac.] **3.** T (5)   Boxing. The champion had his opponent groggy, and finished him off with a right to the jaw. [He scored a knock-out.]

Fit   To adapt for a particular use.

fit up   T (4)   Fit up a work bench. [Supply it with tools.] See **fix up.**

Fix   To put in order or in good condition; to supply something that is needed.

fix up   **1.** T (2)   The parents fixed up the room with a table, a work bench, some shelves and a cupboard. [They supplied those things.] See **fit up.** **2.** T (3, 11)   If you don't have a ticket for the opera tonight, I can fix you up. [I have a ticket I can give or sell you.] **3.** T (4)   They fixed up their quarrel, and are good friends again. [Came to an understanding, an agreement.] **4.** T (2) Can you fix up our power mower. [Repair it so it will function.]

Fizzle   To make a hissing or sputtering sound, that dies out weakly.

fizzle out **1.** I (8) The firecracker fizzled out. [It didn't explode.] **2.** I (8) Fig. We had great plans for the holidays, but they fizzled out when unexpected guests arrived. [They came to an end.]

Flag To use a flag, or some other object, as a signal.

flag down **1.** T (4) Railroading. The brakeman walked ahead on the track to flag down the on-coming train. [Wave a red flag downward as a signal to stop.] **2.** T (4) When our car broke down we flagged down a passing truck and rode to the next town. [Waved to the truck to stop, making a downward motion with the arm.]

Flake To form flakes.

flake off I (1) We'll have to have the house repainted this summer. The old paint is flaking off on the south side. [It is falling off in small pieces.]

flake out **1.** I (9) Slang. The kids flaked out after the picnic. [They fell asleep, had to take a nap.] **2.** I (6) Slang. Jack is the one who suggested the mountain climbing but he flaked out at the last minute. [He didn't go.] See **cop out.**

Flame To burn with a flame, to blaze. See **blaze, flare, flash.**

flame out (1,2) A sheet of fire flamed out over the roof tops after the bomb exploded. [Appeared suddenly.]

flame up **1.** I (5) The fire on the hearth flamed up when the pine branches were thrown on. [Became very bright.] **2.** I (5) Fig. The anger of the mob flamed up to a high pitch when they heard a man had been shot. [Became intense.]

Flare To blaze with a sudden burst of flame.

flare back **1.** I (1) The cannon flared back. [A blast of flame came from the breech after firing.] **2.** *flare-back* N. The soldier flinched at the flare-back.

flare up **1.** I (5,6) The smoldering mass of ruins suddenly flared up when an oil drum exploded. [Burst into flames.] **2.** I (5) He flared up in anger when they accused him of being a traitor. [He became very angry.] **3.** I (5) Violence flared up in the populace when they heard their leader had been shot. [It broke out with intensity.] **4.** T (6) His old rheumatic pains flared up once more. [His joints became sore and inflamed.] **5.** *flare-up* N. (6) A recurrence of an old malady or illness.

Flash To break into sudden flame or light.

flash back **1.** I (4) Play. Cinema-Novel. At the critical moment, the author flashed back to the hero's childhood. [Inserted a scene showing it.] **2.** *flash-back* N. (4) An earlier scene or event so inserted.

flash out I (9) He flashed out at the mention of his wife's name in connection with the scandal. [He expressed his anger.]

Flatten To make flat.

flatten back T (1) The mule flattened back his ears and lunged at his tormentor. [An angry reaction to a challenge.]

flatten out **1.** T (9) The boxing champion flattened out his opponent with a haymaker. [Knocked him down, so that he lay flat on the ground.] **2.** I (10) Beyond the range of hills the land flattened out into a fertile valley. [It became level, flat.]

Fledge Of a young bird, to acquire the feathers necessary for flight.

fledge out I (9) When we next looked into the robin's nest, the young birds were all fledged out. [Their bodies were covered with feathers.] See **feather out**.

Flesh To acquire more flesh on the skeleton.

flesh out **1.** I (11) The young calves are fleshing out very nicely. [They are taking on weight.] **2.** T (11) Fig. The author fleshes out his plots by introducing interesting minor characters. [Makes his stories more complex and longer.]

Flicker To burn unsteadily, shine with a wavering light.

flicker out I (8) The light (the lamp, the candle, etc.) slowly flickered out, and all was dark. [The light died.]

flicker up I (1,2) A small blue flame flickered up from the dying fire. [It shone very briefly.]

Fling To throw, cast or hurl with force or violence.

fling aside T (1) When his wife called him, he angrily flung aside his book and rose from his chair. [Threw it to one side.]

fling down T (5) The opposing candidate flung down a challenge to debate the question. [In the manner of knights in the days of chivalry, who flung down a glove as a challenge.]

fling off **1.** T (2) He flung off his coat and stood ready to fight. [Removed it and threw it aside.] **2.** T (2) Fig. He flung off all restraints and began to campaign in earnest. [He refused to let anything stop him.]

Flop To fall suddenly, especially with a noise.

flop down I (1) Informal. John flopped down on the couch (the bed, the floor, the chair, etc.) and refused to get up.

Flunk To fail in a course or examination and be unable to continue in school.

flunk out I (4,9) James flunked out last quarter. [He was not allowed to continue his studies in college.]

Flush I To redden, to blush.

flush up I (4) Mary flushed up when she was asked about the boy who took her to the dance. [She was embarrassed and she blushed.]

Flush II Hunting. To cause a bird or small animal to leave its hiding place.

flush out **1.** T (1) The hunter's dog flushed out a covey of quail. [Made them fly up out of their hiding place.] **2.** T (3) He keeps his thoughts pretty well to himself, but I think we can flush him out. [Get him to express them.]

Fly To move through the air on wings as a bird. May be used with all the elements, showing the direction of movement.

fly away **1.** I (2,3) Fly away with me. [Let's escape to more glamorous surroundings.] **2.** *fly-away* A. Frivolous or flighty. [She was a giddy, fly-away type of person.]

fly-back   N. (3,4)   Electronics. The return to the starting point of the electronic beam in a cathode ray tube.

fly by   **1.** T (2)   Aviation. The captain directed the formation to fly by the reviewing stand. [Demonstrate their skill by flying past it.]   **2.** *fly-by* N.   See **fly over.**

fly in   **1.** I (1)   The club will fly in to Akron. [Gather there.]   **2.** *fly-in* N.   A sporting and social event for private plane owners. [Having a fly-in.]

fly-off   N. (1,2)   Meteorology. Evapotranspiration. The process of transferring moisture from the earth by evaporation of water and transpiration of plants.

fly over   **1.** T (1)   Army planes flew over the parade. [Took part in it by flying above it in formation.]   **2.** T (1)   The bombers flew over the target.   **3.** *fly-over* N.   (1)   A low-altitude flight of aircraft. See **fly by.**

fly up   **1.** I (2)   Girl Scouts. The Brownies will fly up tonight. [Get their wings as intermediates.]   **2.** *fly-up* N.   A promotion ceremony for Brownie Scouts.

Fob   Archaic. To cheat.

fob off   (2)   He fobbed off a cheap watch on me. [He deceived me into buying a watch of little value.] See **palm off.**

Fog   To become obscured with fog.

fog up   **1.** I (2,4)   Weather. It's fogging up. [The fog is becoming thick.] **2.** I (4)   The windshield fogged up so that we could not see out. [Fog formed, either on the outside or the inside of the glass.]

Fold   To bend over on itself.

fold in   T (5)   Cooking. She folded in the egg whites with a spatula. [Worked them into the cookie batter without a stirring motion.]

fold over   T (3)   The secretary took the document, folded it over, and placed it in the files. [Bent it so that one half covered the other half.]

fold up   **1.** T (3,11)   After the conference on strategy, the experts folded up their maps and put them in their briefcases. [Folded them neatly and compactly.] **2.** I (8)   Cards. To place one's cards face down on the table, as a sign of withdrawing from the play.   **3.** I (8)   Business. I hear that the Boston Store (the Smith Company, International Motors, etc.) is folding up. [Withdrawing from business operations.] See **fold up 2**.   **4.** I (4,6)   When he heard two witnesses testify they had seen him at the site of the murder, he folded up. [He no longer tried to defend himself.] See **give up**.

Follow   To come after in sequence, order of time, etc. May be used with all the elements, showing the direction in which the action moved.

follow out   T (7)   I think we should follow out the plans (orders, ideas, instructions, etc.) that were given to us by our adviser. [Carry them through to a conclusion.] See **carry out**.

follow through   **1.** I (3,4)   Now that we have made a good beginning in our campaign, we must follow through vigorously if we want to win. [Keep working hard until the election.]   **2.** I (4)   Sport. To complete the stroke or swing of a club (golf) or racket (tennis). **3.** *follow-through* N.A. (4) a. A continued effort. [A good beginning is important, but a good follow-through is equally important.] b. Sports. A completed action. [The aspiring golfers and tennis players spend much time perfecting their follow-through. Their technique in completing their strokes with club or racket.]

follow up **1.** T (9,10) The Marines followed up their early advantage by a direct attack on the enemy strong points. [Pursued the fight closely.] **2.** T (9,10) The speaker followed up his opening statement, with a full discussion of the history of the problem. [Pursued the subject, adding further ideas or evidence.] **3.** T (5,10) After the plan had been decided on, the chairman said he would follow up with a letter to the Mayor. [Make that additional effort.] **4.** *follow-up* N.A. a. (5) Pursuit of an advantage. [The follow-up resulted in complete defeat of the enemy.] b. (4,8) A supporting action or activity. [A follow-up letter was sent to all who had received the first announcement.] [Job Corps trainees may receive follow-up training once they are employed.] c. (4,8) Journalism. A news story containing further information. [Did a follow-up on flood damage in the area.] d. (4,8) Medicine. Subsequent treatment. [Follow-up is necessary for many patients after they leave the hospital.]

Fool To act like a fool, to joke, to play.

fool around **1.** I (2) Johnny is always fooling around in class. [He doesn't pay attention, he does things he shouldn't do.] **2.** *fool around (with)* I (2) He spends all his time fooling around with the other boys (the girls, the car, etc.). [He plays with them, does nothing seriously.]

fool away T (3,6) He just fools away the time (his money) to no good purpose. [He wastes, spends foolishly.]

Force To compel, constrain, or oblige (oneself, somebody, or something) to do something. Often with "one's way" as the direct object. See **fight one's way**.

force aside T (1,2) A large man was standing in the doorway, but I forced him aside and went in. [Made him move out of the way.]

force back **1.** T (1) Two men rushed up to take hold of the boy, but we forced them back. [We made them retreat, step backward.] **2.** T (1,5) She forced back her tears and tried to smile. [Made an effort not to weep.]

force down T (1,5) When the big dog jumped up on him he forced him down. [Down to the ground, by exerting force.]

force in T (1,2) The plug was too large for the hole. I had to force it in with a hammer. [Into the hole.]

force off T (1,2) He insisted on sitting on the platform with us. We had to force him off. [Off the platform.]

force on T (I 1) His shoes were very tight fitting. He had to force them on with a shoe-horn. [Onto his feet.]

force out T (1) Enemy troops had occupied the village. It took many hours to force them out. [Out of the village.]

force over   T (5)   The tree was almost ready to fall. We all pushed hard and forced it over. [Caused it to fall.]

force under   T (2)   We had to exert all our strength to force the pole under the fallen horse. [Shove it beneath him.]

force through   **1.** T (1)   The leather was so tough it was hard to force a needle through. [Through the leather.]   **2.** T (4)   The President had to call on all the loyal party members to force through the Civil Rights law. [Through the legislature.]

force up   T (2)   Inflation will force up stock prices. [Make them go higher.]

Fork   Informal. To hand over, deliver, give, pay.

fork out   T (1)   The campaign manager asked each of us to fork out $100 as our contribution. [Make a donation.]

fork over   T (3)   Imagine it! I had to fork over $50 to get my car tuned up. [Pay rather unwillingly.]

fork up   I (4,9)   You promised you would give $20 to help us out. Now fork up! [Hand it over right now.]

Foul   To make foul, dirty; to spoil, interfere with.

foul out   I (6,7)   Baseball. He fouled out. [He hit a foul ball that was caught by an opposing player.] See **be out 4.**

foul up   **1.** T (6)   Slang. He's always fouling up the works. [He spoils everything, brings confusion and disorder to everything.]   **2.** T (6)   The heavy snowstorm fouled up our plans to drive to Denver. [Spoiled.]   **3.** *foul-up* N. (6)   a. A condition of disorder or confusion brought about by stupidity or inefficiency. b. Failure of a mechanical part to operate effectively. See **ball up. gum up, hash up, jam up, louse up, mess up, mix up, muck up, screw up, snarl up,**

Frame   To obtain false evidence by fraud or deceit.

frame up   N. (6)   John was the victim of a frame-up. [Ex. When he entered his hotel room there was a naked woman lying in the bed. A policeman or a hired photographer forced his way in and took photographs.]

Freak   N. A sudden and apparently causeless change or turn of events, the mind, etc. Used as a verb only in the expression **freak out**.

freak out   I (9)   Slang. Psychedelic experience. To pass out of a normal state of consciousness into one induced by LSD or some other drug or narcotic. Ex. Two of the group had already freaked out and were wandering about unconscious of the others present.

G

Gag   To use word play or horseplay for comic purposes.

gag up   T (2,6)   Slang. Instead of playing the scene "straight", the actors decided to gag it up. [Use gags and comic actions to change the nature of the scene.] See **ham up**.

Gamble   To play at any game of chance for stakes.

    gamble away   T (3,4)   He was a rich man's son who had gambled away his inheritance (the family fortune, all he possessed, etc.). [Lost everything through gambling.]

Gang   To form or act as a gang.

    gang up   **1.** I (3,10)   Boys in a slum neighborhood have a tendency to gang up in opposition to other groups of boys. [Form exclusive groups or gangs.]   **2.** *gang up (on)*   I (3,10,11)   The boys on B Street ganged up on one of the boys on A Street. [They got together to beat up (punish, hurt, drive away) the boy from A Street.]

Gas   To fill the gasoline tank of an automobile or truck.

    gas up   I (4,11)   When we reached Omaha we had to gas up. [The tank was empty and we had to have it filled.] See **tank up.**

Gash   To make a long deep cut in, to slash.

    gash up   T (6)   His face was all gashed up from the knife battle with his attacker. [It had many deep cuts.]

Gasp   To make short convulsive utterances.

    gasp out   T (2)   When the police found her lying on the floor, she gasped out a few incoherent words and expired. [She died trying to tell them something.]

Gather   To bring together into one group, collection, or place.

    gather about (around)   I (1)   As the two men started to fight a big crowd gathered about (around). [They formed a circle around the fighters.]

    gather in   **1.** T (1)   It's going to storm. I think we'd better gather in the children. [Bring them into the house (the bus, the shelter, etc.)]   **2.** T (1)   Football. The end gathered in the pass and headed for a touchdown. [Caught the forward pass and started toward the goal line.]

    gather up   T (3,10,11)   It's getting dark. Let's gather up our things and start for home. [At a picnic or outing; collect equipment, clothing, remains of food, etc.] See **pick up 1**.

Gavel   To use a gavel, as a sign of authority.

    gavel down   T (1,4)   At the meeting an angry old man stood up to make charges of unfairness, but the chairman gaveled him down. [Banged his gavel, called him out of order and forced him to sit down.] See **rap down.**

Gentle   To tame, to make gentle.

    gentle down   T (2,6)   It will take a lot of training to gentle down the mustang so that we can saddle it and ride it. [Tame its wild spirits, make it gentle.]

Get   To come into possession of, receive; to arrive at, or bring oneself to or into a place, position, or state.

    get about   **1.** I (1,2)   After ten weeks in the hospital he is now able to get about without help. [Move here and there.] **2.** I (2) She gets about a great deal. [Goes out socially.]

get across **1.** I (1) They came to a river and they couldn't get across. [Go from one side to the other.] **2.** T (1) I'll try to get my ideas across, at the meeting. [Transfer them from my mind to the minds of other people.] See **put across.**

get along **1.** I (1) We must be getting along. [We must leave now, and go to some other place.] **2.** I (1,3) Get along with you! [Go away from here! An angry or impatient remark.] **3.** I (2) They get along very well. [They are friendly with each other.] **4.** I (2,3) They are getting along nicely in their new business. [They are prospering.] See **get on 4, make out 6.**

get around **1.** I (1,2) He's now able to get around on his bad leg. [He can walk about the house; go to work, etc.] **2.** I (5) My brother Charles gets around a lot. [He has an active social life.] **3.** I (1,2) The scandal about the Smiths has gotten around. [It is being talked about in many places.] **4.** T (1) Get the children around. I want to show them something. [Bring them close to me.]

get aside **1.** T (1,2) You'll have to get him aside and tell him the facts in the case. [Take him to a place away from the other people.]

get away **1.** I (1) We got away at nine o'clock. [We left home, or some other place.] **2.** I (2) The animals got away, when the keeper wasn't looking. [They escaped.] **3.** *getaway* N. (2) The bandits made a quick getaway. [They escaped in a hurry.] **4.** *getaway* A. (2) Their getaway car was waiting for them at the corner. **5.** *get away (from)* I (3) Don't bother me! Get away from me! [Leave me. Go some place else.] **6.** T (3) He grabbed my gun, but I got it away from him. [I managed to recover it.] **7.** *get away (with)* I (1) You think your plan will defeat me, but I won't let you get away with it. [I won't let you succeed.] **8.** I (3) He gets away with murder. [He succeeds in doing many bad or wrong things, without punishment.]

get back **1.** I (3) I'm glad to see you. When did you get back? [When did you return?] **2.** I (3) Get back in the car. We're leaving. [Take your place in the car.] **3.** T (5) Did you get your money back? [Did someone return it to you?] **4.** T (5) He got his suit back from the cleaners. [It was delivered to him.]

get by **1.** I (2) Please let me get by. [Let me pass by you.] **2.** I (4) I'll get by, as long as I have you. [I'll be O.K. I'll get by the difficulties of life.] **3.** *get by (on)* I (2) He gets by on a very small income. [He lives rather comfortably.] See **make out 1, squeak by, worry through.** **4.** T (2) We got him by without too much trouble. [We took him past the gatekeeper.]

get down **1.** I (1) Please get down (from the tree, the ladder, the roof). [Come down to the ground.] **2.** I (1) We didn't get down till 9 o'clock. [Come downstairs.] **3.** I (1) Let's go back before the sun gets down too far. [Down to the horizon.] **4.** *get down (to)* I (3,5) Let's get down to business. [Let's start to work. Let's discuss financial terms.] **5.** T (1) Get the books down from the shelf. [Bring them down.] **6.** T (2) This cold weather is getting me down. [It makes me low in spirits.] **7.** T (7) We must get his report down (on paper). [Make a written record of his report.]

get in **1.** I (1) He opened the car door and got in. [He entered the car.] **2.** I (1) They were at the airport when we got in. [When we arrived.] **3.** I (1) They were there when the plane got in. [When the plane arrived.] **4.** I (4) He was refused membership in the club several times, but he finally got in. [He was elected to membership.] **5.** T (1) The car was so full, we couldn't get all the children in. [Into the car.] **6.** T (1) They got the hay in before the rain came. [They put it in the barn.]

get off **1.** I (1) When the bus stopped, got off. [Off the bus.] **2.** I (2) When did you get off? [When did you leave?] See **be away, be off, start off. 3.** I (4) What time do they get off? [Stop working.] **4.** I (1,2) Get off (of) me! [I don't want you on top of me.] **5.** T (2) His feet were so swollen it was hard to get his shoes off. [Off his feet.] **6.** T (2) He got his hat off in the elevator. [Off his head.] **7.** T (1,2) We got the family off on the evening train. [We started them on their trip.] **8.** T (2,3) We got off our Christmas cards a week earlier than usual. [We mailed them.]

get on **1.** T (I 1) When the train stopped, we hurried to get on. [Onto the train.] **2.** I (I 2,3) It was a program (a team, a show) he wanted very much to get on. [Take part in, be a member of.] **3.** I (II 1) It's late. We must be getting on. [We must leave, to go some place else.] See **get along 1. 4.** I (II 1) Write and tell us how you're getting on. See **get along 4. 5.** *get on (with)* I (II 2) He told us to stop playing and get on with our work. [Proceed to do our work.] **6.** T (I 1,5) The bus will stop long enough for us to get our bags on. [On the bus.] **7.** T (I 1) His gloves were so small he had trouble getting them on. [On his hands.]

get out **1.** I (1) Do we have time to get out for some pictures? [Out of the bus to take pictures.] **2.** I (4) When do they get out? [From school, prison, work, the theater, etc.] **3.** I (2) My parents don't get out very much. [They don't leave home for visits, entertainment, etc., very often.] **4.** I (1,9) Get out! Don't bother me. [Leave this place!] **5.** T (2) They have gotten out a new edition of the book, (a new issue of the magazine, a pamphlet, a petition). [Published, printed it.] **6.** T (1) He got out his pen and signed the check. [Took it from his pocket.] **7.** T (1) Johnny got a splinter in his foot but the doctor soon got it out. [Extracted it.] **8.** *get out (of)* I (6) Having made a promise to help her, he couldn't get out of it. [He had to keep his promise.] **9.** T (7) The lecture was good. We got a lot out of it. [We learned a great deal.]

get over **1.** I (3) The bridge was closed, so they couldn't get over. [Over the bridge to the other side.] **2.** I (3) Thanks for the invitation, but I'm afraid we can't get over tonight. [Come, across some distance, to a person's house.] **3.** *get over (it)* Not a true two-word verb. Over is here a preposition, *followed*

by its object. I (8)   He had a bad cold, but got over it soon. [He recovered.]
4. I (3)   I hear that they lost all their money. I just can't get over it. [I feel very sorry for them.]   **5.** T (3)   They tried to put the bridle over the horse's head, but couldn't get it over.   **6.** T (3)   I argued and argued, but couldn't get my idea over. [I couldn't make people understand.] See **get across 2**.   **7.** *get it over (with)* T (8)   This quarrel must stop. Let's get it over with. [Let's bring it to an end.]

get through   **1.** I (1)   Why can't you get through? Because the gate is locked. [Through the gate.]   **2.** I (3,4)   When did you get through? [When did you finish your work (a paper, an exam, a project)?]   **3.** T (1,4)   She bought some jewelry in Japan, and had trouble getting it through. [Through the customs.]   **4.** T (1)   I couldn't get my finger through. [Through a hole or opening.]   **5.** *get through (to)* I (1,4)   I can't get through to her. [She doesn't listen to, or won't understand what I say. There are mental or emotional barriers.]   **6.** *get through (with)* I (4)   Let's get through with this unpleasant job at once. [We must finish it now.] See **get over 1**.

get under   **1.** I (2)   He got out of the car and got under to examine the brakes. [Under the car.]   **2.** T (2)   The nurse lifted the patient's head and got the pillow under. [Under his head.]

get up   **1.** I (1)   He got up at eight o'clock. [Up and out of bed.]   **2.** I (1)   He got up. [From a sitting position or from a lying down position.]   **3.** I (2)   He got up in the world. [He became important, well known.]   **4.** I (16)   The temperature got up to 80°. [It rose to that point.]   **5.** T (1)   She got the children up in time for breakfast. [She woke them and had them get out of bed.]   **6.** T (1)   Let's get up a party (a picnic, a bridge game, an entertainment, etc.). [Arrange, organize.]   **7.** T (15)   He got himself up as an Indian prince. [He dressed in that fashion.] See **tog out, trick out**.   **8.** *get-up* N. (15)   His was a perfect get-up. [It was the "real thing".]   **9.** (15)   What an awful get-up! [Said of a costume in bad taste.] See **get up 7**.   **10.** *get-up-and-git* N. (2,5)   Coll. That man is full of get-up-and-git. [He's full of ideas and energy.]

Give   To deliver freely, bestow, hand over, grant, show, present, furnish, etc.

give away   **1.** T (3)   St. Francis gave away all his earthly possessions and took the vow of poverty. [Gave them to the poor.]   **2.** T (3)   At a wedding the father, or some male relative, gives away the bride. [Gives her to the groom.]   **3.** T (4)   She kept her engagement a secret until her kid brother gave it away. [Said something that revealed the engagement.]   **4.** *give (oneself) away* T (4) He claimed to be innocent of the crime, but gave himself away when answering two of the prosecutor's questions. [Said something that proved him guilty.]   **5.** *give-away* n. (4)   His answer to the second question was a dead give-away. See **give away 3, 4**.   **6.** *give-away* N.A. (3,4)   Radio and television give-away programs have been very popular. [Programs at which prizes are given to those who answer questions correctly.] **7.** *give-away* N. (3,4) An item given free to a customer who has made a purchase.

give back T (5) When she broke her engagement she gave him back all the presents he had given to her. [She returned them to him.]

give down T (1) Something is the matter with that cow. She won't give down. [Give her milk.]

give in **1.** T (1) Be sure to give in your time cards before you leave tonight. [Give them to the clerk.] See **hand in**. **2.** I (3) The walls of the trench gave in and buried three of the workmen. [Collapsed, fell in.] See **cave in**. **3.** I (6) When the votes were counted the losing candidate refused to give in. He wanted a recount. [Refused to acknowledge defeat.] See **give up**.

give off T (1,2) The lilacs gave off a sweet perfume. The burning tires gave off an acrid smoke and odor of sulphur.

give out **1.** T (1,2) They are giving out prizes (citations, propaganda leaflets, free literature, notices, etc.) at the meeting tonight. [Giving them free of cost.] **2.** T (2) The Press Secretary gave out information about the President's future plans. [Gave it to the reporters, the public.] **3.** T (1,9) The cowboy gave out a yell. The lion gave out a roar. [Out of the body, into the open air.] **4.** I (8) Our supply of coffee, sugar and canned goods gave out before the end of our trip. [The supply was exhausted.] **5.** I (8) During the hike his legs gave out. [He was unable to continue walking.] **6.** I (8) The teacher's patience gave out and she scolded Johnny severely. [It came to an end.] **7.** *give out (with)* I (2,9) At the end of the meeting our favorite folk singer gave out with a rousing ballad. [Sang it loudly and gaily.]

give over **1.** T (3) My bachelor uncle gave over all his interest in the estate to my mother. [Transferred it.] **2.** T (8) Mother gave herself over to tears when she heard about his generosity. [She began to weep.] **3.** T (8) The evening was given over to dancing. [All the other activities were stopped.]

give up **1.** T (4) Formal and archaic. He lay back, murmured a few final words, and gave up the ghost. [He died.] **2.** T (4,9,10) After a long and hard chase the bandits finally gave themselves up. [They surrendered to the police.] **3.** I (4) After giving six wrong answers to the question (the puzzle) I finally gave up. [I stopped trying. I surrendered.] See **fold up, give in. 4.** T (4) The doctor has advised me to give up smoking. [Not to smoke anymore; to quit.] **5.** *give oneself up (to)* T (4) People with no hope for the future may give themselves up to despair and thoughts of suicide. [Surrender to those ideas.] **6.** T (4,5) He sold all his business interests and gave himself up to charitable activities. [Devoted himself to them.]

Gleam To appear suddenly and clearly like a flash of light.

gleam out **1.** I (2,10) From the light-house a ray gleamed out over the dark waters. [It spread out.] **2.** I (2) Ext. At the peace talks a ray of hope gleamed out on a troubled world. [It appeared as a ray of light in the darkness.]

Gloss To make a faulty explanation of something to cover up a mistake.

gloss over **1.** T (2) She glossed over her own errors of judgment in selling the family property. [She made it appear that she had not made any mistakes.] **2.** T (2,3) When he made his report to the committee, he glossed over the stupid way he had managed his assignment. [Explained away his stupid actions, as though they were not stupid.]

Glue To use glue for a purpose.

glue on T (I 3) The label on the package had come loose, so he glued it on with mucilage. [Attached it to the package.]

glue up T (6) The children's hands and clothing were all glued up after using mucilage (glue, paste) to make their paper designs. [Smeared over with glue.]

Gnaw To wear away, or remove by persistent biting or nibbling.

gnaw away **1.** I (6) We heard a mouse gnawing away in the kitchen cupboard. [Continuously.] **2.** I (6) Ext. Fear of being discovered kept gnawing away at his feeling of security. [Reducing little by little his confidence.]

Go To move on a course to, towards or into a place, position or state. The opposite of *come*.

go about I (1,2) She is the type of woman who goes about doing good. [It is her nature to be helpful.]

go across **1.** I (1) They came to the river and decided to go across on the ferry, instead of by the bridge. [To the other side.] **2.** I (1) His speech went across very well. [The audience listened with interest to what he said.] See **get across, go over 3.**

go along **1.** I (2) The Smiths are driving to Philadelphia. They want us to go along. [Accompany them.] **2.** I (1) As we were going along, we heard a strange noise in the back of the car. [Moving ahead, forward.] **3.** *go along (with)* I (2) I'll go along with you if you need my help. [Accompany you.] **4.** I (2) You have made a very good suggestion. I'll go along with it. [I'll agree to it, and act with you.] See **come along, come around, come over, fall in.**

go around **1.** I (3) Father is in back of the house. If you want to talk to him, just go around. [Circle the house.] **2.** I (2) A rumor is going around that the war will soon be over. [Here and there.] **3.** I (3) Here's a piece of cord to tie up your bundle. I think it's long enough to go around. [Around the bundle.] **4.** I (1,3) I'm afraid we don't have enough coffee to go around. [Enough for each person in the group to have a cup.] **5.** *go around (with)* I (5) a. I hear that John is going around with Mary Brown these days. [He is dating Mary; taking her to social events.] b. I don't want you to go around with that gang of boys. They're not the right sort for you. [Don't be friendly with them, or join in their activities.]

go aside I (2) The two men went aside for a moment, and seemed to be arguing about something. [They left the group.]

go away **1.** I (2) We always go away for two months in the summer. [Leave home for a vacation.] **2.** I (2)   Go away! I don't want to be bothered. [Leave me alone. Go someplace else.] **3.** I (3)   I wish this headache would go away. [Stop. Leave me.]

go back   1. I (3)   I miss my parents very much. I think I'll go back for a visit next month. [Return home.] **2.** I (4)   The use of tobacco goes back hundreds of years. [It originated then.] See **date back**. **3.** *go back (on)* I (1)   His friends went back on him when they learned how badly he was treating his wife. [They turned their backs on him; turned against him.] **4.** I (1)   He's a man who never goes back on his promises. [He keeps them; he is faithful to them.]

go by   1. I (2)   The parade (the train, the bus, the procession) went by while they were in the house. [Past the house.] **2.** I (2)   They became more friendly as the years went by. [Passed.] **3.** I (2)   You mustn't let this opportunity (chance, occasion, etc.) go by. [You must take advantage of it.] **4.** *go-by* N. (2)   Slang. I waved to him when I saw him in the street, but he gave me the go-by. [He refused to notice me. He went on without greeting me.]

go down   1. I (1)   When you go down don't forget to bring in the milk. [Downstairs.] **2.** I (2)   Prices are going down. [Prices of stocks, food, clothing, etc.] **3.** I (1,4)   He went down fighting. [Said of a boxer, a candidate for office, a debater, or anyone struggling against an opponent.] **4.** I (1,2)   Bridge. We went down two tricks on the last hand. [We lost. We took two tricks less than our contract called for.] **5.** I (1)   Her chocolate cake goes down easily. [We enjoy eating it. It is "easy to take".] **6.** I (1)   That idea of yours doesn't go down with me. [I don't like it. I can't take it; accept it.] **7.** I (7)   Martin Luther King will go down in history as a great peacemaker. [His name will be found in history books.]

go in   1. I (1)   We'd better go in now, it's getting dark. [Into the house.] **2.** I (1)   This key won't go in. It must not be the right one. [Into the lock. It does not fit the lock.] **3.** I (4)   He went in as a volunteer. [Into the army.] **4.** *go in (for)* I (9)   He goes in for sport (for camping, for politics, etc.). [He is enthusiastic for it; he gives much attention to it.] Often used with *in* omitted. There's a girl I could go for. [Be enthusiastic about.] Trained the dog to go for burglars. [Attack them energetically.] **5.** *go in (with)* I (4)   After he left college he went in with his father. [He entered the business his father conducted.]

go off   1. I (1,2)   They went off without saying goodbye. [They left us.] **2.** I (4)   Where were you when the lights went off? [Stopped functioning.] See **go out**. **3.** I (8)   The gun, (the pistol, the firecracker) went off in his hand. [Exploded.] **4.** I (8)   What time was it when your alarm clock went off? [Rang loudly.] **5.** I (8)   The interview (the lecture, the recital, the meeting, the conference) went off very well. [It functioned successfully.]

go on   1. I (I 1)   The stage wasn't lighted when she went on. [Onto the stage.] **2.** I (II 4)   The lights went on after a few seconds. [Began functioning.] **3.** I (II 2)   The performance (the show, the discussion) went on for two hours.

[Continued.] See **drag on**. **4.** I (II 3) Informal. Oh, go on! You're kidding. [Expression of disbelief and annoyance at a speaker's remarks.] **5.** I (II 5) What's going on here? [What's happening?] **6.** I (II 5) If you keep going on like that you'll drive me crazy. [Keep talking excitedly, acting strangely, being unreasonable.] **7.** *goings-on* N. (II 5) I've never heard such goings-on before. [All this talk, noise and crude activity is new to me. It annoys me.]

go out **1.** I (2) We're going out for dinner tonight. [Out of the house.] See **eat out**. **2.** I (2) The Holdens go out quite often. [They have many social engagements.] **3.** I (8) The lights went out suddenly and we were in the dark. [Stopped functioning.] See **go off 2**. **4.** I (8) He went out like a light. [He suddenly lost consciousness, from a blow or a shock.] **5.** I (4) The steel-workers threaten to go out on strike. [Leave their jobs.] **6.** I (4) Cards. We went out with a score of 125. [We won the game with that total of points.] **7.** I (4,9) I hear that Mr. Jones is going out of business. [He is giving up his business.]

go over **1.** I (3) The bridge is so weak it's dangerous to try to go over. [Cross it to the other side.] **2.** I (5) The huge tree went over with a crash. [Fell to the ground.] **3.** I (3) Did my speech (my lecture, my argument, my discussion) go over? [Was it successful in reaching my listeners?] See **get over, go across**.

go under **1.** I (1) John lifted the flap of the tent so we could go under. [Under the flap, into the tent.] **2.** I (4) They tell me that the Wilson Hardware Store has gone under. [It has failed and gone out of business.] **3.** I (4) How long did it take her to go under? [Under the influence of the anesthetic.] **4.** I (3) The body who had fallen into the water went under for the third time and was seen no more. [Under the surface of the water.]

go through **1.** I (1) He opened the gate and went through. [Through the opening.] **2.** I (4) The Civil Rights bill went through with a big majority. [It was passed.] **3.** *go through (with)* I (4) We intend to go through with our plan (project, scheme, idea, proposal) to the very end. [Work hard until it has been achieved.]

go up **1.** I (1) When Mother heard a noise in the children's bedroom she went up to see what was the matter. [Upstairs.] **2.** I (2) Stock prices (groceries, meats, rents) are going up. [Rising in price.] **3.** I (7) There's a large office building going up on the corner. [Being built.] **4.** *go up (to)* I (13) I went up to the policeman and asked him the way to the Post Office. [I came close to him.]

Gobble To swallow or eat hastily or hungrily in large pieces; gulp.

gobble down T (1,5) The children gobbled down their food and ran out to play. [They ate like hungry animals.]

gobble up **1.** T (4) Ext. After two months of travel in Iron Curtain countries tourists gobble up the news in the Western magazines. [They devour the news eagerly.] **2.** T (46) The big corporations have gobbled up many small business-es. [They have "swallowed" them, absorbed them.]

Goof   To act like a goof (a stupid or lazy person).

goof around   I (2)   Slang. He does nothing worthwhile. He just goofs around. [He has no purpose in life.]

goof off   I (5,10)   Slang. We goofed off over the weekend. [We slept a lot; we did nothing constructive; amused ourselves.] See **cop out.**

goof up   T (6)   Slang. Bob was supposed to organize the sports event but he goofed it up. [He spoiled it by bad management.] See **foul up, mess up.**

Grab   To seize suddenly or eagerly; snatch. See **nab.**

grab away   T (3)   Johnny picked up his sister's doll, but she grabbed it away and ran. [Took it from him.]

grab off   1. T (1,2)   Johnny had his cap on his head, but Bob grabbed it off and threw it on the floor. [Off his head.]   2. T (1)   Slang. I'm tired. I think I'll grab off a little sleep. [Have a quick nap.]

grab up   T (1,11)   Informal. We haven't time to eat much. Let's just grab up a sandwich and have something more later. [Eat in a hurry.]

Grease   To put grease on; lubricate.

grease up   1. T (2)   It's time you had your car greased up. [Your car is in need of a lubrication job.]   2. *grease-up* N.A.   (2.4)   My service station always does a good grease-up job. [They know how to lubricate carefully and accurately.]

Grind   To reduce to fine particles by pounding or crushing.

grind down   T (6)   The telescope lens was too thick. They had to grind it down. [Reduce the thickness by a grinding process.]

grind up   T (2,11)   She was grinding up some almonds to put in her cake. [Reducing them to small pieces by grinding.]

Groan   To utter a deep mournful sound, expressive of pain or grief; moan.

groan out   T (1)   When they asked him if he were badly hurt, he groaned out a weak reply. [He answered with pain in his voice.] See **cry out.**

Grope   To feel about with the hands, feel one's way.

grope around   1. I (1,2)   We saw him groping around on the floor for his glasses, which had fallen off. [Trying to find them with his hands.]   2. I (1,2) Ext. When we asked him why he had done such a terrible thing, he groped around for an excuse. [Tried to find an excuse.]

Ground   To come to or strike the ground.

ground out   I (4)   Baseball. The third man at bat grounded out. [He was put out at first base after hitting a ground ball to the infield.]

Grow   To increase in size or height; develop.

grow away (from)   I (3)   I'm afraid our children are growing away from us. [They are becoming independent, no longer close to us.]

grow out (of)   1. I (1)   A crooked branch grew out of the oak tree standing in front of our house. [It developed there.]   2. I (2,10)   The "sit-in" grew out of the determination of young Negroes to secure equal rights. [It developed from that feeling.] **3.** I (11) Johnny has grown completely out of his old suit. [He has become too large for it.]

grow up 1. I (1,2) Johnny is growing up like a weed. [He is getting taller and bigger very fast.] **2.** I (1,8) Many large industrial cities are growing up in the wilds of Siberia. [They are developing.] **3.** *grown-up* N.A. (4) Johnny will soon be a grown-up (boy). [He will be an adult person.]

Growl To utter a deep guttural sound of anger or hostility.

growl out T (1,9) When he was charged with throwing the Molotov Cocktail, he growled out a denial. [He said angrily that he had not thrown it.]

Grub To dig, to clear of roots, stumps, etc.

grub out 1. T (1,9) Pioneer farmers spent much of their first two years grubbing out roots and stumps to clear the land for planting crops. [Removing them by hard labor.] **2.** T (1) Early New England settlers grubbed out a meager living from the stony hillsides. [Labored hard on their stony land to make a living.]

grub up T (1,4) In the arid West the land had to be cleared by grubbing up the deep-rooted sage brush. [Remove it by deep digging.]

Gulp To swallow eagerly, in large drafts or mouthfuls.

gulp down T (5) We scarcely had time to gulp down our sandwiches (soup, coffee, beer, etc.) before the bus arrived. [Swallow them fast.] See **hog down.**

Gum To clog with, or as with, some gummy substance.

gum up 1. T (6) Our shoes were all gummed up with the fresh tar from the roadway. [Covered and sticky with the tar.] **2.** T (6) Informal. We thought Albert would take good care of the problem, but he gummed up the works. [He was very inefficient. He spoiled everything.] See **foul up.**

Gun To shoot with a gun.

gun down T (1,4) As the bank robber ran to his getaway car, the police gunned him down. [They shot him and he fell to the ground.]

Gush To go out, issue suddenly, copiously, or forcibly, as a liquid from confinement.

gush out I (1,9) Blood gushed out of the wound in the bandit's chest. [Came out with force, and in quantity.]

gush up I (5) Under an overhanging cliff a crystal spring gushed up and tumbled down the slope. [Came up with force and in quantity.]

H

Hack To cut, notch, slice, chop, or sever something with heavy, irregular blows.

hack away 1. T (2) It was necessary to hack away a thick cover of vines and bushes in order to reach the entrance to the cave. [Remove them by hacking.] **2.** I (6) He hacked away for an hour or more before the tree fell. [Continuously.]

hack down   T (4,6)   You'll have to hack down all those lilac bushes if you want to make a flower bed. [Cut them down.]

hack off   T (2)   The tree surgeon hacked off three big branches of the elm tree that hung over the roof of the house. [Removed them by hacking.]

hack out   T (8)   The soldiers hacked out a path through the thick jungle growth. [Used machetes to cut down bamboo, bushes, vines, etc.]

hack one's way   See **fight one's way**.

Ham   Slang. To act with exaggerated expressions of emotion; overact.

ham up   **1.** T (2,6) Theater. The director told the actors to ham up the bar-room scene. [Make it a comic scene by overacting.]   **2.** *ham it up*   T (2,6)   The night we saw that melodrama the actors hammed it up in wonderful fashion. [They overplayed the emotional scenes.] See **camp up, gag up.**

Hammer   To beat or drive (a nail, a peg) with heavy blows of a hammer.

hammer away   **1.** I (6)   The workmen kept hammering away all night, trying to finish the job before morning. [Pounded continually with their hammers.]   **2.** I (6)   Ext. His wife kept hammering away at him to get him to start digging the garden. [Using repeated urgings and reminders.]

hammer down   T (1)   The cover on the chest (box, well head, etc.) came loose. He had to hammer it down. [Make it tight by pounding with a hammer.]

hammer in   T (1)   Ext. My students are very poor in English grammar. I try to hammer it in, but I don't get very good results. [Force it into their heads.]

hammer out   **1.** T (1)   I took my car to the garage to have them hammer out the dent in my fender. [Return it to its original shape by hammering.]   **2.** T (7) The diplomats spent three months hammering out a treaty (an agreement, a solution to the problem). [Working hard to reach agreement.]

Hand   To deliver or pass with the hand; to give.

hand along   T (1)   Here are some pamphlets on the subject of the lecture. Please help yourself and hand them along. [Take one and give the rest to people near you.]

hand around   T (2,3)   She took the pamphlets and handed them around to the other people in the room. [To persons who were sitting or standing around in the room.]

hand back   T (5)   Mr. Jones took one of the pamphlets then handed it back, because he already had one. [Returned it to the giver.]

hand down   **1.** T (3,7)   When he died Mr. Brown handed down his business to his sons. [Gave it to them in his will.]   **2.** T (1)   Ext. That tradition has been handed down from generation to generation. [Down through time.]   **3.** *hand-me-down* N.A. (1) a. An article of second hand clothing. [Johnny, as a youngster, was always wearing hand-me-downs that had been worn by his father, or other male relatives or friends.] b. Cheap, ready-made clothing. [Our family was very poor. We always wore hand-me-downs. Clothing handed down from the store shelves.]

hand in   T (1)   The teacher asked us to hand in our papers (tests, compositions, etc.) at the end of the hour. [Give them to her at her desk.] See **give in, turn in**.

hand on   **1.** T (II 3)   Here is the book you asked me about. When you've read it hand it on to someone else. [Do not return it to me.]   **2.** T (II 1)   Each generation hands on certain beliefs to the succeeding generation. [Transfers them.]

hand out   **1.** T (2)   At the political rally a group of pretty girls were handing out campaign literature. [Giving it to those coming to the meeting.]   **2.** T (2) The Red Cross workers were handing out food and clothing to the flood victims. [Distributing them.]   **3.** *hand-out* N.   (1)   a. Free food or money. [A beggar came to the back door and asked for a hand-out.] b. Free gifts for promotional purposes. [Merchants often use hand-outs as a means of attracting customers. These might be samples of their products or inexpensive gadgets.] See **dish out**.

hand over   **1.** T (3)   When he had finished looking at the photograph, he handed it over to me. [Held it out to me in his hand.]   **2.** T (2)   They caught the boy who had stolen their car, and handed him over to the police. [Gave him into their custody.]

Hang I   T.   To fasten or attach a thing so that it is supported only from above or at a point near its top; suspend.

hang on   **1.** T (1,3)   In decorating the Christmas tree they hung the ornaments on with little copper wires. [Attached them to the tree.]   **2.** *hang one on*   T (1,3) Slang. Boxing. The champion hung one on his opponent that knocked him down for the count. [Landed a heavy blow on him.]   **3.** T (1,3)   Slang. The defeated boxer was so despondent he went to a night club and hung one on. [He got very drunk.]

hang out   **1.** T (2)   People in houses along the street hung out their flags in preparation for the parade. [Out of their windows.]   **2.** T (2)   Where's mother? She's hanging out the wash. [Hanging the washed clothes on a line in the open air.]

hang over   **1.** (c) I (4)   We haven't time to discuss finances at this meeting. We'll let it hang over till the June meeting. [Postpone the discussion.] See **put off**. **2.** I (4)   When Congress adjourned in December they left the President's tax bill hanging over until January. [No action could be taken until January.]   **3.** *hangover* N.   (9)   a. Something remaining behind from a former period or state of affairs. [The tax bill the Senate is voting on is a hangover from the previous session.] b. The disagreeable after effects of drunkenness, usually felt several hours afterwards. [The following morning he had a terrible hangover and couldn't go to work.]

hang up   **1.** T (1)   Mother has a hard time getting the children to hang up their clothes. [Hanging them on pegs, brackets, or clothes hangers.]   **2.** T (6)   A traffic jam hung us up for half an hour at Main and Center. [Kept us as if suspended. We couldn't move.]   **3.** T (4)   Telephone. You shouldn't forget to hang up (the receiver) when you finish talking. [Put the receiver back on its hook, or stand, to break the connection.] **4.** *hang up (on)* I (6,8) Telephone. Mary and her boyfriend were having an argument over the telephone. She finally hung up on him. [Hung up the receiver while he was still talking.] **5.** T (6) Slang. His infatuation with the pretty blonde hung him up for weeks. [Kept him as if suspended, unable to think about anything else, act normally.] **6.** *hang-up* N. (6) Slang. Jack has a hang-up about that girl. [He is completely absorbed by thoughts of her. He has an obsession.] **7.** *hung-up* A. (6) Slang. Jack is sure hung-up [About girls, surfing, pot, foreign cars, etc.]

Hang II I. a. To hold on for support, cling.
   b. To be doubtful or hesitant.
   c. To remain in contact, persist, linger.

hang around   **1.** (c) I (1)   Informal. Why are those boys always hanging around? [Staying in the neighborhood.] **2.** I (1)   Informal. Hang around and I'll show you my colored slides. [Stay here.] See **stick around.**

hang back (b)   I (1)   My little niece hung back when we asked her to sing for us. [She was shy, a bit afraid, did not come forward.]

hang on   **1.** (a,c) I (II 2)   He fell through the thin ice but grabbed the ladder which rescuers slid out to him and hung on till he was dragged to safety. He kept his hold on the ladder.] See **I hold on.**   **2.** I (II 2)   Sorry you don't like your job, but you'd better hang on for a while and be looking for another. [Keep working at your present job.] **3.** I (II 2)   My cold has been hanging on for three weeks. [It has been with me.] **4.** *hang on (to)* (c)   I (II 2)   I think I'll hang on to my present car till next year's models come out. [Keep it.] **5.** *hanger-on* N. (II 2)   A person who remains in a place or with a group, another person, etc., especially past the point when his presence is desired, or in the hope of gaining some personal end; an unwanted and frequently parasitic individual. Ex. Hangers-on at the end of a party; political hangers-on.

hang out   **1.** (a) I (2)   Johnny hung out the window to watch the parade go by. [He leaned out, clinging to the window frame to keep from falling.] **2.** I (10) That big branch of the maple tree hangs out too far over the road. We'll have to cut it off. [Out from the trunk into the public street.] **3.** (c) (2)   Slang. Their oldest son hangs out at the pool room every night. [Goes there regularly and stays a long while.] **4.** (2)   Slang. In New York the rich hang out on Park Avenue. [That is the street many of them live on. It is their social center.] **5.** *hang-out* N. (2)   Slang. A place where a person goes out of habit, for companionship, relaxation, gaming, living, etc.]

hang up (c)   T (6)   The passenger train was hung up for five hours in the mountain pass, waiting for the landslide to be cleared away. [It could not proceed.]

Happen   To come or go casually or by chance. May be used with many of the second elements.

happen along   I (1)   Our car broke down on a desert road. Fortunately another car happened along and we got some help. [Arrived unexpectedly.]

happen in   I (4)   We were talking about our vacation plans when the Joneses happened in. See **drop in**.

Harden   To make hard or harder.

harden up   T (2)   You should do some mountain climbing to harden up your muscles. See **tone up**.

Hark   To return to a previous subject or point; revert.

hark back   I (4)   When we talk about the problems of college life he always harks back to his years at Harvard. [Refers to problems of those days.]

Harness   To put a harness on a horse or draft animal; attach him to a vehicle.

harness up   **1.** T (4,11)   The coachman was given orders to harness up two teams of horses. [Have them ready, with harness on.]   **2.** *harness up (to)*   T (3,11) Later the coachman harnessed them up to the carriage.

Hash   To make a mess, or confusion.

hash over   T (7)   Slang. When we went up to their room they were hashing over the events of the night before. [Talking in not very orderly manner about what happened.]

hash up   **1.** T (2)   She hashed up the vegetables to put them in the stew. [Chopped them up.]   **2.** T (6)   Slang. John certainly hashed up that meeting last night. [He did a poor job of conducting it.] See **foul up**.

Hatch   To come forth from an egg; to bring forth or produce.

hatch out   I (1)   Our little chicks hatched out on the 21st of April. [They came out of the shell.]

hatch up   T (7,11)   I wonder what those two are hatching up. They've been whispering to each other all evening. [What they are plotting.] See **cock up**.

Haul   To pull or draw with force; move by drawing; drag. May be used with many of the second elements. See **drag, I draw**.

haul off   **1.** T (2)   We hired a man to haul off the rubbish piled up in front of the house. [Take it away in a wagon or truck.]   **2.** I (1)   Informal. The two men were shouting angrily at each other when one of them hauled off and hit the other a resounding blow. [Drew back his arm and hit him hard.] See **pull off**.

haul up   **1.** T (9)   Informal. Old Jones is always getting in trouble. They've hauled him up before the judge five times for drunkenness. [Made him appear in court.]   **2.** I (13)   Informal. The car caravan hauled up in front of the Bluebird Restaurant. [Came to a stop.] See **pull up**.

Have   To entertain or possess.

have in   **1.** T (1)   Have the neighbors in for tea. [Invite them.]   **2.** *have (it) in (for)*   T (9)   Informal. He never speaks to me anymore. He must have it in for me. [He has a grudge against me. He doesn't like me.]

have on   T (I 3)   Don't bother to dress up. Just come in the clothes you have on. [The clothes you are now wearing.]

have it out   T (9,10)   Father was very angry with Robert for what he said to his mother. They had it out for an hour or more. [They had an angry discussion.]

Head To move forward toward a definite point; go in a certain direction. May be used with all the second elements. See **go**.

head off T (2) The stampeding cattle were headed straight for the river. The cowboys circled the herd to head them off. [Make them change their direction.]

head up T (9) John was chosen to head up the agency. [Be its leader.]

Heal To become whole or sound; get well.

heal over I (2) The wound he had received in battle was healing over nicely. [The area of the wound was going back to normal.]

heal up I (2,3) The sores on his arm healed up quickly after an application of antibiotics. [They disappeared completely.]

Hear To listen, pay attention to.

hear out T (7) He wanted to explain his part in the unpleasant affair and we decided to hear him out. [Listen to everything he had to say about it.]

Heat To make hot; to become hot.

heat over T (7) The soup (the coffee, the stew, etc.) has gotten cold. You'll have to heat it over. [Make it hot again.] See **warm over**.

heat through T (1) Put the rolls (the buns) in the oven for five minutes to heat them through. [Make them warm all the way through.]

heat up **1.** T (2,11) The water from the tap is only lukewarm. Heat some up on the stove for your shave. [Make it hot enough.] **2.** I (2,6) As we drove up the mountain our engine began heating up badly. [It became too hot.]

Heave To raise or lift with effort or force; throw. May be used with all second elements. See **throw, push, pull**.

heave out T (1) Heave out the lifeline! [Throw a rope to the drowning man.]

heave up **1.** T (6) They heaved up the anchor and set sail. [Pulled it up from the sea floor.] **2.** T (1) On hearing that all was well, he heaved up a sigh of relief. [Up from his lungs.] **3.** I (1) Informal. He was sick at his stomach. He heaved up several times during the night. [He vomited.]

Hedge To enclose with, or separate by a hedge.

hedge about **1.** T (3) Mr. Adams wanted to protect his patio from public view so he hedged it about with tall lilac bushes. [Planted them all around the edges of the patio.] **2.** T (3) Fig. The offer of a peace treaty was hedged about with so many conditions that peace seemed hopeless. [The conditions acted like a hedge.]

hedge in T (3) The small nation was hedged in by enemies. [Surrounded.]

hedge off T (3) Mr. Adams hedged off a part of his yard to make a patio. [Separated it from the rest of the yard by planting a hedge.]

Heel To cover temporarily the roots and part of the stem of a plant with soil, prior to permanent planting.

heel in T (1) Mr. Adams bought two dozen lilac bushes for his patio and heeled them in till he could prepare the ground for planting.

Help To assist someone in doing something, especially to move in some direction. May be used with all the second elements.

Ex. He helped her across. [He helped her to go (get, walk, climb, step, etc.) across.] He helped her up. [He helped her to get up (go up, step up, climb up, etc.).]

help along T (1) She had trouble walking over the rough stones but her oldest son helped her along. [Helped her to progress.] See **get along 4.**

help out T (5) The newlyweds had a hard time making ends meet, but their parents helped them out for the first year. [Supplemented their income.]

Hem To enclose or confine; to finish off with a hem.

hem about T (3) The small nation was hemmed about with enemies. [It was surrounded.] See **hedge in.**

hem in T (3) Our valley is hemmed in by mountains on three sides. [Enclosed.]

hem up T (8,11) Sister is busy hemming up the skirt she'll wear at the party. [Finishing it by turning up the bottom edge.]

Hide To conceal from sight.

hide away **1.** I (3,5) The bandits hid away in a remote part of the forest. [Concealed themselves from the authorities.] **2.** T (3,5) Mother hid the presents away from the children till the Christmas tree was put up. [In a secret place.] **3.** *hideaway* N. (3,5) The bandits felt safe in their hideaway. [Their secret refuge.] **4.** *hideaway* A. (3,5) To accommodate guests they have a hideaway bed in the living room of their small apartment. [A bed that can be hidden when not in use.]

hide out **1.** I (9) The members of the gang hide out during the day in a suburban apartment. [They keep out of sight.] **2.** *hide-out* N.A. (9) a. A hiding place. [The police are sure they have located the counterfeiters hide-out.] b. A secluded retreat. [My friend Charles has a charming little hide-out in the Catskills where he can escape the crowds and social life of the city.]

Hill To pile up soil for a purpose, especially cultivation of plants.

hill up T (3,11) It is good practice to hill up the rose bushes to protect them in winter. [Pile soil around them.] See **mound up.**

Hire To furnish service for payment.

hire on I (II 4) Last summer our young cowboy friend hired on as pick-up man for the rodeo. [He took that job.]

hire out **1.** I (2) She used to hire out as part-time cook. [Sell her services as cook.] **2.** T (5) The Nelson Implement Company hires out tractors to farmers who do not want to own one. See **rent out.**

Hiss To make or emit a sharp sound like that of the letter S.

hiss down T (1,4) When a man in the audience stood up to criticize the speaker, the audience hissed him down. [Made him sit down by hissing at him.] See **shout down.**

hiss off T (2) The audience did not like the performance of the actor who played the villain. They hissed him off. [Made him leave the stage by hissing.]

hiss out   T (4)   We knew that he had come to the meeting to make trouble. We hissed him out. [Made him leave by hissing.]

Hit   To give a blow or stroke.

hit back   **1.** T (5)   Johnny hit Bob and Bob hit him back. [Returned the blow.] **2.** *hit back (at)*   I (5)   When the Republican candidate questioned the Democratic candidate's loyalty, the latter hit back at him, accusing him of corruption. [Attacked him in return.]

hit off   **1.** T (8)   In his newest play the dramatist hits off perfectly the absentminded professor. [Represents him accurately.]   **2.** T (8)   The new comedy at the Broadway Theater hits off the stupidities of the political reactionaries. [Satirizes them, makes fun of them.]   **3.** *hit it off*   T (10)   Those two people are just the opposite of each other. They don't hit it off at all. [They don't agree, get along with each other.] See **get along**.

Hitch   To fasten or tie, especially temporarily; to harness an animal to a vehicle.

hitch up   **1.** T (3,11)   The farmer hitched up his team and drove to town. [Hitched the team of horses to the wagon.]   **2.** T (3)   Slang. When did you two get hitched up? [When did you get married?]

Hoard   To accumulate money, food, etc., in a secret or safe place, for future use.

hoard up   **1.** T (2,11)   It is useless to spend your life hoarding up riches. You can't take it with you. [Saving all your money, not spending it for useful and enjoyable things.]   **2.** T (2,11)   Housewives begin to hoard up sugar, tea, and coffee when there is a war scare. [Buying and storing them in large quantities.]

Hog   To eat like a hog.

hog down   T (5)   Slang. Those men simply have no table manners. They hog down their food like animals. [Eat greedily and gluttonously.] See **gulp down, swill down, wolf down**.

Hoist   To raise or lift especially by some mechanical appliance.

hoist on   T (I 1)   The men carried the cotton bales to the truck and hoisted them on. [Onto the truck.]

hoist over   T (3)   Two men stood by the fence to hoist the heavy cast-iron pipes over. [Over the fence.]

hoist up   T (1)   The warehouse has an automatic lift for hoisting up heavy crates. [Lifting them into position for storage.]

Hold I   T.   To maintain a grasp on something with or as if with the hands.

hold away   T (2,3)   The leader of the explorers asked his helpers to hold away the branches that blocked the entrance to the cave. [Hold them aside.]

hold back   T (1)   Two of my companions grabbed my attacker and held him back. [Prevented him from moving forward toward me.]

hold down   T (1)   My companions threw my attacker to the ground and held him down. [Kept him on the ground.]

hold on   T (1)   The wind blew so strongly I had trouble holding on to my hat. [Keeping it on my head with my hand.] See **hang on.**

hold off T (2) She picked up the shirt, held it off, and examined it carefully. [Held it away from her.]

hold out **1.** T (1,10) He held out his hand (the letter, the watch, the knife, etc.) so all could see it. [Out toward the others.] **2.** T (2) The weatherman holds out hope of clear skies tomorrow. [He offers hope to the public.]

hold under T (3) He dragged his opponent into the water and held him under. [Under the surface of the water.]

hold up **1.** T (1) John held up his father's head and gave him a drink of water. [His father was lying down and John lifted his head.] See **II hold up 1.** **2.** T (1) The teacher held up the picture (model, instrument, art object, etc.) so the students could all see it. [Up in the air, to show it.] **3.** T (1) Ext. All in favor of the motion hold up your hands. [Up in the air.] **4.** T (1,9) Fig. John held up his father as a good example of what a father should be. [Up before other people.] **5.** T (1,9) Fig. Some candidates try to hold their opponents up to ridicule. [Make them appear ridiculous.]

Hold II T. To keep control of, restrain, detain.

hold away T (2,3) At the scene of the accident the police formed a circle to hold the crowd away. [Keep them from coming too close.]

hold back **1.** T (1,3) The people watching the parade from the sidewalk began to surge into the street. The police formed a cordon to hold them back. [Keep them on the sidewalk, out of the street.] **2.** T (1,4) More troops are needed to hold back the enemy invasion. [Keep them from invading.] **3.** T (5) She tried bravely to hold back her tears (her sighs, her sobs, her emotions). [Keep them from coming out.] **4.** T (1) They say that the government is holding back certain information about the war. [Not giving out all the information.] **5.** *hold back (on)* I (2) Jane and her husband didn't act natural tonight. I think they're holding back on us. [There is something they don't want to tell us.] **6.** T (1) The Radio Corporation is holding back twenty percent of its profits for future expansion. [Not paying that money out as dividends.] **7.** *hold-back* N. (3) The company's hold-back will be spent for building a new factory. See **II hold back 6.**

hold down **1.** T (1,4) In hospitals they use special harness equipment to hold down delirious patients. [Keep them from getting out of bed.] **2.** T (2,3) The President asks for a tax increase to hold down inflation (buying power, spending, etc.). [Keep them from rising.] **3.** T (2,6) You'd better hold down your speed on this road. There are a lot of traffic officers on patrol. [Stay within the speed limit. Keep your speed down.] **4.** T (1,4) The government is calling up more troops to hold down the rebellion. [Keep it from spreading.] **5.** T (3) Ext. John is now holding down a job with General Motors. [He is working regularly.] **6.** *hold-down* N. (6) The commanding officer ordered a hold-down on bombing. [An order not to increase the bombing.]

hold in **1.** T (1) The teacher held Johnny in after school because he had behaved badly. [Kept him in the school for punishment.] **2.** T (1,3) He held in his breath for a moment, then slowly let it out. [Kept it in his lungs.] **3.** *hold oneself in* T (1,6) He was angry at the way his boss spoke to him, but he held himself in. [He controlled himself, did not speak out angrily.]

hold off **1.** T (1) Our troops held off the enemy attack, until reinforcements arrived. [Kept the enemy at a distance.] **2.** T (1) A tax increase will help to hold off inflation. [Prevent it happening.] **3.** T (8) I received a letter from her a week ago, but held off replying till yesterday. [Delayed answering her letter.]

hold on **1.** I (I 4) We threw a life belt (a rope) to the man who had fallen overboard. He grabbed it and held on while we pulled him in. [Kept his hold on it.] **2.** I (I 4) Hold on! [Keep holding to someone or something — a rope, a moving object, especially something that will help in some way.] **3.** *hold on (to)* I (II 2) He can't hold on to his money. He's always in debt. [He spends everything he earns.] **4.** I (II 2) Dr. Martin Luther King held on to the doctrine of non-violence in spite of the militant spirits. [He continued to believe in it.]

hold out **1.** T (1) There was a rope barrier in front of the entrance to hold people out. [Keep them from entering.] **2.** T (4) The professor gave his collection of art books to the university library, but held out ten of his favorite volumes. [Kept them for himself.] **3.** T (9) By the check-off an employer holds out a percentage of the pay check of union members and gives it to the union. [Deducts it and gives it to the union as membership dues.]

hold over **1.** T (7) That film was so popular that the management held it over for two weeks. [Kept showing it.] **2.** T (4) The tax law was not passed in December. They held it over until Congress reconvened in January. [They delayed action on it.] **3.** *hold-over* N.A. (4) A. The act of holding over something or somebody to a future date. (4) B. A person or thing held over from a previous time.

Ex. A hold-over Cabinet member.

A film that has been held over.

Hold-over legislation. See **lay over.**

hold under T (3) The jaguar dragged its victim into the water and held it under until it drowned. [Under the surface of the water.]

hold up **1.** T (1) Father held up his head so he could drink the water his son brought for him. [He was able to raise his head by himself.] See **I hold up 1**. **2.** T (6) An accident on Main Street held up traffic for an hour. [Kept it from moving. Caused it to stop.] **3.** T (6) We're sorry to be late. The down town traffic held us up. [Kept us from driving.] **7.** T (6) Informal. Let's get going! What's holding us up? [Let's start to do what we planned to do. What is keeping us from acting?] **5.** T (6,11) The robber held up the train (the stage coach, the bank, the gas station, etc.) and got away with a thousand dollars in cash. [They stopped the train (the stage coach) by a show of arms, and took the money.] Now used for any armed robbery. The command "Hold up your hands" or "Hands up" used by robbers may have some connection with the form **hold up 5.** But the present day equivalent command is "Stick 'em up." **6.** *hold-up* N.A. (6) a. Armed robbery. See **stick-up.** b. A stopping of traffic. c. A delay of a meeting or other activity.

Hold III I. To continue in the same state or manner; remain; stay.

hold away I (2) Hold away from me! You're interfering with my experiment. [Don't stay so close to me.]

hold back **1.** I (2) We invited them to join with us in our project, but they held back. [Did not come forward to join us.] **2.** I (2) We walked on toward the exit, but Mary held back for a last look at the Picassos. [She stayed behind for a while.]

hold in I (1,6) Henry was extremely angry at what Mary said. But he held in and changed the subject. [He remained outwardly calm. He kept his feelings to himself.]

hold off **1.** I (2) We wanted him to work with us on this project, but he held off for some reason or other. [He did not cooperate, he stayed away from it.] **2.** *hold off (on)* I (2) He gave us some of his time and some good advice, but held off on contributing money. [Did not want to give money.]

hold on **1.** I (II 2) The discussion (argument, debate, meeting, etc.) held on till past midnight. [It continued.] **2.** I (II 2) James is deathly ill. I hope he can hold on till his daughter gets here. [Continue to live.] **3.** I (II 2) Hold on! [Stop! Halt! Do not continue to say or do what you started to say or do.] From an early use of the verb hold, in the sense of halt.

hold out **1.** I (9) Our troops held out for ten days against the enemy attack. [Remained in their position. Continued to fight.] **2.** I (8) The supplies we took on our camping trip held out to the end. [We had enough for the whole trip.] **3.** I (4) The star pitcher of the Boston Red Sox held out for double his previous year's salary. [Refused to sign a contract for the following year, except on those terms.] **4.** *hold-out* N. (4) a. A person who holds-out on an agreement or contract. b. The act of holding out.

hold over **1.** I (4) Discussion of the tax bill will hold over till the next session of Congress. [It will be postponed.] **2.** I (7) The Academy Award film was held over for two months at the Capitol Theater. [It continued to be shown.]

hold up **1.** I (12) Our car held up very well during our trip across the desert. [It functioned well.] **2.** I (1,10) The market (prices, stocks, etc.) held up well in spite of the war scare. [They did not fall, become less in value.] **3.** I (12) Considering all the sickness she has had lately, Mother is holding up quite well. [She is in fairly good health now, and in good spirits.] **4.** I (1,4) I hope the good weather will hold up. We're planning a trip this weekend. [Continue.]

Hole To enter a burrow or pit in the ground; stay in a confined area.

hole out   I (4)   Golf. The next player holed out in five, one over par. [Took five strokes to drive the ball into the hole. Four strokes was normal.]

hole up   **1.** I (3,11)   The groundhogs have holed up for the winter. [Have gone into their holes to wait for spring.]   **2.** I (3,11)   The robbers holed up in their hide-out until the police gave up the chase. [They took refuge there.]   **3.** I (3,11) Informal. We were so tired after a full day's driving we decided to hole up at the next motel we came to. [Take lodging for the night.] See **put up 1**.

Hollow   To form by making a hollow.

hollow out   **1.** T (1)   At Halloween time we always hollow out a pumpkin to make a jack-o'lantern. [Remove the inside of the pumpkin.]   **2.** T (1)   The Indians used to hollow out logs to make canoes. [They cut, burned, or dug out the inside of logs.]

Home   To move towards, as to a home, or home base.

home in (on)   I (1)   As the robbers' car turned onto the highway, the police homed in on it. [Came toward it from various directions.]

Honey   To talk flatteringly or endearingly to.

honey up (to)   I (3)   Informal. The pretty young secretary honeyed up to her boss, hoping he would give her a raise in pay. See **cozy up**.

Hook   To fasten with a hook; connect apparatus to a source of power.

hook in   T (5)   Larry decided to subscribe to cable T.V. and asked the company to hook him in. [Connect him with the system.]

hook up   **1.** T (3,11)   The garage mechanic hooked us up to his tow car and pulled us into town. [Fastened our car to the tow car with a hook and chain.]   **2.** T (7)   A service man came this morning to hook up the telephone. [Make the connections necessary for it to operate.]   **3.** T (7)   The gas stove hasn't been hooked up yet. [Connected with the gas pipe.]   **4.** *hook-up* N. (10)   a. Electronics. A diagram of electronic apparatus and circuits showing the connection of the different elements in one assembly or device. b. The elements as set up for operation. c. Any combination of related parts; a connection. d. A network, as of radio or television stations.

Hoot   To cry out, or shout, especially in disapproval.

hoot down   T (1,4)   The people at the meeting hooted down a proposal to increase membership dues. [Shouted their opposition, and the proposal was lost.] See **shout down**.

hoot off   T (1)   The actor was so bad the audience hooted him off. [Off the stage.]

Hop   N.   Slang for opium. Used as a verb only in the expression **hop up**, with the meaning of to stimulate, excite, make enthusiastic.

hop up   **1.** T (2,5)   Slang. The young protesters hopped up the crowd with violent denunciations of the Establishment. [Aroused their emotions to a high degree.] **2.** T (2,5)   Ext. James has hopped up the motor of his racing car. [Increased its speed, rate of turnover.]   **3.** *hopped up* A.   (2,4)   In a state of excitement, stimulation. [A hopped up crowd, a hopped up motor.]

Horn To butt or gore with or as if with horns.

horn in (on) **1.** I (4) Slang. My brother-in-law is always horning in on our conversations. [Interfering with them; talking when we haven't invited him.] **2.** I (4) Slang. Three fellows horned in on the party last night. [Came without being invited.] See **butt in.**

Horse To fool around; indulge in horse play.

horse around I (2) Slang. Harry is always horsing around. He makes himself a nuisance. [He plays roughly, noisily, interrupts what other people are doing.] See **fool around.**

Hose To water, wash, spray, or drench by means of a hose.

hose down T (5) The sailors were busy hosing down the deck (of the ship). [Cleaning the deck by spraying water and scrubbing.]

hose off T (2) Instead of raking the leaves from his lawn he hoses them off. [Removes them by a strong stream of water from the hose.]

hose out T (1,9) A workman was busy hosing out the oil drums with a jet of steam. [Removing the remains of the oil by steam action.]

Hot To heat or warm a liquid.

hot up T (2) Informal. Let me hot up your coffee (tea, soup, toddy, etc.). [Add some hot coffee, tea, etc., to what you already have in your glass or cup.]

Hound To hunt or track with hounds; to pursue or harass without respite.

hound down T (4,5) The posse went out to find the horse thief and finally hounded him down. [They caught him after a long search.] See **hunt down.**

hound out (of) T (1,9) After he was convicted of stealing cattle the angry citizens hounded him out of town. [Made it so uncomfortable for him he had to leave town.]

Howl To make a loud noise like an animal howling.

howl down T (1,4) The people who had come to hear the candidate speak howled down a heckler who stood up to challenge the speaker. [Made him sit down by howling.] See **boo down, shout down.**

Huddle To crowd together closely.

huddle around I (1) There was a big fire in the fireplace so we all huddled around and warmed ourselves. [Gathered close around the fire.]

huddle down I (1) The children huddled down under the covers, and were soon asleep. See **snuggle down.**

huddle up I (3) Three little kittens were huddled up in a corner of the basket. [Lying close together.]

Hum To make a low continuous droning sound.

hum along I (2) As the orchestra played our favorite melody we hummed along. [Accompanied the orchestra with humming.]

hum away I (6) He was humming away to himself as he worked in the garden. [He kept humming.]

hum through I (3) We told him we didn't know the song so he hummed it through for us. [Hummed the whole melody.]

Humor To act sympathetically toward a person's humor or mood.

humor along T (2,3) He was in a bad mood but we humored him along, and he came out of it. [We acted sympathetically, and his mood changed for the better.]

humor up T (2,5) Informal. Poor John has had the blues for a week. Let's go over and humor him up. [Help him to get rid of the blues.] See **cheer up**.

Hump To raise the back in a hump.

hump over T (5) Poor Uncle Ted is all humped over with rheumatism. [He is bent over, because of the pain.] See **bend over**.

hump up T (2) We found our playwright humped up over his writing table, working on the last act. [His back was arched.]

Hunch To thrust out or up.

hunch up T (1) When we told the workman we didn't like what he had done he hunched up his shoulders and left. [Showed his indifference by shrugging.]

Hunt To search for, to try to find.

hunt around I (2) When we moved to Boston we had to hunt around for three weeks to find a place to live. [Look here and there for an apartment.]

hunt down T (4,5) The police are busy hunting down the killer. [Making an effort to find him.] See **hound down, track down.**

hunt out T (3) The political parties are busy hunting out prospective candidates for local office. [Trying to persuade people to run for office.]

Hurl To throw or fling with great force or vigor. May be used with most of the second elements. See **throw, toss**.

hurl back T (3) The troops hurled back the enemy. [Made them retreat.]

Hurry To move, proceed or act with haste. May be used with all of the second elements. See **go, come**.

hurry up I (2) Hurry up! We're already late for the party. [Increase your speed. Don't delay.] See **step on 2**. **2.** T (5) The jockey used his quirt on the horse to hurry him up. [Make him go faster.] **3.** *hurry up (to)* I (3) She hurried up to us and told us where we were expected to sit. [Came quickly to where we stood.]

Hush To become or be silent.

hush up **1.** T (2,13) The children at first were very noisy when the guests arrived, but Mother hushed them up. [Made them be quiet.] **2.** I (2,13) The children hushed up when Mother spoke to them. [They became quiet.] **3.** I (13) Hush up! Children. We want to visit with our guests. [Keep completely quiet. A stronger command than "hush!"]

Hustle To proceed or work rapidly or energetically. See **hurry**. May be used with all of the second elements. See **come, go**.

hustle about I (2) Mother was hustling about in the kitchen, preparing dinner. [Moving quickly here and there.]

hustle out   1. I (2)   As soon as the children came from school they hustled out to play in the yard. [Out of the house.]   **2.** T (2)   The barkeeper took the drunken man by the arm and hustled him out into the street. [Out of the bar.]

I

Ice   To become covered or coated with ice.
  ice over   I (2)   The pond (the pool, the lake, the river) iced over when the temperature went down to ten below zero. [Ice formed over the whole surface.]
  ice up   I (2)   It was cold and foggy as we drove along. The windshield kept icing up. [Ice kept forming on it.]
Idle   To pass the time in idleness; to move slowly.
  idle along   I (3)   The evening sun cast a golden glow on the mountains. We idled along, enjoying the scenery. [We drove slowly so as to watch the sunset.]
  idle away   T 3,6)   On our vacation we just idled away the hours, reading and playing bridge. [Spent the time in leisurely fashion.] See **laze away, trifle away.**
Inch   To move by inches, or by small degrees. May be used with all the elements. Often with "one's way". See **fight one's way.**
  inch along   I (1)   We were caught in the five o'clock traffic on 5th Avenue. We inched (our way) along for two miles. [We moved very slowly.]
  inch in   I (1)   There were hundreds of people standing close to the door, but he managed to inch (his way) in and speak to the manager. [Make slow progress getting in.]
Ink   To mark, stain, cover, or smear with ink.
  ink in   T (2)   After making a first draft of the outline (the sketch, the design, the plan) the artist inked it in. [Made it more clear and definite by using ink.]
  ink over   T (2)   Several sentences in the manuscript had been inked over, so that it was impossible to read what had been written. [Covered, blotted out by the application of ink.]

J

Jack   To lift or move something with a jack.
  jack up   1. T (1)   The garage man jacked up the car and crawled under to examine the brakes. [Raised it, using a jack.]   **2.** T (2)   Ext. Informal. Some merchants jack up their prices just before the Christmas shopping rush. [Raise them unreasonably, knowing that people will probably buy things anyway.]   **3.** T (2)   Ext. Informal. John has been neglecting his studies lately. We'll have to jack him up about that. [Do something to make him study.]
Jail   To put in prison.

jail up T (3,5) It would be a good idea to jail up all the young hotheads who urge the teen-agers to burn and to loot. [Put them securely in jail.]

Jam To press, push or thrust something forcibly into or onto some other thing.

jam in **1.** T (1) Informal. The car trunk was so full we had trouble jamming our golf clubs in. [Forcing them in among the other luggage.] **2.** T (5) Informal. That new film at the Capitol is jamming them in. [It is drawing big crowds.]

jam on T (I 1) He was angry and excited. He jammed on his hat and ran out the door. [Put it on his head with force.]

jam through T (4) Ext. The Democrats jammed through a series of anti-poverty bills in the last week of the session. [Worked hard, and succeeded in having them passed.]

jam up T (6) Slang. He's like a bull in a china shop. He's always jamming up the works. [Using force, without much intelligent activity.] See **foul up**.

Jar To cause to shake, to wobble.

jar off T (2) That's a very fragile vase on the end table. Be careful not to jar it off. [Cause it to fall to the floor by bumping against the table.] See **jolt off**.

Jaw To scold, use abusing language.

jaw away I (6) Slang. I could hear her jawing away at the children for coming into the house with muddy shoes. [Scolding them long and loud.]

jaw down T (4) Slang. That poor man never wins an argument with his wife. She can jaw him down every time. [Defeat him. Have the last word.] See **shout down**.

Jazz To play music in the manner of jazz; to put vigor or liveliness into some activity.

jazz up **1.** T (5) Informal. Sometimes they play Bach, Chopin or Beethoven "straight", but they also get a kick out of jazzing them up. [Giving them a modern touch, by using jazz rhythms.] **2.** T (5) Ext. Informal. The meeting had been very dull. Some of the younger people decided to jazz it up by starting an argument about free love. [Put more life into it.] **3.** T (5) The Smiths are jazzing up their living room. They've gotten rid of all their over-stuffed furniture and are going in for pop art, gay stripes, bright colored hangings, and modernistic light fixtures. [They are "livening up" their living-room.]

Jew To bargain sharply with a seller, to get him to reduce his price.

Jew down T (2,3) Offensive expression. He wanted fifty dollars for a used T.V. set, but I Jewed him down to thirty. [He reduced his price by fifteen dollars.]

Join To take part with others in some activity.

join in I (4) At first she was shy and said she didn't feel like singing, but later she joined in and sang as loud as anyone. [She began singing with us.] See **enter in**.

join up I (10) John had been invited several times to become a member of the Men's Club. He finally joined up in 1965. [He became a full, regular member of the club.] The expression can be used of entering the Army, the Navy, or any organized group.

Jolly   To talk or act agreeably to a person, in the hope of gaining something, or of making him feel better.

   jolly along   T (3)   At first he didn't want to make the effort to go with us but we jollied him along, and he finally agreed. [Persuaded him by talking good-humoredly.]

   jolly up   T (2,5)   He looks so sad and lonesome. Let's jolly him up a bit. [Make him less sad by talking gaily, humorously.] See **cheer up**.

Jolt   To jar, shake, or cause to move, as by rough thrusts or bouncing action.

   jolt off   T (2)   We hit a bump in the road that jolted two boxes off of the truck. [Caused them to fall off.] See **jar off**.

   jolt up   T (6)   We were badly jolted up by that fast ride over the rough country road. [We were shaken up, perhaps bruised.]

Jot   To write or mark down quickly.

   jot down   T (7)   I always keep a little book for jotting down notes (car licenses, phone numbers, addresses, etc.). [Making quick entries for future use.]

Jug   To put into a jug (slang for jail or prison).

   jug up   T (3)   Slang. The third time he was found drunk in the park the police jugged him up. [Put him in jail.]

Jumble   To mix in a confused mass; to put or throw together without order.

   jumble up   **1.** T (6)   His clothes were all jumbled up in a heap in the middle of the room. [Piled together in confusion.]   **2.** T (6)   He jumbled up his words so much that we couldn't understand anything he said. [Spoke without order or precision.]

Jump   To spring clear of the ground, or other support, by a sudden muscular effort. May be used with all the second elements. See **hop, leap, skip, spring**.

   jump in   I (4,9)   Informal. We were having a discussion about the race problem when Jim jumped in with an angry remark concerning riots. [Entered the discussion suddenly and forcefully.]

K

Keel   Nautical. To turn or upset so as to bring the wrong side uppermast; to turn upside down; tip over, overturn.

   keel over   **1.** I (5)   The boat keeled over when a huge wave struck it, and the passengers were thrown into the water. [It turned upside down.]   **2.** I (5)   Ext. It was a very hot day for the inspection. Two of the soldiers standing at attention keeled over and had to be taken to the infirmary. [They fell over in a faint.]

Keep I   I   To continue or remain; stay or stay even; persist.

keep away I (2,3)   My father told me to keep away. He said I was bothering him. [At a distance from him.]

keep back I (1)   The police gave orders to the crowd to keep back, because the walls of the burning building might fall at any minute. [Towards the rear.]

keep down **1.** I (1)   We had to keep down so the enemy machine gunners could not see us. [Down below a protective barrier.] **2.** T (1)   The doctor told Mother to keep Johnny down for a few days till the fever left him. [Make him stay in bed.]

keep in **1.** I (1,5)   Father ordered us to keep in as long as the riots were going on. [In the house.] See **stay in**. **2.** T (4)   Henry retired and transferred his business to his son, but still liked to keep his hand in. [Retain an interest, perhaps give help and advice.]

keep off **1.** I (1)   Keep off the grass. [Stay off it. Don't walk on it.] **2.** We kept the light off so nobody would know we were at home. [Not shining, not functioning.]

keep on **1.** I (II 2)   If you keep on in the way you're going, you'll end up in jail. [Continue to do the things you are doing.] **2.** I (II 2)   They kept on singing (talking, dancing, drinking, etc.) while we played bridge. [Continued.] **3.** T (I 1) Slang. Keep your shirt on! [Don't got excited! Stay calm.]

keep out I (1,2)   There is a sign on the door that says, "Keep out". [Do not enter. Stay on the outside.]

keep up **1.** I (12)   My wife takes part in so many activities. I don't see how she keeps up. [Has enough strength and energy to continue.] See **be up to 10**. **2.** I (3)   He walks so fast I can't keep up. [Stay close to him.] **3.** *keep up (with)* I (4)   I can't keep up with the other students in the class. [Be as good in my studies as they are.] **4.** I (4)   The Smiths try so hard to keep up with the Joneses. [Hold the same social position, by their style of living.] **5.** T (8)   The two friends kept up a correspondence for twenty years. [Continued to write to each other.]

Keep II T.   To hold back or restrain; detain.

keep around **1.** T (3)   Put this rope around the horse's neck, and keep it around till I tell you to take it off. [Circling the neck.] **2.** T (1)   My husband always likes to keep some ready cash around. [Near him.]

keep away T (2,3)   The dog was on a chain to keep him away from visitors. [Restrain him from approaching them.]

keep back **1.** T (1)   The police formed a cordon to keep the people back. [Prevent them from coming forward.] **2.** T (5)   She tried hard to keep back her tears (her sobs, her sighs). [Keep them inside her.]

keep down **1.** T (1)   The workmen sprinkled water on the street to keep the dust down. [Prevent it from flying in the air.] **2.** T (2)   During the war the government set up a Price Control Board to keep prices down. [Prevent a rise in prices.]

keep in T (1,5)   Bars keep the prisoner in. [Restrain him from leaving.]

keep off **1.** T (1)   Fear of seasickness kept him off the excursion boat. [Prevented him from taking the boatride.] **2.** T (2)   They kept off an enemy attack with a heavy artillery barrage. [Prevented it.]

keep on   1. T (I 4)   He kept the goat on a tether so he could not wander away. [He was tied to a stake.] **2.** T (I 3)   The clinic keeps a doctor on call at all times. [Available for emergencies. Restrains his personal liberty.]

keep out   1. T (2)   We put screens at the windows to keep out the flies and the mosquitoes. [Prevent them from entering.] **2.** T (3,5)   When he gave his art collection to the museum he kept out three Picassos. [Retained them, did not give them away.] **3.** T (5)   His name was presented for membership in the club, but two negative votes kept him out. Prevented him from joining.   **4.** T (1) The farmer posted his land to keep out hunters. [Prevent them from trespassing.]

keep under   1. T (3)   She kept her jewelry under lock and key. [Kept it in a strong box to prevent thieves from taking it.] **2.** T (4)   Many a father tries to keep his children too tightly under his thumb. [Insists on strict obedience.]

Key   To bring to a particular degree of intensity or feeling excitement, energy, etc. From the idea of winding up a watch or clock with a key.

key up   1. T (2,5)   The excitement of the political campaign keyed up the voters, who turned out in large numbers. [Aroused their interest, their enthusiasm.] **2.** *keyed up* A. (5)   We were all keyed up after watching the big game. No one wanted to go home to bed. [We were excited, stirred up.]

Kick   To strike with the foot.

kick about   I (2)   Informal. He spent most of his young manhood kicking about from place to place. [He did not settle down to a job or a permanent residence.]

kick across   T (1)   Bob grabbed the football and kicked it across to his team-mate on the other side of the field. [Across the field.]

kick along   T (1)   The two boys found a tin can in the street and went kicking it along till they reached home. [They kept it moving ahead by kicking it.]

kick around   1. T (2)   The players kicked the ball around for half an hour. See **bat around 1.   2.**   T (2)   Informal. I think your idea is a rather good one. Let's kick it around a bit. [Play with it. Consider it from various points of view.] See **kick around 1.   3.** *kick-around* n.   (2)   The coach told them to have a kick-around to get warmed up for the game. See **kick around 1.**

kick aside   T (2)   Harry kicked aside the chair that was standing between them and began to wrestle with his brother. [Out of the way of the two wrestlers.]

kick away   T (2)   John kicked away the bottles standing in front of the door and went in. [Removed them by kicking.]

kick back   1. T (5)   He kicked the ball to his team-mate and his team-mate kicked it back. [Returned the ball by kicking.] **2.** T (5)   Informal. The ward heeler who got him a job working for the city expected him to kick back a part of his salary. [Pay something each month in return for the favor.] **3.** *kick-back* N.   (5)   a. Payment by the receiver of a favor to the person who did the favor. b. Rebate, usually given secretively by a seller to a buyer, or to one who influenced the buyer. c. The practice of an employer, foreman or person higher up, of taking back a portion of the wages due to workers.

kick down T (1)   When the man inside the room refused to open the door, the ruffians kicked it down. [Made it fall by kicking it.]

kick in **1.** T (1)   When the man inside the room refused to open the door the police kicked it in. [Made it swing in by kicking it.] **2.** T (5)   Slang. The fellows who were getting up the party told us all to kick in ten dollars each. [Pay that much as our share.] **3.** I (7)   Slang. The poor old man finally kicked in after a long illness. [He died.] See **cash in 3**.

kick off **1.** I (2)   Football. Our team won the toss up, and the quarterback kicked off at exactly 1:30 p.m. [He started the game by kicking the ball towards the opposing team.] **2.** T (7)   Ext. The supporters of candidate Wilson kicked off his campaign at the Hotel Roosevelt. [Held a meeting to get the campaign started.] **3.** I (5)   The poor old man finally kicked off after a long illness. [He died.] See **kick in 3**.

kick out **1.** T (4,9)   Informal. He was a member of our club but we had to kick him out for not paying his dues. [Force him to leave the club.] See **throw out**. **2.** *kick out (at)* I (9)   The angry mule kicked out at his tormentors. [Tried to kick those who were annoying him.] **3.** I (9)   In his speech, the candidate kicked out at his critics. [Answered them angrily in strong language.]

kick over **1.** T (3)   Football. The quarterback took two steps toward the ball and kicked it over for a field goal. [Over the goal post.] **2.** T (3)   Slang. The gangsters threatened to ruin his business if he didn't kick over ten dollars a week for "protection". [Pay them that sum as a bribe.] **3.** I (7)   When he turned on the ignition the engine kicked over twice and then went dead. [It began to operate and then stopped completely.]

kick up **1.** T (1)   He kicked the ball up and caught it as it came down. [Up in the air.] **2.** I (2,6)   Informal. The car engine is kicking up. I'll have to have it checked. [It is not working right.] See **act up 2**. **3.** I (2,6)   Whenever Albert eats pork, his stomach starts kicking up. [He gets indigestion.] See **act up 2**. **4.** T (5,6)   She kicked up quite a fuss when I told her we couldn't go to the show. [She complained loudly and a bit angrily.] **5.** T (1,5)   The teen-agers really kicked up their heels at the dance last night. [Had a gay and lively time. Acted like young colts in a pasture.]

Kid   To tease, joke with, deceive by joking.

kid around I (2)   Her oldest son is always kidding around. He never takes life seriously. [He teases, plays jokes on people.] See **fool around.**

kid along T (3)   They kidded Henry along for an hour or more then finally told him it was all a joke. [Deceived him into believing something that was not true.]

kid on T (II 3)   He was afraid to ask Mary to the dance, but we kidded him on, and he finally got up the nerve to do it. [We teased him, joked about it, and finally persuaded him.]

Kill   To cause the death of, to slay.

   kill off   **1.** T (5)   Indian and white hunters killed off the buffalo that used to roam over the Western prairies. [Destroyed them completely.]   **2.** T (5)   Genghis Khan gave orders to kill off all the population of cities he conquered.

   kill out   T (10)   Poison chemicals are used to kill out noxious weeds (crab grass, morning glory, etc.). [Get rid of them in cultivated areas.]

Kink   To form or cause to form a tight twist or curl.

   kink up   **1.** I (2,6)   The rope he had unwound kinked up and he had to straighten it out. [Formed many kinks.]   **2.** I (2,6)   She hated the way her hair kinked up in damp weather. [It got frizzy.]

Kiss   To touch or press with the lips in token of greeting, affection, reverence, etc.

   kiss away   T (3)   Little daughter cried bitterly when her doll got broken. Mother kissed away her tears. [Kissed her to make her feel better and stop crying.]

   kiss back   T (5)   John kissed Mary but she didn't kiss him back. [She did not return the kiss.]

   kiss off   **1.** T (3)   Informal. Many people at the meeting spoke against the chairman's action, but he kissed it off as the result of ignorance. [He ignored, rejected their opposition.]   **2.** T (3)   He was the sort of person who could kiss off an insult (a defeat, a loss of money, etc.) as being of no importance. [Act as if it were not important.]

Knock   To give a sounding or forcible blow to. May be used with all the elements.

   knock about   **1.** T (2)   Hockey. The players were warming up by knocking the puck about.   **2.** I (2)   After graduation he spent a year just knocking about with a classmate of his. [Not doing anything constructive.] See **bat around 2**, **kick about**.   **3.** I (2)   He wore his old corduroy pants to knock about in. [For outdoor activities.]   **4.** *knock-about* A. (2) a. Knock-about clothing. Informal wear such as jackets and jeans. b. Knock-about comedy. Rough slap-stick comedy. c. A knock-about type (of male). A shiftless, purposeless person.

   knock around   **1.** I (2)   See **knock about 2,3**.   **2.** T (2)   When they were children they had been knocked around a lot. [They had been treated badly by their parents or other adults.]

   knock away   **1.** T (2)   They had to knock away the snow from the branches before they could pass. [The weight of the snow had bent them downward across the pathway.]   **2.** I (6)   He kept knocking away at the door but nobody came. [He thought surely someone should be home, but they refused to come to the door.]

   knock down 1. T (1)   He knocked his opponent down with a blow to the ribs. [Down to the ground.]   **2.** T (1,6)   Commerce. They had to knock down the large machines (pieces of furniture, heavy equipment) in order to ship them. [Take them apart.]   **3.** T (3)   The auctioneer knocked down the painting (statue, manuscript, art object, etc.) to the highest bidder. [He gave a blow of the hammer or mallet to indicate that the sale was made.]   **4.** T (6)   The electrical appliance merchant has knocked down the prices on his refrigerators. [Reduced them.] **5.** T (3) Slang. The cashier at the National Bank knocked down twenty thousand dollars before he was caught. [Embezzled that sum.] **6.** T (3) Slang. How much do you suppose Henry knocks down per year? See **draw down.** [What is his salary?] **7.** T (5) Slang. I think I knocked down a B in chemistry this quarter. [I earned that grade.] **8.** *knock-down* N. (6) a. A reduction in price sometimes given to employees on merchandise sold by their employer. See **knock down 4**. b. A structure or piece of equipment that can be taken apart for storage or shipment. See **knock down 2**. c. A blow that knocks down. See **knock down 1**. d. Slang. A social introduction. Ex. He gave me a knock-down to his boss. **9.** *knock-down-drag-out* A. (1) John and his father had a knock-down-drag-out argument over the use of the car. [It was a real battle, suggesting a bull fight where the bull is knocked down and dragged out.]

knock off 1. T (2) Slang. Tom was so angry with his opponent he threatened to knock his block off. [Hit him hard enough to knock his head off his shoulders.] **2.** T (4) Slang. The gangsters knocked off a gas station. [They robbed it.] **3.** T (5) Slang. The leader of the gangsters gave orders to knock off the leader of the other gang. [Murder him.] **4.** I (4) Slang. We decided to knock off for the rest of the afternoon and play golf. [Stop work or other activity.] **5.** T (5) Slang. Knock it off, will you! [Stop your noise, your confusion, your annoying actions.]

knock out 1. T (4) Boxing. Joe Louis knocked out his opponent in the fifth round. [He could not get up by the time the referee counted to ten.] **2.** T (9) Slang. His dazzling performance knocked them out. [Won enthusiastic applause.] See **lay out 6. 3.** T (9) Our artillery fire knocked out five machine gun nests (artillery emplacements, etc.). [Put them out of action.] **4.** T (8) He knocked himself out to help his brother find a new job. [He used up a lot of his time and energy.] See **knock out 1. 5.** T (9) Two highballs always knock him out. [Make him intoxicated. Make him pass out.] See **pass out. 6.** T (1) Baseball. The next batter knocked out a fly into right field. [Hit it away from the infield.] **7.** T (7) Slang. The skilled workers knocked out a half dozen T.V. sets in two hours time. [Made them quickly.] **8.** *knock-out* N. (9) Slang. Do you see that pretty girl over there? She's a knock-out! [She knocks you out with her beauty and charm.] See **knock out 1, 4**.

knock over 1. T (5) He knocked over a lamp as he rushed to the door. [He upset it.] **2.** T (5) Ext. The news of her marriage knocked me over when I first heard it. [I was upset emotionally.]

knock up 1. T (6) The children knocked up the furniture and the wood work with their boisterous play. [Damaged them.] **2.** T (6) The heavy fighting at Khe Sahn knocked up our troops badly. [Caused many wounds and injuries.] **3.** T (6) One of the soldiers was charged with knocking up one of the waitresses at the bar. [Making her pregnant.]

Knot   To form a knot or knots.

knot up   T (2,6)   The ropes he was going to use for his tent were all knotted up. It took him an hour to fix them. [Undo the many knots.]

Know   To have knowledge of.

know through and through   T (3)   He thinks I don't know much about him, but I know him through and through. [I have complete knowledge of him.]

Knuckle   To use the thumb and forefinger in shooting marbles.

knuckle down   I (5)   Fig. To apply oneself vigorously and earnestly; become serious. The expression is derived from the game of marbles, in which the knuckles of the thumb and forefinger are involved in action close to the ground. Informal. If you want to make something of yourself, you'll have to knuckle down. [Get busy; work hard.] See **buckle down**.

knuckle under   I (4)   Robert refused for a long time to cooperate with the members of his club. They told him he'd have to knuckle under or get out. [Do what they asked him to do, under pressure.]

L

Lace   To fasten with a lace.

lace up   T (3)   Mother told Johnny to get busy and lace up his shoes. [Tie them securely on his feet by lacing.]

Ladle   To dip or convey with a ladle.

ladle out   T (1)   Mother was busy in the kitchen so sister Mary ladled out the soup. [Out of the soup tureen into the soup dishes.]

ladle up   T (1)   Army. In the mess hall the cook's helper stood by the big kettle ladling up the stew. [Up out of the kettle.]

Lag   To fall behind; hang back; linger.

lag back   I (1)   Most of the students followed the museum guide closely, but Alice lagged back, taking time to examine pictures in detail. [Stayed behind the others.]

Lame   To make lame or defective.

lame up   T (6)   Charles is all lamed up from climbing to the top of the mountain yesterday. [He has difficulty walking, because of injuries or strains.]

Land   To come to rest or arrive in any place, position or condition.

land up   **1.** I (13)   We drove for an hour on unfamiliar back roads, and eventually landed up in Springfield. [We arrived there.]   **2.** I (16)   If you don't obey the traffic laws, one of these days you'll land up in jail. [You will be arrested and put in jail.] See **I wind up.**

Lap   To take up liquid with the tongue, as do cats or dogs.

lap up   **1.** T (1,4)   The hungry kitten lapped up eagerly the milk we had poured into the saucer. [Up from the saucer.]   **2.** T (4,5)   Informal. The music (the lecture, the speech, the performance, the exhibition) was a big success. The audience (the listeners, the viewers) lapped it up. [Listened, looked, took it in, eagerly.] See **lick up.**

Lash I To strike vigorously at someone or something, as with a weapon, whip, etc.

  lash out (at) **1.** I (1,9) The escaped prisoner picked up a stick and began lashing out at the police dogs that had tracked him down. [Trying to hit them with the stick.] **2.** I (2,9) Ext. The author of the book lashed out at the critics who had called his work cheap and not true to life. [He used his tongue to give them a "lashing".] **3.** *lash out (with)* I (2,9) He lashed out with angry words at his critics. [Used angry words to combat his critics.]

Lash II To bind or fasten with a rope, cord, etc. See **tie, bind.**

  lash down T (1) The captain of the ship gave orders to lash down all movable objects on the deck because of the approaching storm. [Fasten them securely with ropes.]

  lash on T (I 1) John put his skis on the car top and lashed them on securely. [Fastened them with ropes.]

Last To go on or continue in time.

  last out **1.** T (8) We have enough firewood to last out the night. [Enough to keep the fire burning until morning.] **2.** T (8) Father is very ill. I doubt whether he will last out the night. [Live until morning.]

  last through I (3) This lecture is very boring. I don't think I can last through. [Stay and listen to it any longer.]

Latch To close tightly, so that the latch is secure; to take fast hold of.

  latch on **1.** I (I 3) Informal. I threw a rope to the boy who had fallen into the water and told him to latch on. [Take fast hold of it.] **2.** I (I 2) Slang. I tried to explain the answer to the problem but she didn't latch on. [She didn't understand, didn't get it.] See **catch on.** **3.** *latch on (to)* I (I 4) Slang. I'd like to latch on to a hundred bucks (dollars). [Get hold of them, have them in my possession.] **4.** I (I 4) Slang. John tried to get away from Ann at the party but she latched on to him for the whole evening. [Kept close to him, demanded his attention.]

  latch up I (3) Be sure you latch up the cages (the pens, the sheds, etc.) before you leave for the night. [Close them carefully so the animals will not escape.]

Lather To form lather; to cover with lather.

  lather up **1.** I (5) That soap lathers up nicely. [It makes good lather.] **2.** T (2,4) He lathered up his face and began to shave. [Covered it with a good lather.] **3.** *lathered up* A. T (4) The horse that won the race returned to the stable all lathered up. [Covered with foam from running so fast.]

Laugh To show mirth, satisfaction or derision by an expression of the face and explosive or chuckling sounds from the throat.

  laugh down T (1,3) The speaker argued his case very seriously, but the audience laughed him down. [They didn't believe what he said and laughed at him, made fun of him.] See **shout down**.

laugh off **1.** T (1) He made a threat to call in the police, but we laughed it off. [We were not worried by the threat, and we laughed at the idea.] **2.** T (1) You mustn't laugh off the possibility of an atomic war. [You must consider it very seriously.]

laugh out I (2) It is bad manners to laugh out (audibly) in class, when the professor makes an embarrassing mistake. [Out in public.]

Launch To plunge boldly or directly into action.

launch out I (2,9) After retiring from business Mr. Smith launched out boldly on a career in politics. [He became vigorously active.]

Lay To put or place in a horizontal position, or position of rest.

lay aside **1.** T (1,2) When his wife told him dinner was ready he laid aside his book and went to the dining room. [Put the book to one side, on a table or stand.] **2.** T (2) Ext. Now that you are grown up you should lay aside your childish ways. [Abandon them and act like adults.] **3.** T (2) He's very thrifty. He lays aside twenty percent of his salary each month. [Puts it in a savings account, in a bank.] See **set aside.**

lay away **1.** T (5) He laid away the money he inherited, as a nest egg for future emergencies. [He did not spend it, but kept it for a purpose.] **2.** T (5) We laid grandfather away in Woodlawn Cemetery. [We buried him.] **3.** T (6) There was a special sale at Macy's. Mother laid away a spring suit. [Had the store save it for her.] **4.** *layaway* N.A. (6) A layaway plan. A method of purchasing, whereby a purchaser reserves an article by making a down payment and claims it after paying the full balance.

lay by T (3) George sold insurance for two years and laid by enough money to put him through college. [Saved it.] See **lay away**.

lay down **1.** T (1) He picked up the sleeping child from the floor and laid her down gently on the sofa. **2.** T (1,7) The college authorities have laid down a series of rules and regulations concerning student social life. [They have been published, put before the students.] **3.** T (1,5) Informal. Last night father was laying down the law to the two boys about staying out late. [He was talking very sternly to them about the matter.] **4.** T (1) Our friend Robert has laid down a wonderful stock of French wine in his wine cellar. [Purchased it and stored it for future use, usually in a cellar.] **5.** T (1) The enemy troops surrendered at daybreak and laid down their arms. [Turned them over to our troops.]

lay in T (1,5) Housewives begin to lay in a supply of sugar, tea and coffee whenever there is a war scare. [Purchase it and store it for future use.]

lay off **1.** T (4) I hear that Ajax Motors is going to lay off six hundred workers. [Dismiss them, perhaps temporarily, because of a slack in business, or changes in models, etc.] **2.** T (1,2) Mr. Black laid off his heavy overcoat and moved close to the fire to warm his hands. [Took it off and laid it aside.] **3.**

T (1)   The landscape architect laid off a baseball diamond (a golf course, a playing field, etc.) for the City Recreation Commission. [Indicated the location, size and limits by marking them.] See **map off. 4.** T (5)   Informal. The doctor told me to lay off cigarettes. [Stop smoking them.]   **5.** T (5)   Slang. Lay off the kidding! (the chatter, the foolishness, etc.) [Stop kidding, chattering, acting foolishly.]   **6.** T (1)   Slang. Lay off me! [Stop annoying me, criticizing me, blaming me.] Perhaps the opposite of II **lay on. 7.** *lay-off* N. (4) a. The act of laying off, especially work or workmen. See **lay off 1.** b. A period of being laid off. See **lay off 1, shut down**.

lay out   1. T (10)   The salesman laid out several beautiful Persian rugs for us to examine. [Spread them at full length.]   **2.** T (1,4)   Mrs. Jones laid out her husband's evening clothes before starting to dress for the party. [Selected them and put them on the bed where he would see them.]   **3.** T (10)   When we saw the undertaker he had just finished laying out the corpse of a former friend of ours. [In a coffin. Preparing it for burial.]   **4.** T (7)   Our young architect friend won the job of laying out the room plan for the new hotel. [Making drawings to show the arrangement of the rooms.]   **5.** T (7)   John's Faculty Adviser laid out a study plan for him that should be a big help. [He outlined a system of study.] **6.** T (9)   Slang. His jokes really laid them out (laid them in the aisles). [Won enthusiastic applause.] See **bring down 4, knock out, mow down 3. 7.** T (4,10) Joe Louis laid his opponent out with a right to the jaw. [Knocked him unconscious.] See **knock-out. 8.** T (9)   Informal. He laid himself out to be agreeable to me. [He did everything in his power.] See **knock-out. 9.** *layout* N. (7,10)   a. The act or process of planning. See **lay out 4, 5, 6.** b. An outline, usually with a diagram providing directions for work. See **lay out 4, 5, 6.** c. The make-up of a book, newspaper, or magazine, etc. d. Slang. Something that is displayed, spread out. [That dinner was a fine layout.] See **set out.**

lay over   1. T (4)   We can take no action on this matter now. We'll lay it over till next meeting. [Postpone it.] See **hold over. 2.** I (8)   On our trip to Yellowstone Park we laid over in the Black Hills for a day or two. [We stopped there for a while.]

lay up   1. T (1,11)   He laid his car up for the winter. [He put it in storage, perhaps up on jacks, and took the battery out of it.]   **2.** T (1,5)   Bees lay up honey for the winter. [They build up a supply of it for food during the winter.]   **3.** T (6) The injury to his leg laid John up for several weeks. [He had to stay in bed, keep off his leg, until it got better.]   **4.** T (1,3)   Basketball. Halimon laid up five shots in the first ten minutes of play. [Made them with one hand, from a point close to the basket, sometimes with a rebound from the backboard.]   **5.** *lay-up* N.   (1,3)   Basketball. Halimon made five lay-ups. See **lay up 4.**

Laze   To idle, or lounge lazily.

laze along   I (1,3)   Driving through the park we just lazed along, enjoying the evening air and the scenery. [Drive very slowly.]

laze away   T (3,6)   On our vacation we just lazed away the hours, strolling along the beach, lying in the sun, listening to the music of the natives. [We spent the time in idleness.] See **idle away.**

Leaf I   To put forth leaves.

leaf out   I (1)   Spring is here. The trees are beginning to leaf out. [The leaves are appearing on them.] See **bud out.**

Leaf II   To turn pages quickly, without paying much attention.

leaf over   I (6)   She spent a half hour in the library reading room, leafing over the latest magazines. [Glancing at the pages, without reading much.]

leaf through   I (3)   Last night I leafed through *The Naked Ape*. I think I'll enjoy reading it when I have more time. [I looked over it from beginning to end, without stopping to read much.]

League   To unite in a league.

league up   I (10,11)   Some African leaders want the newly independent African nations to league up against South Africa. [Form a united front.]

Leak   To let air, water, light, power, etc., escape as through an unintentional hole, crack, or opening.

leak down   I (1)   When we entered the room we found water leaking down through a hole in the roof. [Down into the room.]

leak out   **1.** I (1)   His left front tire was flat. The air had leaked out during the night from a puncture or a faulty valve. [Out of the tire.]   **2.** I (2,3)   Informal. It leaked out that the President was going to fly to Australia for a conference. [The news came out from an unknown source.]

leak through   I (1)   There were holes in the curtain that allowed little rays of light to leak through. [Through the curtain.]

Lean   To incline or bend from a vertical position.

lean across   I (1)   We were sitting on the other side of the aisle from each other. Mr. Brown leaned across to ask me a question about the plot of the play. [Across the aisle.]

lean aside   I (1)   As people came up the stairs I leaned aside to let them pass me. [Bent my body to one side.]

lean back   I (1)   I know you're too tired to pay attention to everything that is happening here. Just lean back and relax. [Rest your back against the back of the chair.]

lean down   I (1)   The sick girl was trying to whisper something to me. I leaned down to catch what she wanted to say. [I bent over.]

lean out   I (2)   As the parade went by our window we leaned out to see the band. [Bent our bodies over the window sill.] See **hang out.**

lean over   **1.** I (3,5)   She leaned over to tell me the news about the wedding. [Inclined herself towards me.]   **2.** *lean over (backward)*   I (5)   He's the sort of man who will lean over backward to make his guests feel at home. [Do everything in his power.] See **bend over backward.**

Leave I To allow to remain.

leave around T (1) I've come back to look for my hat. I've left it around somewhere here, I'm sure. [Here or there.]

leave in **1.** T (3) So she wouldn't hear her husband snoring she put cotton in her ears and left it in all night. **2.** T (4,6) Bridge. When my partner bid three spades and was doubled, I had to leave him in. [In his bid. I could not bid to take him out.] See **take out**.

leave off **1.** T (6) When we made up our guest list for the party, we left the Nelsons' name off. [We did not put it on the list.] **2.** T (4) We leave the lights off when we watch T.V. [We don't turn them on.]

leave out **1.** T (1) John left the car out all night. [He did not put it in the garage.] **2.** T (4) Don't leave out the Smiths when you start inviting people to the party. [Don't omit them.]

leave over T (4) We had to leave the question of elections over till the next meeting. [Postpone it.]

Leave II To cease or refrain from doing something.

leave off **1.** I (5) He began to read at the page where he left off. [Where he had stopped.] **2.** T (5) I think it would be wise for you to leave off criticizing people so much. [Stop doing it.] **3.** I (5) It left off raining just as we got in the car. [The rain stopped.]

Lend To make a loan or loans.

lend out T (5) He made a fortune lending out money to uranium prospectors, at high interest rates.

Lengthen To make or become greater in length.

lengthen out **1.** T (10) The cowboy lengthened out his horse's tether to let it graze on the grass by the river bank. [Made the tether rope reach farther.] **2.** I (10) As June approaches the days are lengthening out. [They are becoming longer.]

Let To allow or permit to do something. **Let**, as a two-word verb, produces forms that are abbreviated expressions from which another verb in its infinitive form has been dropped. Ex. let in = let someone *come in, go in, get in*; let off = let someone *come off, go off, get off*. The meanings of the forms, therefore, can be best understood by knowing the uses of come, go and get, as two-word verbs.

let by T (2) Please let me by. [Let me pass, or go by.] A polite request to be allowed to pass another person.

let down **1.** T (1) Please let the child down. He wants to play. [Let it get down from your arms.] **2.** T (1) The well-cleaner's helper let a rope down to the man working on the bottom. [Down into the well.] **3.** I (6) You've been working too hard. You ought to let down a little. [Reduce the amount of work, and the energy you put into it.] **4.** I (6) Athletics. The team had been winning all its games early in the season, then began to let down towards the end. [Lose some of its games.] **5.** T (1,3) The team let the coach down in the final game.

[They disappointed him by not winning.] **6.** *let-down* N. (6) The team suffered a let-down. [A loss of energy, determination to win.] See **let down 4**.

let in 1. T (1) Please let me in! [Allow me to come, go or get into the house (room, building, etc.).] **2.** *let in (on)* T (4) I asked them to let me in on the secret (the party, the business deal, etc.). [Have knowledge of it, have a share in it.]

let off 1. T (1,2) Please let me off at the next bus stop (the corner, the hotel, the bank, etc.). [Allow me to get off the bus.] **2.** T (8) Johnny let off his father's shotgun, and just missed hitting his brother. [Fired it, perhaps by accident.] **3.** T (8) The road builders let off an explosion of dynamite that shook the neighborhood. [Ignited it.] See **go off 3, set off. 4.** T (9) Ext. The children are being very noisy. They have to let off steam after the long ride in the car. [Let their energy explode in noise and activity.] **5.** T (2) It was the prisoner's first offense so the judge let him off with a light sentence. [Let him go free of a severe penalty.] **6.** T (4) I hear that the Adams Company is letting off some of its employees. [Dismissing them temporarily.] See **let out 6. 7.** I (4) James had promised to help me this afternoon, but I let him off when he said he had to go to football practice. [I excused him from his obligation.]

let on 1. T (I 1) We wanted to take the 9:30 bus, but the driver wouldn't let us on. The seats were all taken. [Allow us to get on the bus.] **2.** I (I 1) Informal. We knew that he was lying to us, but we didn't let on. [We didn't show by our expression that we knew it.]

let out 1. T (1,2) The dog had been in the house all day. We let him out as soon as we got home. [Let him go outside.] **2.** T (1,2) Mother doesn't let us out when it's raining. [Out of the house.] **3.** T (3) They let it out that their daughter had been married for a year. [Let the news of it become public.] **4.** T (1,2) The cowboy let out a yell (a whoop, a shout, etc.) and galloped away. **5.** T (10) On a deep-sea fishing trip, my uncle hooked a tuna and had to let out his line to avoid having it broken. [Release a quantity of the line from the reel.] **6.** T (4,9) The Martin factory has closed down and let out all of its employees. [Dismissed them permanently.] See **let off 6. 7.** T (1) The play director let us out from rehearsal at 9 o'clock. [Excused us.] **8.** I (8) What time does the rehearsal (the show, the play, the practice, etc.) let out? [When are the people free to leave?] **9.** T (10) Mother is busy letting out all of Mary's dresses. She's growing like a weed. [Making them longer and wider.]

let through T (1) We were late getting to the entrance but the guard let us through. [Allowed us to enter.]

let up 1. T (1) Let me up! [Let me get up from the ground (the floor, etc.).] Said by a person who is being held down by another. **2.** I (13) The rain (the snow, the hail, the wind, etc.) is letting up. [It is about to stop.] **3.** I (13) Informal. That man is a fool for work. He never lets up. [He will not stop working.] **4.** I (13) Let's let up for a minute. I'm all tired out. [Stop working so hard and intently.] **5.** *let up (on)* I (13) Informal. I wish you would let up on Alice. You've been treating her very harshly since she dropped out of school. [Stop showing your displeasure, your feelings of anger towards her.] **6.** *let-up* N. (13) A pause, or reduction in activity. [We studied (worked, drove, wrote, danced, etc.) all night without a let-up.] [While we were on our vacation it rained (snowed) without a let-up.]

Level   To make a surface level or even.

> **level down**   T (1)   A bulldozer was used to level down the hummocks in preparing the greens for the new golf course. [Make an even surface for the planting of grass.]

> **level off**   **1.** I (1)   The fighter plane dove down to machine gun the enemy position then leveled off at an altitude of 200 feet. [It continued to fly for a while at that elevation.]   **2.** I (1)   Prices rose for six months and then began leveling off. [They reached a certain height and then continued at that level for a while.]

> **level up**   **1.** T (2,11)   That area (ground, field, etc.) is too uneven for making an air strip. We'll have to level it up. [Make it usable by removing the irregularities in levels.]   **2.** I (2,11)   Slang. You're not telling me the truth. You'd better level up with me, if you want my help. [Be "on the level". Tell me the truth.]

Lick   To pass the tongue over the surface of something.

> **lick off**   **1.** T (6)   The cat sat by the fireside licking off its paws. [Cleaning them by licking.]   **2.** T (6)   The child picked up the spoon its mother had used to stir her cake and licked off all the chocolate batter. [Cleaned it by licking.]

> **lick up**   **1.** T (1,4)   The dog licked up the ice cream that had been spilled on the floor. [Used his tongue to remove it from the floor.]   **2.** T (4,5)   Informal. The candidate sailed into (spoke vigorously against) his opponent, and the audience licked it up. [They listened eagerly and approvingly.] See **lap up 2**.

Lie   To be in a recumbent or prostrate position, as on a bed or the ground; to assume such a position.

> **lie by**   I (3)   After six hours of steady traveling, the wagon train lay by for an hour before starting on. [It stopped for a rest.]

> **lie down**   **1.** I (1)   You look very tired. You'd better lie down for a nap (an hour, a short while) before the company arrives. [Take a rest.]   **2.** I (6)   Informal. We thought John would be a very good leader (worker, helper, etc.) but he lay down on the job. [He did not work, do what we expected of him.]

> **lie in**   I (1)   In modern medical practice mothers do not lie in for long periods after child birth. [They do not stay in bed.]

> **lie over**   I (4)   The question of elections will have to lie over till our next meeting. [It must be postponed, delayed.]

Lift   To move or bring something upward from the ground or other support. May be used with all the second elements.

> **lift off**   **1.** I (1,8)   Aero Space. At the end of the count down the rocket lifted off with a mighty roar. [It left the launching pad and rose into space.]   This is the

only intransitive use of **lift** as a two word verb. The idea is that the rocket rises of itself. The technicians "launch" a rocket. The rocket "lifts off" or "blasts off". **2.** *lift-off* N. (8) a. The action of an aircraft in becoming airborne, or of a rocket in rising from its launching site under its own power. b. The instant when such action occurs. See **go off.**

Light I To set burning, as a candle, lamp, fire, match, cigarette, etc.

light up 1. T (2,4,5) For the king's reception a thousand candles lighted up the ball-room. [They made the ball-room glow with light.] **2.** T (2,4) When she saw her lover in the crowd a smile lighted up her face. [Her face glowed with pleasure.] **3.** I (2,4) When she saw her lover in the crowd her face lit up in a smile. See **light up 2**. **4.** I (7) I asked her if I could smoke and she told me to light up. [Ignite my cigarette, cigar, or pipe.] **5.** I (2,4) The sky suddenly lit up with a flash of lightning (a burst of fireworks). [Became very bright.]

Light II To move quickly in some direction. [From the idea of being light in weight.]

light off I (2,9) The boys who were stealing the farmer's apples lit off through the woods when they saw him coming. [Ran as fast as they could.] See **take off 5.**

light out I (2,9) The robbers lit out for the Mexican border in their getaway car. [Drove as fast as they could.] See **take off 5.**

Lighten To become less heavy; to make lighter, more cheerful.

lighten up 1. T (2,5) The cream colored walls and the gay new drapes lightened up their living room, which had been rather dull and gloomy. [Made it more light and cheerful.] **2.** T (2,11) The mountain climbers lightened up their packs for the final climb to the summit. [Reduced the weight by leaving some of their equipment behind.]

Limber To make or become more limber, flexible, pliant.

limber up 1. I (2,5,11) The athletes were limbering up for the contest by doing special exercises. [Making their muscles more flexible.] **2.** T (2,5) The boys limbered up their muscles by doing push-ups. [Made them more flexible.] **3.** T (2,5,11) You'll have to limber up your wits if you want to compete in the debate (the quiz program, the discussion group, etc.). [Improve your ability to think quickly and accurately.]

Line To take a position in a line; to bring into line mark with lines.

line off T (3) The workmen were busy lining off the football field (the parade route, the seating arrangements, etc.). [Marking them by using lines.]

line out 1. T (7) The committee chairman lined out for the members the plan of activities for the coming year. [He gave them the details verbally or in writing. He gave an outline.] **2.** T (1) Baseball. The next batter lined out a hit into left field. [He drove the ball in a straight line, not far above the ground.]

line up 1. I (3,5,10) Military. The captain ordered his men to line up in front of the barracks. [Take their position in a line.] **2.** T (3,5,10) Military. The captain lined his men up for inspection. [Made them fall in line.] **3.** T (4,11) His committee has the responsibility of lining up speakers (artists, entertainers, athletes, workers, etc.) for the coming year. [Contacting them and getting them to make agreements to appear.] **4.** T (4,11) My lawyer is busy lining up all the evidence (arguments, information, etc.) that will be useful at the trial. [Collecting and organizing it.] **5.** *line-up* N. (3,4,11) a. A particular order or disposition of persons or things as lined up or drawn up for action, inspection, etc. b. The persons or things lined up. [A police line-up.] c. Sports. The list of the participating players in a game, together with their positions — especially the starting line-up announced at the beginning of a game. d. An organization of people, companies, countries for some common purpose. [A line-up of support for the new tax bill.]

Link To join or connect by, or as by a link or links.

> **link up** **1.** T (3,4,10) Aero Space. The world was astounded by the news that two astronauts had linked up two capsules in space. [Joined them together.] **2.** *link up (with)* I (3,4,10) The big financial news is that B. Corporation has linked up with a hotel chain. [It has made a deal that unites the two companies.] **3.** T (2,4,10) The prosecuting attorney has uncovered some evidence that links John Brown up with the Chicago gangsters. [Makes it appear that he is connected in some way with them.] **4.** *link-up* N. (2,4,10) The action of joining two or more persons or things together.

Liquor To furnish liquor to, to ply with liquor.

> **liquor up** **1.** T (2) Informal. Perhaps if you can liquor him up he'll talk freely and you can learn what you want to know about the case. [Get him to drink a large quantity of liquor.] **2.** T (4) After he lost his job he went to a neighborhood saloon and got liquored up. [He got drunk.]

Listen To give attention with the ear, pay attention.

> **listen in** **1.** I (2) You seem to be having a very interesting conversation. Do you mind if I listen in? [May I listen to your discussion?] **2.** I (4) There's a very good program on T.V. at 8 o'clock this evening. Would you like to listen in? [Join us in watching the program.] **3.** I (2) Telephone. We are on a party line (a line that serves more than one subscriber) and we often suspect that someone is listening in. [Listening to our conversation by lifting their own receiver.]

Litter To scatter objects in disorder; to be scattered in disorderly fashion.

> **litter up** **1.** T (2,6) In the poor section of the town beer cans, bottles, scraps of paper, and all sorts of rubbish litter up the streets. [They lie scattered about in the streets.] **2.** T (2,6) Some campers had littered up the camp-site with all sorts of rubbish. [They were "litterbugs". They had left things scattered about.]

Live To be alive; to spend one's life; survive so as to overcome.

> **live down** T (6) As a young man he had earned a bad reputation, but he succeeded in living it down, after marrying and raising a family. [He lived in a way to make people forget his earlier reputation.]
>
> **live on** I (II 2) We didn't expect mother to survive the operation for cancer, but she lived on for three more years. [Continued to live.]

live out T (8) Mother lived out her last three years in great pain and suffering. [She completed those three years.] See **live on**.

live over T (7) We took a lot of pictures on our tour around the world. They help us to live it over, from time to time. [Repeat the experience by looking at the pictures.]

live through I (4) Informal. My sister and her five young children are coming to visit us for two weeks. I hope I live through. [Continue to be alive after they leave.]

live up (to) **1.** I (1,4) We have heard that Nureyev is the world's greatest male dancer. I hope he lives up to his reputation. [Gives a performance that proves he is the greatest.] **2.** *live it up* T (5) Informal. While we were in Paris, we really lived it up! [We had a gay time. We went to the best restaurants, shows, night clubs. We ate and drank the best of everything.]

Load To put a load on or in a conveyance or machine.

load down T (1,2) She came home from a shopping tour loaded down with packages. [She was carrying many, perhaps heavy, packages.]

load in T (1) The bus driver was busy loading in the passengers' luggage. [Putting it in the baggage compartment.]

load on T (I 1) The workers brought the cotton bales to the truck and loaded them on. [Onto the truck.]

load up **1.** I (4) It took them half an hour to load up. [Put all the bales on the truck.] See **load on**. **2.** I (4) Informal. Time to load up! [A father telling his family to get in the car with all the things they will take with them.]

Loan To grant the temporary use of something.

loan out T (5) Movie studios will sometimes loan out to other studios the actors they have under contract. [Permit their actors to work for the other studios.]

Lock To fasten or secure (a door, window, building, etc.) with a lock.

lock in T (1,3) The little boy had gone into the bathroom and locked himself in. [Turned the key or latch that locked the door from the inside.]

lock on I (I 2) Aero Space. The radar beam detected a moving object several miles up and locked on. [Kept contact with the moving object.]

lock out **1.** T (1,2) When her husband returned to their apartment after their quarrel he found that she had locked him out. [Locked the door to keep him outside.] **2.** T (2,4) The company would not accept the demands of the striking employees, and locked them out. [Locked the doors of the factory to keep the employees outside.] **3.** *lock-out* N. (2,4) The action of employers in keeping employees from entering their factory or place of business. See **lock out 2**.

lock up **1.** T (3,11) Did you remember to lock up all the doors and windows (lock up the house)? [Fasten all the doors, etc.] **2.** I (4,8) The bar-tender told us he could serve no more drinks. It was time to lock up. [Close the bar for the night by locking the door.] **3.** *locked up* A. (4,8) Did you succeed in making that business deal (getting support for your plan, arranging for your vacation, etc.)? Yes, I have it all locked up. [I have done everything necessary, and have succeeded.]

Look   To set one's eyes upon something, or in some direction, in order to see.

look about   I (1,2)   If you look about, you will understand why I don't want to live in this part of town. [See the conditions that make the area undesirable.]

look across   I (1)   We drove to the river bank and looked across at the beautiful homes on the other side. [Across the river.]

look around   **1.** I (3)   She looked around and saw that the children were following her. [She turned her head to the rear and looked.]   **2.** I (2)   The saleswoman said "May I help you?", but we told her we were just looking around. [We were not interested in buying but in looking at the merchandise.]

look away   I (3)   She did not meet his glance but looked away when he spoke to her. [Turned her eyes away from him.]

look back   **1.** I (1)   She looked back and saw that the children were following her. [She turned her head, possibly her body, so as to look to the rear.]   **2.** I (4) Ext. When we look back to the 15th century we can see how far science has progressed. [Back in time.]

look down   **1.** I (1)   From the top of the Empire State Building you can look down on all of New York City. [See it from a superior height.]   **2.** *look down (on)*   I (1)   The English aristocracy looked down on the merchant class. [They felt themselves to be superior, in a higher class.]   **3.** I (1)   Many professors look down on athletes as not being intelligent enough to do college work. [They consider them to be intellectually inferior.]

look in   **1.** I (1)   Aunt Mary said she would look in this evening to see how we were getting along. [Make a short visit.] See **drop in**.   **2.** *look in (on)*   I (1,3) In the hospitals the doctors look in on their patients each morning. [Visit them briefly to check on their condition.]   **3.** *look-in* N.   (1)   We'll be over tonight for a look-in. [A short visit.]

look off   I (1)   He looked off to the west where the sun was setting behind the mountains. [Away from where he was.]

look on   **1.** I (II 3)   The bank robber held up the cashier while the other employees looked on helplessly. [Watched the action but did not take part in it.]   **2.** I (II 3) At college athletic events only a few people take part. The majority just look on. [They watch and do not participate.] They are lookers-on.

look out   **1.** I (2)   When she heard the noise in the street, she looked out and saw two men fighting. [Out the window.]   **2.** I (1,10)   She looked out to where the sky met the sea. [To a distant place.]   **3.** I (10)   Their picture window looks out over the whole valley. [Away from their house.]   **4.** I (9)   Look out! There's a car coming! [Beware! Be careful! There is some danger.]   **5.** *look out (for)*   I (9)   John is always looking out for his little brother. [He watches what the brother is doing. He takes care of him, protects him.]   **6.** I (9)   Uncle Robert is always looking out for his health. [He is very careful about avoiding disease, germs, viruses, etc.] **7.** I (10) While you're down town shopping look out for some bargains in men's shirts. [Try to find a store where they have bargains.] **8.** *look out (on)* I (2,10) Her bedroom window looks out on the garden (the cathedral, the park, etc.). [It gives a good view of those things.] **9.** *look-out* N. (10) a. A tower or other structure from which a view can be had of surrounding terrain. Especially for military purposes. b. A person whose function it is to use a lookout. c. Slang. A responsibility, worry or obligation. [That's your lookout!] See **watch out.**

look over **1.** I (5) They walked to the edge of the cliff (the parapet, the platform, etc.) and looked over. [Over the edge and down.] **2.** T (2,6) There are some beautiful Persian rugs on sale at Gimbel's. Let's go down and look them over. [Look at them, examine them to see if we want to buy any.] **3.** T (2,6) Informal. John's fiancee's parents have invited us to dinner. I'm sure they want to look us over. [See whether they approve of his parents.]

look through I (1) That window is so dirty you can't look through. [Through the glass.]

look under I (2) She went to the bed and looked under to see if the cat was there. [Under the bed.]

look up **1.** I (1) She looked up in surprise when someone called her name. [Raised her eyes.] **2.** T (17) Teacher told us to look up the new words in the dictionary. [Try to find them.] **3.** T (17) John said he would look up our friends, the Watsons, when he went to Chicago. [Try to find them.] **4.** I (2,5) Business is looking up as the Christmas buying season approaches. [It is getting better.] **5.** *look up (to)* I (1,4) The boys all look up to their father. [They respect and admire him; consider him as a good example.]

Loom To appear indistinctly; come into view in indistinct and enlarged form.

loom up **1.** I (1) Great black clouds loomed up on the horizon. [They appeared threateningly.] **2.** I (6) Ext. The clouds of war loomed up over Europe in the summer of 1939. [War threatened to break out.]

Loosen To make or become less tight; to relax.

loosen up **1.** T (2) He dug around the old rose bushes to loosen up the soil which had become very hard. [Break up the hard crust.] **2.** T (2) The college authorities loosened up the restrictions on female visitors in the men's residence halls. [Made them less strict, relaxed them.] **3.** I (2,5) When we first were introduced to him he was very formal, but he loosened up after a couple of drinks. [He relaxed, became more friendly.] **4.** I (2) Slang. He finally loosened up and let me have ten dollars. [Became generous.]

Lop I To cut off (branches, twigs, etc.) from a tree or plant.

lop off **1.** T (2) Father lopped off two branches of the maple tree that were shading the flower beds too much. [Removed them by cutting.] **2.** T (6) Ext. The Senate lopped off three items of the President's budget, for a saving of twenty million dollars. [They cut the budget by that amount.]

Lop II   To hang loosely or limply; droop.

   lop over   I (5)   Fred sat up straight in his chair, trying to keep awake, but soon he lopped over and fell asleep. [His body drooped to one side.]

Lose   To suffer a loss or defeat.

   lose out   **1.** I (9)   The candidate won the nomination in the primaries but lost out to his opponent in the election. [He was defeated.]   **2.** I (9)   We thought Bob was going to marry Margaret, but he lost out to Henry. [Henry succeeded in winning her in marriage.] See **miss out.**

Louse   To spoil, make a mess of.

   louse up   **1.** T (6)   Slang. Don't invite the Johnsons. They always louse up the party. [They are the kind of people who spoil a party.] See **foul up.**

Love   To show love or affection.

   love-in N.   (4)   The Hippies (the Flower People) were holding a love-in in Golden Gate Park. [A gathering of a social nature in which those present express feelings of love toward each other.]

Luck N.   Fortune, good or ill. Used as a verb only in the expression "luck out".

   luck out   I (9)   Slang. John lucked out when his motorcycle crashed into the big truck. (He was not seriously injured.) Bridge. We lucked out on the hand we played at three no trump. We should have been set one trick. (We were lucky. The defense was poor.]

M

Machine   To make, prepare or finish with a machine.

   machine down   T (6)   The bolts (pistons, rods, plugs, etc.) were too large. The workmen had to machine them down. [Reduce their size by grinding or abrading them to remove the excess metal.]

Mail   To send by mail; place in the post office or in a mail box for sending.

   mail out   T (2)   The office force was busy mailing out campaign material (advertisements, requests for contributions, propaganda, etc. to all the voters in the community). [Out to the public.]

Make I   To cause to exist; put together by combining parts; create, compose.

   make over   T (8)   Mother used to make over her dresses. She couldn't afford to buy many new ones. [She remodeled them to look new by changing the shape, adding new trimmings, etc.]

   make up   **1.** T (4,11)   The train for San Francisco is made up in Ogden. [The coaches, the diner, the sleeping cars, etc. are put together.]   **2.** T (5,11)   Alice is always making up stories (exercises, fanciful explanations, etc.) to escape being punished. [Inventing them for a purpose.] See **fake up, think up, trump up.**   **3.** I (4,5)   An automobile is made up of many parts. [Constructed.]   **4.** T (2,4,11)   Circus clowns make up their faces by putting on lipstick, face paint, and powder. [They prepare their faces for the performance. They use make-up.] See **black up. 5.** *make-up* N.A. a. The facial cosmetics (lipstick, powder, paint, etc.) used by women to create a beautiful appearance.

b. Cosmetics used on other parts of the body.

c. The application of cosmetics. Ex. She spends hours on her make-up.

d. The ensemble or effect created by such application. Ex. Her make-up was very pleasing.

e. All of the effects used by an actor (cosmetics, costumes, etc.) to present himself in a certain role.

f. The way in which something is organized or put together. Ex. The make-up of an athletic team, of a corporation, of a military group, etc.

g. The physical or mental constitution of a person. Ex. John is of an unusual make-up. He has the make-up of a criminal.

h. The art, technique, or process of making up, as in arranging the type and layout of books, newspapers, advertisements, etc.

i. The appearance of a book, a page, a poster, etc., as determined by the size, shape, color, etc.

Make II   To accomplish, succeed in doing something.

make away (with)   I (1,2)   The robbers made away with $1,000 in cash. [Carried it with them as they escaped.]

make off   **1.** I (2,9)   The robbers made off through the woods. [They escaped, hurried away.] See **take off 5.**   **2.** *make off (with)*   I (1,2)   The robbers made off with the jewelry they had stolen. [Took it with them as they escaped.] See **make away with**.

make out   **1.** T (1,7)   I can't make out the words (the names, the figures, the details on the map, etc.). The print is too fine. I need a magnifying glass. [Recognize them, identify them.]   **2.** T (9)   He used a pen to make out the application blank (the check, the receipt, the report, the resumé). [Complete it by writing the details necessary.]   **3.** T (3,7)   He's a very strange complicated person. I can't make him out. [I can't understand him, discover his make-up.]   **4.** T (3,7)   It is sometimes difficult to make out the meaning of modern poetry. [Be sure of the meaning.]   **5.** T (7)   The teacher tried to make out that I was to blame for the noise in the classroom. [Tried to prove it, insisted that it was my fault.]   **6.** T (8)   Father wrote to ask how I was making out in my school work. [How I was succeeding.] See **get along 4. 7.**   I (10)   She can't make out on $100 a month. [Live comfortably, make a go of it.] See **get by 3.**

make over   **1.** T (3)   Before father died he made over his property (business, stocks, bonds, etc.) to mother. [He signed legal documents that gave the things he owned to her.]   **2.** T (3)   When you sell your car to another person it is necessary to make over the title to the buyer. [Have the name of the new owner legally put on the title.]

make up   **1.** T (4,11)   Mother told Mary to make up the beds in the guest room before the company arrived. [Put them in proper condition for the guests to sleep in.] **2.** T (4,8) I missed the examination (test, quiz, etc.) in chemistry last week. The professor will let me make it up. [Take the examination so as to be up on my work, up with my class.] See **be up on 9**. **3.** T (2,8) He went to bed early last night to make up the sleep he lost the night before. [Gain back the sleep he lost.] **4.** T (2,8) They drove very fast the rest of the evening to make up the time they wasted at the dinner table. [Regain the time they spent eating.] **5.** *make up (for)* I (2,4) We spent an hour and a half eating dinner, so we had to drive fast to make up for lost time. [Do the mileage we lost by taking so long to eat.] **6.** T (4) When the waiter presented the bill for the dinner, I found I didn't have enough money. John made up the difference. [He paid the part of the bill I was unable to pay.] **7.** T (3,4) He couldn't make up his mind to tell his father the truth. [Think how to explain his actions; organize his thoughts.] **8.** I (2,4) The two friends had quarreled about money, but they made up and are the best of friends again. [They settled their quarrel, their differences.] **9.** *make up (to)* I (3,4,11) His wife made up to the president of the company, hoping to get her husband a raise in salary. [She paid a lot of attention to him, tried to please him.] **10.** *make up (with)* I (1,4) Betty had a quarrel with her girl friend, but now she's trying to make up with her. [Become good friends again.] **11.** I (4) You will have to work hard to make up for the damage you did to the machine you broke. [Pay for the damage.] **12.** I (4) The beauty and restfulness of the summer resort made up for the difficulties we had in getting there. [They repaid us for the effort.] **13.** *make-up* N.A. (4,8) Education. An examination or test taken in substitution for one that a person failed to pass or was absent from. See **II make up 2**.

make it (+ second element) To succeed in arriving at or going, coming to or from a certain place or destination. Ex. The race horse made it around (3) in three minutes. [Around the race track.]

We made it **away** (1,2) at 3 o'clock. [Away from home, etc.]

He made it **back** (3) before we did. [Back to his starting place.]

We made it **by** (2) easily. [Past some place or person.]

They made it **down** (1) first. [Downstairs, down a hill, etc.]

The plane made it **in** (1) on time. [Into the airport.]

He made it **off** (2,3) on schedule. [Got away, left.]

We made it **on** (I 1) just in time. [On the plane, the bus, etc.]

She made it **out** (1) in a hurry. [Out of the store, the theater, etc.]

He made it **over** (3) before she did. [Over the fence to the other side.]

We made it **through** (1) before the gate was closed. [Through to the inside.]

They made it **under** (3) just in time. [Under a shelter.]

He made it **up** (1) before the others. [Upstairs, up the hill, etc.]

Make one's way (+ second element). See **fight one's way**.

May be used with any of the second elements, showing the direction in which the person proceeds, without specifying the manner in which he does it.

Ex. He made his way through (1). [Through college, a fence, etc.]

He made his way up (1). [Up the stairs, up the hill, up in the world, etc.]

Mangle   To cut, slash, or crush so as to disfigure.

mangle up   T (6)   The workman's arm had been caught in the machine and was badly mangled up.

Map   To represent or delineate on, or as on a map.

map off   T (3)   The city engineer was instructed to map off certain areas in the park to be used for athletic events. [Mark the boundaries of the playing fields.] See **lay off, mark off, rope off, section off, set off, stake out.**

map out   **1.** T (7,9)   The park commissioners office mapped out the whole area to make the best use possible of the terrain. [Made a complete design or map.] See **lay out.**   **2.** T (7,9)   The candidates for office began mapping out their campaigns six months before the elections. [Making plans for their activities, as to timing, location, speech making, T.V., etc.]

Mar   To damage or spoil to a certain extent.

mar up   T (6)   The spike heels on the women's shoes marred up the beautiful hardwood floors. [They made many ugly marks.] See **scuff up.**

Mark   To make marks for some purpose.

mark down   **1.** T (2,7)   The department store has marked down prices on all electrical goods. [Reduced the prices. Marked the reduction on sales cards.] See **mark up 1.**   **2.** T (7)   Thank you for your contribution. I'll mark you down on my list of contributors. [Down on paper.]   **3.** *mark-down* N. (2)   a. A reduction in price, usually to encourage buying. See **mark down 1.**   b. The amount by which a price is reduced. See **mark down 1.**

mark off   **1.** T (3)   The police marked off the area where no spectators would be permitted. [Used ropes or a barrier.] See **map off.**   **2.** T (6)   The storekeeper marked off a dollar on the price of his electric toasters. [Sold them at a dollar less than a previous price.]   **3.** *mark-off* N. (6)   The storekeeper gave a mark-off on his toasters. See **mark off 2.**

mark out   **1.** T (7,10)   New England farmers marked out the boundaries of their fields by building stone fences. [Made a complete and permanent scheme of boundaries.]   **2.** T (4)   Do you have John Smith's name on your list? If so, mark it out. [Draw a line through his name, to eliminate it.] See **cross out.**

mark up   **1.** T (2)   Some shopkeepers begin marking up their prices before Christmas. [Making them higher.] See **mark down 1.**   **2.** T (6)   Little children often mark up the walls with their dirty hands (the floors with their dirty shoes). [Leave dirty marks on them.]   **3.** *mark-up* N. (2)   With inflation we must expect a mark-up in prices. See **mark up 1.**

Marry   To give a person in marriage; to take a husband or wife.

marry off   T (2)   After our neighbors had married off their two daughters they moved to Florida. [Succeeded in finding husbands for the two daughters. Often implying that the parents felt very much relieved of a burden.]

marry up (with) I (2,5) Humorous. Hillbilly. Lil Abner married up with (got married up with) Daisy Mae. [He married her.]

Marshal To arrange in proper order; to act with control.

marshal in T (1) When the doors to the reception hall were opened there were ushers there to marshal the guests in. [Take them in and seat them in orderly manner.]

marshal up T (4,11) John finally marshalled up courage to ask Mary to marry him. [He got up courage, became brave enough.]

Mash To reduce to a soft pulpy mass.

mash up T (2,11) To make a good puree of potatoes, first mash up the potatoes well, add milk or cream, then whip until fluffy.

Mask To put on a mask, disguise oneself.

mask over T (2) Her feelings had been hurt but she tried her best to mask them over. [Hide her true feelings, as under a mask. Disguise them.]

mask up I (4,11) Our hostess told us all to mask up for the party. [To wear masks.]

Match To equal, be equal to, be of the same type as.

match up I (4) The colors in the rugs and the drapes don't match up. We'll have to change the drapes. [They are not matching colors.]

Mate To join as a mate or mates.

mate up (with) I (5) Informal. They are the last two people in the world I ever thought would mate up with each other. [Become close associates or mates.]

Measure I To mark off or give out while measuring.

measure off T (1) The dry-goods clerk measured off five yards of the cloth for his customer. [Used a tape measure to determine the length of cloth desired.]

measure out T (1,7) The Red Cross worker measured out three pounds of sugar (a gallon of milk, a peck of potatoes, etc.) for each flood victim. [Used scales or containers to determine the portions.] See **deal out, dole out, mete out, parcel out, portion out.**

Measure II To reach a certain standard.

measure up **1.** I (10) The troops of our allies do not measure up to our own troops in military skill. [They are not equal to ours.] **2.** I (4) The results of the military campaign in the North did not measure up to our expectations. [They were not as good as we had hoped.]

Meet To come into the presence or company of someone.

meet up (with) **1.** I (17) Who do you suppose I met up with at the concert last night? [Happened to meet. Ran into.] **2.** I (6) You may meet up with a lot of difficulties traveling alone in a country whose language you do not know. [Run into, happen to meet.]

Melt I To become liquefied by heat; to reduce to a liquid state by heat.

melt down T (1,6) The American Revolutionaries melted down statues of the king to make bullets. [Reduced the statues to molten lead.]

melt off I (7) When the snow melts off you can climb onto the roof to fix the T.V. antenna. [Becomes water and runs off the roof.]

melt up T (2,4) Patriotic citizens were asked to melt up coins and jewelry and give the gold to the government. [Prepare it by melting.]

Melt II To pass, become less, disappear gradually.

melt away **1.** I (3,4) When peace negotiations began the guerilla forces melted away. [They stopped fighting and disappeared.] **2.** I (2,4) The sun began to shine and the clouds melted away. [They disappeared.]

Mess To make a dirty or untidy mess.

mess about/around **1.** I (1,2) Informal. Where's John? Oh, he's out in the kitchen messing around (about). [Trying to prepare something to eat, but doing it inefficiently, making a mess.] **2.** I (5) Informal. I don't like that young man. I don't want him messing around with my daughter. [Becoming intimate with her, in an improper way perhaps.]

mess up **1.** T (6) John always messes up the kitchen when he tries to cook. [Leaves it untidy, in a mess.] **2.** T (6) Harry tried to settle the quarrel between his two friends, but only succeeded in messing it up. [Making it worse.] See **foul up**.

Mete To distribute or apportion by measure.

mete out T (1,7) Formal. It is the business of a judge to mete out justice (punishment, awards, etc.) to those brought before him. [Give to each person what the law requires.] See **measure out**.

Milk To draw milk from an animal.

milk off T (2,9) Ext. The officials of the company were accused of milking off a large share of the year's profits, and lining their own pockets. [Taking much of the company income without reporting it.]

Mill To move around aimlessly, confusedly, as a herd of cattle.

mill around **1.** I (1,2) We watched the cattle milling around in the corral. **2.** I (1,2) After the fire alarm (the parade, the explosion, etc.) people were milling around in the streets.

Mine To dig into the earth for ore, coal, etc.

mine out T (8) That whole section of the area has been mined out. [All of the minerals have been removed by mining.]

Mire To plunge into or as if into mud.

mired down **1.** T (2,3) Driving along the country road after a rainstorm we got mired down and had to ask a farmer to pull us out. [Our car wheels had sunk into the mud.] **2.** T (7) Ext. The peace negotiations got mired down in fruitless arguments about procedure. [The diplomats were unable to reach agreement on questions of procedure.]

Miss To fail to be present at some occasion.

miss out **1.** I (9) You missed out by not going to the picnic. It was a very pleasant afternoon. [You missed, lost out on, something good.] See **lose out**. **2.** *miss out (on)* I (9) I don't want to miss out on Mrs. Brown's cake. She's a wonderful cook. [Fail to get a piece of the cake.]

Mist To become misty.

mist over I (3) The sky is misting over. It will be a bad day for a picnic. [The mist is hiding the sun.] See **cloud over**.

Mix To put together a number of substances in one mass; to confuse.

mix in **1.** T (5) To give added flavor to her jam she mixed in two cups of grated orange peel. [Added them to the mixture.] **2.** I (4) This quarrel is between me and my sister. I don't want you mixing in. [Entering the quarrel.]

mix up **1.** T (3,11) Where's Jane? She's out in the kitchen mixing up some pancake batter (cake batter, cookie dough, etc.). [Putting the ingredients together in preparation for baking.] **2.** T (5) Those boys really hate each other. Whenever they meet, they mix it up. [Get into a fight.] **3.** T (6) Johnny has mixed up the toothbrushes in the bathroom. We don't know which is whose. [He moved them about, out of their usual places. Confused them.] **4.** T (6) Those young friends of yours are so much alike. I'm always mixing up their names. [I use the wrong name when speaking to them.] See **foul up.** **5.** *mix-up* N. (6) a. A great confusion. [There was a terrible mix-up at the meeting last night. Nobody knew who was in charge, or what was to be done.] b. A fight. [Robert got into a mix-up with Ed over the use of the car.] **6.** *mixed up* A. (6) a. Confused. [No, Mother, you're all mixed up (you have it all mixed up). Harry is the one who took the money, not Albert.] b. Emotionally disturbed. [He's just a mixed up kid. Said of a boy in his teens who is having "growing pains". He is disturbed about life, and about himself.]

Mock To imitate, mimic or counterfeit.

mock up **1.** T (4,11) The car designers mocked up the new sports car design for the inspection of the management. [They made a small model of the proposed car made to scale.] **2.** *mock-up* N. (4,11) The management approved the design for the new sports car after examining the mock-up. See **mock up 1**.

Moisten To make or become moist.

moisten up **1.** T (2) He moistened up his dry lips by licking them. [Made them soft.] **2.** T (2) Rain moistened up the parched ground. [Softened it.]

Moon To spend time idly, dreamily.

moon about/around I (1,2) John must be in love. He goes mooning about (around) with a far-away look in his eyes. [He doesn't pay attention to other people or to his work.]

moon away T (6) John just moons away the hours, neglecting his studies and his acquaintances. [His thoughts are on other things. He does nothing constructive.]

Mop To rub, wipe, clean or remove with a mop or some absorbent material.

mop off T (7) The athlete was perspiring freely. He mopped off his forehead (mopped the sweat off) with a towel. [Removed it as with a mop.]

mop up **1.** T (1,4,8) Mother always has to mop up (the bathroom, the water on the bathroom floor, the floor) after the children take a shower. [Clean, remove the water from the floor.] **2.** T (1,4,8) Military. As our troops pursued the enemy forces across the river, a small detachment was left behind to mop up. [Clear the area of scattered or remaining enemy troops.] **3.** *mop-up* N.A. (1,4,8) The action of clearing an area of enemy troops left behind. See **mop up 2**. **4.** *mop up the floor (with)* T (5) Slang. John had no trouble defeating his opponent. He simply mopped up the floor with him. [He defeated him quickly and badly.]

Mother To care for as a mother.

mother up T (2,5) Teddy is such a sad looking little boy. I feel like mothering him up (giving him a mothering up). [Give him loving care and attention.]

Mound To form into a mound.

mound up T (3,11) To prepare rose bushes against the winter weather we mound up the soil around them. [Pile soil close to the stalk.] See **hill up.**

Mount To go up, to climb, ascend.

mount up **1.** I (1) Formal. Biblical. After his resurrection Jesus mounted up into heaven. [He ascended.] **2.** I (2) The cost of food and clothing mounts up almost daily. [It rises.] **3.** I (5) As he thought of the insult, he felt his anger mount up. [His blood pressure rose.] See **boil up.**

Move To go or cause to go from one place to another; to change one's place of residence (move in or out of a house or apartment).

move about/around I (1,2) Has your mother recovered from her accident (her arthritis, rheumatism, etc.)? Yes, but she's just barely able to move about (around). [Walking is still difficult for her.]

move along I (3) There were many curious onlookers standing near the scene of the crime. The police asked them to move along. [To leave the scene.]

move away **1.** I (2) I was standing in front of the burning building, but moved away when the fire department arrived. [Moved far enough not to be in their way.] **2.** I (1) Do the Millers still live here? No, they moved away a month ago. [Went to another part of town, or to a different city.]

move back **1.** I (1) As the soldiers came marching down the street the crowd moved back to let them pass. [To the rear.] **2.** I (3) We left San Francisco five years ago, but moved back last month because of Father's new job. [We again live in San Francisco.]

move down T (1) Mother is too weak to climb the stairs, so we have moved her down. [To a room downstairs.]

move in **1.** I (1,4) After two of the wild dogs had cut the old zebra out of the herd, the rest of the pack moved in for the kill. [Joined the others.] **2.** I (1) Come to see us in our new apartment. We're moving in on the 1st of June. [Into the apartment.] **3.** *move in (on)* I (1,4) Our troops moved in on the enemy position, and soon had complete control of it. [Fought their way to it.] **4.** I (1,4) The Capone gang moved in on the bootleg liquor operations of the West Side gang. [Tried to get control of it by threats or the use of force.] **5.** *move in (with)* I (1) Our house was too large for our small family so we invited a nice young couple to move in with us. [Live in part of our house.]

move off I (2) We waved as the column of troops moved off. [Started to leave.]

move on **1.** I (II 1,3) It's getting late. We'll have to move on. [Get in our car and continue our driving.] **2.** I (II 1,2) The police ordered the crowd to move on. They were blocking the sidewalk. [Start walking away from the spot.]

move out **1.** I (2,9) The owner of the house told the people who had not paid their rent to move out. [Change their residence.] **2.** T (2) The owner threatened to move them out forcibly if they didn't pay their rent. [Put them and their belongings in the street.]

move over I (3) Please move over a little and make room for the old lady to sit down. [Move far enough away on the seat or bench for her to have a place to sit.]

move up **1.** I (1,10) A fresh regiment moved up to replace the tired troops who had been fighting on the front line for two weeks. [Up to the front.] **2.** I (2) Prices are moving up on the Stock Exchange after the recent decline. [Becoming higher.] **3.** T (2) The company is moving John up from Assistant Manager to Manager. [Giving him a raise in position.] **4.** T (1,11) Chess. To protect his knight, he moved up a pawn. [Advanced it.]

Mow To cut or reap.

mow down **1.** T (1,6) The workmen of the Highway Department were busy mowing down the weeds along the roadside. [Removing them by cutting.] **2.** T (1,4) As the enemy troops staged a mass attack on our position, our machine guns mowed them down. [Cut them down as with a scythe.] **3.** T (1,3) Slang. The entertainer (the comedian, the debater) was a great success last night. He just mowed 'em down. [He won enthusiastic applause.] See **lay out 6.**

Muck To make dirty or soil; to ruin, spoil.

muck up T (6) That man is a real menace. He mucks up everything he touches. [He spoils it.] See **foul up.**

Muddle To mix up in a confused manner; to jumble.

muddle along I (3) Everything looks hopeless. I suppose we'll just have to muddle along, doing the best we can. [Continue to act, even if in a confused manner.]

muddle through I (3,4) People say that England will always muddle through. [Finally succeed in what she is trying to do, without much purposeful effort or planned direction.]

Muddy To make muddy, soil with mud.

muddy up **1.** T (6) The children muddied up the floor with their shoes when they came in out of the rain. [Left muddy tracks on the floor.] **2.** T (6) A heavy storm had muddied up the once clear waters of the brook. [Made the water mud colored.] **3.** T (6)   Ext. The war in Viet Nam has muddied up the channels of international diplomacy. [Caused bad relations between nations.]

Muffle   To wrap in a cloak, shawl, coat, muffler, etc., especially to keep warm.

muffle up   T (3,11)   It's cold outside. Be sure to muffle up the children before they go out to play. [See that they are wrapped up warmly.]

Mull   To study, think about quietly.

mull over   T (6,7)   We sat in front of the fire mulling over the events of the day. [Thinking and talking quietly about them.]

Muscle   Informal. To make one's way by force. See **fight one's way.**

muscle aside   T (1,2)   When we tried to get in through the door we were muscled aside by a big brute of a man. [He forced us to step aside.]

muscle in   **1.** I (4)   We were having a nice quiet party when a complete stranger muscled in. [Forced himself upon us.]   **2.** *muscle in (on)* a.   I (4)   The stranger disrupted the party and muscled in on our conversation. [Joined it without being asked.] b.   I (4)   The leader of the West Side gang tried to muscle in on the protection racket of the Capone gang. [Make a deal to get some of the profits by threats or force.]

Muss   To put into disorder.

muss up   **1.** T (6)   His girl friend liked to tease him by mussing up his hair. [Making it look uncombed.]   **2.** T (6)   The youngsters mussed up the living room with their rough play. [Made it look disorderly, untidy.] See **rumple up.**

Muster   To assemble troops.

muster in   T (4)   Henry enlisted in the Marines on June 10th. He was mustered in July 1st. [He was officially taken into the service.]

muster out   T (4,9)   Our company was mustered out on September 5th. [The members were officially released from service.]

muster up   T (2,5,11)   Ext. You must try to muster up courage (strength, will power, etc.) to carry on in spite of your husband's death. [Get control of yourself, show that you have the qualities necessary.]

Muzzle   To put a muzzle on an animal's mouth to prevent it from biting, eating, etc.

muzzle up   **1.** T (3,5)   That dog bit my little daughter the other day. He should be muzzled up. [Have a muzzle put on him.]   **2.** T (3,4,5)   One of the first acts of a dictator is to muzzle up the opposition. [By threats or by decrees to keep those who oppose him from freely expressing themselves.]

N

Nab   To catch or seize, especially suddenly. See **grab.**

nab off   T (1)   I'm very tired. I think I'll nab off a bit of sleep (forty winks) before dressing for the party. [Take a short nap.]

nab up   T (1,11)   We haven't time to eat a big lunch. We'll just nab up a sandwich and eat it while we talk. [Stop somewhere and pick up a sandwich, then continue to talk as we drive along.]

Nail   To fasten with a nail or nails.

>   **nail down**   **1.** T (1)   A floor board had come loose so John got out his tools and nailed it down. [Made it fast to the beam by hammering nails into it.]   **2.** T (3) Informal. Mr. Fisher has nailed down the contract for building the new City Hall. [He has secured the contract.]

>   **nail up**   T (3,11)   Before leaving their summer cabin they always nail up the windows and doors to keep out intruders. [Make them difficult to open by using nails.]

Name   To identify, specify, or mention by name.

>   **name off**   T (6)   The leader of the group named off the people who were to take part in the ceremonies. [Read their names from a list.]

Narrow   To decrease in width; to limit or restrict.

>   **narrow down**   **1.** I (6)   The river narrows down to less than fifty feet in width by mid-summer. [Is reduced in size during the dry season.]   **2.** I (6)   The list of candidates (contestants, competitors, etc.) narrowed down before August. [It became smaller. Some candidates dropped out.]   **3.** T (6)   The F.B.I. narrowed down the search for the murderer to two suspects. [They eliminated a number of suspects.]   **4.** T (6)   The leader of the panel asked the members to narrow down the subjects for discussion. [Eliminate a number of subjects.]

Nick   To make a nick, notch, or chip in something.

>   **nick up**   T (6)   Mrs. Jones was furious at the new maid for nicking up some of her best dishes. [Spoiling them by making nicks or chips in them.]

Nip   To compress tightly between two surfaces or points; to pinch, to bite.

>   **nip off**   **1.** T (1)   He nipped off a bit of the cheese and put it in his mouth to taste its flavor. [Pinched it off with his fingers.]   **2.** T (2)   To get larger peaches (apricots, apples, pears, etc.) it is well to nip off many of the newly formed fruits. [Remove them by a nipping process.]

Noise   To spread reports or rumors by talking.

>   **noise about/around**   T (1,2)   It has been noised about (around) that the President may not seek re-election. [People have been talking here and there about the possibility.]

Nose   To use the nose in some activity.

>   **nose around**   **1.** I (1,2)   The stray dog went nosing around in the back yards of the neighborhood, trying to find something to eat. [Here and there.]   **2.** I (1,2) Informal. That woman is a snooper. She is always nosing around in other people's business.

>   **nose in**   I (1)   The ship nosed (it's way) in through the dense fog. [It came into the harbor, as though following its nose.]

>   **nose out**   **1.** T (4)   Racing. The winning horse nosed out its rivals in the final stretch. [Won the race by a very narrow margin.]   **2.** T (4)   The Democratic

candidate nosed out his Republican opponent in a very tight race. [Won the election.]

Notch   To keep tally by cutting a notch in a stick; add to a record.

notch up   T (5,10)   Our basketball team notched up another victory last night. [Won another game.]

Note   To mark down, as in writing.

note down   T (7)   As the announcer read off the names of the winners, we noted them down. [Put them down on paper.]

Nurse   To treat or handle with care, as a nurse takes care of a patient.

nurse along   **1.** T (1)   Sports. The hockey player nursed the puck along till he found an opening for a shot. [Moved it carefully. Kept control of it.]   **2.** T (1) Informal. Mr. Brown has been nursing along a new business that may turn out to be a big success. [Giving a great deal of care and attention to it.]

nurse back   T (4)   Her husband had been ill for a year, but she nursed him back to health. [Gave him the care and attention necessary to make him well again.]

O

Offer   To present solemnly as an act of worship or devotion to God, a deity, or a saint.

offer up   T (1)   In many religions in past ages the priests offered up human sacrifices to their gods. [In the ceremony the sacrifice was lifted up or sent up towards Heaven.]

Oil   To lubricate or supply with oil.

oil up   T (2)   The motor bearings had gone dry. He had to oil them up to get the motor started. [Lubricate them well.]

Open   To move (a door or window) from a closed position; disclose, reveal.

open in   I (1)   Most outside house doors open in. [Move inward when they are opened.]

open out   **1.** I (2)   The windows of his bedroom opened out. [Moved outward when they were opened.]   **2.** I (2,10)   Her hotel window opened out on a courtyard. [Gave a view out into the courtyard.]   **3.** I (10)   The fan opened out to show a geisha girl under a cherry tree. [The design appeared when the fan was unfolded.]

open up   **1.** I (7,9)   It was his job to open up in the morning and close up at night. [Open the store for business and close it at night.]   **2.** T (7,9)   Rexall Drug Company has opened up a new store on Main Street. [Started business in a new location.]   **3.** I (5,7,10)   Our troops opened up with machine guns as the enemy troops approached. [Began to fire.]   **4.** I (2,5)   When he reached the free-way, he opened up and sped along at 85 miles per hour. [Opened the throttle and went at high speed.]   **5.** I (4)   After the police had been grilling (questioning severely) the prisoner for an hour, he opened up and told everything. [He talked freely.]

Opt To make a choice.

opt out I (4) Our friend Charles was given the opportunity to join the new law firm, but he opted out. [He decided not to join.]

Order To give an order, direction, or command to someone. May be used with all the second elements, with the direct pronoun object of the person to whom an order is given to move in a certain direction.

order about/around T (1,2) I don't like my Uncle John. He's always ordering me around. [Telling me to do this or that, bossing me.]

order away T (2) When the children came too close to the fire engine the firemen ordered them away. [Away from the engine.]

order off T (1) The children were playing around on the stage but the director ordered them off. [Off the stage.]

order out T (2) The soldiers stayed in their quarters till the captain ordered them out. [Out of the barracks.]

order up I (4,11) The restaurant closes at 11 p.m. I think we had better order up. [Give our order to the waiter for what we want to eat and drink.]

Own To confess, admit.

own up **1.** I (9) Someone in this room broke the window. We'll stay here until the one who did it owns up. [Admits that he broke it.] **2.** *own up (to)* I (9) The prisoner finally owned up to having robbed the gas station. [He confessed the crime.] **3.** I (9) I'll own up to having a strong dislike for our manager. [I admit the fact that I do not like him.]

P

Pace To measure by taking paces or steps in some direction.

pace off T (3) He paced off 100 yards to establish the western boundary of the athletic field. [Measured them by taking steps or paces.] See **mark off**.

Pack I To pack goods in compact form; to press or crowd together.

pack down T (5,6) After planting the tree he packed the earth down around it to make it stand straight. [Pressed it firmly.]

pack in T (1,5) Informal. The new film at the Capitol is packing them in. [It is drawing large crowds. The theater is completely filled at all performances.]

pack up T (3,11) We won't be able to come to the meeting. We're packing up for our trip. [Putting things in suitcases, boxes, etc., in preparation for travel.]

Pack II To leave in a hurry; to send a person away in a hurry.

pack off **1.** I (1) They packed off for the mountains where they will do some skiing. [Left hurriedly.] **2.** T (2) As soon as Mother had packed the children off to school she drove to the super market. [Got them ready and sent them to school.]

Package   To put into a wrapper or container.

    package up   T (3)   The super markets package up their meats and vegetables in cellophane. See **bag up.**

Pad   To fill out or stuff with a pad or padding.

    pad out   **1.** T (1,11)   Many clowns pad themselves out with pillows or inflated balloons for comic effect. [Make themselves bigger around the middle.]   **2.** T (1,10)   He is a writer who pads out his stories with material that spoils the plot. [Puts in unnecessary details.]

Pair   To separate into pairs or groups of two.

    pair off   **1.** T (10)   Mrs. Martin is a successful hostess. She pairs off her dinner guests according to their age and tastes. [Arranges for people to sit together who will enjoy each other's company.]   **2.** I (10)   Marie paired off with John in the mixed doubles tennis match. [The two became team mates.]   **3.** I (10)   After dinner the guests paired off and went for a stroll along the beach. [They formed couples.]

    pair up   I (10,11)   Why don't you and Charles pair up for the week-end and give the car a good checking over. [Work together as a team.]

Palm   To dispose of something by fraud; substitute something with intent to deceive.

    palm off   T (2)   The fake art dealer palmed off a poor imitation Picasso as the real thing. [He deceived the buyer.] See **fob off.**

Pan   To wash gravel (sand, etc.) in a pan to separate out gold or other valuable metal.

    pan out   **1.** I (9)   Many of the streams worked by the Gold Rush miners did not pan out. [The amount of gold found was very small.]   **2.** I (7)   Informal. How do you think the peace negotiations will pan out? [What good results may come from them?]   **3.** I (9)   George's business venture didn't pan out. [It was not successful.]

Pancake   Aviation. To drop flat to the ground after leveling off a few feet above it.

    pancake down   I (1)   The plane's landing gear was out of order so the pilot had to pancake down. [Drop to the ground and skid to a stop.]

Paper   To use paper for a purpose.

    paper over   T (2)   The boys' bedroom was papered over with posters, pictures of athletes, airplanes, and space men. [The walls were covered with them.]

Parcel   To divide into or distribute in parcels, or portions.

    parcel out   T (1,7)   The leader of the group parceled out the remaining food supplies to the other members. [Gave to each one his share.] See **measure out.**

Pare   To cut off the outer coating or layer, or a part of something.

    pare away   T (3)   Mother said to pare away the bad spots on the potatoes (the apples, etc.) before putting them on to cook. [Remove them by cutting.]

    pare down   T (2)   The Congress asked the President to pare down the budget if he wanted a tax increase. [Reduce it by cutting government spending.]

pare off T (1,2) The cook pared off the humps on the potatoes before wrapping them in aluminum foil for baking. [Removed them by cutting.]

Partition To divide or separate by interior walls, barriers or the like.

partition off T (3) The carpenters partitioned off the large room so as to make three small offices. [Divide the space into three parts.] See **curtain off.**

Pass I To move past, go by.

pass away **1.** I (4,6) The hours passed away all too quickly and soon it was time to say goodbye. [They went by.] **2.** I (4) The making of homespun cloth passed away with the invention of textile weaving machinery. [It disappeared.] **3.** I (4) Grandmother passed away at the age of 90. [She died.]

pass by **1.** I (2) As the years pass by she thinks less and less of the old home town. [Pass in time.] **2.** I (2) We leaned out the window to watch the parade pass by. [Pass in space.]

pass in I (1) At the church door we stepped aside to let the wedding party pass in. [Enter the church.]

pass off I (8) The evening (the discussion, the social event, the election, etc.) passed off without any trouble. [It took place, ended, successfully.]

pass on **1.** I (II 1) The procession passed on after a brief pause in front of the Town Hall. [It continued on its way.] **2.** I (II 1) As the older generation passes on, new young leaders come to the fore. [Dies.] See **die off 1.**

pass out **1.** I (2) After the wedding we stood near the church steps as the wedding party passed out. [Came out of the church.] **2.** I (8) Informal. It was so hot in the auditorium that several people passed out. [They fainted, lost consciousness.] **3.** I (9) After hours of hovering between life and death, the poor fellow finally passed out. [He died.] See **pass away 3.** **4.** *pass out (cold)* I (9) The fat man had been drinking heavily all evening. He finally passed out cold. [He went into a drunken sleep.] See **knock out 4.**

pass over I (3,8) We'll stay in our car till the storm passes over. [Disappears, stops.]

pass through I (1,2) We can't stay for a very long visit. We're just passing through. [We are on a trip and must continue our journey.]

Pass II To cause or enable to go.

pass about/around T (1,2) The host asked me to help pass the drinks around. [Here and there to people in the room.]

pass along T (1,3) He asked me to pass along the news (the information, the papers, the gossip, etc.) to those who were interested. [Give it to other people.]

pass away T (6) We passed away the hours with music and dancing. [We spent the time in those activities.]

pass back **1.** T (1) Football. The center passed the ball back to the quarterback. [To the rear.] **2.** T (5) Just look at the book for a moment and pass it back. [Give it back to me.]

pass by   T (2)   The guard looked at his badge and passed him by. [He let him through the gate.]

pass down   1. T (1)   The speaker had a supply of pamphlets on the platform. He passed them down to the ushers for distribution. [Down to the floor of the auditorium.]   **2.** T (1)   Each generation passes down some of its beliefs and customs to the next. [Down in time.]

pass in   1. T (1)   After examining our tickets the doorman passed us in. [Allowed us to enter.]   **2.** T (1)   The teacher asked us to pass in our papers as soon as we finished. [In to her desk.] See **hand in**.

pass off   T (1)   Informal. When someone accused him of having beaten his wife, he passed it off as a joke. [He pretended that it was not a serious charge.]

pass on   T (II 1,3)   Someone gave him some pamphlets and asked him to pass them on to the people sitting in his row. See **pass along**.

pass out   T (2)   At the super-market we saw a group of college students passing out campaign literature. [Giving it to the customers at the market.]

pass over   T (3)   When the authorities were giving out prizes they passed over the one man who should have received one. [They ignored him. Did not give him a prize.]

pass up   1. T (1)   The ushers collected written questions and passed them up to the speaker on the platform. [Handed them up.]   **2.** T (4)   Informal. I think I'll pass up the dessert. I've already eaten too much. [I will not have any.]   **3.** T (4)   John passed up a good opportunity (a job, a chance, an advancement, etc.) when he was in Chicago. [He did not take it, make use of it.]

Pat   To strike lightly or gently with something flat, as a paddle or the palm of the hand.

pat down   T (1,6)   She glanced in the mirror and patted down her hair, which had become disarranged during the fast ride in the open car. [Smoothed it down with the palm of her hand.]

Patch   To mend, cover, or strengthen with a patch or patches.

patch over   T (2)   There were worn spots at the elbows of his jacket. He had the tailor patch them over with leather. [Repair the worn spots with leather patches.]

patch up   1. T (2,3)   It keeps Mother busy patching up the children's play clothes. [Mending them so that they can be worn again.]   **2.** T (3,4)   You'll have to patch up the chicken yard fence. The chickens are getting out. [Block the holes in the fence with wire, rope, etc.]   **3.** T (4,8)   John and his wife have succeeded in patching up their quarrel over the damage to the car. [They have settled their quarrel. Are on good relations again.]

Pay   To give money in exchange for goods or services.

pay back   1. T (5)   John paid back the money he borrowed from his father to buy a car. [Returned it to his father.]   **2.** T (5)   He paid his father back within three months.   **3.** I (5)   Ext. I'll pay you back for all your insults. [I will do something unpleasant to you in return for the insults you gave me.]

pay down T (1)   I had to pay 50 dollars down on the new refrigerator we bought. [I made a partial payment at the time of purchase, on condition that I pay the balance in installments.]

pay in T (1,4)   Each one of us paid in 20 dollars to get our names on the list of season ticket holders. [Into the box office.]

pay off 1. T (4)   This month I hope to pay off all my debts (the mortgage, my creditors, the loan, etc.). [Finish paying everything I owe.] **2.** T (4)   The company paid off all its employees and closed down the shop. [Gave to each one everything that was due to him, usually meaning that the employee is discharged.] **3.** I (2)   My investment in oil stocks paid off handsomely. [I made a lot of money by investing.] **4.** I (2)   Our decision to send a representative to the meeting paid off. [We got some good results from it.] **5.** T (9)   That used car dealer cheated me on the price of a Chevvy, but I paid him off well and good by spreading the word around town. [I gave him a bad reputation.] **6.** T (9)   Slang. The contractor paid off the City Commissioner for his help in getting his bid accepted. [He bribed the commissioner.] **7.** *pay-off* N. (2) a. The payment of a salary, debt or wages. b. The time at which such payment is made. c. A settlement or reckoning by way of retribution or reward. d. A profit or reward. See **pay off 5, pay back 3.** e. Informal. The consequence, outcome, or final sequence in a series of events, actions or circumstances. Ex. He had an operation, lost his job, had his mortgage foreclosed. But the pay-off was when his wife divorced him. f. The climax of something, especially of a story or joke. Ex. In the pay-off we find out it's the butler who commits the murder.

pay out 1. T (10)   He has paid out thousands of dollars in doctors' bills and still doesn't know what's wrong with him. [Spent that much for medical advice.] **2.** T (8)   I'll pay him out for all he has done to me. [Get revenge.] See **pay back 3. 3.** T (10)   Fishing. When he hooked a big fish he began paying out his line. [Letting the line slide out from the reel.] See **play out, reel out.**

pay up 1. T (4)   I'll be able to pay up all my bills at the end of the month. [Make a complete payment.] **2.** I (4)   If you don't pay up you will lose your membership in the club. [Pay what is due.] **3.** *paid up* A. (8) a. Thank Heavens. I'm all paid up. [I have paid all my bills.] b. A paid up mortgage is a great help to the elderly. [It reduces the drain on their limited income.]

Peek To look or glance briefly or furtively.

peek in 1. I (1)   We looked toward the window and saw two little children's faces peeking in. [Looking into the room.] **2.** I (1)   Mother went to the bedroom door and peeked in to see if the children were asleep. [Gave a quick glance in the bedroom.]

Peel To remove the skin, rind, or bark from something.

peel off 1. T (1,2)   The little child was having a hard time peeling off the skin of an orange. [Removing it.] **2.** T (1,2)   It was hot out in the garden so Bob peeled off his shirt after ten minutes of digging. [Removed it as one would the peel of an orange.] **3.** I (2) Aeronautics. Two planes in the rear echelon of the formation peeled off, and began to descend towards the watching crowd. [Removed themselves from the formation, usually laterally.]

Peg To work or continue persistently or energetically.

peg away I (6) I know that Russian is a very difficult language, but keep pegging away at it and you'll make out all right. [Work hard and you will succeed in learning it.]

Pen To confine in or as in a pen.

pen in T (1) A small detachment of our soldiers was penned in on all sides by a battalion of the enemy. [Kept within a small area from which escape would be difficult.]

pen up T (3) I think you should ask the neighbors to pen up their chickens. They're ruining our garden. [Put them securely in a pen.]

Pension To cause to retire on a pension.

pension off T (4) Most big companies pension off their workers at the age of 65. [Discharge them but continue to pay them a monthly pension.]

Pep To make spirited, vigorous, lively.

pep up **1.** T (2,5) Informal. This party has become very dull. What can we do to pep it up? [Make it more gay, more lively.] **2.** *pepped up* A. T (2,5) He was all pepped up over the news that our team had won the championship. [He felt happy, enthusiastic, full of life.]

Percolate To pass through a filter, as a liquid.

percolate down **1.** I (1) In an electric percolator the boiling water percolates down through the coffee grounds. [Down to the bottom part.] **2.** I (1) The benefits from new technologies gradually percolate down to the mass of the people. [Down from the people who make use of the discoveries.]

Perfume To give off a pleasant odor or scent.

perfume up T (4) The room was all perfumed up with the smell of roses. [The scent was everywhere in the room.]

Perk To become lively or vigorous, especially after being ill or depressed.

perk up **1.** I (2,5) Mary had been ill all winter, but she perked up when the weather grew warmer. [She began feeling better.] **2.** T (2,5) She perked up her last year's spring suit with a gay colored blouse. [Made it appear more attractive.]

Peter To diminish gradually and then disappear or cease.

peter out **1.** I (8) The firecracker (the roman candle, etc.) fizzed for a moment, then petered out. [It did not continue to the point of exploding.] **2.** I (8) Their interest in (enthusiasm for) building a swimming pool petered out at the beginning of September. [They were less and less interested in it.]

Phone To use the telephone. Can be used with many of the second elements to show the direction of the action.

phone in I (1) The doctor's receptionist told him that Mrs. Brown had phoned in to say that she could not keep her appointment. [Phoned the message into the doctor's office.]

phone over I (3) Aunt Jane just phoned over to tell me she couldn't come to dinner tonight. [Phoned from across the river or some distant part of town, etc.]

Pick I To choose or select.

pick out 1. T (4) While Mary was picking out a new dress, her husband went to the men's furnishings department to pick out some ties. [Making a selection for purchase.] **2.** T (4) From the top of the Empire State Building we were able to pick out the Brooklyn Bridge, the Queensboro Bridge and the Verrazano Bridge. [See and identify them.] **3.** T (4) I could pick out that man's face in any crowd. [Distinguish him from all the others.] **4.** T (4) My husband has already gone to Dallas to pick out a place for us to live. [Locate and decide on the place.]

pick over 1. T (6,8) The tomatoes were not of very good quality. She picked them over, and finally found some that suited her. [Looked at them, felt them all.] **2.** *picked over* A. (6,8) When she finally got to the bargain counter the blouses were already pretty well picked over.

[Other women had been there earlier and taken the best of them.]

Pick II To lift or remove with or as if with the hands, or an instrument such as tweezers, a clamp, a fork, or a vehicle; to make figurative or electronic contact with.

pick off 1. T (2) The gardener was busy picking off the faded blossoms of the iris (the imperfect fruit of the peach trees, etc.). [Removing them with his fingers.] **2.** T (2) Monkeys spend much time picking off lice and foreign matter from each other's bodies. [Removing it with their fingers.] **3.** T (5) Sharpshooters are skilled at picking off enemy soldiers who expose themselves to view. [Killing them with a single shot from their rifle.]

pick out 1. T (1) Jane was busy in the kitchen picking out nut meats with a nut pick. [Removing them from the nut shell.] **2.** T (1) Vultures and other scavenger birds pick out the eyes of dead animals. [Remove them with their beaks.] **3.** T (1) Johnny got a splinter in his foot. Mother picked it out with a needle and a pair of tweezers. [Removed it.]

pick up 1. T (1) The children were busy picking up sticks, fallen branches and dry wood for the bonfire. [Up from the ground.] See **gather up. 2.** T (1) Telephone. He picked up the receiver to answer the call after the second ring. [Up from the bracket.] **3.** T (1) At lunch today my boss picked up the check. [He insisted on paying for the lunch.] **4.** T (2,5,11) Mother just had time to pick up the living room before the guests arrived. [Pick up things that were lying around. Put the room in good order.] **5.** T (1) The bus picked up ten passengers at the hotel. [Took them aboard.] **6.** T (1) We'll pick you up at 8:30. [We'll come to your place and take you with us. Usually in a car.] **7.** T (1) They warn us that it is dangerous these days to pick up hitchhikers. [Stop along the highway and take strangers into the car.] **8.** T (1) The repair man came this morning to pick up our T.V. set. [Take it in his car to the repair shop. Probably in a pick-up truck.] **9.** T (1) On our world tour we picked up a lot of interesting souvenirs. [Bought them here and there in a casual way.] **10** T (1) I've never studied Spanish. I just picked it up, traveling and living in South America for a year. [Learned it informally.] **11.** T (1) On his last trip to Europe he picked up a cold (the flu, a virus, an infection, etc.). [He got it by accident. He didn't try to get it.] **12.** T (1) He picked up the World Series (a Canadian broadcast, B.B.C., the Olympic Games, etc.) on the radio. [He made the connections necessary.] **13.** T (1) He was staggering around drunk at 2 a.m. on Main Street when the police picked him up. [Arrested him and took him to jail.] **14.** T (17) The F.B.I. picked up the trail of the bandits as they were heading for Mexico. [They found evidence that the bandits were going that way.] **15.** T (17) Slang. That's a cute chick I saw you with last night. Where did you pick her up? [Make her acquaintance.] See **pick-up** N.A. **16.** T (1,5) Informal. You look very tired. I think a drink and a little food would pick you up. [Give you a lift. Make you feel better.] **17.** I T (2,12) He had been ill all winter, but began picking up with warm weather. [Picking up strength, good health.] **18.** I T (2) With Christmas approaching, business began picking up. [Getting better.] **19.** T (5) Going down hill he (his car) picked up speed. [Went faster.] **20.** T I (5) As the dance became wilder and wilder the music began to pick up. [Pick up speed.] See **pick up 19**. **21.** T (7) The lecturer picked up the discussion of his subject where he left off the day before. [Started his new lecture at that point.] **22.** *pick-up* N.A. a. Informal. A casual, usually unintroduced acquaintance often made in hope of a sexual relationship. See **pick up 15**.

b. Automobile (1) The capacity for a rapid acceleration. Ex. This car has a quick pick-up. See **pick up 19**. (2) A small truck having a low-sided open body used for deliveries and light hauling. A pick-up truck. See **pick up 8**.

c. Informal. An improvement as in health, work, production, etc. See **pick up 16**, **17, 18, 19, 20**.

d. Sports. The act of fielding (picking up) a ball after it hits the ground.

e. Radio. (1) The act of receiving sound waves in the transmitting set, in order to change them into electrical waves. (2) A receiving or recording device. (3) The place from which a broadcast is being transmitted. (4) Interference with a transmission.

f. Television. (1) The change of light energy into electrical energy in the transmitting set. (2) The device used for making the change. (3) A telecast made directly from the scene of an action.

g. Phonograph and recorder. A device which generates electric or acoustic impulses in accordance with the mechanical variations impressed upon a phonograph record or tape.

h. An instance of stopping for, or taking aboard passengers or freight, as by a train, bus, taxicab, or ship. See **pick up 5**, **6**, **7**, **8**.

i. The taking of freight or a shipment aboard.

j. The person, freight or shipment taken aboard. See **pick up 5**, **8**.

k. Informal. The ability or capacity to receive impressions or ideas. Ex. He's quick on the pick-up. [He responds quickly to what he hears. He understands immediately.]

l. Metal working. The adhesion of particles of metal to the die or plug. **23.** *pick-me-up* N. (1,5) A drink or a bit of food taken to get quick energy, or relief from fatigue. See **pick up 16**.

Piece To complete, enlarge, or extend by an added piece or something additional.

    piece out **1.** T (10) The waist of Jennie's dress was too high, so Mother had to piece it out to make it fit her. [Add some cloth to make the waist lower.] **2.** T (10) She pieced out her collection of antique crystal with two goblets bought at the auction. [Made it more complete.]

Pile I To lay or dispose in a pile or heap; to form a pile or piles.

    pile on **1.** T (I 1) Our teacher is certainly piling on the work these last days of classes. [Giving us a lot of extra assignments.] **2.** T (I 1) Slang. When that woman tries flattery to get what she wants she can really pile it on. [Heap flattery on the person she wants a favor from.]

    pile up **1.** T (1) The children were piling up the fallen leaves in the back yard and jumping about in them. [Making piles of leaves.] **2.** I (1,6) John, the leaves are piling up in the back yard. You'll just have to get busy and rake them. [They are forming piles.] **3.** I (2,6) My work is piling up on me. I can't seem to keep my desk clear. [There are piles of papers on my desk.] **4.** I (1,6) Six cars piled up on the free-way during the snow storm. [There was an accident which caused a collision involving six cars.] **5.** I (2,6) His debts (bills, costs, etc.) began piling up after his second child was born. [His expenses increased greatly.] **6.** I (1,4) Football. On the fourth down the defenders piled up on the ball carrier who was unable to gain ground. See **pile-up 7d**. **7.** *pile-up* N. (2,6) a. The pile-up of work kept him at the office late at least three times a week. See **pile up 3**. b. The pile-up occurred about three miles out of town. See **pile up 4**. c. The pile-up of debts nearly gave him ulcers. See **pile up 5**. d. Football. The pile-up on the five yard line was successful and the ball went to the defenders. See **pile up 6**.

Pile II To get somewhere in a more or less disorderly group.

    pile down I (5) When Father called upstairs to say the Christmas tree was ready, the children piled down in a mad rush. [Came down quickly and noisily.]

    pile in I (1) When the car was packed the family piled in and off we started. [Got in the car with some noise and confusion.]

    pile on I (I 1) Our group of twelve piled on when the bus arrived, all talking and laughing. [Onto the bus.]

    pile out I (1,2) When the bus stopped at Ogden we all piled out for a snack and a cup of coffee. [Out of the bus.]

Pin   To fasten or attach with or as with a pin or pins.

  pin down   **1.** T (1,4)   Wrestling. The wrestler pinned his opponent down (pinned his opponent's shoulders down) to the floor. [Threw him down and held him down.]   **2.** T (1)   The driver was pinned down when his car overturned. [The car was on top of him, holding him down.]   **3.** T (1)   Ext. James doesn't seem to remember his promise to take us to the movies. We'll have to pin him down on it. [Hold him to his promise.]   **4.** T (1)   Ext. He changes his mind so often, it's hard to pin him down in an argument. [Get him to be consistent in what he says.]

  pin on   T (I 3)   His wife was pinning his medals on when the phone rang. [Fastening them to his uniform (his jacket, etc.) with a pin.]

  pin up   **1.** T (1)   The cleaning woman pinned up her skirts before starting to scrub the floor. [Made them shorter by pinning the bottom part up around her waist.]   **2.** T (1)   Soldiers have the habit of pinning up pictures of beautiful girls on the walls of their sleeping quarters. [Attaching them to the walls with pins, tacks, or tape.]   **3.** *pin-up* N. (1)   a. Informal. A picture that is suitable for pinning up on a wall, usually of an attractive girl. See **pin up 2**. b. A girl in such a picture. c. A device or fixture that can be fastened to a wall, such as a lamp.

Pine   To fail gradually in health or vitality, from grief, regret, or longing.

  pine away   I (4)   After the tragic death of her lover, she pined away and was never seen again in public. [She became weak, ill, and unwilling to show herself in public.]

Pipe   To play a musical instrument such as a flute or whistle. Nautical. To blow a whistle to call sailors down from the rigging of a ship.

  pipe down   **1.** T (1)   The boatswain piped the men down after practice drill in the rigging. [Down to the deck of the ship.]   **2.** I (4)   Informal. Pipe down! [Shut up! Be quiet!] A rather rude way of telling people not to talk so much, so loud.

  pipe up   **1.** I (9)   Informal. The meeting had been rather quiet, when all of a sudden a voice piped up in the back row, calling for action. [Someone began to speak, in an assertive tone of voice.]

Pitch   To throw, fling, hurl or toss.

  pitch in   **1.** T (5)   We all pitched in a dollar to help buy the food for the picnic. [Each one contributed that much.] Probably from games of chance, such as poker. See **ante in, chip in**.   **2.** I (4)   After the party we all pitched in to help the hostess. [We rearranged the furniture, cleared the table and washed the dishes, etc.]   **3.** I (7)   I'm behind in my studies. I'll have to pitch in if I want to catch up with the class. [Work hard and steadily.]

Plank   To lay or put down with force — variant, plunk.

  plank down   T (1)   A big cowboy went to the bar, planked down ten dollars, and ordered drinks for everyone in the room. [Put them down with force and perhaps noisily.]

Play   To exercise or employ oneself in diversion, amusement, or recreation.

play along (with)   I (2,3)   We were not sure that he was doing the right thing (had the right idea, knew how to act, etc.) but we decided to play along with him (with the idea, etc.) for the time being. [Cooperate, work with him.]

play around   I (1,2)   Jack hasn't lost his childish ways. He spends his time just playing around. [He is not serious, does childish things.] See **fool around**.

play back   **1.** T (5)   After finishing the tape he played it back to listen for mistakes. [Played from beginning to end.] See **play over**.   **2.** *play-back* N.A.   (5) a. The act of operating a phonograph or tape recorder so as to hear a reproduction of the recording. See **play back 1**. b. In a sound recording device, the apparatus for producing play-backs. c. The recording so played especially the first time it is heard after being recorded.

play down   **1.** T (6)   Although he was the leader in getting the Civil Rights bill passed, he played down his own efforts and gave the credit to others. [He belittled his own activity. Made it seem unimportant.]   **2.** T (6)   The newspapers are playing down the activities of the militant leaders of the demonstrators. [Not reporting their activities with big headlines on the front page.]

play off   **1.** T (5)   Each team had won three games, and were tied for first place. They had to play off the tie to determine the championship. [Play another game, the winner of which would be the champion.]   **2.** T (3)   Jeanette was a clever girl. She played her father off against her mother, and was allowed to have her own car. [Her father won in the contest of wills. She promoted the contest.]   **3.** *play-off* N.A.   (2,4)   a. In competitive sports, the playing of an extra game, round, inning, etc., in order to settle a tie. b. A series of games or matches, as between the leading teams of two leagues, played in order to decide a championship.

play on   I (II 2)   Casey would waltz with a strawberry blonde while the band played on. [Continued to play.] From an old popular song.

play out   **1.** T (7)   Cards. Unless you are sure you can take all the tricks, you should play the hand out. [Not lay your cards all at once on the table, but play each card in proper turn, till all have been played.]   **2.** I (8)   Our food supply played out before the end of our boat trip. [It was finished, exhausted.]   **3.** T (10) When he hooked that big trout he played out his line, not wanting to have it snapped off short. See **pay out 3**.   **4.** *played out* A.   (8)   I'm all played out! I never felt so tired in my life. [I'm exhausted.]

play over   T (6,7)   She played the record over three times before she could understand all the words of the song. [Played it three times more.]

play through   T (3)   Please play the tape (all the way) through. I haven't heard the last part. [From beginning to end.]

play up   **1.** T (1,2)   He always plays up the part he took in securing the playground. [He exaggerates his activities.] The opposite of **play down 1**. **2.** *play up (to)* I (5) She played up to the movie director, hoping to get a good part in the new film. [Did things to win his favor, his attention.] See **cozy up**.

Plot To divide land into plots.

plot out T (7) In the new real estate development they have plotted out the land into half acre lots. [They have laid it out, made a plan or plot.]

Plough (Plow) To turn up the soil with a plow: to make a furrow or groove, as with a plow.

plough back T (3) The Martin Company will plough back this year's profits into an expansion program. [Invest the profits in new plants and equipment.]

plough under T (3) Mr. Black planted two of his fields to clover this year. He will plough it under in the spring for green fertilizer. [Plough the fields so that the clover is turned under.]

plough up **1.** T (2,11) Mr. Black ploughed up ten acres of pasture land and will plant it to corn. [Prepared the land for growing corn.] **2.** T (1,6) The airliner that crash landed at the airport ploughed up a large section of the runway. [Damaged it badly by ploughing up the surface.]

Pluck To pull off or out from the place of growth, as fruit, flowers, feathers.

pluck off **1.** T (1,2) Some women pluck off their eyebrows to make themselves more beautiful. [Remove them by pulling out the hairs.] **2.** T (1) To prepare a chicken for cooking, you first pluck off the feathers. [Remove them by pulling them out.]

pluck out T (1) Vultures will pluck out the eyes of dead animals. [Out of their sockets.]

pluck up **1.** T (1,4) When he returned from his vacation he spent hours plucking up the tall weeds in his garden. [Pulling them up by the roots.] **2.** T (2,4) Ext. He finally plucked up enough courage to ask her to marry him. [He managed to find in himself the courage necessary.] It required an effort to "pull his courage up". See **pluck up 1**.

Plug I To stop or fill with or as with a plug.

plug in T (1,6) He plugged in the radio in time to catch the news program. [Put the plug into the outlet socket to connect the radio with the electric current.] Used with any type of electrical device such as a toaster, percolator, iron, mixer, T.V., etc.

plug up **1.** T (3,11) Before going to bed she plugged up her ears with cotton, so as not to hear her husband's snoring. [Filled the openings with cotton.] See **stop up**. **2.** T (3,4) When the plumber came he plugged up the leak in the water tank. [Put material in the opening to stop the leak.] **3.** *plugged up* A. (6) His nose was so plugged up he couldn't breathe through it. [The inflamed membranes and the mucus blocked the flow of air.]

Plug II To work steadily or doggedly; to move in the same manner.

plug along I (3) The path was rough and slippery, but he plugged along, determined to reach the cabin before night. [Kept walking even though it was difficult.]

plug away   I (6)   Henry is plugging away at his studies. [He continues to work hard and steadily.]

Plummet   To plunge; to fall as if weighted with lead.

plummet down   I (1)   There was a loud explosion and the plane plummeted down from the skies and crashed into the school house. [Fell swiftly and heavily.]

Plump I   To become plump (well filled out, or rounded in form).

plump out   I (11)   Alice was very thin as a little girl, but she's plumping out now that she's in her teens. [Her body is becoming more rounded.] See **round out.**

plump up   T (2,11)   Before climbing into bed she plumped up the pillows. [Patted them to make them rounder and softer.]

Plump II   To drop or fall heavily and suddenly.

plump down   **1.** T (1)   Frank carried in the heavy suitcases and plumped them down on the bed. [Let them fall heavily.]   **2.** T I (1)   Father came home tired from work and plumped down (plumped himself down) in the easy chair. [Let himself fall heavily.]

Pod   To produce pods (seed vessels for peas or beans).

pod out   I (11)   The peas have begun to pod out. [Their seed pods are forming.]

Point   To direct the finger (a weapon, the attention, etc.) at, to, or upon something. May be used with all the second elements showing the direction of the action.

point out   **1.** I (10)   He pointed out to where the workmen were planting trees. [He called my attention to them by pointing toward a group.]   **2.** I (7)   I asked him to point out the leaders of the group. [To indicate in some way who the leaders were.]   **3.** I (9)   Ext. I pointed out to the governor that I was not a member of his political party. [I called his attention to that fact.]

point off   **1.** I (2)   The guide pointed off towards the opposite rim of the canyon. [He pointed his finger to a distant object.]   **2.** T (3)   The math teacher pointed off the figure he had written on the blackboard. [Used dots or points to separate it into its parts.]

point up   **1.** I (1)   The guide pointed up to the top of the tower where there was a T.V. antenna.   **2.** T (5)   Ext. The rioting in the big cities points up the need for jobs and better housing. [Calls attention to, and emphasizes the need.]

Poke   To prod or push, especially with something narrow or pointed.

poke in   **1.** T (1)   Informal. While we were eating dinner our neighbor poked her head in to tell us our car lights were on. [Put her head through the door, but did not come in.]   **2.** T (1)   He picked up the pan and poked his finger in to see if the water was hot. [Into the water.] See **stick in.**

poke out   T (9)   There was a knot in the board fence around the baseball field. Johnny poked it out with a stick so he could watch the game. [Out of the fence.]

poke through   T (1)   I opened the door a little way and poked my nose through to see if there was anyone in. [Through the narrow opening.]

poke up   T (4,7)   It's cold in here. Poke up the fire while I fix a pot of coffee. [Stir it up with the poker. Perhaps add some firewood.]

Police   To clean and keep clean (a camp, parade grounds, a military post).

police up   T I (4,11)   We'll have to police up (police up the place); the Commanding General is coming for inspection. [Put the place in proper order.]

Polish   To make smooth and glossy by rubbing or friction.

polish away   T (2,3)   The sculptor used carborundum paper to polish away the rough spots on the casting. [Remove the spots.]

polish off   **1.** T (10)   Where is your father? He's in the library polishing off the speech he has to give tonight. [Making final changes, corrections, etc.]   **2.** T (5)   Slang. The three of us polished off a fifth of Bourbon. [We drank all of the whiskey in the bottle.]   **3.** T (5)   Boxing. Joe Louis polished off his opponent in three rounds. [He defeated him, quickly.]

polish up   **1.** T (4,5)   "I polished up the handle on the big front door." [I made the handle shine.] A line from a song from "H.M.S. Pinafore", by Gilbert and Sullivan.   **2.** T (4,8)   She's spending a year in Paris to polish up her French. [Improve her ability to use French.]   **3.** T (8,11)   Three of the President's speech-writers are working with him now, polishing up his State of the Union speech. [Helping to put it in its final form, suggesting changes and corrections that will improve it.]

Ponder   To weigh carefully in the mind, consider thoughtfully.

ponder over   T (6,8)   There are many questions to ponder over now that the war has been won. [To think about seriously.]

Pony   To pay money, as in settling an account.

pony over   T (3)   Slang. The members of the robber gang wanted the chief to pony over their share of the loot. [Give each one his share.] See **hand over**.

pony up   I (4)   Slang. If you won't pony up, I'll have to use force. [Pay me what you owe me.]

Poop   Slang. To cease from or fail in something, as from fear or exhaustion.

poop out   **1.** I (4,6)   Slang. He was supposed to help us build the garage, but he pooped out. [He did not help.] See **goof off**.   **2.** *poop out (on)* I (6)   Slang. He pooped out on us (on the deal, on the project). [He failed to take part, as he had promised.]   **3.** *pooped out* A. (8)   Slang. We were all so pooped out after the party (the long day, the day's travel, etc.) that we went straight to bed. [Tired, exhausted.] See **wear out**.

Pop   To make a short, quick, explosive sound; to act suddenly, briefly; move in such a manner.

pop in   T I (1)   Informal. While we were eating dinner she popped in (popped her head in) to say "Hello". [Came in for a moment, or put her head inside the door.] See **drop in**.

pop off   **1.** I (2)   When he put on his World War I uniform for the parade two buttons of his jacket popped off. [The jacket was so tight the buttons came off.]

2. T (2) There were five bottles standing on the fence rail. He popped them off one by one with his sling shot. [Knocked them off the rail.] **3.** I (1,2) Bill was with us during the early part of the evening, but he popped off around 9 o'clock. [Suddenly disappeared.] **4.** I (5) Slang. The old man popped off around midnight. [He died unexpectedly.] See **kick off 3**. **5.** I (9) She became more and more angry as she listened to the argument, and finally popped off about the unfairness of the speakers. [Exploded in an angry speech.]

pop out **1.** I (1) Ext. His eyes popped out when he saw all that money fall out of the machine. [His eyes opened wide and seemed to start out of their sockets.] **2.** I (4) Baseball. The next batter popped out. [He hit a pop fly, which was caught by a player on the opposing team. He was declared out by the umpire.] **3.** I (1) The comedian popped out before the curtain and took a bow. [Appeared suddenly.] **4.** T (3) The comedian popped his head out between the curtains and grinned at the audience. [Made his head appear suddenly.]

pop up **1.** I (1) The slice of bread in the toaster popped up all golden brown. [Came up suddenly.] **2.** I (7) Ext. There is always something new (interesting, unexpected, exciting) popping up at our weekly meetings. [Showing up suddenly.] **3.** I (5) In the center of the auditorium a man popped up to challenge the speaker. [Stood up suddenly.] **4.** *pop-up* N.A. (1) a. A pop-up toaster is one in which the toast pops up when brown. See **pop up 1**.

b. Baseball. A pop fly. A high fly ball hit to the infield just beyond it, that can easily be caught before reaching the ground.

Portion To divide into or distribute in portions or shares.

portion out **1.** T (8) The committee chairman portioned out the propaganda literature to each member. [Gave to each one his share.] **2.** T (8) The chosen leader in the life-boat portioned out the water and food supplies each day. [Gave to each one his share.] See **measure out**.

Pound To strike repeatedly and with great force, as with an instrument, the first, heavy missiles, etc.

pound down **1.** T (1) He tried to pound down the door with his fists. [Cause the door to fall by pounding on it.] **2.** T (1) Vibration caused the railroad spike to work loose and they had to pound it down. [Hammer it in.]

pound out T (9) The pianist pounded out the melody with one finger. [Played it loudly.]

Pour To cause to move in a continuous flow from or as if from one container to another, or into, over or onto something; to move in a stream.

pour down **1.** T (1) The enemy, from the surrounding hills, poured down their fire upon our troops. [Kept a stream of fire directed on them.] **2.** T (1) Informal. He mixed himself a drink and poured it down. [Drank it all at once. Poured it down his throat.] **3.** I (1) There was a clap of thunder, and the rain came pouring down. [Down to earth.]

pour in **1.** T (1,5) If your coffee is too hot pour in some cold water. [Into the coffee cup.] **2.** I (1,4)   For the inauguration ceremonies people poured in from all parts of the country. [Into Washington, the capital city.]

pour on **1.** T (I 1)   To put out a small fire you should pour on water. [On the fire.] **2.** T (II 5)   Informal. When talking about the greatness of his own country he just pours it on. [He uses a great stream of words. He exaggerates.]

pour off T (1)   After boiling a chicken you should pour off the fat. [Remove it by pouring.]

pour out **1.** T (1)   He poured out drinks for everyone in the room. [Out of a bottle or pitcher.] **2.** T (10)   Ext. She poured out her sorrows to her dearest friend. [She talked at length about them. The words came out like a stream.] **3.** I (2,3)   After the political rally the people poured out into the streets. [Came out in a stream.]

pour over I (2,3)   The levees along the river were not high enough. The flood waters poured over and engulfed the village. [Over the levees.]

pour through I (1)   As soon as the gates were opened the crowd poured through. [Went through in a stream.]

Practice   To perform or do repeatedly in order to acquire skill or proficiency.

practice over T (6,7)   I'm not familiar with the piano accompaniments of your songs. I think we should practice them over together several times. [Repeat them.]

practice up I (2,5,11)   Mary spends all of her time practicing up for her recital. [Preparing for it by much practice.]

Precipitate   To cause to separate from a solution or mixture.

precipitate out T (3)   Power companies precipitate harmful substances out of the smoke before it goes out of the smokestack. [They remove cinders and gases.]

Press I   To act upon with steadily applied weight or force.

press down I (1)   He pressed down hard on the accelerator, and the car picked up speed. [Exerted pressure with his foot.]

press out T (1)   A wine press presses out the juice from the grapes.

Press II   To push forward or advance with force, eagerness or haste.

press on **1.** I (II 1)   It was getting dark, so we pressed on to reach our destination while there was still some light. [Kept moving (driving, walking hurriedly.)] **2.** I (II 1,2)   Columbus urged his crew to press on. [Continue to sail westward.]

Pretty   To make pretty, improve the appearance of.

pretty up **1.** T (2,8)   She was busy prettying up her room (her hat, her dress, her face). [Doing things to make them look prettier.] **2.** *prettied up* A. (2,8) Informal. You're all prettied up tonight. Are you expecting your boy friend? [You have made yourself look very pretty.] See **doll up.**

Price   To fix the price of.

price down T (2)   The merchant priced his goods down after the holidays. [He reduced the price of them.]

price out T (9)   He priced himself out of the market. [He asked so much for his services that no one would buy them, pay him what he asked.]

price up   T (2)   The artist had been selling his sculptures at an extremely modest price. His friends advised him to price them up. [Put a higher price on them.]

Prick   To cause to stand erect or point upward.

   prick up: **1.** T (1)   The dog pricked up his ears when he heard the car coming. [Raised them to hear better.]   **2.** T (2,5)   Ext. Informal. When Mrs. Jones started to tell about the neighborhood scandal all the ladies pricked up their ears. [They listened eagerly for a bit of juicy gossip.]

Primp   To dress or adorn oneself with care.

   primp up   I (2,8,11)   Informal. Where are the girls? They're upstairs primping up for their dates. [Dressing carefully, combing their hair, putting on make-up.] See **doll up**.

Print   To cause (a manuscript, text, etc.) to be published in print.

   print off   T (1)   He gave instructions to the duplicating service to print off 500 copies of the price schedule. [Make that number of copies from the original.]

   print up   T (7)   For the first edition of the novel they will print up 20,000 copies. [Produce that number of copies, while keeping the plates for future editions.]

Pull I   To draw or haul towards oneself (or itself) in a particular direction. May be used with all of the second elements to indicate the direction of the action.

   pull down   **1.** T (1)   They pulled down the old house and are going to build a new one on the same location. [Brought it to the ground.]   **2.** T (3)   Informal. How much does he pull down a month? [What is his salary?] See **draw down**.

   pull in   **1.** T (1)   After fishing for two hours he pulled in a big one. [He caught it on his line, and drew it in towards himself.]   **2.** T (1)   The police pulled him in for disturbing the peace. [Arrested him and took him to jail.]

   pull off   **1.** T (2)   He pulled off his sweater (his shoes, boots, trousers, etc.) and put on his pajamas. [Removed them by pulling.]   **2.** T (8)   Informal. Clyde pulled off three bank robberies in three days. [He succeeded in robbing three banks.]   **3.** T (8)   The two partners pulled off a big business deal (a merger, a shady deal, a clever trick, etc.) without anyone knowing about it. [Successfully completed it, perhaps dishonestly.]

   pull on   **1.** T (I 3)   He pulled on his boots and his sweater and went out to shovel snow. [Put them on by pulling.]   **2.** *pull-on* N.A.   (I 3)   A garment or other wearing apparel that has to be pulled on.

   pull out   **1.** T (1)   The car slid into a road-side ditch and had to be pulled out. [Out of the ditch.]   **2.** T (1)   The dentist pulled out two of Johnny's front teeth. [Extracted them.]

   pull over   **1.** T (3)   She reached for the lamp on the other side of the table and pulled it over towards her. [From one side to the other.]   **2.** *pull-over* N.A.   (5) A sweater or other garment that has to be pulled over the head. See **slip over**.

   pull through   T (4)   Albert nearly died of typhoid fever but Dr. Smith pulled him through. [Gave him treatment that made him well again.]

Pull II   To move as if being drawn or hauled. Arrive at a destination or result.

pull aside   I (1,2)   He saw a big truck coming towards him on the narrow road, so he pulled aside to let it pass. [Drove to one side, out of the way.]

pull around   I (3)   When the traffic cop saw a suspicious looking truck go by he pulled around and followed it. [Made a complete turn.]

pull away   I (1,2)   We pulled away at 6:30 a.m. [We drove away from the hotel or motel where we spent the night.]

pull back   **1.** I (3)   The troops pulled back from the hill they had captured the day before. [Back to a previous position.]   **2.** I (4)   Ext. After having agreed to joining in the demonstration, he pulled back from the idea. [He withdrew; he did not like the idea.]   **3.** *pull-back* N.   (1,4)   a. The act of pulling back. b. That which pulls back, or impedes its forward movement.

pull by   I (2)   We waited on the edge of the road and watched a long line of military trucks pull by. [Go past us.]

pull in   **1.** I (1)   The train (the bus, the boat, etc.) pulled in a half hour late. [Arrived.]   **2.** I (1)   Informal. I went to bed early last night. What time did you pull in? [Come home. Come into the house.]

pull off   **1.** I (1,2)   When are you pulling off? [What time do you leave?]   **2.** I (2)   The first man pulled off and hit the other one a blow with his fist. [He moved back far enough for a swing.] See **haul off.**

pull out   **1.** I (1)   The train (the bus, the ship, etc.) pulled out on time. [It left the station, the dock, etc.]   **2.** I (4)   Ext. After working for three years with that organization (company, group, political party, etc.) I decided to pull out. [Leave it, resign.]   **3.** *pull-out* N.A.   (4)   Aviation. A flight maneuver in which an aircraft levels into horizontal flight following a dive.

pull over   **1.** I (8)   The traffic cop who stopped us told us to pull over. [Over to the curb, to the side of the road.]   **2.** I (8)   When we heard the fire engine (the ambulance, the police patrol siren) we pulled over. [Moved into the slow lane.]

pull through   I (4)   John pulled through nicely after his operation, thanks to Dr. Wilson's good care. [He recovered, became well again.]

pull up   **1.** I (13)   We pulled up at the hotel an hour before dinner. [We came to a stop.] See **drive in, rein, roll up.**   **2.** I (1)   Weeds pull up easily after rain. [You can pull them out of the ground.]   **3.** *pull up (with)*   I (4,10)   We walked along slowly so our companions could pull up with us. [Come alongside of us.] See **catch up.**   **4.** *pull-up* N.A.   (1)   a. An exercise consisting of chinning oneself, as on a horizontal bar attached at each end to a post. b. Aviation. A flight maneuver in which an aircraft climbs sharply from level flight.

Put   To place in a specified position or relation.

put about   I (3)   Nautical. To change direction. When we saw the storm approaching, we put about and headed for the shore.

put across   T (1)   I hope I can put my ideas (my plan, my proposal, my point of view) across. [Get other people to understand it.] See **get across.**

put around   T (1,3)   She carried the presents to the Christmas tree and began to put them around. [Around the tree.]

put aside   **1.** T (1)   Put aside your homework and help me with the dishes. [Leave your homework.]   **2.** T (2)   Father had put aside a good deal of money for the children's education. [He put it in the bank, or made investments for that purpose.] See **set aside.**

put away   **1.** T (2,3)   She put her knitting away, for the moment, and answered the telephone. [She laid it aside.]   **2.** T (2,5)   Teach the children to put away their playthings before going to bed. [Put them in a special place.]   **3.** T (5) After his death they put all his things away in the attic.   **4.** T (5)   They are putting away something for a rainy day. [They are putting money in the bank or making investments.]   **5.** T (5)   He was mentally ill, so they had to put him away. [In a mental institution.]   **6.** T (5)   They put her away in Woodlawn Cemetery. [They buried her.]   **7.** T (5)   Informal. He put away a big meal last night. [He ate a large quantity of food.]

put back   **1.** I (3)   Nautical. The boat put back into the harbor. [It reversed its direction.]   **2.** T (5)   Put that back. It doesn't belong to you. [Return it to the place you took it from.]   **3.** T (1)   The dog put back his ears and began to growl. [Toward the rear.]   **4.** T (4)   Atomic war would put civilization back 10,000 years. [Return it to an earlier time.]   **5.** T (2)   Informal. That new overcoat put me back $60. [It reduced my finances that much.] See **set back. 6.** T (4)   I'll put you back on the line. [The telephone operator will give you your connection again.]

put by   **1.** T (3)   We need to put by something every month to take care of taxes. [Save some money.]

put down   **1.** I (1)   The plane put down at Ogden at 5:30. [It landed.]   **2.** T (1) Put Johnny down! He wants to play with the other children. [Don't hold him in your arms.]   **3.** T (1)   He put his book down and joined the conversation. [He placed it on the table, his lap, or somewhere.]   **4.** T (4)   The police put down the riot. [They controlled or stopped it.] See **stamp out, trample out. 5.** T (1) Informal. The athlete put down a big meal after the game. [He ate heartily.] See **put away 7. 6.** *put down (for)*   T (7)   How much shall I put you down for? Put me down for $100.00. [I pledge $100.00.] See **be down (for), set down, write down.**

put in   **1.** I (1)   Nautical. The boat will put in at Saybrook. [It will stop at that harbor.]   **2.** T (1)   He located the lock and put the key in. [Into the keyhole.] **3.** T (1)   Go to the door and put your head in. [Inside the door.]   **4.** T (1,5) How much do you want to put in? [Into a bank, a fund, a business deal, a company, etc.]   **5.** T (4)   The votes of the minority groups put him in. [Helped him win the election.]

put off   **1.** T (2)   When the train stopped the conductor put the children off. [Off the train.]   **2.** T (2)   Having put the newspapers off, the bus driver started his motor. [Off the bus.]   **3.** T (1)   Put those dishes off to one side. [Away from a point.]   **4.** T (4)   So few people came that we put the meeting off. [We postponed it.] See **hang over, put over. 5.** T (1)   She put me off, with a polite "No, thanks". [She kept me at a distance.]   **6.** T (1)   I was much put off by his remarks. [I was annoyed, perhaps deceived.]

put on   1. T (I 1)   When the bus stopped, we put our luggage on. [In the bus.] **2.** T (I 1)   Put your clothes on, it's time to leave. [On your body.]   **3.** T (I 1) Put the kettle on. We'll all have tea. [On the stove, the fire, the hot plate.] **4.** T (II 4)   Jones is putting on a new play. [On the stage.]   **5.** T (II 4)   Just a moment. I'll put you on. [On the telephone line. Said by the operator to the caller.]   **6.** T (II 5)   Informal. I think you are putting us on. [You are "kidding" us, deceiving us.] See **a put-on 8**.   **7.** T (II 5)   She puts on airs when she comes to our house. [She acts very superior.] See **put on 6**.   **8.** *put-on* N.   Informal. Now she's doing a put-on. [She is acting, putting on an act; pretending.] See **put on 7**.

put out   1. I (1)   Nautical. They put out to sea in very fair weather. [They went away from the shore.]   **2.** T (1)   Did you put the cat out? [Out of the house.]   **3.** T (1)   They were so noisy the barkeep put them out. [Out of the bar.]   **4.** T (10)   To signal a turn you should put your hand out. [Out of the car window.]   **5.** T (8)   Put the light out, please. I want to get to sleep. [Extinguish it.] See **II turn off 1**.   **6.** T (8)   You should always put out a blaze (a candle, a cigarette, a coal, an ember, a flame, a lamp, a pipe, a spark, or a torch) when there is danger of starting a forest fire.   **7.** T (8)   He often puts himself out to help his neighbors. [He goes out of his normal way to be helpful.] **8.** T (4)   Baseball. The catcher put the runner out at home plate. [Out of the game for one inning.]   **9.** *put-out* N.   (3,6)   Baseball. The catcher made the put-out. See **put out 8**.   **10.** *put out* A.   (6)   We were much put out when he failed to come. [We were annoyed, inconvenienced. We were out of good humor, out of our plans and hopes.]

put over   1. T (3)   She rode her horse up to the hurdle and put him over. [Made him jump the hurdle.]   **2.** T (3)   She held the bridle close to the horse's head and tried to put it over. [Over the head.]   **3.** T (8)   Mr. Brown put over a big business deal yesterday. [He succeeded, against some opposition.]   **4.** *put over (on)*   T (2)   Informal. He put one over on his opponents. [He did something clever, perhaps dishonest, to succeed.]   **5.** T (4)   We'll have to put the meeting over to next week. [Postpone it.] See **put off 4**.

put through   1. T (1)   She cut a hole in the cloth and put her hand through. [Through the cloth, the hole.]   **2.** T (2)   Please put this message through at once. [Send it by telephone or telegraph, through to the receiver.]   **3.** T (4) Our senator tried to put through a bill for pay increases. [Get the Congress to pass it.]

put under   1. T (1)   He walked to the table and put his hand under. [Under the table.] **2.** T (2)   Lift the patient's head so I can put the pillow under. [Under his head.]   **3.** T (4)   It took the doctors five minutes to put him under. [Under the influence of the anaesthetic.]

put up   **1.** I (3)   In Washington we put up at the Willard Hotel. [We stayed there during our trip.]   **2.** I (3)   We put up with some old friends in Seattle. [We stayed in their home.] See **hole up.**   **3.** T (1)   Put up your hands! [A robber speaking to his victim.]   **4.** T (1,4)   The Boy Scouts learned to put up their tents in a few minutes. [Make them stand up.]   **5.** T (2)   The storekeeper put up his prices on all electrical goods. [He raised them.]   **6.** T (3,11) Mother always used to put up tomatoes, corn, and peaches. [She preserved them in jars or cans.]   **7.** T (1,9,10)   His constituents wanted to put him up for governor. [They wanted to nominate him.]   **8.** T (3,11)   Before going to bed she would put her hair up in curlers.   **9.** T (9)   I'm planning to put my house up for sale. [Up before the public.]   **10.** T (3,10)   Can you put us up for the night? [Can you let us stay with you?]   **11.** T (1,7)   I hear that the May Company will put up a new building. [Build one.]   **12.** T (10)   John put up a thousand dollars to get a share in that business. [He offered that much.]   **13.** *put up (to)*   T (4)   I put it up to you. Shall we do it or not? [The decision is yours to make.]   **14.** T (4,6)   She put me up to saying those words. [She persuaded me.] Often referring to a bad action.   **15.** *put up (with)*   I (5)   I'll not put up with him any longer. [I want nothing to do with him. I don't want to be near him.] See **put up 2, 10.**   **16.** I (5)   You'll just have to put up with him. [You must accept him, and what he does.] See **bear up.**   **17.** [*put-up* A.   (7) Informal. I'd call that a put-up job. [I think there has been some trickery in what was done, in order to deceive us.]

Q

Queue   To form a line while waiting.

   queue up   I (3,11)   When we reached the theater, people were already queueing up at the ticket window. [Lining up, forming a waiting line.]

Quiet   To make or become quiet.

   quiet down   **1.** T (4,6)   The children are terribly noisy tonight. Can't you do something to quiet them down? [Make them be more quiet.]   **2.** I (4,6)   The children quieted down when grandmother said she would read them a story. [Became quiet.] See **hush up.**

R

Race   To engage in a contest of speed; run a race; run at high speed; engage someone in a race. May be used with all of the second elements to show the direction of the movement.

race around   T (3)   "I'll race you around", said Bill. [Run a race with you around the house (the race track, the city square, etc.).]

race back   T (3)   "I'll race you back", said Bill. [Run a race with you back to where we came from.]

Rack I   Pool. To put the balls in a rack.

rack up   T (3,10)   Before starting the next game Jack racked up the balls. [Put them in position for the game to start.]

Rack II   To draw off wine or cider from the lees.

rack off   T (7)   I think it's time to rack off the new batch of wine. [Remove it from its container, usually by siphoning and allowing the sediment to remain.]

Radio   To send a message by radio. May be used with many of the second elements to show the direction of the movement.

radio in   T (1,4)   The scout troops radioed in the position of the enemy patrol. [Sent the message in to headquarters.]

Raffle   To dispose of by a raffle, selling chances as in a lottery.

raffle off   T (1)   The Lion's Club is raffling off a Mustang convertible at the County Fair tomorrow. [Selling lottery tickets. The lucky ticket will win the Mustang.]

Railroad   To send or push forward with great or undue speed.

railroad through   T (4)   The Democratic Party leaders are trying to railroad through a new tax bill. [Doing everything possible to have it passed quickly by the legislature. Perhaps without much consideration for the opposition.]

Rain   To fall or cause to fall like rain.

rain down   **1.** I (1)   Ashes from the volcano rained down on the countryside, destroying much of the plant and animal life. [Came like rain from the skies.] **2.** T (5)   Ext. The prophet (the preacher, the priest, etc.) rained down curses on the heads of the wicked people of the land. [Called God's curses down from Heaven upon them.]

rain out   T (4)   The game (the contest, the race, the performance, the picnic) was rained out. [It rained so much, the game had to be abandoned, postponed.]

Raise   To elevate or lift up; bring to maturity.

raise up   **1.** T (1)   The nurse turned the crank on the hospital bed to raise the patient up to a sitting position. [Up from lying on his back.] **2.** I (1)   He raised up enough to see out of the window. [Up from a reclining position.] **3.** T (7)   God raised up prophets to lead His people in olden times. [Set them before the people, to lead them.] **4.** T (2,12)   It is hard to raise up a family in the slums. [Train the children to become good, useful citizens.] See **bring up.**

Rake   To gather or scratch with or as if with a rake.

rake in   **1.** T (1)   Gambling. The croupier raked in the chips and paid off the winners. [Drew the chips toward himself with his rake.] **2.** T (1)   Informal.

Mr. Allen marketed his invention and has been raking in a fortune ever since. [Taking in large profits.]

rake off **1.** T (2) Informal. The prosecuting attorney accuses him of raking off a cool million in his subway construction operations. [Taking that money illicitly from the public funds.] **2.** *rake-off* N.A. (2) a. A share or amount taken illicitly. as in connection with a public enterprise. See **rake off 1.** b. Slang. A share in the profits of a business or enterprise. c. A discount in the price of a commodity. Ex. My wife got a rake-off of 20% when she bought this refrigerator.

rake over T (3,8) Informal. When my wife learned I had spent $100 for a new hunting rifle she really raked me over. [Scolded me, criticized me severely.]

rake up T (3) Every time I rake up the leaves the wind blows and scatters them around again. [Rake them into piles.]

Ram To drive or force by heavy blows.

ram down T (1) To build the pier they first rammed down heavy pointed logs into the river bed. [Used a pile driver to drive them down.]

ram through T (4) Ext. The Senate liberals think they have enough votes to ram through the open housing bill. [Push it through to a successful vote.]

Rant To speak or declaim extravagantly or violently; talk in a wild or vehement way.

rant away I (6) When we came into the meeting a red-faced man was ranting away about the newest Supreme Court decision. [Talking wildly in opposition to the decision.]

rant on (and on) I (II 2) He tried to make his wife keep quiet, but she ranted on and on, for hours. [Kept talking angrily and violently.] See **rave on.**

Rap To strike, especially with a quick, smart, or light blow.

rap down T (1,4) The little man in the third row stood up to challenge the vote, but the chairman rapped him down. [Struck the table with his gavel to force him to sit down.] See **gavel down.**

rap out T (1,9) Ext. When the officer rapped out a command to the squad of soldiers they did an about face, and marched away. [Spoke quickly and sharply.]

Rasp To utter with a grating sound.

rasp out T (1,9) The sergeant rasped out an angry refusal when the private asked for a midnight pass. [Spoke harshly, in a raspy tone of voice.]

Rate To estimate the value or worth of something.

rate down T (6) Many people consider her to be the best actress in the movies today, but I would rate her down among the second best. [Consider her inferior to the best.]

rate up T (2) He used to be classed as a second rate artist, but the critics are now rating him up among the very best. [Calling him a first class artist.]

Rave To talk wildly, as in delirium.

rave on I (II 2) Informal. She couldn't stop talking about the wonderful time she had in New York. She raved on about it till we were worn out. [Talked enthusiastically and at length.] See **rant on.**

Reach   To stretch or hold out; extend.

reach around   I (1,2)   She got in the car and reached around for the seat belt. [Felt here and there with her hand to find it.]

reach back   I (1)   From the front seat of the car she reached back for her purse on the rear seat. [Extended her hand to pick up the purse.]

reach down   I (1)   From the pier he reached down to give a hand to the tired swimmer. [Take hold of the swimmer's hand to help him out of the water.]

reach in   I (1)   Opening the clothes closet door, she reached in to get her rain coat. [Extended her arm into the closet.]

reach out   T (10)   When we came into the living room the hostess reached out her hand to greet us. [Extended it.] See **stretch out.**

reach over   I (3)   As I took my seat at the theater someone reached over and touched my arm. [Over from several seats away.]

reach up   I (1)   My hat is on the top shelf. Will you please reach up and get it for me? [Extend your arm up to the shelf.]

Read   To peruse and apprehend the meaning of something written, printed, etc.

read back   T (5)   When I finished dictating the letter I asked the stenographer to read it back to me. [Repeat the letter aloud so I could make corrections or changes, etc.]

read down   I (1)   When we saw the list of club members we read down to see how many names were familiar to us. [We started at the top and looked down the list.]

read in   I (1,5)   Our son is learning how to read in at the computer training school. [Introduce information into a computer.] See **read out 3**.

read off   T (6)   The club secretary read off the names of those who had not paid their dues. [He read them from a list.]

read out   **1.** T (2)   The secretary read out the names of the new members. [Out in public.]   **2.** T (4)   Last night at a special meeting, James Nelson was read out of the party. [He was declared no longer a member, by the reading of a statement.]   **3.** I (6)   Our son will also learn how to read out. [Retrieve infor-formation from a computer.] See **read in**.

read over   **1.** T (2,6)   Will you please read over what I have written and tell me what you think of it? [Take time to read it.]   **2.** T (7)   I've read it over three times and I think it's very interesting. [Repeated the reading.]

read through   T (3)   I haven't had time to read it through yet, but will do it after dinner. [From beginning to end.]

read up (on)   I (2,11,12)   I'll have to read up on Russian history before we take our trip to the U.S.S.R. [Improve my knowledge of it.]

Ready   To make ready; prepare.

ready up   T (4,11)   Informal. The guest room has been readied up for the bride and groom. [Prepared to receive them.]

Rear   To rise on the hind legs, as a horse. In the folk speech sometimes heard as "rare".

   rear up   **1.** I (1)   The great stallion reared up, pawing the air with his fore legs. **2.** I (6)   Ext. Informal. When John was accused of betraying a family secret he reared up (on his hind legs) and denied it fiercely. [Showed hot resentment in his denial.]

Reason   To think or argue in a logical manner.

   reason out   T (7)   Now just reason it out. If Mother has to go to a meeting and I have to go back to the office, one of you will have to stay home and mind the baby. [Use logic. Use your head.]

   reason through   T (3)   After reasoning it through we reached the decision to keep our present system of operation. [Thinking carefully.] See **think through**.

Reckon   To count, compute, or calculate, as in number or amount.

   reckon back   I (4)   He reckoned back and decided that Mother was right. They had been here for two years when the flood occurred. [Counted the years carefully.]

   reckon up   T (4)   The two business partners reckoned up their accounts and then one of them withdrew from the business. [Made an accurate accounting.]

Redden   To become red in color; to blush.

   redden up   I (4)   The pretty teen-age girl reddened up when they asked her if she had ever been kissed by a boy. [She blushed.]

Reel   To pull or draw by winding a line on a reel, as in fishing.

   reel in   T (1)   I watched from the river bank as he reeled in a five pound trout. [Drew it in towards him by winding his reel.]

   reel off   T (10)   Ext. Informal. He is a very entertaining person. He can reel off stories (jokes, wise cracks, etc.) one after the other, and they're all amusing. [Tell them quickly and easily, the way a reel allows the line to unwind.]

   reel out   T (10)   When the big fish struck he reeled out his line to avoid having it break. See **pay out**.

Refer   To direct the attention or thoughts.

   refer back   **1.** T (5)   When I talked to the Dean about my failing grade in Chemistry he referred me back to the professor. [Told me to talk to the professor again.] **2.** I (1,2)   The note at the bottom of page 97 refers back to the first paragraph of Chapter II. [Calls attention to it.]

Rein   To check or guide (a horse or other animal) by exerting pressure on a bridle bit, by means of the reins.

   rein in   T (7)   The stagecoach driver reined in his horses when the bandits appeared suddenly on the road. [Pulled them to a halt.] See **pull up**.

Remain   To continue in the same state. May be used with all the second elements to indicate the position or state of the subject after having gone, come or been put in such a position or state. See **to be**.

Rent To grant the possession and enjoyment of property in return for a payment or payments to be made at agreed times.

    rent out **1.** T (2,5) After the children married and left home they rented out the upstairs bedrooms. [Made some money by taking in roomers.] **2.** *rent out* T (2,5) The farmer had two tractors which he sometimes rented out to neighboring farmers. [Charged them money for the use of the tractors.] See **hire out.**

Report To make a statement concerning something, to a person or persons in authority.

    report back **1.** I (3) The Bureau Chief told him to report back as soon as he had returned from Europe. [Appear personally at the Bureau.] **2.** T (3) It was his job to report back any information he gathered about the race riots. [Do the work of a reporter. Send news items to the editors of the paper.]

    report in I (1) When Jones reports in, tell him to come to my desk. [When he comes to work, or returns from an assignment.]

Rest To refresh oneself, as by sleeping, lying down, or relaxing.

    rest up I (4) We had to rest up before dinner after the hard day's driving (the heavy garden work, the long walk through the woods, etc.). [Relax for a while.]

Return I. To go or come back as to a former place, position, state, etc.

    T. To put, bring, take, give, or send back to the original place, owner, etc.

In the folk speech the Latin origin of this verb is not felt. The Latin prefix "re" signified "back", but the folk speech makes use of the element "back" to indicate a complete, perhaps permanent, return.

    return back **1.** I (3) Mr. Jones is returning back to San Francisco after living in the East for two years as company representative. [He will be permanently located in San Francisco.] **2.** T (5) You have no right to keep that book. You should return it back to the original owner. [Put it in his possession.] Said of a book that has been loaned to a third party.

Rev To accelerate sharply the speed of an engine, or other device. [An abbreviation of the noun "revolution".]

    rev up **1.** T (2) He revved up the motor and listened carefully to check for faulty spark plugs. [Increased the speed.] **2.** T (2,5) Ext. Candidate McCarthy's young supporters, spurred on by the victory in Oregon, said they would rev up the campaign in California. [Increase the speed and intensity of their efforts.]

Revert To return to a former habit, practice, belief, custom, condition, etc.

    revert back I (4) After gaining their independence some of the new African nations reverted back to a state of turmoil, due to ancient tribal rivalries. [Returned to that state.] See **return back 1**.

Rid To clear, disencumber, or free of something objectionable.

    rid out T (1,9) Mother spent the morning ridding out the closets and cupboards during her spring housecleaning. [Removing unwanted objects.] See **clear out.**

    rid up T (1,9) Mother asked Father to rid up the attic, and throw away all of the useless stuff that had accumulated over the years. [Clear out the unwanted objects.] See **clear out 1.**

Ride I   To be carried on the back of an animal or in a vehicle. May be used with all the second elements to show the direction of the movement.

ride off   I (1,2)   They rode off in a brand new convertible. [Departed.]

ride up   I (13)   She rode up on a beautiful black thoroughbred. [Came to a stop near us.]

Ride II   To carry a person on something (as a horse, an automobile, a bicycle, or other conveyance). May be used with all the second elements to show the direction of the movement.

ride around   T (2)   He rode his little sister around on his bike. [Took her for a ride.]

ride back   T (3)   They walked over the bridge to our house and we rode them back in our new station wagon. [Returned them to their home.]

Ride III   To perform with or as if with a conveyance under control.

ride down   **1.** T (1)   The man on horseback spurred his mount towards the leader of the mob and rode him down. [Knocked him to the ground by bringing his horse in contact with him.]   **2.** T (4,5)   The sheriff's posse pursued the fleeing bank robber and finally rode him down before he could cross the river. [Caught up with him. Overtook him.]

ride out   **1.** T (10)   Marine. The ship had difficulty riding out the storm, which was one of the worst of the season. [Remaining afloat on the surface of the water.]   **2.** T (10)   Ext. The French government is searching for changes in policy that will help it to ride out the series of violent demonstrations and strikes that threaten it. [Remain in control.]

Rig   To put in proper order for working or use.

rig out   T (7)   The Watson Sporting Goods Store told him they could rig him out for the summer cruise. [Supply him with the clothing and equipment necessary.]

rig up   **1.** T (7)   John is very clever with his hands. He can rig up a sail, a mowing machine, a canoe, a moose trap; anything you can think of. [Equip and set it up for use.]   **2.** T (7)   Ext. I'm suspicious of those two fellows. I think they're rigging up a plot to take over the meeting. [Doing the secret planning necessary to gain control.]

Rile   To cause (water) to become muddied, raily; to irritate or vex.

rile up   **1.** (4)   The waters of the brook were all riled up after the heavy storm. [They were muddied.]   **2.** *riled up* A.   (2,4)   James is all riled up over something. Do you know what's wrong? [His emotions are stirred. He is excited, angry.] See **roil up.**

Ring   To give forth a clear, resonant sound, as a bell when struck.

ring back   T (5)   Telephone. I'm sorry I can't talk to you now. We're just sitting down to dinner. I'll ring you back. [I'll call you (return your call) later.]

ring down   **1.** T (1)   Theater. When one of the actors became ill on the stage the manager gave the order to ring down the curtain. [Lower the curtain.] In early days the signal was given by the ringing of a bell. **2.** T (4) Theater. Ext. They rang down the curtain just before midnight. [The show came to an end. The curtain was lowered.] **3.** *ring down (on)* T (1) The recently announced Supreme Court decision rings down the curtain on various abuses of power by the police. [Brings an end to them.]

ring in T (1) Crowds always gather at Broadway and Forty-Second Street to ring the New Year in. [Celebrate the coming of the New Year with bells, horns and noise-makers of many sorts.]

ring off **1.** I (4) Telephone. She talked for half an hour before she rang off. [Stopped talking and hung up the receiver.] **2.** I (4) Ring off! Will you? [Impolite way of telling a person to stop talking.] See **shut up**.

ring on I (II 2) The phone (the bells) rang on for five minutes. [Continued to ring.]

ring out **1.** I (2) The church bells ring out on Christmas Day. [Out in public.] **2.** I (9) His voice rang out over the crowd as he appealed to them for their support. [Sounded loud and clear.]

ring up T (14) I'll ring you up as soon as I hear any further news about the wedding. [Give you a ring. Call you. Call you up.]

Rinse To wash lightly, as by pouring water into or over, or by dipping in water.

rinse off T (7) You should always rinse off the plates before putting them in the automatic dishwasher. [Remove matter that is on the surface by pouring water over the plates.]

rinse out **1.** T (1) It is a good idea to rinse out the tea towels (the coffee pot, the wash bowl, the bathtub, etc.) as soon as you finish using them. [Wash them lightly with clean water.] **2.** T (1) She puts her washing through two waters to rinse out the soap (the detergent).

Rip To cut or tear apart in a rough or vigorous manner.

rip away T (3) It is time to rip away the masks of those who pretend to be our friends, and see them as they really are. [Expose them as one would by removing a mask.]

rip down T (1,5) When our troops captured the enemy stronghold they ripped down their flag and put up our own. [Tore it from its place.]

rip off **1.** T (1) He ripped off his shirt and threw it on the floor. [Pulled it off in a violent manner.] **2.** T (9) Ext. He ripped off a string of oaths that made the ladies blush. [Uttered them angrily, and loudly, one after the other.]

rip out **1.** T (1) Mother ripped out the lining of her last winter's coat and put in another. [Cut the stitching to remove it.] **2.** T (1) In ancient warfare the victorious soldiers would at times rip out the bowels of their enemies. [Use swords and daggers to cut open their bellies.] **3.** T (9) He ripped out an oath as he lunged towards his assailant. [Uttered one oath, violently and loudly.] See **rip off 2**.

rip up **1.** T (2,4) The nurse ripped up an old sheet to make bandages. [Tore it into many pieces.] **2.** T (6) The plane that crashed yesterday ripped up a corn field not far from town. [Tore up the soil and did much damage.]

Ripen To make or become ripe.

  ripen through I (1) That pineapple is too green to eat now. Wait till it ripens through. [Becomes ripe all the way through.]

  ripen up I (4,11) The peaches we bought for canning are still hard. We'll let them ripen up a bit. [Get ripe enough for canning.]

Rise To become active in opposition or resistance; rebel against something.

  rise up **1.** I (5,10) After years of suffering, the people suddenly rose up against the dictator and threw him out. [Started a rebellion.] **2.** I (1) Several people rose up in meeting to protest against the unfair decisions of the chairman. [Stood up to speak against his actions.]

Roar I To utter a loud, deep cry or howl, as in excitement, distress, anger, gaiety, etc.

  roar out I (9) He roared out in pain as the doctor twisted his arm to put his shoulder back in place. [Uttered a loud cry.]

Roar II To function or move with a loud, deep sound; as a locomotive, automobile, truck, etc. May be used with most of the second elements to indicate the direction of the movement.

  roar by I (2) We waved to the soldiers as the train roared by. [Went past us with a roar.]

  roar off I (1,2) At the starting gun the racing cars roared off. [Started the race with a roar.]

  roar through I (1) The huge trucks roared through all night long. [Through the village (the gate, the forest, etc.).]

Roil To render (water, wine, etc.) cloudy by stirring up sediment.

  roil up T (6) Two big dogs had been splashing around in the pool. They roiled up the water so badly we couldn't see the goldfish. [Caused the water to be muddied.] See **rile up.**

Roll I To move along a surface by revolving or turning over and over, as a ball or wheel. May be used with all the second elements, both transitively and intransitively, to indicate the direction of the movement.

  Ex. I. The ball rolled about. [Here and there.]

  T. We rolled the ball about. [Here and there.]

  I. Ol' Man River just keeps rollin' along. [Continues to roll.] From a popular song.

  T. Roll out the barrel. [Out from storage, or from the inn.] From a popular song.

  T. Ext. The Democratic candidate rolled up a big majority. [Won the election by much more than half the votes cast.]

Roll II To move in some direction in a vehicle on wheels. May be used with all the second elements to indicate the direction of the movement.

roll in I (1)   What time did you roll in? [Get to your destination.] See **get in 2**.

roll up I (13)   We were leaving the house just as they rolled up. [Reached our house and stopped in front of it.] See **pull up**.

Roof   To provide or cover with a roof.

roof over T (2)   They roofed over their terrace with plastic, to make an outdoor living room. [Built a roof over the terrace.]

Root I   To turn up the soil with or as if with the snout.

root about/around 1. I (2)   The pigs were rooting about in the orchard looking for mushrooms and succulent roots. [Here and there.] **2.** I (2)   Informal. Dagwood was rooting around in the refrigerator to find things to make a sandwich with. [Hunting, looking into various containers and packages.]

root up 1. T (1)   In France, farmers train pigs to root up truffles. [Dig them up with their snouts.] **2.** T (1)   The pigs had gotten out of their pen and were in the vegetable garden rooting up all the newly planted seeds. [Turned up the seeds with their snouts.] **3.** T (6)   When the family returned they found the pigs had rooted up the entire garden plot. [Turned the soil up with their snouts.]

Root II (1)   To take root or form roots. (2)   To remove by the roots. In its second meaning the verb is often confused with **I root.**

root down 1. I (1)   The shrubs we planted two weeks ago are beginning to root down. [They are sending roots down into the soil.] **2.** *rooted down* A. (1) Ext. I think the Wilson's will never come back to Omaha. They seem to be rooted down in California. [They have sent down roots there. They are permanently established.] **3.** (5)   Ext. Those people are so rooted down in their prejudices, it's no use arguing with them. [Their opinions are fixed, unchangeable.]

root out 1. T (1,9)   It took him three days to root out the tall weeds that grew up in his garden while he was on vacation. [Remove them by pulling or digging them up by the roots.] **2.** T (9)   Ext. The committee says that it is determined to root out all subversive and disloyal employees from the government. [Remove them by exposing them.] **3.** T (9)   Ext. It should be the responsibility of every citizen to help the police root out crime in our cities. [Remove it by exposing it and taking action against it.]

root up T (4)   Sage brush has very long roots. It requires deep plowing to root it up. [Up from below the soil.]

Rope   To pull, bind or fasten with or as if with rope.

rope in 1. T (1)   Informal. The swindler roped in at least twenty unsuspecting investors before he was exposed. [Persuaded them to invest some money in stock that had no value or that was fraudulent.] [The expression probably comes from the roping or lassoing of cattle by a cowboy.] **2.** T (4)   Maybe you can rope in a few of your young friends to help with the decorating of the gymnasium. [Persuade them to join you in your project.]

rope off T (3)   The police roped off a space in front of the platform for special guests. [Used ropes to enclose the space.] See **map off**.

rope on   T (I 1)   They put the canoe on top of the car and roped it on securely. [Fastened it with rope.]

rope up   T (3)   They threw the captured bandit to the ground and roped him up. [Tied ropes around him so that he couldn't move.]

Rot   To undergo decomposition; decay.

rot away   I (3,4)   The front door-step of the old house had rotted away. [It was no longer useable; was not attached to the doorway.]

rot down   I (1,2)   The stump of the big oak tree that used to stand in the front yard had rotted down, so we dug it out and planted an elm. [Decayed sufficiently to make it easy to remove.]

rot off   I (2)   That tree hasn't long to live. Several branches have already rotted off. [Died and fallen off.]

Rough I   To handle roughly, give a beating to.

rough up   T (6)   The angry mob broke up the meeting and began roughing up the speaker. [Pushing him in a rough manner, perhaps beating him.]

Rough II   To make a plan, outline, or design in unfinished, incomplete fashion.

rough in   **1.** T (2)   The artist roughed in the outline of the human figures on the canvas to give us a general idea of the composition of the painting. [Drew the figures with light strokes.]   **2.** T (6)   The novelist roughed in the conversation in his new novel. [Put it in in sketchy, tentative form.]

rough out   T (7)   The architect roughed out a diagram for the location of buildings in the proposed city park. [Drew lines and put in marks to show the possible locations of the buildings.]

Roughen   To make or become rough or rougher.

roughen up   **1.** T (6)   The snowfall and the freezing temperature had roughened up the surface of the outdoor skating rink. [Made it uneven, rough.]   **2.** *roughened up* A.   (6)   Her hands had become all roughened up from so much garden work and dishwashing. [They had lost their smoothness.]

Round   To make round.

round off   **1.** T (1,7)   We asked the carpenter who was building our kitchen cabinets to round off all the corners. [Make the corners curved, not sharp.]   **2.** T (7) The students in the math class were told to round off all the figures in their final calculations. [Eliminate the fractions, leaving a whole number.]   **3.** T (7) When multiplying, we were told to round off the product. [Express it as a round number, usually the closest multiple of 10.]

round out   **1.** I (11)   As a teen-ager Alice was very thin, but she's rounding out as she grows older. [Putting on weight, filling out.] See **plump out**.   **2.** T (7)   Mrs. Roberts is rounding out her collection of antiques by some purchases she made in Boston. [Making it more complete.]   **3.** T (11)   The president rounded out his White House Staff by making three new appointments last week. [Filled three vacancies; added three staff members.]

round up   **1.** T (3,10)   The cowboys are out on the range rounding up the cattle.

[Gathering them into herds and driving them to the corrals.] **2.** T (10,11) It's getting dark. We'd better round up the children and start for home. [Find them and get them together.] Said at a picnic, outing, etc. **3.** T (4,10) The police were given orders to round up all the suspicious characters who might endanger the President's life. [Take them into custody.] **4.** T (4,10,11) John is out rounding up support for the new golf course. [Finding people who will approve and help finance it.]

Rouse To bring out of a state of sleep, unconsciousness or inactivity; to stir or incite to strong indignation or anger.

rouse out T (1) It's nine o'clock, and the people in the next cabin show no signs of life. I'm going over and rouse them out. [Wake them up, and get them started on the day's activities.]

rouse up T (2,5,10) The agitators were doing their best to rouse up the townspeople to demand better sanitation service. [Stir their emotions and their will to act.]

Rout To cause to rise from bed.

rout out T (1) At the ranch they routed us out at 5:30 in the morning for breakfast. [Made us get up at that time.]

Route To arrange a tour; to send or forward by a particular route.

route back T (3) The travel agent routed us back through Yellowstone Park. [Planned our return trip to include a visit to the park.]

route out T (1) The travel agent routed us out by way of Canada. [Planned our trip to the West so that we went through Canada.]

Rub To subject the surface of something to pressure and friction, as in cleaning, smoothing, polishing, etc.

run down **1.** T (1,5) Father rubbed the antique table down with sandpaper before giving it a coat of varnish. [Removed the old paint or varnish by rubbing.] **2.** T (1,5) After the race the stable boys rub down the horses. [Remove the sweat and dirt from them by rubbing with sponges, straw, etc.] **3.** T (1,5) Part of the duty of a trainer is to rub down the athletes after sports events. [Give them a massage to relieve muscle strain, and relax the body.] **4.** *rub-down* N. (1,5) The action of rubbing down horses, athletes, etc. See **rub down 2, 3**.

rub in **1.** T (2) In giving a facial massage the barber rubs in a rolling massage cream after applying hot towels to the face. [Rubs the cream into the pores of the skin with his hands.] **2.** T (2) Slang. I know I played that hand badly but don't rub it in. [Don't keep talking about it; criticizing my playing of the cards.]

rub off **1.** T (1) The teacher wrote one problem on the blackboard, then rubbed it off to make room for another. [Erased it.] **2.** T (1) He rubbed off the sweat from his forehead with his sleeve. [Removed it by a rubbing movement.] **3.** I (1) Mother was furious when the varnish on the newly finished chair rubbed off on her best dress. [Became attached to the dress by friction.] **4.** I (8) Ext. I hope that some of the good manners of the Smith children will rub off on our youngsters. [I hope that by associating with the Smith children, our children will learn good manners.]

rub on   T (I 1)   He rubbed on liniment to take the soreness out of his shoulder. [Used friction to make the liniment penetrate to the muscles.]

rub out   **1.** T (9)   She found she had made a mistake in addition, so she rubbed out the figures and started over again. [Erased them.]   **2.** T (8)   Slang. The leader of the gang gave orders to rub out the member who was suspected of being a stooge. [Murder the man who was thought to be working secretly for the police or for another gang.] See **bump off.**

Ruff   Cards: to trump, when unable to follow suit.

ruff out   T (10)   The dummy held four trumps, so he was able to ruff out his diamonds. [Lead his diamonds and trump them all in the dummy.]

Rule   To exercise authority; govern.

rule out   **1.** T (8)   The faculty ruled out smoking in the classrooms. [Declared that smoking would not be permitted.]   **2.** T (4,9)   Sports. The referee (the umpire) ruled out the last play. [Said that it should not be counted.]   **3.** T (4,9) You say that you are looking for a good bridge player? That rules me out. [The fact that I am not a good player excludes me from your group.]   **4.** T (9) When we were discussing where to send Henry to college, Father ruled out California. [Excluded that state from the possibilities.]   **5.** T (9)   Do you think Mr. Brown will run for Senator again? I wouldn't rule that out as a possibility. [Exclude it from the realm of possibility.]

Rumple   To ruffle, tousle, put in disorder.

rumple up   T (6)   His girl friend liked to rumple up his hair, just to tease him. [Make it look uncombed, disordered.] See **muss up.**

Run   The verb "run" has a long history in the English language. It has acquired many different meanings and uses. A recent unabridged dictionary has 116 separate paragraphs listing the various meanings and uses. In this dictionary the uses of "run" as a two-word verb have been organized into three main groups. Group I (1) shows the earliest meaning. Group I (2) shows an extension of that meaning. Group II gives a still wider extension, and Group III the more modern pattern of usage. Groups I and II show the intransitive patterns, and Group III the transitive patterns. Careful study and repeated practice of the example sentences will give a good understanding of the two-word verb as it has developed in English.

Run I   (1)   To go faster than a walk, with springing steps so that for an instant in each step all feet are off the ground.

This is the original meaning of the verb. It may be used in this meaning with all the second elements, to indicate the direction of the movement.

run about/around   I (1)   The children were running about in their bathing suits. [Here and there.]

run away   **1.** I (2)   He ran away when I called to him. [Away from me.]   **2.** I

(4,6)   As she was riding in the park her horse was frightened by an explosion and ran away. [Got out of control and ran, fast and furiously.]

run back   I (3)   She ran back to her mother. [To the person from whom she went away.]   (2)   To move quickly; make a quick trip or a short stay; associate freely.

run along   **1.** I (3)   Run along now, children. I want to talk to your father. [Leave us now, and don't come back for a while.]   **2.** I (1)   I have to be running along. I must have dinner ready by six o'clock. [Leave immediately.]

run around   **1.** I (1)   Run around to the grocery store and get a loaf of bread and some milk. [Go quickly. Around the corner.]   **2.** I (1)   We'll run around to see you before you leave. [Make a quick visit to your place from our house.]   **3.** I (5)   The children are running around with a group of young people I don't approve of. [Spending a lot of time in their company.]   **4.** I (5)   James Wilson is running around with another man's wife. [He is having a love affair with her.]   **5.** *run-around* N.   (3)   Informal. I asked the boss for a raise, and he gave me the run-around. [He did not say yes or no. He treated me evasively.]

run away   **1.** I (2,3)   I'll have to run away now. I'll come back later to see how you are getting along. [Leave at once.]   **2.** I (2,3)   When Robert was six years old he ran away from home twice. [Left home and did not intend to return.]   **3.** *run away (with)*   I (2,4)   Our neighbor's daughter ran away with the captain of the football team. [She eloped with him.]   **4.** I (2,4)   The bank cashier ran away with $20,000 in cash and bonds. [He absconded; stole the money and the bonds.]   **5.** I (2)   Our oldest daughter ran away with the first prize in the Beauty Show. [She won it easily.] See **run off with, skip out**.   **6.** *runaway* N. (2,4)   a. One who runs away; fugitive; deserter. b. A horse or team that has broken away from control. c. An act of running away. d. A film produced abroad by a U.S. company.   **7.** *runaway* A.   (2,4)   a. Having run away; escaped: become a fugitive. [Runaway prisoner]. b. Having escaped from control of the rider or driver. [Runaway horse.] c. Pertaining to or accomplished by running away or eloping. [Runaway bride.] d. Easily won, as a contest. [A runaway victory at the polls.] e. Of, pertaining to or characteristic of a film produced abroad by a U.S. company. f. Commerce. Characterized by a rapid uncontrolled price rise. [Runaway inflation.]

run back   I (3)   I believe I left my purse at the Smith's. I'll run back and get it. [Return there quickly.]

run down   I (1)   When we're in Boston we'll run down to New York to see a play or two. [Make a quick visit.] [Down from North to South.]

run in   I (1)   If you are ever in this part of town I hope you'll run in for a little visit. [Spend a short time with us; make a social call.] See **drop in**.

run off   **1.** I (1,2)   Don't run off! I have so many things to tell you. [Don't leave so soon!]   **2.** *run off (with)*   I (2,3)   The treasurer ran off with $10,000 worth of bonds. [Escaped with them.]   **3.** I (1,2)   John Jones ran off with our neighbor's daughter. [Eloped.] See **run away (with)**.

180

run on I (II 3)   I have to run on now. My husband is waiting for me at the office. [Leave at once.]

run out I (1)   The Nelsons have a new home in the suburbs. We must run out to see them one of these days. [Make a quick trip.]

run over I (3)   The Nelsons have bought a home in New Jersey. We must run over to see them one of these days. [Over the Hudson River from New York City.]

run through **1.** I (3)   Theater. When several of the actors missed their cues in the second scene the director had them run through again. [Repeat the scene.] **2.** *run-through* N. (3) a.   The performance of a series of actions as a trial practice or rehearsal for the final performance.   b.   A quick outline or review. Ex. The surgeon gave his assistants a run-through of the medical history of the patient.

run up **1.** I (1)   When we're in New York we'll run up to Boston for a few days. [Make a short trip.] [Up from South to North.] **2.** I (13)   As we were leaving the party Alice ran up to remind us of the dinner at her house. [Came quickly to us.] **3.** *run-up* N. (9) Sports. a.   The running up to the jump line by a broad jumper.   b.   The running up of the ball in soccer or polo, towards the goal.   c.   The running up of a golf ball towards the putting green. **4.** *runner-up* N. (9,10)   The competitor, player or team finishing in second place as in a race, contest, tournament, election, etc.

Run II   To move on or as if on wheels; pass or slide freely. (Used of motor or spring-driven devices, moving liquids, wind, time, etc.)

run about **1.** I (1,2)   The robot machine ran about over the floor, guided by the electric signals given to it by the inventor. [Here and there.] **2.** *run-about* N.A. (1,2) a.   A small, light automobile or other vehicle, usually with an open top; a roadster.   b.   A small pleasure motorboat.   c.   One who roves around from place to place, or group to group.

run away **1.** I (4,6)   The locomotive ran away when the engineer dropped dead from a heart attack. [Ran without control.] **2.** *runaway* N.A. (2,6)   The runaway locomotive was finally stopped by the brakeman.

run down **1.** I (1)   Water from a leak in the roof ran down onto the living room floor. [Down from the roof.] **2.** I (4,6)   His watch had run down, so he didn't know what time it was. [The spring had unwound. The watch had stopped.] **3.** *run-down* A. (4,6)   His watch was run-down. [The spring was unwound; it was not functioning.]

run in I (1)   When the flood waters reached the door sill they ran in, and soon the floors were covered with a foot of water. [Into the house.]

run off **1.** I (1)   She spilled hot water on the stove and it ran off onto the floor. [Off the stove.] **2.** *run-off* N. (1,2)   The spring run-off has begun, and the river is at flood stage. [Water from melting snow in the mountains is draining down to the river.]

run on **1.** I (II 1,2)   Time was running on and still the meeting had not begun.

[The hour was getting late.] **2.** I (II 1,2) The years run on so swiftly, and we are old before we know it. [Pass quickly.] **3.** I (II 1,2) The lecture ran on for almost two hours. [It continued.] **4.** I (II 2) The speaker ran on (and on). We thought he would never stop. [He kept talking for a long time.]

run out **1.** I (1) Johnny upset the milk pitcher and the milk ran out all over the table. [Out of the pitcher.] **2.** I (8) Our milk (coffee, sugar, paper, money, etc.) has run out. [We have used all of it. There is no more.] **3.** I (8) Time is running out. [There will soon be no more time for what we want to do.] **4.** I (8) My subscription to *Time* runs out next month. [It will be finished then.] **5.** *run out (of)* I (8) We are running out of milk (coffee, sugar, paper, money, etc.). [The supply of them is almost ended.] **6.** I (8) We are running out of time. [There will soon be no time left.] **7.** *run out (on)* I (1,5) He ran out on his wife. [He abandoned her; left home for good.]

run over **1.** I (3,5) The water in the pitcher (the pail, the cup, etc.) ran over. [Over the edge and down.] **2.** I (3) Ext. The pitcher (the pail, the cup, etc.) ran over. [The water in it ran over and down.] **3.** I (3) Ext. Her cup of happiness was running over. [She was extremely happy.] **4.** I (4) The lecture (the class, the performance, etc.) ran over at least a quarter of an hour. [It lasted a quarter of an hour longer than expected.]

run up **1.** I (2) Our expenses on our vacation ran up higher than we expected. [Became greater.] **2.** I (13) Johnny's temperature ran up to 100 degrees last night. [Mounted to that level.]

Run III To produce an act or effect by applying motive power. For instance, to deliver, chase or collide with someone or something. The force may be applied by a person (or other animal), a self-propelled vehicle, forces of nature, circumstances, etc.

run around T (3) Mother asked me to run the car around for her before I left. [From the rear of the house to the front.]

run away T (1,2) We trained our shepherd dog to run the chickens away from the vegetable garden. [Chase them off. Keep them at a distance.]

run back **1.** T (3) Football. At the kick-off our quarter-back ran the ball back fifty yards. [Back towards the goal line of the opponents.] **2.** T (3) You can come to our house by the bus. I'll run you back after dinner. [Take you in my car back to your house.] **3.** *run-back* N. a. (3) Football. 1) A run made by a player towards the goal line of the opponents, after receiving a kick, intercepting a pass, or recovering an opponent's fumble. 2) The distance covered in making such a run. b. (2) Tennis. The space on a tennis court, between the base line and the back stop.

run down **1.** T (1) The driver of the car (the truck, etc.) ran down an old lady who was crossing the street. [Struck her and knocked her down.] See **run over 4.** **2.** T (4) The police ran down the criminal (the runaway horse, the escaped animal, etc.). [They pursued and captured the criminal, etc.] **3.** T (4)

Baseball. The second baseman, the third baseman and the shortstop ran down the base runner. [Chased him and tagged him with the ball.]   **4.** T (4)   John spent the evening in the library running down information on the proposed tax increase. [Searching, trying to find it.]   **5.** T (2,6)   That woman makes me furious. She's always running down her neighbors. [Criticizing them; saying bad things about them.]   **6.** *run-down* N.   (4)   a. This brief run-down of the events of last night may help you to make your decision. [A quick review of the main points of the happenings.] b. Baseball. A play in which a base runner is caught between bases by two or more players of the opposing team.   **7.** *run-down* A. (2,6)   a. She looks terribly run-down. She should see a doctor. [Weary, exhausted, tired.] b. He was in a run-down condition from months of overwork. [In poor health.] c. The house they bought was badly run-down. They spent a lot of money making repairs. [In neglected condition, in disrepair.]

run in   **1.** T (1)   Informal. The old drunkard was shouting and swearing in the middle of the street. The police ran him in for disturbing the peace. [Took him to jail.]   **2.** *run-in* N.   (8)   James had a run-in with the school principal about his conduct in the laboratory. [A sharp exchange of words; a quarrel.]   **3.** (5) Printing. Material that is added to a text, especially without indenting for a new paragraph. An insertion.

run off   **1.** T (1,2)   Some gypsies had parked their wagons in one of Mr. Brown's fields. He got the sheriff to run them off. [Away from the field.]   **2.** T (8)   The office manager had the duplicating service run off 200 copies of the price list. [Reproduce them from the original copy.]   **3.** T (8)   Our young composer friend ran off a new song for the company show. [Composed it quickly, easily.] **4.** *run-off* N.A.   (5)   a.   A final contest held to determine the victor, after earlier contests have eliminated the weaker contestants.   b.   A deciding final contest held after one in which there has been no decisive victor as between two contestants who have tied for first place.

run on   T (2)   Dictionaries usually run on idiomatic phrases following the main entry. [Add them at the end.]

run out   **1.** T (1,2)   The angry citizens ran the confidence man out of town. [Forced him to leave in a hurry.]   **2.** T (7)   He ran the figures out to the fourth decimal point. [Made the calculation to that point.]

run over   **1.** T (4)   The news story was too long for one column. The type-setter had to run it over to the next column (page, section, etc.). [Finish the story in the next column.]   **2.** T (3,7)   To pack the soil down firmly he ran it over several times with his tractor. [Drove over it with the purpose of doing something to it.] Note. If you say, "He ran over it", you use over as a preposition showing direction. It does not express purpose or determination.   **3.** T (7)   They ran the record (the tape) over several times to make sure they understood the words. [Repeated the action.]   **4.** T (5)   The cat was run over by a car. [The car rolled over the cat's body.] **5.** *run-over* N. (4) Printing. Type matter for a given article (story, column, etc.) that exceeds the space allotted for it.

run through **1.** T (1) The more skillful of the duellists finally found an opening, and ran his opponent through. [So that the point appeared on the other side of his body.] **2.** T (2) Better run the car through the car wash before the trip. [Move it mechanically.] **3.** T (3) Theater. At the final rehearsal the director had us run the last scene through four times. [Play it from beginning to end.]

run up **1.** T (2) The wage increase granted to the union members will run up costs considerably. [Increase the cost of things manufactured.] **2.** T (2) While he was in college he ran up large bills (debts) at many of the local shops. [Increased his indebtedness greatly.] **3.** T (1,7) They have torn down many old houses and are running up high-rise apartments. [Building them hurriedly.] See **throw up 5.** **4.** T (7,11) Mother is going to run up some curtains for the living room before the guests arrive. [Sew them rapidly to have them ready.]

Rustle To find, gather, or assemble by effort or search.

rustle up T (7,11) Informal. I'm hungry. Do you think we could rustle up something to eat? [Find something in the refrigerator or cupboards.]

S

Sack To put into a sack or sacks.

sack out I (9) Slang. I'm very tired. I think I'll sack out. [Go to bed, go to sleep.] The meaning is the same as in the slang expression "Hit the sack." Sack is slang for mattress.

sack up T (3) The grocery clerk was in the back room sacking up potatoes. [Putting them in sacks.] See **bag up**.

Saddle To put a saddle on a horse.

saddle up T (4,11) The stable boy was told to saddle up six horses for the riding party. [Have them ready by putting saddles on them.]

Sag To sink or bend downward by weight or pressure.

sag down I (1) The car sagged down under the weight of six passengers and all their luggage. [The springs bent, letting the car body down.]

Sail To travel in a vessel conveyed by the action of wind, steam, etc.; to move in a manner suggesting sailing. May be used with all of the second elements transitively or intransitively to indicate the direction of the movement.

Salt To season with salt; **to** cure, preserve, or treat with salt.

salt away **1.** T (5) Early settlers on the American plains would salt away buffalo meat for their winter food supply. [Preserve it with salt, and store it.] **2.** T (5) Ext. Robert is salting away half of his weekly pay check to help pay for his college expenses. [Putting it in the bank.]

salt down   T (1)   Sauerkraut is made by salting down raw cabbage in vats or crocks. [Adding a thin layer of salt to each layer of shredded cabbage.]

salt out   T (1)   To separate a dissolved substance from a solution by the addition of salt.

Sand   To smooth or polish with sand, sandpaper, or some other abrasive material.

sand down   T (1,6)   After sanding down the antique table, Father gave it a coating of wax. [Removing old paint and imperfections by rubbing with sandpaper.] See **smooth down.**

Save   To keep, retain for a purpose.

save out   T (4)   When you give away the peaches, be sure to save out enough for our own use. [Keep them.]

save up   **1.** I (5,11)   Mary is saving up to buy a tape recorder. [Putting money aside.]   **2.** I (2,11)   Don't work so hard! You'd better save up for the party tonight. [Save your strength, your energy.]

Saw   To cut with, or as with a saw.

saw off   **1.** T (2)   I wish you would saw off that big branch that hangs over the front door. [Remove it by sawing.]   **2.** *sawed-off* A. (2)   a. Having a very short barrel. [Gangsters make use of sawed-off shotguns to rub out (eliminate, kill) their enemies.] b. Informal. Short. [He was a sawed-off, skinny little runt. He was very short and thin.]

saw through   T (1)   The branch fell with a crash when he sawed it through. [Made a cut through the branch.]

saw up   T (2,11)   When we reached camp, Jack got busy sawing up firewood for the stove. [Making a supply of firewood.]

Say   To utter, pronounce, speak.

say out   T (9)   If you think the committee decision is wrong you should say it right out in meeting. [Express your opinion publicly.]

say over   T (7)   I've said over and over that she never should have married him. [Repeated it many times.]

say through   T (3)   Have you memorized the speech? Can you say it through without a mistake? [From beginning to end.]

Scale   To reduce or increase in amount according to a fixed scale.

scale down   T (2)   The union contract makes no provision for scaling down wages if the cost of living goes lower. [Reducing them.]

scale up   T (2)   The union contract calls for scaling up wages to meet increased living costs. [Increasing them.]

Scar   To mark with a scar.

scar up   T (6)   Those sportsmen have scarred up my beautiful hardwood floors with their hobnail boots. [Made ugly marks, scratches, on the floors.]

Scare   To frighten, alarm.

scare away   T (2)   He fired his shotgun to scare away the birds that were eating his cherries. [Cause them to fly away.]

scare off   T (1,2)   The burglar alarm sounded and scared off the would-be robbers. [Caused them to run off.]

scare up   T (7,11)   Informal. We're trying to scare up enough money for a trip to Hawaii. [Doing everything possible to find it.] See **scrape up.**

Scatter   To separate, disperse, go in different directions.

scatter out   I (1,9)   The soldiers scattered out over the rice fields in search of enemy snipers. [Away from their base in many directions.]

Scent   To fill with an odor or perfume.

scent up   T (3,4)   A huge bowl of roses scented up the whole room. [Gave off a sweet perfume.]

Scoop   To take up or out with, or as with a scoop.

scoop out   T (1)   The children scooped out a hole in the sand and buried their toys in it. [Dug the sand out to make a hole.]

scoop up   T (3)   Sports. One player scooped up the ball and threw it (ran with it). [Caught it close to the ground, in his glove or with his hands.]

Score   To keep a score of a game.

score up   T (9)   Baseball. The scorekeeper scored up three runs for the Dodgers in the eighth inning. [Made the official tally.]

Scour   To remove dirt, grease, etc., with a rough or abrasive material.

scour off   T (1)   The cook scoured off the table top (the stains on the table top) before starting to prepare dinner. [Removed the dirt, etc., by scouring.]

scour out   T (1)   The cook had to scour out the pot (the material sticking to the inside of the pot) before she could use it. [Remove the material by scouring.]

Scout   To seek, search for.

scout around   I (2)   The first thing we'll do when we get to Chicago is scout around for a place to live. [Hunt up an apartment, etc.]

scout out   T (3)   Informal. The next time you go to the library, scout out a couple of good books for me on the subject of wine making. [Try to find them.]

scout up   T (7,11)   Informal. John's roommate wants him to scout up a date for him for the dance. [Find a partner.]

Scrape   To remove something from a surface by drawing an instrument over it.

scrape off   T (1)   Bobby, go back outside and scrape off your shoes (the mud off your shoes) before you come in the house. [Remove the mud by scraping.]

scrape out   T (1)   The children were busy scraping out the insides of the pumpkin in order to make a Jack-o-lantern. [Removing them by scraping.]

scrape through   T (4)   Ext. That test was a hard one. I think I barely scraped through. [Passed it with some difficulty.]

scrape up   T (7,11)   Ext. He was barely able to scrape up enough money to pay for his bus fare. [Find it by careful effort.] See **scare up, scratch up.**

Scratch   To break or mar the surface; to mark by rubbing or scraping.

scratch along   I (3)   When we were first married we scratched along on very little money. [We had trouble finding enough money to pay our expenses.] [From the idea of a chicken scratching for food.]

scratch out **1.** T (5)   Henry told the secretary to scratch out the names of five people who had failed to make a money contribution. [Remove the names from a list by scratching.] **2.** T (5)   She told me she was so angry at her boy friend she could scratch out his eyes. [Dig them out with her fingers.]

scratch up **1.** T (6)   The cat scratched up the table leg, trying to sharpen its claws. [Made ugly scratches on it.] **2.** T (7,11)   The unemployed miner had all he could do to scratch up the rent. [Find enough money to pay it.] See **scrape up.**

Scream   To utter a loud piercing cry.

scream out T (1,9)   She screamed out an angry "No!" when he accused her of deceiving him. [Out from inside.] See **screech out.**

Screech   To utter a harsh shrill cry.

screech out T (1,9)   She screeched out her hatred for the man who had struck her. See **scream out.**

Screen   To shelter, protect, conceal, or remove with or as with a screen.

screen off **1.** T (3)   In hospitals they screen off the beds of dying patients. [Place screens around them to conceal the dying person from other patients.] **2.** T (3)   They decided to screen off a part of their porch to make an outdoor dining room. [Use screening to enclose part of the porch.] See **partition off.**

screen out **1.** T (1)   They put heavy drapes over the windows to screen out the strong sunlight. [Keep the strong light from entering.] **2.** T (1,9)   They ran the lettuce seed through a sieve to screen out the foreign matter. [Remove it.] **3.** T (4)   They gave a series of intelligence tests to screen out the poorer students. [Eliminate them from the group.]

Screw   To fasten, tighten, force, etc., by or as by a screw; to twist or contort by a screwing action.

screw around I (2)   Slang. Ext. That fellow never does anything constructive. He just screws around. [Wastes his time in foolish activities.]

screw down **1.** T (1)   To be sure the box would arrive in good condition, Robert screwed the lid down tight. [Used screws to hold the lid on.] **2.** T (2)   Informal. The shopkeeper asked fifteen dollars for the lamp, but we screwed him down on his price. [Forced him to sell it for less.]

screw up **1.** T (3)   When we offered him ten dollars for the lamp, he screwed up his mouth and shook his head as a sign of refusal. [Brought his lips tightly together.] **2.** T (5,11)   Informal. Do you think you can screw up courage to ask your father for a new car? [Force yourself to act bravely.] **3.** T (6)   Slang. Jack screwed up all our plans for a pleasant week-end at the beach. [Ruined them by his stupid actions.] See **foul up.**

Scrub   To rub hard with a brush, cloth, etc., or against a rough surface.

scrub off T (7)   It took her ten minutes to scrub off the front steps (the mud on the front steps.) [Remove it with a brush or broom and water.]

scrub out   T (1,9)   Don't forget to scrub out the bath tub when you're through. [Clean it by scrubbing.]

scrub up   T (2,11)   Informal. Tell the children to scrub up now. It's nearly time for dinner. [Wash themselves well.]

Seal   To close by any form of fastening that must be broken before access can be gained.

seal off   T (3)   A heavy iron chain and a string of mines sealed off the harbor from enemy submarines. [Blocked the entrance to the harbor.]

seal up   T (3,4)   There were cracks in the bottom of the boat that had to be sealed up before we could use it. [Filled with some caulking substance to keep the water out.]

Scuff   To mar a surface by scraping or hard use.

scuff up   T (6)   The floor was all scuffed up by the heavy boots of the soldiers. [The surface was badly marred.] See **mar up**.

Search   To go or look through (a place, area, etc.) carefully in order to find something missing or lost.

search about/around   I (1,2)   He searched around for his glasses, not remembering where he had put them. [Hunted, looked for them.]

search out   T (3)   Before condemning the accused prisoner, we must search out all the facts in the case. [Hunt for them until they are discovered.]

search through   T (3)   I've searched his novel through, and still I can't find the statement you referred to. [Hunted from beginning to end.]

Season   To heighten or improve the flavor of food by adding spices, condiments, etc.

season up   T (2,11)   This bean dish is too tame (bland, lacking in spicy flavor). I think I'll season it up a bit for our Mexican guests. [Add more spice.]

Section   To cut or divide into sections.

section off   T (3)   The seating in the auditorium was sectioned off so that the delegates from each state could sit together. [Separated into special sections, by using ropes or signs.] See **map off**.

See I   To use the eyes for looking at or toward.

May be used with many of the second elements to indicate the direction of the action.

Ex. Can you **see across**? [Across the river, etc.]

Can you **see back**? [Behind the car as we travel.]

Can you **see down**? [Down in the well.]

Can you **see in**?   [Into the room.]

Can you **see out**? [Out the window.]

Can you **see over**? [Over the wall.]

Can you **see under**? [Under the bed.]

Can you **see through**? [Through the curtain.]

Can you **see up**? [Up to the top of the building.]

See II To escort or watch as a courtesy or safeguard; encourage by accompanying to a point of departure. See **show II**.

see across T (1) I'll see you across. [Help you go across (the street, the bridge, the river, etc.)]

see around **1.** T (1,3) I'll see you around. [Go with you around the museum, the garden, the shopping center, etc.] **2.** T (5) Informal. I'll see you around. [A pleasant way of taking leave of a person you expect to meet again casually.]

see back T (3) Don't worry about having to take the subway to your hotel. My husband will see you back. [Go with you; perhaps drive you back.]

see by T (2) Take hold of my arm. I'll see you by. [I'll go with you past the dangerous or frightening place.]

see down T (1) My son will see you down. [Go down the elevator or the stairs with you.]

see in T (1) They sat in their car and saw us in. [Waited until we had gone into the house safely.]

see off T (10) We went to the pier to see our friends off. [Be with them as they boarded the ship.]

see on T (I 1) We drove her to the airport and saw her on. [Helped her with getting on the plane.]

see out **1.** T (1,2) Our host saw us out. [He politely went to the door with us as we were leaving.] **2.** T (8) It was a long, hard evening, but we saw it out to the bitter end. [We stayed in spite of the unpleasantness.]

see over T (3) I didn't know how to get to Berkeley from San Francisco, but Harry said he would see me over. [Go with me to the other side of the bay.]

see through **1.** T (1) There will be no problem at the Romanian border. Your Tour Guide will see you through. [Be with you to take care of any difficulties.] **2.** T (4) He hadn't earned enough to pay for his last year in college but his father saw him through. [Furnished the money necessary for him to complete his studies.] **3.** T (4) He had several set-backs after his operation, but his doctor saw him through. [Took such good care of him that he got well.] **4.** T (4) This is going to be a hard year for our family, but we'll see it through somehow. [Keep up our courage and do everything possible to come out allright.]

see up T (1) My son will be waiting for you at the entrance. He will see you up. [Bring you up to our apartment, by the elevator or the stairs.]

Seek To go in search of, try to find.

seek about/around I (2) When they asked me why I hadn't taken the trouble to call my lawyer I had to seek around for an answer. [Try to think of an explanation.]

seek out T (3) When they moved to San Francisco they sought out the little restaurants where the food and the wine were of the best. [Made an effort to find them.]

Select To choose in preference to another or others.

select out T (6) Peace Corps. Three volunteers for Nigeria were selected out after their three months training period. [They were dropped from the group. They were not thought to be good prospects for the work.]

Sell To give up or make over something to another person for a price.

sell off **1.** T (2) Father sold off all his real estate holdings and invested in stocks. [He disposed of them.] **2.** I (6) Stocks are selling off today at the Stock Exchange. [The prices are lower than they were yesterday.]

sell out **1.** T (4) The storekeeper sold out all of his refrigerators and discontinued the line. [He disposed of them by sale.] **2.** T (4) Tickets for tonight's performance of Hamlet are all sold out. The theater is sold out. [All the tickets have been sold.] **3.** T (6) Informal. He was a traitor. He sold out (sold out his country, sold out his country's secrets) to the enemy. [He betrayed his country, gave away secrets.] **4.** T (6) The basketball team sold out to the gambling ring. [Accepted a bribe not to win the game.] **5.** *sell-out* N. (4,6) The act or an instance of selling out.

Send To cause, permit, or enable to go. May be used with all the second elements to indicate the direction of the movement.

send along **1.** T (2) When you go to the store I'll send Johnny along to help carry the packages. [Send him with you.] **2.** T (1) When I get a letter from Aunt Mary, I'll send it along to you. [Put it in the mail so that you will receive it.]

send in T (1) The radio announcer invited the listeners to send in their questions (their contest entries, etc.). [In to the radio station.]

send off **1.** T (10) When the Joneses left for Europe we sent them off with a gay party just before sailing time. [Expressed our good wishes with a party for them.] **2.** T (2) I must send off a letter (telegram, package, etc.) to them. Their wedding anniversary is on the 10th. [Get it ready and mail it right away.] **3.** *send-off* N. (10) a. A demonstration of good wishes. [We gave them a good send-off when they left for Europe.] b. A good start. [Her father bought a house for the newly-weds. That was quite a send-off for the young couple. A good start for them as they began married life.]

send out **1.** T (1,2) The secretary was told to send out notices of the next meeting. [Inform people by mailing them a letter or post card.] **2.** T (1,2) The campaign manager sent out pamphlets and campaign literature to all the county chairmen. [Issued it, distributed it.]

send up **1.** T (1) The fire at the automobile repair shop sent up a huge cloud of black smoke and an odor of burning rubber. [Caused them to rise.] **2.** T (1,9) The people living in the slum area sent up an appeal to the mayor for better garbage service. [Make a request to the high officials, to the city government.] **3.** T (9) He was convicted of armed robbery and the judge sent him up for twenty years. [Sent him to prison.]

Serve To perform a duty or service; to serve food or refreshments.

serve out   **1.** T (9)   The prisoner was unable to obtain a pardon. He had to serve out his sentence. [Remain in prison the full time to which the judge had sentenced him.]   **2.** T (9)   The President was assassinated before he could serve out his term. [Complete his term of office.]

serve up   I (4,11)   Is everybody ready for dinner? We're going to serve up. [Put the food in dishes and place it on the table.]

Set   To put something or someone in a particular place; to establish; to start an activity.

set about   I (4)   As soon as he arrived in town he set about organizing a tennis club. [He began to organize one.]

set around   T (2)   Take the chairs into the living room and set them around wherever there is a space. [Place them here and there.]

set aside   T (2)   He sets aside ten percent of his monthly salary for the children's college education. [He does not spend it.] See **put aside, lay aside**.

set back   **1.** T (4)   We set our watches back one hour when we reached New York. [Turned the hour hand back.]   **2.** T (4)   Informal. That dinner at the hotel set him back $25. [Cost that much; reduced his cash by that amount.] See **put back**.   **3.** T (4)   If the reactionary forces win the election it will set progress back 100 years. [Return the country to the outmoded conditions of 100 years ago.]   **4.** T (4)   Having to take time out to earn his tuition set him back a year in college. [Delayed him.] See **throw back 2**.   **5.** *set-back* N.   (4)   a. A check to progress; a reverse; a temporary defeat. b. Architecture. The upper part of a building which recedes from the building line.

set down   **1.** T (7)   Now that we have reached an agreement let's set it down in black and white. [Write, print, or type the agreement on paper.]   **2.** T (1)   She brought the refreshments into the living room and set them down on the coffee table. [Placed them.]   **3.** T (1)   The pilot set his plane down (he set down) in field. [He landed.] See **touch down**.   **4.** T (7)   He looks shifty. I'd set him down as a crook. [In my opinion he is dishonest.] See **put down**.   **5.** T (2)   That man is too boastful. I'd like to set him down a notch. [Humble or humiliate him.]

set in   **1.** I (1)   When we reached home darkness was setting in. [It was beginning to get dark.]   **2.** I (9)   Before we reached home it was setting in to rain. [It was beginning to rain.]   **3.** *set-in* A.   (5)   Something that is made separately and inserted or placed in another unit. Ex. Set-in sleeves in a dress.

set off   **1.** I (2)   We set off on the return trip. [We started.] See **set out 1, take off 3, take out**.   **2.** T (2)   The engineers set off an explosion that rocked the countryside. [Ignited the powder, dynamite, T.N.T.]   **3.** T (2)   A thief tripped on the wire that set off the burglar alarm. [Caused it to ring.] See **go off, let off, touch off**.   **4.** T (10)   Her dark blue evening gown sets off her lovely pink complexion. [Makes it more lovely by contrast.]   **5.** T (5)   Conservationists set off the marsh as a bird refuge. [Preserved it from commercial development.] See **map off**.   **6.** *set-off* N.   (6)   a. Accounting. A counterbalancing debt or claim. b. Architecture. A reduction in the thickness of a wall. A flat sloping projection on a wall. c. Printing. Offset. Something placed off a center line.

set out   **1.** I (3) It is time we set out for home. [Started to go home.] See **set off 1.**   **2.** I (2,8) In his lecture he set out to prove that life on other planets is possible. [He began with the intention of establishing the fact.]   **3.** T (2,8) The city engineer set out a plan for improving the street lighting. [Produced a design, a pattern.]   **4.** T (10) The judge asked the defense attorney to set out more clearly his line of argument. [Explain, describe it.]   **5.** T (1) We always set out our petunias (annual plants, etc.) around the middle of May. [Transplant them into the flower beds.]   **6.** T (10) In the presence of the Mayor the architect set out the plan for the new municipal building. [Laid it out in actual size on the building site.] See **layout**.

set up   **1.** T (1,3) They used to hire boys to set up the pins in bowling alleys. Now they have machines to set them up. [Raise them into position.]   **2.** T (4) Hitler set himself up (the Nazi Party set him up) as a dictator. [Put him in a high, powerful position.]   **3.** T (1,2) We need carpenters to set up the platforms (scaffolding, booths, stages, etc.) at the County Fair. [Construct, erect, assemble them.]   **4.** T (7,9,11) Each candidate for office has to set up an organization (a method of procedure, a schedule, a plan of action, etc.) before the campaign starts. [Establish, put in order, etc.]   **5.** T (4,7) His father said he would set him up in business as soon as he graduated from college. [Furnish money, give him the help he needs.]   **6.** T (1,4) Slang. He told the bar-tender to set up drinks for everybody. [Serve a drink to each person present at his expense.] He was treating them to a drink.   **7.** T (2,5) He was all set up by the good news from Wall Street. [He felt happy, elated.]   **8.** T (7) The college authorities set up certain rules (conditions, principles) in regard to the social life of the students. [They advanced, established them.]   **9.** T (7,11) Slum conditions set up the conditions for rioting. [They cause people to want to riot.]   **10.** T (7,11) Bridge. My partner trumped spades twice in dummy to set up his spade suit. [Make it possible for his remaining spades to take tricks.]   **11.** *set-up* N. (5) 1) a. Organization; arrangement. [They have a very good set-up for their political campaign.]   b. Everything required for an alcoholic drink except the liquor — glass, ice, soda water, etc. — as served to persons who provide their own liquor.   c. An arrangement of all the tools, parts, apparatus, etc., necessary for a specific job or purpose. [Their auto repair shop has a complete set-up for taking care of every kind of repair work.]   d. A plan or projected course of action. Ex. The committee chairman spent an hour and a half explaining the set-up for winning approval of the proposed new sewer system. 2) (6) a. Informal. An undertaking or contest deliberately made easy. [Some of the questions asked on T.V. quiz programs are pure set-ups. They are so easy that the contestant is sure to win.] b. Sports. A match game arranged with an opponent who can be defeated without effort. [Wrestling matches on T.V. are frequently suspected of being set-ups rather than serious contests.] c. An opponent easy to defeat. Pushover. d. A shot or play that results in a puck, shuttlecock, ball or balls being so positioned as to provide a player with an easy opportunity for a winning shot. e. The position of such a ball, etc. f. The puck or ball itself. **12.** *setting-up* A. (2) Setting-up exercises. Any of various exercises, as deep knee bends and push-ups, for improving one's posture, muscle tone or limberness, or for reducing one's weight.

Settle   To place in or assume a desired or permanent position.

settle back   I (1)   He sat down in a big chair in front of the fire, settled back, and began to read the evening paper. [Rested his back against the back of the chair.]

settle down   **1.** I (4)   The pioneer family, after moving farther west in three separate stages, finally settled down in Iowa. [Made Iowa their permanent home.]
2. I (1)   He got up to stretch his legs and pour himself a drink, then settled down to write another chapter of his book. [Remain seated at his desk for a while.]   **3.** I (4)   The children had been very active and noisy, but they settled down when Father threatened to send them to bed. [They became quiet.]
4. I (2)   John had been rather wild as a young man, but he settled down when he got married. [Became a good husband and father.]

settle in   I (1)   They rented a cottage at the seashore, and settled in for a three month's vacation. [Prepared to stay for a while.]

settle out   I (9)   Harry poured the solution into a bottle and waited for the solid matter to settle out. [Fall to the bottom of the bottle, out of the liquid.]

settle up   **1.** T (4)   I told the grocer that I would be able to settle up my account with him at the end of the month. [Pay what I owed him, meet my obligations.]
2. I (4)   If you don't settle up I'll have to consult my lawyer. [Pay me what you owe me. Keep your promise to me.]

Sew   To join or attach by stitches.

sew on   T (1)   He gave his wife his shoulder patches (his sergeant's stripes) and asked her to sew them on. [Attach them to his uniform by sewing.]

sew up   **1.** T (3,4)   After the operation the surgeon sewed up the incision with thirty stitches. [Closed the wound by sewing the skin together.]   **2.** T (4,10)   The senator's campaign manager has sewed up the votes of all the county delegates. [He has persuaded the delegates to vote for the senator.]   **3.** T (4)   Slang. Have you succeeded in getting that job you were talking about? Yes, it's all sewed up. [It has been promised to me. I have done all that was necessary to get it.]

Shake   To move or sway with short, quick, irregular vibratory movements.

shake down   **1.** T (1)   We shook down some apples (nuts, oranges, etc.) from the tree and put them in baskets. [Down to the ground.]   **2.** T (5)   Ext. They shook down their new yacht on a trip along the Atlantic seacoast. [Made a trial voyage to test the new yacht.]   **3.** T (5)   Slang. The gangsters shook down all the storekeepers in the area once a month. [Threatened them with damage to their store or their person, if they did not pay for protection.] **4.** T (4) Slang. The police shook down all the prisoners taken in the round-up. [Searched them for stolen goods or concealed weapons.] **5.** *shake-down* N. 1) (1) a. An act or process of shaking down. [It takes an occasional shake-down of the ashes to keep a coal furnace burning well.] b. A bed, as of straw or blankets, spread on the floor. c. Any makeshift bed. d. A cruise or flight intended to prepare a new vessel or aircraft for regular service, by training the crew to operate it, and by breaking in and adjusting the machinery, etc. 2) (5) a. An act or instance of extortion, as by blackmail or threats of violence. b. A thorough search of prison cells or of suspects for concealed weapons.

shake off **1.** T (1) When they came back from the beach, Mother told them to shake off the sand before coming into the house. [Remove it by shaking.] **2.** T (1) Informal. After their candidate lost the election they threw a wild party to shake off the blues. [Get rid of their feelings of sadness and disappointment.] **3.** T (2) The escaping bandit shook off his pursuers by swimming a mile down stream. [Made them lose his trail.]

shake out **1.** T (1) They picked up their blankets from the beach and shook out the sand. [Removed it by shaking.] **2.** *shake-out* N. (3) Commerce. a. An elimination of business concerns, products, etc., as a result of intensive competition, in a market of declining sales, or rising standards of quality. b. A rapid decline in the values of certain securities sold in stock exchanges or the like.

shake up **1.** (6) That long fast ride in the truck over the desert road shook us up quite a bit. [Jolted and jarred us; bounced us around.] **2.** (6) The assassination of the President shook me up terribly. [Agitated, disturbed me mentally and emotionally.] **3.** T (4,11) When we reached home John shook up some Martini's (cocktails, mixed drinks, etc.) for everybody. [Mixed the elements by shaking.] **4.** *shake-up* N. (4) a. A jolting, jarring, etc., from a ride in a vehicle. b. A thorough reorganization of a business, a department or the like. [When the new man takes office, the staff expects a shake-up.] **5.** *shaken-up* A. (6) a. I never saw such a shaken-up group of people in my life. [People emotionally upset by a tragedy, an accident.] b. She was terribly shaken-up after her husband's death in the plane crash. [The shock of the accident left her mentally and emotionally upset.] **6.** *shook-up* A. (6) Slang. I'm all shook up. [My composure is disturbed. I am upset, nervous, agitated, unhappy, etc.]

Shape To give definite form, shape, organization, or character to; fashion or form.

shape up **1.** I (5,11) In Viet Nam things are shaping up for a showdown in the central highlands. [The military situation is developing towards a big battle to determine the control of the highlands.] **2.** I (12) Our football team is beginning to shape up. [Starting to play well as a team. Beginning to win some games.] **3.** I (2,11) Father told Robert he would have to shape up if he wanted money for a college education. [Show by his conduct, his interest in studying, that he deserved it.] See **ship out**. **4.** I (10) Longshoremen shape up at 6:30 each morning. [Get into line, or formation, in order to be assigned the day's work.] **5.** *shape-up* N. (4,5) The forming of the line. The line itself formed by the longshoremen.

Share To divide or apportion by shares.

share up (with) **1.** T (4) Mother gave Mary a dozen cookies and told her to share up. (Share up with the other children.) [Give some (a share) to each child.]

Sharpen To make sharp.

sharpen up **1.** T (2,11) The bridge tournament director had his daughter sharpen up all the pencils before the afternoon session. [Make them ready by sharpening.] **2.** T (2,11) You'll have to sharpen up your wits if you want to win an argument with him. [Do some studying, some clear thinking.]

Shave To remove a growth of beard or hair with a razor.

shave off **1.** T (1) His sweetheart begged him to shave off his beard. [Remove it by shaving.] **2.** T (6) Ext. To attract more customers he shaved off a few cents from the price of all his canned goods. [Reduced the price.]

Shear To remove by or as if by cutting or clipping with a sharp instrument.

shear off **1.** T (2) He sheared off a fender when he collided with a big truck on the highway. [The fender was cut, or torn off by the impact.] **2.** T (2) The anti-aircraft fire sheared off a wing of the fighter plane. [Cut it off.]

Sheer To deviate from a course; swerve.

sheer away **1.** I (3) The little motor boat sheered away from the approaching steamer just in time. [Changed its course to avoid a collision.] **2.** I (3) Ext. The preacher is always warning the young people to sheer away from evil companions and liquor. [Avoid them.]

Shell To take out of the shell, pod, etc.

shell out **1.** I (1,9) Slang. The hold-up man told his victim to shell out or else. [Take money from his pocket or purse and give it to the hold-up man.] **2.** T (1) Slang. We had to shell out $10.00 apiece for the tickets. [We were forced to pay what seemed to be an excessive amount.]

Shift To transfer from one position to another. May be used with all the second elements to indicate the direction of the movement.

Shin (or Shinny) To climb by holding fast alternately with the hands and arms, and the legs, thus drawing and shoving oneself up.

shin up I (1) The kitten had climbed up a telephone pole. Jack shinned up and brought it down. [Up the pole.]

Shine I To give forth or glow with light.

shine on I (II 2) Oh, shine on, shine on, harvest moon, up in the sky. [Keep shining. Continue to shine.] From a popular song.

shine out I (1) A beacon lantern (a light from a window) shone out in the darkness. [Gave out light.]

shine through I (1) The sky was very cloudy but now and then the sun shone through. [Sunlight pierced through the clouds.]

Shine II To put polish or a gloss on something.

shine up **1.** T (2) Informal. Shine 'em up for you? [May I shine your shoes?] A bootblack asks the question of people passing by. **2.** *shine up (to)* I (5) Informal. Henry is shining up to his boss these days, hoping to get a raise in pay. [He is being very agreeable, friendly, eager to please.] **3.** I (5) John is shining up to Margaret. [Trying to make a favorable impression, wanting to be her boyfriend.]

Ship To travel by ship; to send by ship or other conveyance. May be used with many of the second elements to indicate the direction of the movement.

ship off T (2) Informal. We shipped the kids off for summer camp this morning. [We sent them away.]

ship out **1.** I (1) Albert writes us that he's shipping out for Brazil next Tuesday. [Leaving his home country for a foreign land.] **2.** T (1) The Army is shipping Henry's regiment out next week. [Sending it to a foreign destination.] **3.** I (4) Informal. Shape up or ship out! [Become a good, useful worker, or be fired (lose your job).] See **shape up 3**.

Shoot I To hit, wound, damage, kill, or destroy with a missile discharged from a weapon.

shoot down **1.** T (1) Each hunter shot down five ducks as the flock flew overhead. [Brought them down to earth by firing a gun at them.] **2.** T (1,4) The police shot down the escaping robber. [Caused him to fall.]

shoot off **1.** T (1) William Tell put an apple on his son's head, then shot it off. [Off the head of his son.] **2.** T (2) In the gun battle one gunman shot off a finger of the other gunman's right hand. [Severed it from the hand.]

shoot up T (6) In Western movies there is often a scene in which outlaws or drunken cowboys shoot up the town (the barroom, the saloon, etc.). [Cause great damage, fear, and confusion by firing pistols and guns.]

Shoot II To fire a gun or missile; detonate explosive material; cause to move as though propelled by an explosion.

shoot away (6) As the flock of ducks rose from the water the hunters began shooting away for dear life. [Firing their guns as rapidly and as often as possible.]

shoot back **1.** (5) Write to me as soon as you reach home, and I'll shoot a letter back. [Answer immediately.] **2.** T (5) He accused her of stealing, and she shot back an angry "That's a lie!" [Spoke the words quickly and sharply.]

shoot off **1.** T (8) At the officer's command the soldiers shot off their rifles in unison. [Pulled the trigger and fired their rifles.] **2.** T (8) At Cape Kennedy yesterday they shot off a rocket into space. [Ignited the fuel that forced the rocket up into space.] **3.** T (9) Slang. I can't stand that man. He's always shooting off his mouth. [Talking boastfully as if he knows all the facts in a case, but really does not.]

shoot out **1.** T (10)   When the boy started running past us John shot out his arm and stopped him. [Reached his arm out quickly.]   **2.** T (8)   The robbers holed up in an abandoned house and shot it out with the police. [Had a long gun battle.]   **3.** *shoot-out* N.   (8)   During the shoot-out one robber was killed and two policemen wounded.

shoot through   (2)   Commerce. As soon as we receive your order for the books we'll shoot it through. [Fill the order and mail the books to you immediately.]

Shoot III   To move quickly in some direction as if fired from a gun, or propelled by an explosive.

shoot by   I (2)   The noise was terrific as the racing cars shot by. [Went past with a flash and a roar and at top speed.]

shoot off   I (1,2)   At the end of the count-down the huge rocket shot off into space. [Off the launching pad.]

shoot out   **1.** I (1)   When we opened the door the cat shot out and ran into the street. [Came out as if fired from a gun.]   **2.** I (9)   As the racers approached the finish line Griffin shot out into the lead. [Made a spurt that put him ahead of the others.]

shoot up   **1.** I (2)   After the explosion flames shot up to a height of fifty feet. [Rose suddenly.]   **2.** I (2)   After the warm rain the plants shot up overnight. [They started growing very fast.]   **3.** I (2)   Johnny has been shooting up like a weed this past year. [Has kept growing very rapidly.]

Shop   To visit shops and stores for purchasing or examining goods.

shop about/around   **1.** I (2)   We're not sure we want to buy anything. We're just shopping around. [Looking here and there to see what you have in the store.]   **2.** T (2)   You would do well to shop around for ideas on home building before you hire an architect. [Read books and magazines, talk to people who have built homes.]

Shore   To support by a shore or shores (a pole or prop, or beam).

shore up   **1.** T (2)   The bridge had to be shored up after the flood had weakened its foundations. [Strengthened by steel beams, concrete, sandbags, etc.]   **2.** T (2)   The President called in experts to figure out means for shoring up the economy. [Giving support to the sagging economy.]   **3.** T (2)   After World War II the U.S. shored up her weakened allies. [Gave them support.]

Short   Electricity. To short-circuit.

short out   I (8)   The whole city was plunged in darkness when a main power line shorted out. [Failed to function due to a short circuit.]

Shorten   To make short or shorter.

shorten up   T (2)   The program you have planned is too long. I advise you to shorten it up a bit. [Cut out some of the numbers. Make the program shorter.]

Shoulder   To push with or as with the shoulder, especially roughly. Usually with "one's way" as the direct object. Can be used with all elements. See **fight one's way.**

shoulder aside T (1)   When I tried to talk to the candidate one of his body guards shouldered me aside. [Used his shoulder to make me move away.]

Shout   To call or cry out loudly and vigorously. May be used with most of the second elements to indicate the direction of the action.

shout back   I (5)   I called after him as he started to run down the street and he shouted back that he couldn't wait. [Back to me.]

shout down   **1.** I (1)   When he got to the top of the stairs he shouted down to tell me everything was allright. [Down to me on the ground floor.]   **2.** T (1,4)   When a man rose in the meeting to heckle the speaker the audience shouted him down. [Made him sit by shouting.] See **boo down, hiss down, hoot down, howl down, jaw down, laugh down.**

shout out   **1.** T (9)   The captain shouted out an order loud enough to be heard over the noise of the machine gun fire. [Gave the order in a very loud voice.]   **2.** I (2,4)   You'll have to shout out if you want to be heard. [Holler.] See **belt out, sing out.**

Shove   To push; to move by applying force from behind. May be used with all the second elements to indicate the direction of the movement. Often used with "one's way" as the direct object. See **fight one's way.**

shove off   **1.** I (2)   When the boat was full we shoved off and started for the fishing grounds. [Pushed the boat away from the shore.]   **2.** I (2)   Slang. It's time for us to shove off. [Leave, depart, start off.]

Shovel   To take up and cast or remove with a shovel. May be used with all the second elements to indicate the direction of the movement.

shovel away   T (2,3)   James went out early to shovel away the snow from the garage door. [Remove it.]

shovel in   T (1)   Slang. The hungry youngsters sat down at the table and began shoveling it in. [Eating their food greedily, as if with a shovel.]

shovel off   T (7)   The sidewalks and the driveway were under four feet of snow. It took an hour to shovel them off. [Remove the snow with shovels.]

Show I   To cause or allow to be seen.

show-down   (With *down*, usually used as a noun.) N.   **1.** (1)   Cards. The placing of cards face up on the table, as in poker, to see who wins.   **2.** (5)   A conclusive settlement of an issue or difference in which all resources are balanced off. [At the ceasefire negotiations yesterday there was a show-down that may produce some fruitful action. Each side reviewed its advantages.]

show off   **1.** T (10)   Her children are very talented musicians. She likes to show them off. [Have them perform for her friends and guests.]   **2.** I (9)   Uncle James is always showing off at parties. [He talks a lot about himself, performs parlor tricks, tries to amuse and entertain the other guests.]   **3.** *show-off* N. (9)   a. Uncle James is a show-off. [He likes to attract attention.] b. His performance last night was quite a show-off.

show out I (9) Bridge. When trumps were led for the third time my partner showed out. [He was out of trumps, could not play one.]

show through 1. I (1) Her blouse was so thin that her slip showed through. [It could be seen through the blouse.] **2.** *show-through* N. (1) Paper making. a. The visibility through paper of what is printed on the other side. b. A measure of the opacity of the paper.

show up 1. T (4,6) The riots, burning, and looting show up some of the weaknesses in our society. [Expose them to public view.] **2.** T (4,6) Informal. In the T.V. debates our candidate showed up his opponent as a weak, badly prepared speaker. [Made him appear inferior.] **3.** I (5) White shows up well against a blue background. [It stands out; is seen clearly.] **4.** I (9) John showed up at the meeting a half hour late. [He appeared, arrived.]

Show II To guide, escort, or usher. See **See II.**

May be used with many of the second elements to show the direction of the movement. Ex. Our guide will show you about (around, back, by, down, in, out, through, up).

Shriek To utter a loud, sharp, shrill cry.

shriek out T (2,9) She shrieked out a denial when they accused her of stealing. [Out in public.] See **cry out.**

Shrink To draw back, as in retreat or avoidance; to decrease in size, as cloth.

shrink back I (1) The sight of the blood on the accident victims caused her to shrink back in horror. [Move backward, away from them.]

shrink up I (6) His woolen shirts were all shrunk up from being washed in hot water. [Much reduced in size.]

Shrug To raise and contract the shoulders, expressing indifference, disdain, etc.

shrug off 1. T (1) Mr. Nelson shrugged off the criticism of his policies, as being ignorant and biased. [He paid no attention to it.] **2.** T (10) He was able to shrug off the after effects of the drug the doctor had prescribed for him. [Recover from the after effects.]

Shut To put a door, cover, etc., in position so as to close or obstruct.

shut down 1. I (1,6) The factory shut down, (T. They shut down the factory) in order to install new machinery (prepare for the new models, make changes in the structure of the building, etc.). [Closed temporarily, with the workers laid off.] See **lay off. 2.** I (2) Ext. The clouds (the fog) shut down over the hill, making it impossible to see the top. [They formed a cover.] **3.** *shut-down* N. (1,6) The temporary closing of a shop or factory. See **shut down 1.**

shut in 1. T (1,3) She shooed the chickens into the hen house and shut them in. [Closed a door or gate to keep them inside.] **2.** *shut-in* N. (1,3) Mrs. Jones has been a shut-in for three long years. [She has been ill, an invalid, and unable to leave the house.] **3.** *shut-in* A. (1,3) Psychology. The psychiatrist found his patient to have a shut-in personality. [The patient was "in on himself", not outgoing, friendly.]

shut off **1.** T (4)   Did you shut off the water (the electricity, the gas, etc.) before you left on your trip? [Close the outlets.] See II **turn off**. **2.** T (2)   Their peculiar religious beliefs shut them off from contact with modern life. [Prevented them from adapting to new ways; isolated them.] **3.** T (3)   The police placed barriers at all cross streets to shut off traffic during the parade. See **block off**. **4.** *shut-off* N. (4)   A device such as a valve, electric switch or plug for closing an outlet, interrupting service.

shut out **1.** T (1)   He closed the door of the living room so as to shut out the children (the noise, the insects, the light, etc.). [Keep them from entering.] **2.** T (1,9)   A high fence (hedge, bush, etc.) shut out the view of the street. [Hid the view from sight.] **3.** T (9)   Baseball. The pitcher shut out the Dodgers in the third inning. [Kept them from scoring.] **4.** *shut-out* N.A. (9)   Baseball. Dazzy Vance pitched a shut-out (a shut-out game) for the Dodgers on the final day of the season. [A game in which the opposing team did not score.]

shut up **1.** T (3,4)   Everybody out! It's time to shut up shop. [Close for the night.] **2.** T (3,4)   Mr. Thomas used to have a drugstore on Main Street but he shut up shop and moved away. [He went out of business, closed permanently.] **3.** T (3)   The police were given orders to shut up (lock up) all suspicious characters in preparation for the President's visit to the city. [Put them in jail, confine them.] **4.** I (4)   Informal and rude. Shut up! [Close your mouth; don't say anything more.] I wish you would shut up about that. [Not mention it again.] You can't shut him up. [Keep him from talking.] See **clam up, dry up, ring off.**

Shy   To draw back or recoil.

shy away **1.** I (2,3)   The little girls shied away from the donkey. They were afraid to touch it. [Drew back, or to one side.] **2.** I (2,3)   The government is shying away from the idea of sending more troops to Viet Nam. [It doubts that sending them would be wise, the right thing to do.]

shy off   I (2)   The horse shied off when Dick attempted to saddle it. [Moved away nervously.]

Side   To favor or support, or refuse to support one group or opinion against another; to take sides.

side in (with)   I (4)   We decided to side in with the younger members of the club. [Accept their ideas, their program, etc.]

Sigh   To express or utter with a sigh.

sigh out   T (1)   She sighed out her sorrow (her grief, her complaint) in a voice heavy with pain. [Out of her breast.]

Sign   To write one's signature as a token of agreement, obligation, receipt, etc.; to give a signal of some sort.

sign away   T (4)   The eldest son had signed away his rights to any share in his father's estate. [Signed a legal document giving up his rights.]

sign in **1.** I (1)   Girls who live in college dormitories must sign in when they return to the dormitory late at night. [Write their name in a book or on a list to show that they have returned.] Opposite of sign out.

sign off   1. I (4)   Radio and Television. Station WQZ signs off at midnight. [Gives a signal that it is stopping its broadcasts.]   **2.** I (4)   Informal. I've been studying for eight hours and I'm tired. I think I'll sign off. [Stop studying, working, etc.]   **3.** *sign-off* N.   (4)   Radio and Television. It's just five minutes before sign-off. [After five minutes the broadcasting will stop.]

sign on   1. I (II 4)   He signed on as a pitcher with the Dodgers. [He signed a contract with the management of the Dodgers.]   **2.** T (II 4)   The management signed him on for two years. [Gave him a two-year contract.]

sign over   T (3)   Before he went to the hospital for his operation he signed over all his property to his wife. [Signed a legal document giving all his property to her.]

sign up   1. I (10)   Instead of waiting to be drafted, he signed up with the Marines. [He enlisted, joined the Marines.]   **2.** I (10)   At the age of twenty-one he signed up with the Dodgers. [He signed a contract to play baseball with that team.]   **3.** T (4)   John is a very good organizer. We've signed him up to take charge of the campaign for the Community Chest. [We have persuaded him to accept the responsibility of organizing the campaign.]

Silk   To develop or form silk.

silk out   I (1)   The corn is silking out already. [The silk is beginning to show at the tips of the ears.]

Silt   To become filled or choked up with silt.

silt up   I (6)   After the spring rains the harbor (the river bed, etc.) silts up badly. It will have to be dredged. [Becomes full of silt.]

Simmer   To keep a liquid in a state approaching boiling.

simmer down   1. T (6)   The cook simmered down the meat broth to make soup stock. [Reduced the amount of water by simmering.]   **2.** I (6)   Father is still angry about the damage you did to the car. Wait until he simmers down before you try to explain it. [Becomes less angry, less "hot and bothered".]

Sing   To produce musical tones by use of the voice.

sing out   1. I (1,9)   The choir sang out at the top of their voices. [Sang with full power.]   **2.** I (9)   As soon as our boat came within earshot we heard a voice sing out a greeting. [Sound loud and clear.] See **shout out.**

Sink   To fall, drop, or descend to a lower level.

sink back   I (1)   Lighting his pipe and picking up a book he sank back in his chair for a comfortable evening of reading. [Leaned his back against the back of the armchair.]

sink down   I (1)   The condemned murderer sank down and toppled over at a blast from the firing squad. [His knees gave way, buckled under him, and he fell to the ground.]

sink in   1. I (1)   Informal. At first she didn't understand the joke, but it finally

sank in and she began to laugh. [It penetrated her mind; she understood it.]
2. *sunken-in* A. (1) His cheeks (his eyes) were all sunken in as a result of his
long, painful illness. [They were hollow, as if pressed into his skull.]

Single To pick or choose out from others.

> **single out** **1.** T (4) The school principal singled out a red-haired boy as the
> leader of the disturbance in the hallway. [Picked him out of the whole group of
> students.] **2.** T (3) I wouldn't single out any one cause for the student riots.
> [There are many causes. I would not limit it to one.]

Siphon To convey or pass through a siphon.

> **siphon off** T (2) Father is down in the cellar siphoning off his new batch of
> home-made wine. [Drawing it from one container to another by means of a
> siphon.]
> **siphon out** T (1) The pool had no bottom drain so we had to siphon the water
> out in order to clean it. [Remove the water by siphoning.]

Sit To rest with the body supported by the buttocks or thighs; be seated.

> **sit around** I (1,2) We just sat around doing nothing, until it was time for the
> program to start. [Here and there.]
> **sit back** **1.** I (1) Sit back and relax. I'll call you if I need your help. [Rest
> yourself comfortably with your back against the back of the chair.] **2.** I (1)
> Ext. We can't sit back and do nothing when there are so many problems to be
> solved. [Take it easy, not be concerned about the world's problems.]
> **sit down** **1.** I (1) Won't you sit down? [A polite way of asking a person who is
> standing to be seated.] **2.** I (1) The audience sat down when the dignitaries
> had taken their seats. [Took their seats.] **3.** I (1) Ext. The plane sat down in
> an open field. [It alighted, landed.] **4.** T (1) Ext. The military forces sat down
> at the approaches to the city. [Took their position.] **5.** *sit-down* N.A. (1) A
> sit-down strike. [One in which the workers occupy their benches, their places of
> work, and refuse to work until the strike is settled.]
> **sit in** **1.** I (1) The civil rights workers plan to sit in at lunch counters in the
> department stores, until they are desegregated. [Protest the exclusion of Negroes
> by occupying seats at the lunch counters.] **2.** *sit in (on)* I (4) We were
> invited to sit in on the conference (the lectures, the classes, the discussion, etc.).
> [Be present, sometimes to take part.] **3.** *sit-in* N.A. (1) A sit-in demon-
> stration. [One in which a group of people remain seated in a forbidden place, in
> protest against the custom or rule that excludes certain people, especially Negroes.]
> **sit out** **1.** T (10) The play (the lecture, the concert, etc.) was very boring, but we
> sat it out to the very end. [We remained in our seats.] **2.** T (8) The orchestra
> is starting to play a rhumba. Let's sit this one out. [Let's not dance, but remain
> seated while they play it.]
> **sit through** I (3) The play was so boring that we could hardly sit through. [Stay
> till the very end.]
> **sit up** **1.** I (1) When we came into the room he tried to sit up, but we told him

to stay the way he was. [Rise to a sitting position.] **2.** I (1) When our friends were here for a visit we sat up till long after midnight talking. [Did not go to bed at our usual time.] **3.** I (1,3) Mother told Johnny to sit up straight and not lean his elbows on the table. [Hold himself erect, upright.] **4.** I (2,5) Informal. They all sat up and took notice when the beautiful girl went to the mike and began to sing. [They became very much interested, astonished, etc.] **5.** *sit up (with)* I (1) James is going to sit up with his friend tonight. [The friend is ill and James will spend the night watching him, taking care of him.] **6.** *sit-up* N. (1) An exercise in which a person, lying flat on his back, and with the legs straight, lifts the torso to a sitting position without bending the legs. [Sit-ups are good for strengthening the stomach muscles.]

Size To estimate the size or quality of; to meet requirements as to size or quality.

    size up **1.** T (4) Father wants to meet Mary's boy friend in order to size him up. [Get some idea of his character and abilities.] **2.** I (4) If her boy friend doesn't size up to her parents' expectations, they will be upset. [Show good qualities, character.] **3.** *size-up* N. (3,4) An appraisal or estimation. [The Manager asked for a size-up of the production capacity for the next six months.] [We're going to the museum to make a size-up of a young Italian painter's exhibit.]

Sketch To make a rough design.

    sketch in T (2) The painter sketched in the minor figures on his canvas before finishing the head of the central figure. [Indicated them by light lines.]

    sketch out T (7) We asked the landscape architect to sketch out the general plan for our formal garden. [Draw a rough design of it.] See **trace out.**

Skin To strip or deprive of skin.

    skin out **1.** T (9) The hunter skinned out the bobcat on the spot. [Removed the pelt to collect the bounty but left the carcass.] **2.** I (1,2) Slang. We hoped to have a chat with Harry, but he skinned out before we could catch him. [He left in a hurry. Escaped by a slim margin.]

    skin up T (6) Little Alice skinned up her knees when she fell while jumping rope. [Scraped the skin off her knees. Damaged the surface.]

Skip To go away hastily and secretly, without asking permission or giving notice.

    skip out I (1,5) Informal. The cashier skipped out with the bank president's daughter and $10,000 dollars in cash. [Eloped with the daughter, taking $10,000 of the bank's money.] See **I run away.**

Slack To make or allow to become less active, vigorous, or intense.

    slack down I (6) Production of new cars has slacked down, due to strikes and business uncertainty. [It has become less.]

    slack off **1.** I (2) The rain slacked off and the sun began to shine. [It stopped gradually.] **2.** I (2,4) The captain told the mate to slack off and prepare to come about. [Loosen the line holding the sail in place and let the boom swing to the other side. Tack.]

slack up   **1.** I (2)   He had been driving at 65 miles per hour, but slacked up as he approached the town. [Began to move more slowly.] See **slow up, slow down.** **2.** I (2)   You're working too hard. You'll get ulcers if you don't slack up a bit. [Stop working so hard.]

Slam   To dash, strike, etc., with violent and noisy impact.

   slam down   T (1,5)   James was very angry. He slammed his book down on the table and stalked out. [Showed his anger by banging it on the table.]

Slap   To dash or cast forcibly.

   slap down   **1.** T (1,5)   Mary didn't like it when her mother scolded her for coming home so late. She slapped her books down on a chair and ran out of the room. See **slam down.** **2.** T (1,4)   Ext. Informal. The boss slapped down the suggestion of a coffee break in the afternoon. [Refused roughly to consider it.]

Sleep   To take repose or rest; cease being awake.

   sleep away   T (6)   It was cold and rainy. We decided to sleep the day away and hope for better weather in the morning. [Spend the day in sleep.]

   sleep in   **1.** I (1)   We have an extra bedroom so the maid sleeps in. [Sleeps at our house.] **2.** I (1)   We stayed so late at the dance that we all slept in this morning. [Slept beyond our usual hour for rising.] **3.** *sleep-in* N. (1) a. Sleeping at a place of employment. b. The person who sleeps in.

   sleep off   **1.** T (4)   She had a terrible headache. We told her to take some aspirin and try to sleep it off. [Get rid of it by sleeping a bit.] **2.** T (4)   John drank too much last night. He's upstairs in bed trying to sleep off a hangover. [Get rid of it by sleeping in.] See **hangover** N.

   sleep out   **1.** I (1)   We don't have an extra bedroom so our maid sleeps out. [She goes home at night.] See **sleep in. 2.** I (2)   The boys have put up a tent in the back yard. They're sleeping out every night. [They do not sleep in the house.]

   sleep through   I (3)   The alarm must have gone off, but I slept through and didn't waken till 9 o'clock. [Through the sounding of the alarm clock.]

Slice   To cut into slices (thin, broad pieces of bread, cheese, meat, etc.).

   slice off   T (2)   The host sliced off thick pieces of the beef roast and laid them on the serving tray. [Cut them off with his carving knife.]

   slice up   T (2,4)   That roast is very small for this large group of people. You'll have to slice it up thin. [Make thin slices in order to serve everybody.]

Slick   To make sleek or smooth.

   slick up   I (2,11)   Informal. After the long hot hike they just had time to slick up a bit before the guests arrived. [Wash, comb their hair and put on fresh clothing.]

Slide   To move along in continuous contact with a smooth or slippery surface. May be used with all the second elements to show the direction of the movement.

Slim   To make or become slim.

   slim down   **1.** I (6)   She was much overweight when he first met her, but she has slimmed down to a neat 120 pounds. [Reduced her weight.] **2.** *slimming-down* N.A. (6) Her slimming-down exercises, plus a strict diet, helped her to lose 20 pounds. See **thin down.**

Slip To move, flow, pass, or go smoothly or easily; glide; slide. May be used with all the second elements to indicate the direction of the movement.

slip away I (4,6) In such good company the hours slip away before you know it. [Pass by.]

slip by I (2) The years (time, the hours, life, etc.) slipped by and still she did not give up hope for the return of her loved one. [Went past.]

slip off T (1,2) The doctor asked him to slip off his shirt to get ready for the chest examination. [Remove it quickly and easily.]

slip on **1.** T (I 1) He slipped on his sweater before going out into the cold. [Pulled it quickly over his head.] **2.** *slip-on* N.A. (2) a. His mother made him a slip-on (a slip-on sweater) for Christmas. b. Any garment that is designed to be put on easily.

slip out **1.** I (1,4) Robert slipped out of the meeting before it was over. [Left hurriedly without being noticed.] **2.** I (1) She slipped out of her dress and put on a bath robe. [Took off her dress quickly and easily.]

slip over **1.** T (3) He held the horse's head and slipped the bridle over. [Over the head of the horse.] **2.** T (3) Ext. I don't trust that man. I think he's trying to slip something over on me. [Deceive me, play a trick on me.] **3.** *slip-over* N.A. (1) A garment that can be slipped on over the head. See **pull-over.**

slip up **1.** I (6) Henry slipped up when he reported that there were only forty people who voted in favor. There were forty-five. [He made an error; failed to count correctly.] **2.** *slip-up* N. (6) Henry's slip-up was noticed by three people at the meeting. [His error, his wrong judgment.]

Slop To spill over the rim of a container, as of a liquid.

slop over **1.** I (5) When he bumped against the table his coffee (milk, beer, wine, etc.) slopped over onto the tablecloth. [Ran over the rim of the cup or glass and down.] **2.** I (5) Ext. Informal. She's the type of person who slops over when she talks about vivisection. [Lets her emotions come to the surface and spill over.]

Slough To dispose of, get rid of.

slough off **1.** T (1) In the spring rattlesnakes slough off their last year's skin. [Abandon it, work their way out of it.] **2.** T (1) Ext. My old uncle advised me to slough off my old companions (former associates, fears, feelings of inferiority, etc.). [Abandon them; leave them.]

Slow To make or become slow or slower.

slow down **1.** I (2) He slowed down when he saw the traffic cop approaching. [Reduced the speed of the car.] **2.** T (2,6) The heavy traffic on Fifth Avenue slowed him down. [Kept him from making rapid progress.] **3.** I (2,6) The doctor told him he would have to slow down if he wanted to avoid another heart attack. [Not work so hard; take time for rest and relaxation.] **4.** *slow-down* N.A.

(2,6) A delay in progres or action; especially a deliberate slowing of pace by workers to win demands from their employers.

slow up **1.** I (2) Business is slowing up now that Christmas shopping is over. [The stores are not selling goods as rapidly as before.] **2.** I (2,11) Slow up! We're coming to a sharp curve (a narrow bridge, an intersection, a bit of rough road, etc.). [Reduce your speed! There is danger ahead.]

Note. "Slow down" usually refers primarily to a reduction "in speed".

"Slow up" usually refers to a purposeful slowing. The distinction is not always clear.

Slumber To sleep, doze, especially lightly.

slumber away T (6) It was a warm, lazy day. We slumbered away the afternoon, waiting for the cool canyon breeze to start up. [Spent the time in sleep.]

slumber on I (II 2) Slumber on, My Little Gypsy Sweetheart. [Keep sleeping.] Title of a popular song.

Slur To pass over lightly or without mention or consideration.

slur over T (2) In his report to the meeting he slurred over the failures (the bad state of finances, the disagreements, etc.). [Did not call attention to them, covered them up.]

Smash To break to pieces with violence and often with a crashing sound.

smash up **1.** T (6) Informal. He smashed up his car when he ran off the road and hit a telephone pole. [Wrecked it, causing great damage.] **2.** *smash-up* N. (6) A wreck of one or more vehicles, resulting in considerable damage.

Smell I To perceive the odor or scent of, through the nose.

smell out **1.** T (3,10) Many animals have a highly developed sense of smell. They can smell out their prey in the darkness of night. [Discover it by smelling.] **2.** T (3) Ext. The secret police have many special devices for smelling out subversive agents (enemy spies, criminals, etc.). [Finding, detecting, identifying them.]

Smell II To produce an offensive odor.

smell up T (6) The burnt toast (the boiled cabbage, etc.) smelled up the whole house. [Filled it with an unpleasant odor.]

Smoke To create smoke; to use smoke for a purpose; to draw into the mouth and puff out the smoke of tobacco or other substances.

smoke down T (6) He smokes his cigars (cigarettes) down to the last inch. [Till they are reduced to an inch in length.]

smoke out **1.** T (2) The police tossed tear gas (smoke bombs) into the building to smoke out the gangsters. [Force them to leave the building.] **2.** T (3) Ext. The district attorney and several reporters joined forces to smoke out the gang leaders (the spy ring, the conspirators, the grafters, etc.). [Force them into public view, expose them.]

smoke up **1.** T (6) A log from the fireplace had fallen onto the hearth and smoked up the living room. [Filled it with smoke.] **2.** I (7) Our host offered us cigars and told us to smoke up. [Begin smoking.]

Smooth   To make smooth of surface; to make free of hindrances or difficulties.

smooth back   T (1)   With a quick gesture he smoothed back his hair, then straightened his tie and brushed himself off. [Passed his hand over his hair to make it lie back.]

smooth down   T (1,6)   He smoothed down the table top with sandpaper before applying shellac. [Made the surface smooth.] See **sand down**.

smooth out   **1.** T (1,9)   She smoothed out the wrinkles in her dress before answering the doorbell. [Passed her hand over the wrinkles to eliminate them.] **2.** T (7,9)   Ext. Our ambassador to the U.S.S.R. is attempting to smooth out the difficulties that have arisen over the consular treaty. [Eliminate them.]

smooth over   T (2)   Ext. Do you think the marriage counselor will be able to smooth over the difficulties (misunderstandings, quarrels, etc.) between Mr. Smith and his wife? [Eliminate them; make them less troublesome.]

Snap   To perform quickly an act such as biting, taking, breaking, speaking (often accompanied by a sharp snapping sound.).

snap back   **1.** T (1)   Football. The center snapped the ball back to the quarterback. [He flipped the ball between his legs to the player crouched behind him.] **2.** T (5)   When her husband accused her of being unfaithful to him she snapped back an angry denial. [Answered sharply that it was not true.]   **3.** I (4)   He was very ill all winter long but has snapped back with the coming of spring.   **4.** *snap-back* N.   (4,1)   a. A sudden rebound or recovery. b. Football. The action of snapping the ball back.

snap down   T (1)   When he had finished packing his trunk he snapped the lid down and locked it. [Brought the lid down quickly.]

snap in   **1.** T (1)   Many top coats are provided with a special lining that you can snap in. [Fasten to the inside of the coat by means of snaps.]   **2.** *snap-in* N.A. (1)   This coat has a snap-in (lining).

snap on   **1.** T (I 1)   This typewriter has a cover that you can snap on.   **2.** *snap-on* A.   (I 1)   This typewriter comes with a snap-on cover.

snap out   **1.** T (1,9)   When I asked him to help me with my work he snapped out a refusal. [He spoke sharply, unpleasantly.]   **2.** T (1,9)   The captain snapped out an order, and the soldiers marched off. [Gave a sharp command.]   **3.** *snap out (of)* I (1,9)   Informal. He had been very sorry for himself. I told him to snap out of it, and start doing something positive. [Give up feeling sorry for himself.]   **4.** *snap-out* N.   (1)   An order form with perforated sheets that can be snapped in or out of a notebook.

snap up   **1.** T (5)   Informal. He had been making unpleasant remarks about her family when she suddenly snapped him up. [Interrupted his remarks sharply.]   **2.** T (5)   The store had a bargain sale on electric toasters and the customers snapped them up in two hours time. [Bought them quickly.]   **3.** T (5)   When

John's friend invited him to go hunting, John snapped up the invitation. [Accepted it quickly.]

Snarl To bring into a tangled or confused condition.

snarl up T (6) The kitten managed to snarl up her thread by playing with the spool. [Unwound it into a tangled mess.] **2.** *snarled up* A. a. Tangled. [Traffic around the Arc de Triomphe is usually snarled up during rush hours. It is slowed to a crawl by the general confusion.] b. Blocked. [Peace negotiations have been snarled up for three months. There has been no progress towards a settlement because of general discord.] See **foul up.**

Sneak To go in a stealthy or furtive manner. May be used with all the second elements to show the direction of the movement.

sneak up (on) I (13) Johnny sneaked up on the big boy who had hurt his little brother, and hit him with a stick. [Moved quietly and so as not to be seen.]

Sniff To search out by smelling, as a dog.

sniff around I (1,2) She is a busybody who is always sniffing around in other people's private affairs. [Trying to find some scandal, something to gossip about.]

sniff out T (3) She is an expert in sniffing out a scandal. [She often succeeds in finding one.]

Snow To cover, obstruct, impede, etc., with snow.

snow in **1.** T (3) That last big storm snowed in many of the farmers in the Middle West. [The snow blocked their driveways so that they could not reach the highways.] **2.** *snowed in* A. T (1) Many of the farmers were snowed in for five days. [They were unable to leave their homes for that length of time.]

snow under **1.** T (3) Slang. The rush of orders for the Christmas trade snowed the office staff under. [Gave them so much work they had difficulty taking care of it.] **2.** *snowed under* A. (3) I'm completely snowed under with 300 examination papers to correct and grade. [I have no time to do anything else.]

Snuff To extinguish, especially a candle.

snuff out **1.** T (8) We were careful to snuff out all the candles before going to bed. [Extinguish them.] **2.** T (9) Ext. The government succeeded in snuffing out the revolt by capturing the leaders. [Crushing it, suppressing it.]

Snuggle To draw or press closely against, as for comfort or affection.

snuggle down I (1) The children snuggled down under the warm covers and were soon fast asleep. [Down in their beds.]

snuggle up (to) I (3) Little Marie snuggled up to her mother, feeling safe and free from fears. [Pressed closely against her.]

Soak To penetrate (as a liquid); to absorb a liquid.

soak in **1.** I (2) The ground was so hard and dry it took an hour for the water to soak in. [Penetrate the soil.] **2.** I (2) Ext. The lesson (the idea, the suggestion, the story, etc.) was so new and surprising, it took some time for it to soak in. [Penetrate the mind, the consciousness.]

soak off T (1)   You can use warm water and a detergent to soak off the old sticker (paper, plaster, etc.). [Remove it by wetting it thoroughly.]

soak out   **1.** T (1)   You can soak out the stain from the napkin (the handkerchief, the tablecloth, etc.) by putting it in cold water for a while. [Remove it by soaking.] **2.** T (1)   Soak the ache out of tired feet with a foot bath. [Relieve it.]

soak through   **1.** T (1)   The heavy rain soaked us through before we reached the house. [Penetrated all our clothing.]   **2.** *soaked through* A.   (1,5)   We were soaked through (through and through) by the downpour. [All of our clothing was soaking wet.]

soak up   **1.** T (1,4)   She used a blotter to soak up the spilled ink. She used a dish towel to soak up the spilled milk. [Absorb it.]   **2.** T (1,4)   Informal. Our neighbors have gone to Paris to soak up a little culture. [Acquire some culture by absorption.]

Soap   To rub, cover, lather, or treat with soap.

soap up I (4)   Just when he had soaped up for his shower the telephone rang. [Covered his body with lather from soap.]

Sob   To weep with a sound caused by a convulsive catching of the breath.

sob out T (1)   She went home to Mother and sobbed out her story of the quarrel she had had with her husband. [Told the story while sobbing.]

Sober   To make or become sober, especially after being drunk.

sober up   **1.** I (2,4)   We'll have to wait until Harry sobers up before driving home. [Recovers from drunkenness.]   **2.** T (4)   His host gave him some black coffee to help sober him up. [Make him recover from his drunken condition.]

Sock   To use, or manipulate, as if using a sock.

sock away T (5)   Slang. He was able to sock away fifty bucks (dollars) each month. [Save that much. Put it in a savings account.]

sock in T (3)   He was socked in at the airport. [Unable to fly his plane because of bad weather conditions.]

Soften   To make soft or softer.

soften up   **1.** T (2,4)   To soften up hard putty you can mix it with linseed oil. [Make it pliable.]   **2.** T (2,4)   The gardener softened up the hard clay soil by mixing in humus, wood ashes and sand. [Made it easier to work with.] **3.** T (4,11)   The captain called for a bombing strike (an artillery barrage, etc.) to soften up the enemy positions. [Reduce their numbers and their capacity to resist attack.]

Sop   To take up (liquid) by absorption.

sop up   **1.** T (1,3,4)   After finishing his meal he used a piece of bread to sop up the gravy that was left on his plate. [Take it up off the plate.]   **2.** T (1,3,4) Mother sopped up the spilled milk with a towel (paper napkin, sponge, etc.). [Removed it from the table (floor, chair, etc.).]   **3.** T (1,3,4)   Ext. Informal. They are over in Europe this year sopping up culture. [Touring museums and galleries to steep themselves in it.]

Sort   To arrange or select according to sorts, kinds.

   sort out   T (7)   After their father's death the daughters spent a lot of time sorting out his belongings. [Dividing them into groups, deciding who would receive what items.]

   sort over   T (6)   Some of the apples in the basket were spoiled. We sorted them over and threw away the bad ones. [Examined all of them.]

Sound I   To make or emit a sound.

   sound off   **1.** T (9)   Military. The sergeant gave the command "Sound off!" and the soldiers shouted "One! Two! Three! Four!" in sequences of fours. [Spoke loudly and clearly.]   **2.** I (9)   Jack is the sort of person who will sound off at the slightest provocation. [Speak loudly; complain about things; object to things.] **3.** I (9)   He's always sounding off about how much he knows, what he can do, how wrong other people are, etc. [Talking arrogantly.] See **blow off.**

   sound out   I (1,9)   From the back of the hall a deep voice sounded out. [It made itself heard.]

Sound II   To measure or try the depth of water by some mechanical device.

   sound out   T (3)   Ext. I'm not sure whether Mr. Jones is a Republican or a Democrat. I'll have to sound him out. [Try to learn his views.] See **feel out.**

Soup   Slang. To add to the efficiency or speed of an engine or motor, through improvement in fuel or adjustment of the engine.

   soup up   **1.** T (2,5)   Teenagers are always looking for some way to soup up the motors of their jalopies (their old second hand cars). [Increase the power by use of additives or some mechanical means.]   **2.** T (2,4)   Ext. Informal. The local committee plans to soup up the political rally with a pop band and a bevy of pretty girls. [Make the rally more lively, more entertaining.]

Spade   To dig, cut, or remove with a spade.

   spade under   T (3)   Father is out in the garden spading under the manure and the year's collection of humus. [Turning them under with his spade.]

   spade up   T (2,11)   Father spaded up the garden last weekend so he can now begin to plant the seeds. [Made it ready by spading.]

Speak   To utter words; to talk.

   speak out   I (5)   If you want your representative in Congress to vote for gun control laws, you must speak out. [Express your opinion openly and firmly.]

   speak up   I (5)   When grandfather asks you what you want for Christmas, don't be bashful. Speak up! [Tell him.] See **answer up, ask up, talk out, talk up.**

Speed I   To move, cause to move, go, or proceed with speed.

   speed up   **1.** T (2)   He stepped on the gas to speed up the engine. [Cause it to go at a greater speed.]   **2.** I (2)   He (the car, the motorcycle, etc.) speeded up on the freeway. [Increased speed.]   **3.** *speed-up* N. (2)   a. An increase of speed. b. Labor. An imposed increase in the rate of production of a worker without corresponding increase in the rate of pay.

Speed II To move, go, or proceed with speed in a vehicle. May be used with all the second elements to indicate the direction of the action.

    Ex. The motorcade **sped across**. (1) [Across the bridge.]

        The big cars came **speeding by** (2) [Past us.]

        He **sped on** (II 1,2) through the night. [Continued.]

        The trucks **sped through** (1) at seventy miles an hour. [Through the town.]

Spell I To name, write, or otherwise give the letters in order of a word (a syllable, etc.).

    spell down **1.** T (2,4) Johnny won the spelling match. He spelled down fifteen other students in the contest. [Outlasted them.] **2.** *spell-down* N. (2,4) A spelling competition which begins with the contestants standing, and which ends when all but one, the winner, have been required to sit down due to a specified number of misspellings. Also called a spelling bee.

    spell off T (10) The leader of the group spelled off the duties of each member, so that all should know what was expected of them. [Made a detailed statement of each one's duties.]

    spell out **1.** T (7) Will you please spell out that name (that word, that title, etc.)? I didn't hear it very distinctly. [Give the letters in order.] **2.** T (7) I spelled out the telegram for the telegraph operator. [Gave the whole telegram by spelling.] **3.** T (9) Ext. You say you are not sure you understand the plan. I'll spell it all out for you in detail. [Give you all of the information about it I possess.]

Spell II To take the place of someone in some activity; relieve.

    spell off **1.** T (4) I could see that he was very tired after two hours of hard work so I spelled him off. [I let him rest, and did his work for him.] **2.** T (4) When driving long distances we spell each other off every hundred miles. [We take turns driving.]

Spice To prepare or season with a spice or spices.

    spice up **1.** T (2) Your chili recipe is very mild. You'll have to spice it up for our Mexican guests. [Add more spice.] **2.** T (2) Ext. Informal. He always spices up his conversation with little off-color stories. [Adds color and interest to it.]

Spill To fall or cause to fall from a container.

    spill out **1.** T (1,2) The truck overturned and spilled out its contents onto the highway. [Out of the truck.] **2.** I (1,2) When the show is over the people spill out onto the sidewalks. [Come out like water from a container.]

    spill over **1.** I (3) She forgot to turn down the heat and the boiling soup spilled over onto the floor. [Over the rim of the kettle and down.] **2.** I (4) There were not enough seats for everyone at the meeting. It spilled over into the lobby. [Some people had to stand in the lobby.] **3.** I (3) In the rainy season, water spills over the dam. [It rises to the top and flows over it.] **4.** I (3) The glowing happiness of the bride and groom spilled over to the wedding guests. [It was contagious. Everyone felt happy looking at them.]

Spin I To revolve, or cause to revolve, or rotate rapidly.

spin around **1.** I (3) When I shouted to him he spun around and started looking for the source of the shout. [Turned about quickly.] **2.** T (3) Boxing. His opponent hit him a heavy blow that spun him around on his heels. [Made him rotate.]

Spin II To draw out and twist into thread; produce or eliminate by drawing out.

spin off **1.** T (3) Commerce. After acquiring a rival concern, the company was required to spin off about a third of its assets. [To divest itself of some of the new company's assets by distributing them to stockholders as dividends without detracting from or affecting the relative size or stability of the parent company.] **2.** *spin-off* N. (2) Commerce. A process of reorganizing a corporate structure, whereby the capital stock of a division or subsidiary of a corporation or of a newly affiliated company is transferred to the stockholders of the parent corporation, without an exchange of any part of the stock of the latter. See **split-off, split-up.**

spin out **1.** T (10) The spider spun out a long thread as it dropped from the ceiling. [Extruded a thread behind it.] **2.** T (10) He spun out the story at great length, adding details we hadn't heard before. [Made a long story of one that had been much shorter when first told.]

Splash To scatter water, mud, or other liquid about.

splash down **1.** I (1) Aerospace. The nose cone of the space vehicle splashed down 20 miles from target. [Landed in the sea, with a splash.] **2.** *splash-down* N. (1) The splash-down occurred at 12:45 P.M.

splash out I (1) When Mary dropped the milk pitcher, the milk splashed out all over the table. [Scattered, spread in all directions.]

splash up T (6) The long drive in the rain splashed up the car. [Covered it with mud and water.]

splash one's way To make one's way through a liquid with a splashing sound. Can be used with all elements. See **fight one's way.**

    Ex. He splashed his way down the stream. [Waded to a good fishing spot.]

Split To divide or separate from end to end; to separate by cutting or chopping, usually lengthwise.

split off **1.** T (2) The woodcutter split off long sections of the log to make a rail fence. [Cut them off lengthwise.] **2.** I (2) Ext. After the Reformation many small sects split off from the Mother Church. [Separated from it.] **3.** *split-off* N. (2) a. An act or process of splitting away. b. A group or product so formed. c. Spin-off.

split up **1.** I (2,11) Mother told the boys to get busy and split up enough kindling and firewood to last for five days. [Chop large pieces of wood into the proper size for burning in stove and fireplace.] **2.** I (6) Ext. I hear that Robert and Marie have split up. [They are no longer close friends. Possibly they are separating or getting a divorce.] **3.** I (6,10) After the opening ceremonies the meeting split up into discussion groups. [Separate groups were formed.] **4.** I (2) The steamer received such a pounding from the thirty foot waves that it split up in mid-ocean. [Broke into two pieces.] **5.** *split-up* N. (4,11) a. An act or instance of splitting. b. Spin-off.

Spout   To emit or discharge forcibly in a stream.

   spout out   **1.** T (1,10) In Yellowstone Park we watched Old Faithful Geyser spout out great clouds of steam and vapor. [Out of an opening in the ground.] **2.** T (2,7) Ext. If you give him half a chance he'll spout out his opinions on all the world's problems. [Out in public.]

   spout up   I (1) The Daisy Geyser was quiet when we got there, but after a short wait, it spouted up in a beautiful display. [Up from the ground.]

Spread   To draw, stretch, or open out in extent.

   spread out   **1.** T (10) The eagle spread out his wings and floated high above the tree tops. [Opened them to their widest extent.] **2.** T (10) He spread out the road map on the table and showed us the best route to Chicago. [Unfolded it and laid it out on the table.] **3.** I (6,10) The soldiers spread out over the countryside, searching for hidden machine gun nests. [Scattered so as to make a clean sweep of the area.]

Spring   To rise, leap, move, or act suddenly or swiftly.

   spring back   I (3) The soldier stepped into the clearing, but sprang back when a sniper's bullet grazed his helmet. [Jumped backward.] **2.** I (1) When you press the catch, a small panel springs back, revealing the contents. [It slides into a slot out of the way.]

   spring out   **1.** I (3) As we approached the door, a cat sprang out of the bushes and ran around the house. **2.** T (1) On the hour a little bird springs out of the cuckoo clock. [Appears suddenly from the inside on a spring.]

   spring up   **1.** I (1) After the warm rain we found mushrooms springing up all through the orchard. [Up from the ground.] **2.** I (1) There are many new houses springing up in the suburbs. [Being built rapidly.] **3.** I (1) He sprang up from his chair when the doorbell rang. [Rose hurriedly.] **4.** I (1,9) Ext. News came to the capitol city that a revolt had sprung up in the provinces. [Started suddenly.] **5.** I (1) When you release the catch on the lid, the jack-in-the-box springs up. [It pops into view.]

Sprout   To begin to grow, shoot forth, as a plant from a seed.

   sprout out   I (1) We could see that the horns on the young deer were just beginning to sprout out. [Appear on his head.]

   sprout up   **1.** I (7) Seedlings from the Siberian elm were sprouting up all over the garden. [Beginning to grow.] **2.** I (7) It takes many years for the seeds of democracy to sprout up in countries that have lived for hundreds of years under despotism. [Begin to grow.]

Spruce   To make oneself neat, smart in appearance.

   spruce up   **1.** I (2,11) You can't go to the party looking like that. You'll have to spruce up a bit. [Improve your appearance; dress up.] **2.** T (5,11) The Joneses are sprucing up their living room with a new set of furniture. [Improving its appearance.]

Spy   To observe secretively or furtively, with hostile intent; do the work of a spy.

   spy out   T (7,9)   The commanding officer sent scouts ahead to spy out the terrain. [Get useful information concerning the enemy.]

Square   To face directly; prepare for action; settle accounts.

   square away   **1.** I (1)   The captain called "Square away!" [Set the sails to run before the wind.]   **2.** I (1)   The wrestlers squared away for the first fall. [Took positions face to face.]   **3.** I (1)   It's time to square away (get squared away) for the evening's activities. [Prepare ourselves for them.]

   square off   I (8)   Boxing. The opponents squared off and began looking for an opening. [Assumed their posture for beginning the fight.]

   square up   I (4)   After breakfast Father squared up with the cashier (of a hotel or motel) and we checked out. [Paid our bill; settled our account.]

Squeak   To succeed in some activity by a very narrow margin.

   squeak by   I (4)   Informal. John's salary is just enough for the two of them to squeak by. [Live without going into debt.] See **get by.**

   squeak through   I (4)   That was a very hard exam, but I think I squeaked through. [Managed to pass it, with some difficulty.]

Squeeze   To press forcibly together or exert pressure on; compress.

   squeeze by   I (2)   There were many people standing in the doorway. There was just enough room to squeeze by. [Go past the people, into the room, by pressing against them.]

   squeeze in   **1.** T (1)   Our car seats five people comfortably, but we can squeeze in a sixth if necessary. [Make room for another by pressing close together.]   **2.** I (3)   The bus was so full we had trouble squeezing in. [Getting in by pushing against the other people.]   **3.** T (5)   Baseball. The Dodgers squeezed in a run at the very end of the ninth inning. [Managed to make a run just before the end of the inning.]

   squeeze off   **1.** T (2)   The cook squeezed off a lump of dough, patted it into shape and put it in the baking pan. [Pinched a piece from the mass of dough.]   **2.** T (2)   Ext. When the cowboy shook my hand it seemed as though he was going to squeeze it off. [He had a strong handclasp.]

   squeeze out   **1.** T (9)   She squeezed out the juice of six lemons and made a big pitcher of lemonade. [Removed the juice by using a squeezer.]   **2.** T (1)   To brush your teeth, first squeeze out some toothpaste onto the brush. [Force it out of the tube.]   **3.** T (3)   The big automobile manufacturers have squeezed out many small companies. [Eliminated them by competitive pressure.]

   squeeze through: **1.** I (1)   They reached the gate just at closing time, but managed to squeeze through. [Through the gate.]   **2.** I (4)   In his senior year he found the competition very hard, but he managed to squeeze through. [Finish success-fully by a close margin.]

squeeze up   I (10)   I think we can make room for another person in our car if we squeeze up. [Sit very close together.]

Stack   To pile or arrange in a stack; arrive at an orderly total.

stack up   **1.** T (10)   Aeronautics. The flight control tower stacks up the incoming planes. [Controls the flight patterns of planes waiting to land at an airport so that each circles at a designated altitude.]   **2.** I (4)   Slang. She doesn't stack up to you, baby. [She can't compare with you for looks.]   **3.** I (4)   Slang. Your story just doesn't stack up. I don't believe you are telling the truth. [The facts don't fit together into a logical total.]

Stake   To mark with, or as with stakes.

stake off   **1.** T (3)   He staked off a corner of his yard, to make a rose garden. [Used stakes to mark where it would go.]   **2.** T (3)   The manager of the Fair Grounds staked off the refreshment concession for a friend of his. [Set aside that activity, reserved it for his friend.] See **map off.**

stake out   **1.** T (1)   In the early days of the uranium (gold, silver, oil, etc.) boom he had staked out a claim in the Moab area. [Took the legal steps necessary to establish his claim.]   **2.** I (2)   He stakes out his tomatoes every spring. [Plants them with stakes for support.]   **3.** T (10)   Slang. The sheriff has the suspected robber staked out. [The suspect is under constant surveillance.]   **4.** T (4)   Slang. The sheriff staked out five deputies to keep an eye on the suspect. [Assigned them to watch all his movements.]   **5.** *stake-out* N. (10)   Slang. An act or instance of surveillance by the police, as in anticipation of a crime, or the arrival of a wanted criminal. [Set up a stake-out across the street from the criminal's hideout.]

stake up   T (1,3)   Our gardener always stakes up the tomatoes. [Ties the tomato vines to stakes to hold them off the ground.]

Stall   To delay, by ruse or deception.

stall around   I (2)   John stalled around for weeks before making up his mind to enlist in the Navy. [He delayed making the decision.]

stall off   T (2)   Henry was able to stall off the landlady by promising to pay his rent when he got a check from his father. [He got her to extend the due date.]

Stamp I   To trample with or as if with the feet.

stamp down   **1.** T (2,5)   After moistening the loose soil around the newly planted tree the gardener stamped it down firmly. [Stepped hard on it to make it compact.]   **2.** T (1,5)   The police say they plan to stamp down hard on the young hood-lums. [Treat them firmly and severely.]

stamp out   **1.** T (8)   A small fire was started by a spark in the dry grass but we stamped it out quickly. [Used our feet to put it out.]   **2.** T (8)   He dropped his cigarette butt on the floor and stamped it out. [Extinguished it by stepping on it.]   **3.** T (8)   Ext. Be sure to stamp out your cigarette before you leave the room. [Extinguish it by pressing it with your fingers into the ash tray.] **4.** T (8) The government succeeded in stamping out a rebellion in the southern province. [Crushing it.] See **put down**.

Stamp II To walk with forcible, heavy, resounding steps. May be used with all the second elements to indicate the direction of the movement.

Ex. He **stamped out** angrily. [Out of the room.]

He **stamped through** without even saying "Hello". [Through the group.]

Stand I I. To assume or keep an upright position on the feet; to remain firm in a position or belief, or cause.

stand around I (1,2) In the public square there were many people standing around waiting for the parade. [Here and there.]

stand back **1.** I (1) When the doctor arrived at the scene of the accident he asked the onlookers to stand back. [Step back from around the injured man.] **2.** I (1) When you have a good idea to present to the meeting, don't stand back, but speak up. [Don't hesitate to present your idea.]

stand by **1.** I (1) We stood by as the police came and began investigating the accident. [Close to the scene.] **2.** I (1) The doctor asked me to stand by in case Father asked for me when he came to (recovered consciousness). [Be present in order to help.] **3.** I (1) The radio (television) announcer asked the listeners to stand by for a special bulletin. [Keep the radio or television set tuned to the same station.] **4.** I (1,3) The program director told him to stand by, as it was nearly time for him to appear on the program. [Get ready to speak, participate.] **5.** *stand-by* N. (1,3) a. One who can be relied on. [Mr. Smith is one of our old stand-bys. He is always there to be counted on.] b. One that is dependable. [My 1959 Ford is my stand-by for vacation travel.] c. Something or someone held in reserve for emergency, especially a substitute radio or television program used in case of cancellation of a regularly scheduled program. [When a snow-storm kept the band from reaching the studio, they used a film as a stand-by.] d. A state of readiness. [The flight was full but they put the passenger on stand-by in case there was a cancellation.] [Hearing rumors of invasion, the ruler put the troops on stand-by.] **6.** *stand-by* A. (1,3) Available for use as a replacement. [A stand-by player.] [A stand-by medical team.] b. Composed of those available. [A stand-by line at the airport.] [A stack of stand-by recordings.]

stand down I (1) Law Court. After giving his testimony the witness was asked to stand down. [Come down from the witness stand, and go to his seat.]

stand in **1.** I (4) At the rehearsal for the wedding the bride's sister stood in for her because of a slight illness. [Took her place.] **2.** *stand in (with)* I (9) I understand that Robert stands in with (in well with) his boss. [He is on friendly terms, enjoys the confidence of his boss.] **3.** I (4) The former police inspector stood in with the leader of the bootleg ring. [Conspired with him, to protect him from the law.] **4.** *stand-in* N. (4) a. A person employed to replace an actor during the preparation of lighting, cameras, etc., or in dangerous scenes. b. Any substitute. [Mary was a stand-in for her sister at the wedding rehearsal.] c. Informal. A position of favoritism. [He has a stand-in with the boss.]

stand off **1.** I (2) When the street riot started most of the older people stood off at a distance. [They did not come close to the rioting.] **2.** I (2) She put the flower vase on the piano, and stood off to study the effect. [Stepped away from the piano.] **3.** *stand-off* N. (2) a. An act of standing off; aloofness. b. A prop for holding the top of a ladder away from the vertical surface against which it is leaning. **4.** *stand-off (stand-offish)* A. (3) a. He had a stand-off attitude towards civil rights. [He held himself apart, did not take a stand in favor of civil rights.] b. Not friendly, not cooperative, not interested. [The new neighbor was very standoffish. She showed no desire to make our acquaintance.]

stand out **1.** I (10) The pier stands out from the harbor wall. [It projects, extends out to sea.] **2.** I (9) You will be sure to recognize my grandfather. He always stands out in a crowd. [He is conspicuous; can be seen easily.] **3.** I (10) Senator Jones stood out against the proposed gun law. [He continued to oppose it.] **4.** *stand-out* N. (4) a. Something or someone remarkably superior to others. [Albert was a stand-out in the track events.] [The new play is a stand-out among this seasons productions.] b. Informal. One who defies the majority by refusing to conform with their actions, opinions, or wishes. [All of us voted for the measure except Brown. He was the only stand-out.] **5.** *stand-out* A. (4) Excellent, superior. [The pianist gave a stand-out performance last night.]

stand over I (3) The usher asked us to stand over a little, to make room for two more people. [Move to the right or left.]

stand up **1.** I (1) When the President came to the platform, the audience stood up to applaud. [Rose from their seats.] **2.** I (1) There were not enough seats in the auditorium so we stood up during the whole performance. [Remained standing.] **3.** I (4,5) Our old car stood up well during the trip across the continent. [Continued to function well.] **4.** I (4,5) Mrs. Adams stood up well during her husband's last illness. [She carried on; was able to endure the pain and distress.] **5.** *stand up (for)* I (1,5) The minority groups have to stand up for their rights. [Defend them; try to secure them.] **6.** I (1,5) At John's wedding his cousin Charles stood up for him. [Served the bridegroom as best man.] **7.** *stand up (to)* I (5,9) In Nazi Germany there were few people who dared to stand up to Hitler. [Speak their minds, act fearlessly.] **8.** *stand-up* A. (1) a. Stiff, upright. [The old man wore a stand-up collar.] b. Absorbed or eaten while one is standing. [A stand-up meal. A stand-up lecture.] c. Designed for or requiring a standing position. [A stand-up lunch counter.] d. Boxing. Characterized by the rapid exchange of many blows, toe to toe. [A stand-up fight.] e. Theater. Giving a comic monologue while standing alone in the center of the stage. [A stand-up monologuist.]

Stand II To place or keep someone or something in a standing position; repel an advance or fight to a draw.

stand off **1.** T (3) Yesterday our troops stood off an enemy attack for three hours. [Repulsed the attack, prevented an enemy advance.] **2.** *stand-off* N. (3) An equal contest. a. The battle between our troops and the enemy was a stand-off. [Neither side was able to advance.] b. Sports. The game resulted in a stand-off. [The result was a draw, a tie. Neither side could claim a victory.] c. The T.V. debate between the two candidates was a stand-off. [Neither man could claim a victory.]

stand up **1.** T (1) He stood his little son up on the table so all could admire him. [Placed him in standing position.] **2.** T (1,6) Slang. I had made a date with Alice for the dance, but she stood me up. [She did not keep her word. She figuratively left me standing.]

Stare To gaze fixedly and intently, especially with the eyes wide open. May be used with all the second elements to indicate the direction of the action.

stare down T (1,4) I turned around to look at the elderly lady at the table next to us but she stared me down. [Made me drop my eyes, turn my head away, by gazing steadily at me.]

Start I To begin to move in some direction. May be used with all the second elements to indicate the direction of the movement. The verbs "come" and "go" are understood between the two elements.

Ex. She **started around**. [Started to go or come around.]

She **started back**. [Started to go or come back.]

Start II To initiate an action or activity; cause to move or operate.

start in **1.** I (9) As soon as the bell rang he started in to work. [Began at once.] **2.** T (4) The laboratory assistant came to John's table and started him in. [Showed him how to begin the experiment.] **3.** I (9) After a brief lull, his headache started in again. [His head began throbbing again.]

start off **1.** I (8) The speaker started off by saying how glad he was to be in Portland. [Began his speech.] **2.** T (8) The speaker's remarks about race riots started off a long, heated argument. [Caused it to begin.] **3.** *start-off* N. (2) We're going down to the big meeting for the start-off of Mr. Nelson's campaign for the Senate. [The beginning of the campaign.] See **get off**.

start out **1.** I (7) Mary started out to apologize for her being late, but we told her it didn't matter. [Began.] **2.** T (9) His father had promised to start him out in business as soon as he had his degree. [Furnish the capital necessary to make a start.]

start up **1.** I (1) He started up from his chair on seeing the President enter the room. [Rose quickly.] **2.** T (7) Mr. Adams is starting up a new business (a law practice, etc.) the first of the year. [Beginning.] **3.** I (5,7) The engine started up with a roar at the third turn of the ignition switch. [Began to function.] **4.** *start-up* N. (2,5) a. The act or fact of creating something. b. An act or instance of setting in motion.

Starve To weaken or die for lack of food; to deprive of sustenance.

starve off I (5) People in Biafra are starving off by the thousands. [Dying from starvation.]

starve out T (1,8) The besiegers hoped to starve out the defenders of the city by cutting off all food supplies. [Cause them to surrender from hunger.]

Stash Informal. To put by or away for safekeeping or future use, usually in a secret place.

stash around T (2) The squirrels at this season of the year are busy stashing nuts around, getting ready for winter. [Hiding them here and there.]

stash away T (5) Slang. I'll bet he has stashed away a million or so in the Swiss banks. [Put the money there where people will not find out about it.]

Stave To break or crush inward; to keep off an attacker with or as if with a club.

stave in **1.** T (2,3) His boat was staved (stove) in when it was struck by the prow of the steamship. [The side of the boat was crushed inward.] **2.** T (2,3) A vicious kick by the horse staved (stove) in his ribs. [Cracked them and bent them inward.] **3.** *stove in* A. (3) That was a hard day's work in the fields yesterday. I'm all stove in. [I feel as though I have been crushed. I'm terribly tired.]

stave off **1.** (2) The last battalion succeeded in staving off the enemy attack until help arrived. [Defending itself, as if with staves or clubs.] **2.** (2,4) I hope we can stave off the rent collector (the foreclosure, hunger, illness, misfortune, etc.) for another month. [Keep them from our door.]

Stay To remain in a place, situation, company, etc. See **be, remain**. May be used with most of the second elements to show the location of the action.

stay back I (2) This man has been seriously injured. Stay back! [Don't come near, give him plenty of room.]

stay down I (1) He had a bad virus infection. The doctor advised him to stay down for several days. [Stay in bed.]

stay in **1.** I (1) Johnny can't come out to play. He has to stay in for several days. [In the house, because of illness.] See **keep in. 2.** I (4) Poker. I think I'll stay in. [Continue to play the hand.]

stay off I (1) Mother told Bobby to get off the table and stay off. [Not to get on it again.]

stay on **1.** I (I 1) Father put me on the bus and told me to stay on until we reached Denver. [Not to get off.] **2.** I (II 2) Uncle John left Sunday evening but Aunt Louise stayed on for a week. [Remained at our house.]

stay out **1.** I (2) The children were so noisy, Mother ordered them to go out and stay out till she called them. [Out of the house.] **2.** I (4) Poker. Henry stayed out on the next deal. [He did not play the hand.] **3.** T (8) Although it was nearly midnight we stayed the performance out. [Stayed till the end.]

stay over I (7) We urged Aunt Louise to stay over for a week. [Extend her visit.]

stay under I (4) They gave her a very strong anaesthetic. She stayed under for an hour and a half. [Was unconscious from the anaesthetic.]

stay through I (3)   The meeting (lecture, concert, etc.) is going to be very long. I think we'll not stay through. [Remain till the end.]

stay up I (1,5)   During our vacation we stayed up till two a.m. every night. [We did not go to bed.] See **wait up.**

Steal   To move, go, or come secretly, quietly, or unobserved. May be used with all the second elements to show the direction of the movement.

steal away I (2)   Before the party was half over we stole away and went to a night club. [Left unobserved.]

steal by I (2)   The years steal by and before you know it you're an old man. [Go quietly, unobserved.]

steal out I (2)   Mary stole out by the back door where her boyfriend was waiting for her. [Went out so as not to be observed.]

Steam   To move under (or as under) steam power. May be used with all the second elements to show the direction of the movement. The verb describes the energy of steam used to propel machines, and by extension, the manner in which an angry person behaves under pressure.

steam away I (2)   The passenger ship steamed away with its list of 1,200 passengers. [Left the harbor.]

steam in I (1)   When the candidate heard that he had lost the election by twenty votes, he steamed in and demanded a recount. [Came in full of anger; all steamed up.]

steam out I (3)   The ship steamed out on its first trans-Atlantic voyage. [Out of the harbor.]

steam up **1.** T (4)   The vapor from the boiling kettles steamed up the kitchen windows. [Covered them with steam.] **2.** *steamed up* A. T (4)   He was all steamed up over the decision of the election chairman. [Very angry.] See **steam in.**

Step   To move by taking a step or steps. May be used with all the second elements to indicate the direction of the movement.

step aside I (1,2)   The party officials asked the older man to step aside and allow a young lawyer to become the nominee for the Senate. [Not to run for office.]

step down **1.** I (1)   He had been president of the company for many years when he stepped down in favor of the sales manager. [Resigned, and let the sales manager become president.] **2.** T (2,6)   The motor ran at too high a speed. It had to be stepped down. [Have adjustments made to reduce the rate of speed.] **3.** *step-down* A.   (2,6)   Electronics. A step-down transformer serves to reduce or decrease the voltage. See **step down 2.**

step in **1.** I (4)   The fight had been going on for an hour when the police stepped in and took over. [Came to the scene of the fight and took control.] **2.** *step-in* N.A. (1)   Any garment that can be put on by stepping into it. [Step-in shoes, slippers, panties.]

step off **1.** I (1)   He walked to the door of the bus and stepped off for a breath of fresh air. [Off the bus.] **2.** I (2)   The band struck up and the regiment stepped off to the tune of Stars and Stripes Forever. [Started marching briskly.] **3.** T (2,4)   The architect stepped off the distance between the house foundation and the street. [Measured the distance by stepping.] **4.** *step-off* N.   (2)   An abrupt drop, as from a shoreline into deep water.

step on **1.** T (I 3)   He stepped on the accelerator and passed the bus. [Gave the car more gas by pressing the pedal.] **2.** T (II 4)   Step on it! We're late. [Increase your speed.] See **hurry up. 3.** *step-on* A.   (I 3)   Operated by means of a pedal. [A step-on garbage can.]

step out **1.** I (2)   Is your husband in? No, he has just stepped out. [He has left the house (the store, the office, etc.) for a moment or two.] **2.** I (9)   The soldiers were marching along listlessly, but when the band began playing they stepped out briskly and sang as they marched. [Began to move at a more rapid pace.] **3.** I (2)   We're stepping out tonight. [We're going to have a gay, lively time socially.] **4.** *step out (on)*   I (5)   I hear that Jones is stepping out on his wife. [He's having an affair with another woman.]

step up **1.** I (9)   When your name is called, please step up and get your tickets (cards, equipment, etc.). [Come forward.] **2.** I (2,12)   John is stepping up in the National Bank. [He is getting a promotion.] **3.** T (2,5)   American Motors is stepping up both the quality and quantity of its car production. [Increasing them.] **4.** T (2)   The electric company will step up its voltage to take care of the new street lighting system. [Increase it.] **5.** *step-up* N.   (1,2)   a. An increase in size or intensity. [Step-up of a war.] **6.** *step-up* or *stepped-up* A.   (1,2) Causing or resulting in an increase. [A step-up program.] [Stepped-up production, bombardment, etc.]

Stick I   To fasten or attach into position by means of a pointed object, or some adhesive material such as glue, mucilage, etc.; to remain fastened or attached in a position by such means.

stick around   T (1,2)   I gave him the posters (notices, announcements, etc.) and told him to stick them around on all the bulletin boards. [Here and there.]

stick in   T (5)   Johnny was busy with his stamp album, sticking each new stamp in according to the country. [Into the album.]

stick on   T (I 1)   He pressed each stamp with his thumb to make it stick on. [Adhere to the envelope, the document, etc.]

stick up **1.** T (1)   He stuck up the notices on all the bulletin boards. [Fastened them there with pins, thumb tacks, adhesive tape, etc.] **2.** *stuck-up* A.   (4,6) a. Informal. She's so stuck-up she wouldn't accept an invitation to our party. [Conceited, self-important.] b. My hands (hair, clothing, etc.] were all stuck-up after papering the living room. [Covered with paste used in applying the wallpaper.]

Stick II   Informal. To remain in a place; continue in some attachment; to stay put.

stick along   I (2)   If you'll stick along with us we'll take you home after the game. [Go with us.]

stick around   I (1)   We asked him to stick around for a while to see what would happen. [Stay with us.] See **hang around.**

stick it out   T (7)   It was a very long and boring meeting but we decided to stick it out. [Stay to the very end.]

stick it through   T (3)   The meeting lasted for two hours, but we stuck it through. [From beginning to end.]

Stick III   To push or thrust as if with a pointed object.

stick down   T (1)   He stuck his hand down into his pocket, and pulled out a small knife.

stick in   T (1)   He came to the door and stuck his head in to say "Hello". [Into the room.]

stick out   I (1)   He opened the car window and stuck his head out to ask directions from the traffic cop. [Out of the window.]   **2.** I (10)   His ears stick out straight from his head. [They protrude.]   **3.** I (9)   His ambition to be president sticks out like a sore thumb. [It is very evident, can be seen by everyone.]

stick up   **1.** I (1)   Informal. She stuck up her nose at the idea of having dinner in that cheap restaurant. [Turned her nose up as a sign of dislike.]   **2.** I (6) His hair stuck up where he had slept on it. [He couldn't make it lie flat.]   **3.** T (1)   "Stick 'em up!" said the robber to his victim, pointing a gun at him. [Put up your hands!]   **4.** *stick-up* N.   (1)   "This is a stick-up!" said the robber to the bank teller. [An armed robbery.] See **hold up.**

Stiffen   To become stiff, rigid.

stiffen up   **1.** I (6)   His leg muscles stiffened up so that he could hardly walk. [Became stiff after some unusual exercise.]   **2.** I (2,6)   At first he was very friendly but he stiffened up when he learned that I was not a good Republican. [He became cool, stiff, in his attitude towards me.]

Stink   To emit, give off a strong offensive smell.

stink out   T (2)   They threw rotten eggs into the meeting hall to stink the audience out. [Cause them to leave because of the bad odor.]

stink up   T (6)   The odor of stale beer, limburger cheese, and cigar butts stunk up the living room. [Made it smell very bad.]

Stir   To move briskly; to arouse to action.

stir around   I (1,2)   When we awoke at seven o'clock, people were already stirring around downstairs. [Moving about briskly.]

stir up   **1.** T (11)   Mother was in the kitchen stirring up pancake batter. [Preparing it by stirring.]   **2.** T (2,4)   Hitler and Goebbels were past masters at stirring up, the war spirit in Nazi Germany. [Arousing it.] See **whip up.**   **3.** *stirred up* A.   (2)   We were all stirred up on hearing that our brother had been chosen to lead the campaign. [Excited, enthusiastic.]

Stock   To furnish with a stock or supply.

stock up (on)   I (4,11)   We should stock up on coffee (sugar, liquor, etc.). They say that prices are going up. [Purchase a good supply at present prices.]

Stoke   To poke, stir up, and feed a fire.

   stoke up   **1.** T (2,5)   While you stoke up the fire, I'll go to the kitchen and mix some drinks. [Stir it and put on more wood or coal.]   **2.** I (2,4)   Informal. Let's stop at the next hamburger stand and stoke up. [Get something to eat and drink.]

Stop I   To come to a stand, as in a course or journey; to halt.

   stop by   I (1)   When you are on your way down town I hope you will stop by. [Make a brief stop at our house.] See **drop by**.

   stop in   I (1)   We can't stay very long. We just stopped in to welcome you back. [Came for a short visit.] See **drop in**.

   stop off   **1.** I (2)   On our way to Los Angeles we stopped off in Las Vegas to try our luck with the one-armed bandits (slot machines). [Made a short stop.]   **2.** *stop-off* N. (2)   We made a stop-off in Las Vegas.   **3.** *stop-off* A. (2)   We had stop-off privileges in Chicago and Denver. [Our ticket permitted us to make short visits there.]

   stop over   **1.** I (7)   On our way to New York we stopped over in Rome where we spent two weeks. [Stopped for a brief visit, usually a little longer than a stop-off.]   **2.** *stop-over* N. (7)   During our stop-over we took a side trip to Milan.   **3.** *stop-over* A. (7)   We had stop-over privileges in all the capital cities of the countries we visited.

Stop II   To reduce or prevent passage of something.

   stop down   T (6)   Photography. He stopped down the lens of his camera. [To reduce the diaphragm opening, to allow less light to enter.]

   stop up   **1.** T (6)   A collection of grease and hair had stopped up the wash basin. [Blocked it; kept the water from flowing out.]   **2.** *stopped-up* A. (6)   My nose is stopped up. [The membranes are swollen.] See **block up, dam up, stuffed up**.

Store   To accumulate or put away for future use.

   store away   T (5)   When we returned from the trip we stored away our luggage. [Put it in the attic (the basement, the storeroom,) till the next trip.]

   store up   **1.** T (3,11)   The squirrels are busy storing up nuts for the winter. [Hiding them under the ground or in their nests.]   **2.** T (3,11)   Ext. We were so tired after our thousand mile drive that we needed several good nights rest to store up energy for the long drive home. [Acquire the needed energy.]

Stow   To put away in a safe or convenient place; store.

   stow away   **1.** T (5)   When we left our summer cabin we stowed away all the bedding and supplies in trunks and closets. [Made them safe from prowlers and animals.]   **2.** I (5)   A fifteen-year-old boy had stowed away in the ship's hold (the baggage compartment of the plane, etc.). [He had concealed himself in order to obtain free transportation or to escape pursuers.]   **3.** *stow-away* N. (5)   A secret passenger.

Straighten   To make or become straight in direction, form, position, character, conduct, etc.

straighten out   **1.** T (10)   The engineers are preparing plans for straightening out the river channel (the curves on the highway, etc.). [Making them straight and better suited for traffic.]   **2.** T (7)   Robert had the wrong idea about how to work the experiment. The professor straightened him out. [Showed him the correct method.]   **3.** T (9)   Our oldest son has been behaving very badly. Father is going to give him a good talking to. I hope it will straighten him out. [Make him change his ways for the better.]

straighten up   **1.** I (1,2)   Johnny was hunched over with his elbows on the table. Father told him to straighten up. [Sit up straight, with his shoulders back.]   **2.** I (2,4)   Mr. Nelson had been a rather loose-living irresponsible person in his early life, but he straightened up after he married. [Became a sober and responsible man.]   **3.** T (2,11)   We just had time to straighten up the living room before the guests arrived. [Put it in good order, arrange the furniture, etc.]

Strain   To filter, percolate.

strain off   T (2)   After the vegetables are cooked, we strain off the liquid and save it for making soup. [Remove it by a straining process.]

strain out   T (1)   When the meat that has been boiling in the kettle is tender, we strain it out and save it for making hash. [Remove it with a strainer.]

Strap   To fasten or secure with a strap or straps.

strap down   T (1)   He closed the lid of the trunk and strapped it down securely. [Buckled the straps tight.]

strap on   T (I 1)   He put the skis on top of the car and strapped them on tight. [Used straps to secure them.]

strap up   T (3,4)   The doctor found that Bob had two cracked ribs. He strapped him up and gave him some sedatives to take. [Wrapped a tight bandage around his chest.]

Stretch I   To extend; cause to continue or last.

stretch out   **1.** T (10)   He stretched himself out on the couch and soon was fast asleep. [Lay at full length.]   **2.** T (10)   She stretched out her hand to touch the little girl's hair. [Extended it.] See **reach out**.   **3.** T (10)   Our camping supplies are nearly exhausted. Maybe we can stretch them out till the end of the week. [Use them carefully; make them last.]   **4.** I (10)   The meeting stretched out till nearly midnight. [It kept going on, lasted.]   **5.** *stretch-out* N.   (6)   Industry. a. A deliberate extension of time for meeting a production quota. b. A method of factory management by which employees do additional work without a proportional increase in wages.

Stretch II   To spread widely over a distance or area, or a period of time.

stretch back   **1.** I (1)   Our farm stretches back to the foot of the mountains. [Back from the road.]   **2.** I (4)   His memory stretches back to the days before the telephone. [Back in time.]

stretch down   I (1)   Our property stretches down to the river front. [Down the slope.]

stretch off I (2)   Our view stretches off to the horizon. [Away from the house.]

stretch out I (10)   The forest stretches out in all directions. [Extends far.]

stretch over I (3)   Their ranch stretches over to the other side of the mountain. [Over the mountain.]

stretch up I (1)   Their range land stretches up to the timber line. [Up the mountain.]

Strike I   To deal a blow or stroke to a person or thing, as with a fist, a weapon, a hammer; to hit.

strike back **1.** I (5)   Ext. When his enemies accused him of making false statements, he struck back hard. [He defended himself vigorously.]   **2.** *strike back (at)* I (5)   He struck back at his accusers. See **strike back 1**.

strike down **1.** T (1,4)   The assassin struck down the President with three shots from a rifle. [Killed him.]   **2.** T (1,4)   A severe heart attack struck him down. [Injured him seriously. Incapacitated him.]

strike in I (4)   Ext. As we were discussing the problem, Dr. Jones struck in with the suggestion that we should hold up making a decision for a few days. [He interrupted our discussion.]

strike off **1.** T (1)   The printers struck off 1000 copies of the bulletin. [Printed them.]   **2.** T (8)   The typist struck off the five letters and got them in the 4 o'clock mail. [Finished them quickly.]   **3.** T (8)   Congress passed a bill to strike off a medal for Lindbergh. [Have it made.]   **4.** T (6)   When he looked at the list of members (contributors, delegates, etc.) he noticed with surprise that someone had struck his name off. [Removed it from the list by the stroke of a pen.]

strike out **1.** T (4)   He found that his name on the document was spelled incorrectly. He struck it out and inserted the correct spelling. [Removed it by a stroke of the pen.]   **2.** I (9)   He struck out at his attacker and knocked him back. [Hit him with his fist.]   **3.** I (9)   In his speech the senator struck out at all the opponents of his bill. [Attacked them with words, arguments, etc.]   **4.** I (4)   Baseball. When Jackson came to bat in the third inning he struck out. [Swung his bat at three pitched balls, and missed.]   **5.** T (4)   Baseball. The pitcher struck Jackson out in the third inning. [Pitched three balls to him, which he swung at and missed.]   **6.** *strike-out* N. (4)   Baseball. An out made by a batter or a pitcher. See **strike out 4, 5**.

strike up **1.** I (7)   The band struck up as the visiting diplomat got off the plane. [Began to play.] [Probably from the idea of the drummer striking the drum.]   **2.** T (5)   The band struck up "Hail to the Chief" as the President came onto the platform. [They began to play the traditional melody used to salute heads of state.]   **3.** T (7)   Joseph struck up a friendship (an acquaintance) with the son of Senator Chase. [Began.]

Strike II   To make one's way, advance; especially to start in a new direction.

Ex. We **struck down** (1) towards the river.

He **struck in** (1) towards the canyon waterfall.

They **struck off** (2) towards the West.

He **struck out** (1) at dawn.

We **struck over** (3) to where the two rivers meet.

String   To lead or pull with or as if with a rope; resemble a rope.

string along   **1.** T (3)   Slang. I don't believe a word he says. He's just stringing us along. [Deceiving us by telling us things he thinks we may believe.]   **2.** T (3) Slang. Henry kept stringing us along till we finally decided he never would pay back the loan. [Making promises, remarks, but never paying.]   **3.** I (2)   I'll string along with you. [I have confidence in you, will follow your lead, your suggestions.]

string out   **1.** I (10)   The parade strung out for two miles. [It made a line two miles long.]   **2.** I (10)   The payments strung out over three years. [There were three years in which to pay the full amount.]   **3.** T (7)   He strung out his account of the accident till everyone was bored with it. [Talked long and in great detail.]

string up   T (1)   Informal. The enraged citizens strung up the horse thief on the nearest tree. [They hanged him.]

Strip   To deprive of covering.

strip back   T (1)   At a corn roast you strip back the husks of the corn and use them as a handle. [Pull them back in a bunch, exposing the ear.]

strip down   I (6)   The doctor told his patient to strip down to his shorts. [Take off all his clothing except his shorts.]

strip off   T (2)   A strip-tease artist strips off her garments one by one, to the accompaniment of music. [Takes them off.]

Study   To apply oneself to the gaining of knowledge.

study out   T (7)   That's a very complicated (difficult, complex, etc.) problem. I'll have to study it out and tell you what conclusions I reach. [Do a thorough, complete study of all the possibilities.]

study over   T (6)   I doubt that I can accept the offer of the presidency. Give me time to study it over. [Think about the matter for a while.]

study up   I (5,11)   This is the last week of school. Students are all studying up for exams. [Preparing themselves by concentrated study.]

Stuff   To cram to capacity; fill or block.

stuff in   T (1)   The youngsters were over at the picnic table stuffing it in at a great rate. [Eating hungrily; pushing food into their mouths.]

stuff up   **1.** T (3)   I hate it when hay fever stuffs up my nasal passages. [Blocks them so I can't breathe.]   **2.** *stuffed-up* A.   (6)   My nose is all stuffed-up. [It is blocked with mucus and inflammation.] See **stopped-up**.

Suck   To draw into the mouth by applying the lips and tongue to create a vacuum.

suck around   I (1,2)   Slang. I can't stand that fellow. He's always sucking around you. [Fawning on you; flattering you.] See **suck up**.

suck in **1.** T (1) He sucked in his breath in short gasps. [Drew it into his lungs.] **2.** T (1) Slang. The sergeant told the private to suck in his guts and stand straight. [Draw his abdomen inward by muscular action.] **3.** T (4) Slang. I didn't want to join their club, but I got sucked in. [I was deceived into joining it.]

suck up **1.** T (1) Elephants suck up water into their trunks, then squirt it into their mouths. [Draw it up by sucking.] **2.** *suck up (to)* I (6,11) Slang. He sucked up to the boss, hoping to get a promotion and an advance in pay. [He toadied to him, made himself agreeable; flattered him.] See **suck around**.

Sugar To make sugar from the sap of maple trees.

sugar off I (7) They are sugaring off now, up in Vermont. [Completing the boiling-down process, so as to bring the syrup to the point of granulation.]

Sum To combine figures or facts into a total.

sum up **1.** T (4) Now, pupils, sum up the figures you have written down and give me the answer. [Add the figures together.] **2.** T (4) He spent the evening summing up his various assets in preparation for getting a loan from the bank. [Estimating their value as guarantee for the loan.] **3.** T (10) At the end of the lecture the professor summed up in brief form the points he had made. [Put them together as a unit or sum.] **4.** T (4) It only took a few minutes of conversation with that man to be able to sum him up. [Make an estimation, a judgment as to his character and ability.]

Swallow To take into the stomach through the mouth and esophagus; to envelop as if by swallowing.

swallow down T (1) The patient had great difficulty in swallowing down the tube the doctor inserted in his mouth. [Down into the stomach.]

swallow up T (4) Ext. We watched him as he walked down the street. He was soon swallowed up in the crowd. [He disappeared from sight, as though swallowed.]

Swear To make a solemn promise; take an oath, usually with a deity as witness.

swear in **1.** T (4) The Chief Justice swore in the President at the Inauguration ceremonies. [Administered the oath of office.] **2.** *swearing-in* N. (4) The swearing-in ceremonies are followed by an address given by the President. His family usually attends the swearing in.

swear off T (2,4) Informal. His wife persuaded him to swear off drinking (smoking, gambling, etc.). [Take an oath (make a promise) to stop.]

swear out T (7) The policeman swore out a warrant for the arrest of the man suspected of robbery. [Took the legal action, under oath, to secure a warrant.]

Sweat To excrete moisture through the pores of the skin; perspire.

sweat off T (7) After five weeks of daily workouts in the gym, followed by steam baths, he had sweated off twenty pounds. [Lost them through exercise and heat treatments.]

sweat out **1.** T (10) Slang. After the voting booths closed, the candidates sweated out the long waiting for the results. [They were anxious and worried.] **2.** T (9)

Slang. John was sweating it out in the hospital waiting room, while his wife was giving birth to their first child. [He was nervous, anxious, perhaps sweating, until the baby came.]

Sweep I To remove with or as if with a broom or brush.

sweep aside T (1) Ext. The senator swept aside the objections to his bill with a wave of the hand. [Rejected the arguments of his opponents.]

sweep away T (2) Ext. The flood swept away ten houses situated on the banks of the river. [Removed them from their foundations.]

sweep down T (1) The cleaning woman swept the cobwebs down from the walls. [Removed them by a downward movement of a broom or brush.]

sweep off T (7) The clerk swept off the sidewalk in front of the store. [Removed the dirt by sweeping.]

sweep out T (1) Before sweeping off the sidewalk, he swept out the store. [Removed the dust and dirt from the floors of the store.]

sweep up 1. T (1) Mother told her daughter to sweep the broken glass up. [Up from the floor.] **2.** I (2,4,11) It was the clerk's job to sweep up in the mornings. [Sweep the floors, in preparation for the day's business.] See **tidy up**.

Sweep II To move steadily, strongly, or swiftly. May be used with most of the second elements to indicate the direction of the movement.

sweep along I (1) The parade swept along with band playing and flags flying. [Moved rapidly, steadily.]

sweep by I (2) As the big cars swept by, the people waved to the President. [Moved rapidly, steadily.]

sweep down I (1) The eagle swept down and carried off one of the chickens. [Descended swiftly.]

sweep out I (1,4) The angry old lady rose from her chair and swept out of the room [Moved with quick, firm steps.]

Sweeten To make sweet, as by adding sugar.

sweeten up T (2) This lemonade is too sour. You should sweeten it up a bit. [Make it sweeter.]

Swell To increase in volume; to grow larger; dilate.

swell out T (9) A sudden breeze from the West swelled out the sails of our ship. [Made them look larger, stretched them.]

swell up I (2,6) After he was stung by a bee his face swelled up to half again its size. [Became that much larger.]

Swill To consume greedily like a pig; guzzle.

swill down T (5) At the fraternity party, the brothers swilled down great quantities of beer. [Drank a lot in a short time.] See **hog down**.

Swoop To sweep through the air, as a bird or a bat, especially down upon prey; lift with a sweeping motion.

swoop down I (1) The eagle swooped down and carried off one of our chickens. [Descended swiftly.]

swoop up T (1) He swooped his little daughter up in his arms and kissed her. [Lifted her.]

T

Tack To fasten by a tack or tacks.

> **tack down** T (1) The workmen were busy tacking down carpet (a rug, matting, etc.) on the living room floor. [Making it secure with tacks.]
>
> **tack on** T (4) Ext. The opponents of the gun control bill tried to kill it by tacking on certain amendments. [Make the bill unacceptable by adding amendments.]
>
> **tack up** T (1) He tacked up a picture of an airplane over his desk, (a notice on the bulletin board). [Fastened it up with a tack.]

Tag Informal. To follow closely.

> May be used with most of the second elements to indicate direction.
>
> **tag about/around** T (2) Their little brother was always tagging them around. [Following them everywhere they went.]
>
> **tag along** I (2) When the girls went for a walk, little Jane tagged along. [Followed closely.]

Tail To follow close behind, in order to observe, or hinder the escape of someone. May be used with most of the second elements to indicate the direction of the movement.

> **tail across** T (1) The escaped convicts rowed to the other side of the river, and the police tailed them across. [Across the river.]
>
> **tail out** T (2) When John and his girlfriend left the party a jealous rival tailed them out. [Followed them to watch what the two of them would do.]

Take To get into one's hands, possession, control, etc., sometimes by force or artifice; to remove or move from one place to another.

> **take away** **1.** T (2,3) He took the knife away from the boy, for fear he would hurt himself with it. [Removed it from his possession.] **2.** T (3) That fast ride down the mountain (the view of the ocean, the sound of the waterfall, etc.) took my breath away. [Almost made me stop breathing.] **3.** T (2) He took his children away to summer camp. [Away from home.]
>
> **take back** **1.** T (5) After their engagement was broken he took back many of the presents he had given her. [He regained possession of them.] **2.** T (3) The sewing machine she bought had something wrong with it so she took it back. [Returned it to the store, perhaps to exchange it for a good one.] **3.** T (4) He left his wife after a quarrel, and she said she would never take him back. [Allow him to return to her; accept him.] **4.** T (4) Those old movies take you back to your childhood. [Make you remember.] **5.** T (5) He apologized, saying he would take back all the bad things he had said about me. [Retract, withdraw them.]

take down **1.** T (1) I hired a man to take down the tree that was blocking our view. [Remove it.] **2.** T (6) Henry is very good at taking down a motor (a machine, a structure of any kind). [Taking it apart, dismantling it.] **3.** T (7) A reporter was at the meeting, taking down notes on everything that was said and done. [Down on paper.] **4.** T (6) Doctor Jones is very conceited, thinks he knows everything. I'd like to take him down a notch or two. [Do or say something to make him humble, less sure of himself.] **5.** *take-down* N. (6) a. An act or instance of taking down. b. A fire-arm designed to be swiftly assembled or disassembled. c. The point of separation of two or more of the parts of a take down fire-arm or other device. d. Informal. An act or instance of humiliation. [Having another student correct him was a take-down.]

take in **1.** T (4) He wanted to become a member of our club, and we finally took him in. [Accepted him, admitted him.] **2.** T (1) Marie lost a lot of weight during her illness. She has to take all her dresses in a bit. [Alter them, making them smaller.] **3.** T (1) The lady next door is going to take in roomers (boarders). [Provide lodging (board) for pay.] **4.** T (4) The Deep South takes in five states. [Includes, is made up of.] **5.** T (1,9) The lecturer spoke so rapidly and used such big words that I couldn't take in half of what he said. [Understand, grasp the meaning of it.] **6.** T (1) He hurried to take in his sails before the storm struck. [Furl them, make them secure.] **7.** T (8) Informal. That book salesman surely took me in. [Tricked, deceived, cheated me.] **8.** T (1,9) We took in the view (his remark, the situation, etc.). [We noticed, became aware of, paid brief attention to it.] **9.** T (1,9) When we were in New York we took in the sights (some shows, concerts, museums, exhibitions, etc.). [Visited them, were present at them.] **10.** *take-in* N. a. (8) Informal. That deal with the book salesman was a real take-in. [A fraud, a deception.] b. (1) What was the take-in last night? [The amount of money paid in at the ticket window, or the entrance.]

take off **1.** T (2) He took off his hat and coat and hung them in the closet. [Removed them from his body.] **2.** T (2) The kidnapers took the young boy off to their hide-out. [Away from home.] **3.** I (2,7) Our guests took off for New York. [Started their journey.] See **set off.** **4.** I (2,7) We waved to them as their plane took off. [Left the ground, starting on its way.] **5.** T (4,5) The thief saw the policeman coming and took off. [Escaped as fast as he could.] See **clear out, dig off (out), light off (out).** **6.** T (4) She took time off to eat her lunch. [Away from work.] **7.** T (8) The Black Plague took off millions during the Middle Ages. [Removed them by causing their death.] **8.** T (6) The electric appliance dealer took 20% off all his merchandise for the big clearance sale. [Made a reduction in his prices of 20%.] **9.** T (2) Informal. Ext. At the variety show one of the actors took off the Vice-President. [Did an amusing imitation of him.] **10.** *take-off* N. (1,2) a. An act or instance of taking or setting off; a jump or ascent, as beginning a flight in an airplane. b. The place or point of departure. c. Machinery. A shaft geared to a mainshaft for running auxiliary machinery. d. A branch connection to a pipe, electric line, etc. e. A homorous or satirical imitation; burlesque. [It is easy to do a take-off of a drunk. Everyone recognizes the symptoms.]

take on   **1.** T (I 1)   The bus stops at every corner to take on passengers. [Allow them to get on.]   **2.** T (I 2)   Father has taken on too many responsibilities (jobs, problems, etc.) at the office. [Assumed them, taken them "on his shoulders".]   **3.** T (I 2)   The war has taken on a new aspect (meaning, seriousness, etc.) for many of our citizens. [Acquired it.]   **4.** T (II 5)   The drunken man shouted that he would take on anyone in the place. [Fight with anyone who wanted to fight.]   **5.** I (II 2)   Informal. The old lady took on at a terrible rate about the boy who had broken her window. [Became very excited, talked loud and angrily.] See **carry on 6**.

take out   **1.** T (1)   He took out his handkerchief and wiped his forehead. [Out of his pocket.]   **2.** T (4)   The doctor advised him to take out an insurance policy (naturalization papers, etc.). [Make application at the proper office or with an agent.]   **3.** T (6)   Bridge. When he was doubled, his partner took him out. [Bid another suit to rescue him.] See **leave in.**   **4.** T (2,3)   When we were in Florida a Naval officer took our daughter out every day. [Took her on a date; dated her outside the home.]   **5.** I (2)   The youngsters put on their bathing suits in a hurry, and took out for the beach. [Started in a hurry.] See **set out.**   **6.** *take it out (of)*   T (8)   That hard work in the hay fields took it out of him. [Exhausted, tired him out.]   **7.** *take it out (on)*   T (9)   She was angry because her father wouldn't let her have the car. She took it out on her kid brother. [Treated him meanly, to express her feelings of disappointment and frustration.]   **8.** *take-out* N.   (3)   a. The act or fact of taking out. b. Something taken out or made to be taken out. [You can buy the restaurant's famous home-made bread as a take-out.] c. A magazine section designed to be removed intact. [The take-out this month was a set of art reproductions.] d. Machinery. A device for removing a manufactured product from a machine after processing. e. Cards. 1) A bridge bid in a suit or denomination different from the one bid by one's partner. 2) Poker. The minimum poker wager with which a player can begin.

take over   **1.** T (3)   Mother baked a cake for our neighbor and asked me to take it over. [Over to the neighbor's house.]   **2.** T (3)   When Mr. Adams retired from the family business, his elder son took over. [Assumed the management, the responsibility of the business.]   **3.** T (3)   Slang. That used car salesman really took me over. [Cheated me; sold me a bad car.]   **4.** *take-over* N.   (3)   After Hitler's take-over in Germany the Jews were persecuted and millions of them were killed. [After he seized power and got complete control of the country.]

take up   **1.** T (1)   He took up a handful of earth and examined it carefully. [Up from the ground.]   **2.** T (11)   After getting his bachelor's degree he took up medicine (law, art, music, etc.). [Began to study it.]   **3.** T (4)   A grand piano takes up a lot of space in a living room. [Occupies, covers it.]   **4.** T (4)   Her large family takes up all her time (energies, attention, etc.). [Requires, demands, etc.] **5.** T (7) At our next meeting we will take up the question of money. [Bring it up for consideration.] **6.** I (8) At the next meeting we will take up where we left off at the last one. [Begin the meeting.] **7.** T (10) The newly elected officers will take up their duties at the first meeting in December. [Begin to function in their new positions.] **8.** *take up (with)* I (2) Informal. Robert has taken up with the daughter of our new neighbor. [Has become friendly with her, is keeping company with her.] **9.** *take-up* N. (1,10) a. An act of taking up (as by absorption). Machinery. b. The contraction of fabric resulting from the wet operations in the finishing process. c. A flue leading up from below; uptake. d. Any of various devices for taking up slack, winding in, or compensating for the looseness of parts due to wear.

Talk To employ speech, perform the act of speaking.

talk around T (4) At first he didn't like our plan for the evening but we talked him around to it. [Brought him over to our way of thinking by talking to him.] See **bring around 2**.

talk away T (6) On our ocean voyage we often talked away the afternoons with an interesting couple we met. [Spent the time in talking.]

talk back I (5) Mr. Smith's children are very rude. They talk back to their father when he asks them to do some work around the house. [Answer in a rude and disrespectful manner.] See **answer back**.

talk down **1.** T (4) I was trying to persuade a group of people to vote for the proposed sewer system but they talked me down. [Spoke loudly and forcefully against my point of view till I stopped talking.] **2.** T (2,4) The leaders of the opposition party talk down the achievements of the present administration. [Belittle them; say they are not important.] **3.** T (1) Because the weather conditions at the airport were very bad the control tower talked the pilot down. [Gave him oral instructions on how to land his plane.] See **talk in**. **4.** *talk down (to)* I (2) The speaker gave the impression that he was talking down to his audience. [Speaking condescendingly; using very simple language, as to inferiors.]

talk in T (1) The control tower talked the pilot in. [Gave him oral instructions on how to bring his plane in to the landing area.] See **talk down 4**.

talk out **1.** I (9) You'll have to talk out if you want to be heard in all this noise. [Talk loudly.] See **speak out**. **2.** T (7) This is a very difficult problem. I suggest you talk it out with a good lawyer. [Discuss it fully and perhaps reach a solution.] **3.** *talked-out* A. (9) After two hours of pleasant conversation we were all talked out. [We had nothing more to talk about.]

talk over **1.** T (6) Let's talk over the whole situation. I haven't heard all the details. [Consider everything that happened.] **2.** T (3) At first he was against the sewer proposal, but we talked him over to our side. [Persuaded him to accept our idea.] See **bring around**.

talk up   **1.** T (2,5)   He traveled around the state talking up the need for paved roads. [Discussing it enthusiastically, trying to stir up interest in it.]   **2.** I (5,9) If you really want to have that job that has become vacant you should talk up now, and not wait for another chance. [Tell the boss immediately that you want it.] See **speak up.**

Tally   To count or reckon up.

  tally up   T (4)   He tallied up his earnings (his losses, his sales account, etc.) to see where he stood financially. [Made a complete count.]

Tame   To make gentle, manageable.

  tame down   T (6)   That saddle horse is a bit too spirited for the girls to ride. We'll have to tame him down first. [Train him to be more gentle, easier to handle.]

Tamp   To force in or down by repeated rather light strokes.

  tamp down   T (1)   After watering thoroughly the soil around the newly planted tree he tamped it down firmly with his foot. [Compacted it.] See **tramp down.**

  tamp in   T (1)   He filled his pipe with tobacco and tamped it in with his forefinger. [Pressed the tobacco down into the pipe.]

Tank   To put or store in a tank.

  tank up   I (4,11)   We'll stop at the next gas station and tank up. [Have the tank filled with gas.] See **gas up.**

Tap   To strike a light but audible blow or blows.

  tap in   T (1)   He made a wooden peg to fit the hole and tapped it in with his hammer. [Into the hole.]

  tap out   **1.** T (2)   The telegrapher tapped out the message in Morse Code. [Out over the wire.]   **2.** T (2)   As the orchestra played, Bob tapped out the rhythm with his knife on the table top. [Out in the open air.]

Tape   To tie up, bind, or attach with tape.

  tape on   T (I 1)   She wrote out an address label for the package then taped it on. [Attached it with adhesive tape.]

  tape up   T (3,4)   The doctor discovered that Jack had a cracked rib, so he taped him up. [Wrapped tape or a tight bandage around his chest.]

Taper   To become smaller or thinner at one end.

  taper off   **1.** I (2)   The peninsula tapers off to a narrow point. [Becomes smaller and smaller.]   **2.** I (2,5)   The doctor told him he was smoking too much. He advised him to taper off gradually and then stop completely. [Reduce the number he smoked; cut down on his smoking.]

Taxi   To ride or transport in a taxi cab; (of an airplane) to move slowly over the surface of the ground or water, under its own power.

  May be used with all the second elements to show the direction of the movement.

  taxi out   I (1)   We taxied out to the airport. [Out of town.]

  taxi in   I (1)   The plane taxied in from the landing strip. [Into the unloading area.]

Team   To join together in a team or close association.

team up   I (5,10)   The two service clubs teamed up to equip the city playground. [Joined together, cooperated.]

Tear I   To pull apart or in pieces; pull or snatch violently.

tear down   **1.** T (1,6)   They are tearing down many old houses in the slum area, and will make a park where the houses stood. [Demolishing, pulling down.] **2.** T (1,6)   She enjoys tearing down people she has taken a dislike to. [Disparaging them, saying unkind things about them.]

tear off   **1.** T (1)   She tore off the wrapping of the package and opened it eagerly. [Removed it by tearing it.] **2.** T (1,2)   He tore off his shirt and threw it on a chair. [Pulled it off with a violent gesture.] **3.** T (8)   Slang. He tore off a poem (an imitation, a little speech, etc.) to the amusement of everyone. [Recited, performed it rapidly, casually.]

tear out   T (6)   She tore out an article in the newspaper to show to her friend. [Removed it by tearing.]

tear up   **1.** T (2,4)   Mother tore up an old bed sheet to make cleaning rags. [Made many pieces of it.] **2.** T (4,5)   The baseball player tore up his next year's contract when he learned that another player had received a better one. [Canceled it.] **3.** T (4,5)   Slang. We're going to tear up the town tonight. [Have a wild party; go on a spree.]

Tear II   To move with violence or haste, or both.

May be used with many of the second elements to show the direction of the movement.

tear across   I (1)   When they reached the bridge they tore across in hot pursuit of the black roadster. [Rushed over the bridge.]

tear by   I (2)   Ten leather-jacketed young fellows tore by on their motorcycles. [Went by with a rush and noise.]

tear in   I (1)   We were sitting quietly by the fire when Henry tore in to get his coat and tore out again. [Entered with a rush and went out in the same manner.]

Tee   To strike a golf ball from a tee at the start of a hole; to commence.

tee off   **1.** I (1,2)   Martin teed off first with a long hard drive. [Struck the ball from the tee.] **2.** T (8)   Slang. They teed off the program with a lively number from the orchestra. [Started the program.] **3.** I (8)   Boxing. Gonzalez teed off with a powerful blow to his opponent's head. [Started the fight.] **4.** *tee off (on)*   I (8)   Baseball. Willie Mays teed off on a fast pitch and drove the ball into left field. [Hit the ball hard.] **5.** I (9)   Slang. Mr. Jones teed off on his son for wrecking the car. [Scolded, reprimanded him.] **6.** *teed-off* A. (1)   Mary was teed off because her boyfriend was a half hour late for their date. [She was angry; disgusted.]

tee up   I (11)   The champion was nervous as he teed up for the eighteenth hole. [Put the ball on the tee and prepared to hit it.]

Telegraph   To transmit or send a message by telegraph.

May be used with many of the second elements to indicate the direction of the action.

telegraph back   I (3)   We asked our son to telegraph back as soon as he arrived at camp. [Back to us.]

telegraph in   T (1)   The editor told the reporter to telegraph in any new developments in the murder case. [Into the newspaper office.]

Telephone   To speak by telephone; send a message by telephone.

May be used with many of the second elements to indicate the direction of the action.

telephone around   I (2)   When I got home, Alice was telephoning around trying to find a fourth for bridge. [Here and there.]

telephone back   I (3)   When she arrived in New York she telephoned back to say everything was O.K. [Back home.]

telephone over   I (3)   Aunt Jane just telephoned over to say she can't come to dinner tonight. [To our house from across the river, or another part of town.]

Tell   To make known by speech or writing; announce; proclaim.

tell off   **1.** T (6)   The sergeant began to tell off the members of the company who were to be assigned to special duty. [Read their names from a list; announce the names.]   **2.** T (1)   Informal. That man has gone too far with his trouble making. It's about time that someone told him off. [Gave him a rebuke; denounce him for his actions.]

Test   To subject to a test or trial of any kind.

test out   **1.** T (9)   When the bridge damaged by the flood was repaired, they ran a heavy truck over it to test it out. [Make a test of its safety.]   **2.** T (9)   John protested to his girlfriend that he was not jealous by nature. She decided to test him out by having a date with Robert. [Putting him to the test.]

Thaw   To become free of the physical effect of frost or extreme cold.

thaw out   **1.** I (9)   When we came in out of the blizzard (the heavy snow storm), we sat by the fire for a while to thaw out. [Get warm, lose the feeling of extreme cold.]   **2.** I (6)   Ext. The cold war is beginning to thaw out. [Relations between the U.S.S.R. and the U.S.A. are becoming warmer, more friendly.]

Thin   To become thinner; to reduce the number of.

thin down   I (6)   Jane has thinned down considerably since going on her diet. [Become less stout, slenderized.] See **slim down, trim down.**

thin out   **1.** T (4)   It's time to thin out the carrots (onions, beets, etc.). [Remove the excess plants from the rows.]   **2.** I (4)   After the rain started the crowd in the football stadium began thinning out. [People began to leave the stadium.]

Think   To use the mind, especially the intellect, actively; cogitate, meditate, reason.

think back   I (4)   She asked him to think back to the day they were married, and what he had promised her. [Back in time.]

think out   **1.** T (7)   You should think out the problem, and not act until you know for sure what is best. [Examine all the possibilities carefully.]   **2.** T (7)

I hope the Johnsons will think out a way to settle their marriage difficulties. [Discover, devise by thinking.]

think over   T (6)   Thanks for the suggestion (the invitation, the offer, etc.). We'll think it over and let you know what we decide. [Give some thought to it.]

think through   T (3)   That was an interesting statement Henry made, but I don't believe he has thought it through carefully. [Made a close, logical examination of the whole matter.] See **reason through.**

think up   **1.** T (7,11)   She's very good at thinking up ways to entertain children. [Preparing, devising them.]   **2.** T (7,11)   The Nelsons want us to play bridge at their house tonight. Can't we think up an excuse. I'm too tired to go out. [Concoct, give an excuse that may be false.] See **make up.**

Thrash/Thresh   To deliver blows as with a flail, beating out grain.

thrash about   I (2)   Ext. I didn't get to sleep till 6 a.m. I was thrashing about all night. [Tossing from side to side in bed.]

thrash out   **1.** T (1)   We watched the peasants threshing out the wheat by hand. [Using flails to separate wheat from the husks.]   **2.** T (9)   We greatly hope the delegates to the peace conference will succeed in thrashing out all the difficulties between the two countries. [Resolving them.]

thrash over   T (7)   We spent the evening thrashing over the problems that had come up at the afternoon meeting. [Discussing them a second time.]

Thread   To make one's way between closely spaced objects (as in a forest or crowd) like a thread through the eye of a needle. See **fight one's way.**

May be used with most of the second elements to indicate the direction of the movement.

thread (one's way) along   T (3)   We threaded our way along through the bamboo thicket. [Moved forward in a narrow path.]

thread (one's way) out   T (1,2)   He threaded his way out through the crowd. [Move in and out among the people, seeking a path.]

Throw   To project or cast in any way, especially to project or propel from the hand by a sudden forward motion, or straightening of the arm or wrist.

May be used with all the second elements to indicate the direction of the action.

throw around   **1.** T (2)   Marvin just throws his money around. He never saves a cent. [Spends it recklessly, foolishly, unwisely.]   **2.** T (2)   Ext. He was the sort of person who enjoyed throwing his weight around. [Using his power, strength, influence, etc., in a showy, offensive manner.]

throw away   **1.** T (2,3)   I threw away my only hat in 1954 and haven't owned one since. [Discarded it, disposed of it.]   **2.** T (2,3)   Allan is throwing away his talents, working in an office. He could be a fine musician (artist, actor, etc.). [Wasting them, neglecting to use them.]   **3.** T (2,3)   As a young man-about-town he threw away a fortune on horses, women, and sporty cars. [Wasted the fortune he inherited.]   **4.** *throw-away* N.A. (2,3)   Any advertisement, as a folder or broadside, passed out on streets, slipped under doors, etc. [The store hired young boys to distribute throw-aways (throw-away sheets) announcing the big sale.]

throw back   **1.** T (5)   Jack threw the ball to Bob and Bob threw it back. [Returned it by throwing.]   **2.** T (2)   Maryjane's long illness threw her back one year in school. [Put her a grade behind.] See **set back 4.**   **3.** T (4)   The death of her young husband threw her back on her parents for support. [Caused her to return to her parents.]   **4.** T (4)   Ext. Her red hair and blue eyes throw back to her great grandmother. [Come from genes inherited from the great grandmother.]   **5.** *throw back (at)*   T (5)   He accused her of being unfaithful, and she threw back at him that he had been stepping out on her himself. [Replied angrily.]   **6.** *throw-back* N.   (4)   a. An act of returning an object by throwing, as a ball. b. A set back or check. c. The reversion to an ancestral or earlier type or character. [Her red hair was a throw-back.] d. One that is defective. [Inspectors reject the throw-backs.]

throw in   **1.** T (5)   When we bought pears from our fruit man he always used to throw in some big red apples. [Give them to us without charge.]   **2.** T (5)   At the Greenlodge Motel they throw in breakfast with the room. [Give a free breakfast.]   **3.** T (5)   At the meeting last night Dr. Strong threw in a few remarks (suggestions, ideas, etc.) about the need for more Public Health services. [Spoke informally and briefly.]   **4.** T (7)   Poker. Smith threw in his hand on the second round of bidding. [Threw his cards into the center of the table as a sign that he was not bidding.]   **5.** T (1)   Boxing. After the sixth round Carnera threw in the towel (the sponge). [Tossed a towel or a sponge into the ring as a sign that he was giving up the fight.] See **toss in.**

throw off   **1.** T (2)   He went to the edge of the swimming pool, threw off his bathrobe and plunged in. [Removed his bathrobe quickly and tossed it aside.]   **2.** T (2)   I've been trying to throw off the flu (a cold, a headache, etc.) by staying in bed and dosing myself with aspirin. [Get rid, free of it.]   **3.** T (3)   The robbers threw the pursuing police off by taking a narrow side road and turning back to town. [Eluded them; threw them off the trail.]   **4.** T (3)   When you start using all those big scientific words you throw me off. [Confuse me; make it impossible for me to follow the discussion.]   **5.** T (1)   The garbage dump threw off an acrid smoke and an odor of burning rubber. [Caused them to spread about.]   **6.** T (8)   The entertainer threw off a few jokes and wisecracks before the curtain went up. [Performed, spoke them with ease.]

throw on   **1.** T (I 1)   The fire is nearly out. Please throw on some more wood. [Add it to the fire.]   **2.** T (I 3)   When the bell rang she threw on her dressing gown and went to the door. [Put it on quickly.]   **3.** T (II 4)   Electronics. The engineer threw on the main switch and suddenly all the street lights began to glow. [Moved the switch so that electric current began to flow.]

throw out   **1.** T (4)   They sorted over the apples and threw out all the bad ones. [Discarded them, removed them from their containers.]   **2.** T (1)   I would like to throw out a few suggestions (ideas, proposals, etc.). You may find them helpful. [Bring them before you for consideration.] **3.** T (9) We can't throw out the possibility that this is not a murder, but a suicide. [Reject the idea, put it out of our minds entirely.] **4.** T (4) Baseball. The alert short-stop caught the ball and threw the runner out at third base. [Threw the ball so that the third baseman caught it and tagged the runner, putting him out of the game.] **5.** T (4,9) The bouncer in a bar has the job of throwing out customers who become too noisy and offensive. [Putting them out into the street, etc.] See **kick out.**

throw over **1.** T (3) He picked up the ball and threw it over to the other side of the field. [Over or across the field.] **2.** T (8) Informal. She threw over her first husband for a handsome young athlete. [She abandoned him, divorced him.]

throw up **1.** T (1) He spent ten minutes throwing the ball up and catching it in his left hand when it came down. [Up in the air.] **2.** T (1) Informal. We gave the patient some hot soup, but he threw it up a few minutes after swallowing it. [Vomited it out.] See **toss up 4.** **3.** T (1) Rachel threw up her hands at the sight of all the damage caused by the explosion (the children's rough playing, the wind storm, etc.). [Raised her hands in a gesture of despair, dismay, etc.] **4.** T (4) He became angry at the way the boss treated him, and threw up his job. [Gave it up, abandoned it.] **5.** T (1,11) When the oil boom started the real estate people began throwing up houses to take care of the increased population. [Building them hastily.] See **run up 3.** **6.** T (1) Falconry. His falcon threw up in a flash and soon struck down the pigeon. [Flew suddenly upward.] **7.** *throw up (to)* T (6,9) Informal. His wife threw it up to him that he had been mistaken before about the chances of finding a motel vacancy. [Reminded him of his mistake; criticized him for it.]

Tide Carry as the tide does.

tide over T (3,7) Could you lend me fifty dollars to tide me over until next pay day? [Supply me with enough money to enable me to carry on.]

Tidy To make tidy or neat, in good order.

tidy up T (3,11) I want to tidy up the kitchen before Aunt Mary comes. [Wash things, sweep, make the kitchen presentable.] See **sweep up.**

Tie To bind, fasten, or attach with a cord, string or the like, drawn together and knotted; to fasten, join, or connect in any way.

tie back **1.** T (1) She always ties her hair back with a ribbon. [Back from her forehead.] **2.** T (1) She used a heavy gold braid to tie her living room drapes back. [Back from in front of the windows.] **3.** *tie-back* N. (2) a. A band, strip or loop of material, heavy braid, or the like used for holding curtains back to one side. b. A curtain having tie-backs.

tie down **1.** T (1) The robbers gagged him and tied him down on the couch (his chair, etc.). [Fastened him so that he couldn't rise.] **2.** T (1) Ext. Her husband's illness tied her down so that she couldn't attend evening classes. [Kept her very busy.] **3.** T (1) Our artillery fire tied down the enemy tanks so that they could not prevent our seizure of the bridgehead. [Kept them from advancing.] **4.** *tie-down* N. (1) a. A device for tying something down. b. The act of tying down.

tie in **1.** T (5) Surveying. To establish the position of a point, not part of a survey control but coordinated with it. **2.** I (5) The defendant's story ties in with that of the second witness. [There is a close correspondence between the two.] **3.** T (5) In his summary the lawyer tied the defendant's past crime record in with his employer's testimony. [Showed a relationship between the two.] **4.** *tie-in* N. (5) a. Something that serves as a direct or indirect link, relationship or connection. [The tie-in between smoking and cancer] b. A tie-in sale or advertisement. c. An item in a tie-in sale. **5.** *tie-in* A. (5) a. Pertaining to or designating a sale in which the buyer in order to purchase one desired item must purchase one or more usually undesired items. b. Of or pertaining to two or more products advertised, sold, obtained or allotted together. [I bought the table, and the store gave me the lamp on a tie-in deal.]

tie off T (3) Surgery. To tie a cord or suture around a vein, blood vessel or the like, so as to stop the flow of blood.

tie on **1.** T (I 1) He put the camping equipment on the roof of his car and tied it on with a heavy rope. [On the car.] **2.** T (II 5) Slang. When his girl broke their engagement he went out with an old drinking companion and tied one on. [Got very drunk.]

tie up **1.** T (3) They always tie up their dog when the neighbor's children come to play in the yard. [Fasten him securely.] **2.** T (3,11) She spent the evening tying up Christmas packages. [Putting fancy wrappings and ribbons on them.] See **bag up.** **3.** T (6) Cross-town traffic was tied up by the parade on Fifth Avenue. [It could not move, was hindred, impeded.] **4.** T (6) A strike tied up the subway (the telephone service, the garbage collection, etc.) for five days. [Brought it to a stop, made it inactive.] **5.** T (4) He couldn't lend me $5,000 because he had tied up all his spare cash in a new business venture. [Invested it in such a way that he couldn't use it for other purposes.] **6.** T (4) A court order had tied up the assets of the company (its real estate, its inventory, etc.) until the law suit against it was settled. [Made it impossible to sell, trade or dispose of the assets.] **7.** T (3) The ship was tied up beside the dock during repairs. [Moored; fastened with ropes to the dock.] **8.** T (6) I'm sorry I can't play bridge with you. I'm tied up tonight. [I have another engagement, am busy.] **9.** *tie-up* N. (6) a. (6) A temporary stoppage or slowing of business or traffic. [The strike resulted in a state-wide telephone tie-up.] b. (3) A mooring place. [A tie-up for cabin cruisers.] c. (4,10) An involvement or connection. [There is some kind of a tie-up between Company A and Company B.] [We suspect him of having a tie-up with the crime syndicate.]

Tighten To make or become tight or tighter.

tighten down T (1) As the storm approached the seamen were busy tightening down the hatches and all other objects on deck. [Securing them with locks, ropes, etc.]

tighten up **1.** T (2)   The ropes securing the cars to the deck had to be tightened up. [Made tighter, less loose.]   **2.** T (12)   The primary concern of the new business manager was to tighten up the organization (the procedures, the regulations, the work schedule, etc.). [Make things more efficient; change the loose habits and ways of operating.]   **3.** I (2,6)   The witness tightened up and refused to answer the questions the lawyer put to her. [Became tense, was emotionally disturbed.]

Tilt   To cause to lean, incline, slope, or slant.

tilt back   T (1)   He tilted back his chair and put his feet on the table. [Made it lean backward on the two rear legs.] See **tip back.**

Time   To ascertain, record the time or duration of an act or movement, especially in racing or athletic events.

May be used with many of the second elements to indicate the direction of the movement.

time around   T (3)   We timed him around at three minutes and fifty seconds. [We noted that he circled the track in that time.]

time back   T (3)   I timed him back at 5:10. [Noted that he returned at that time.]

time by   T (2)   As the racing car passed the judge's stand they timed him by at 256 miles per hour. [Noted that he was going at that rate of speed.]

Tip I   To cause to assume a slanting or sloping position; overturn, upset.

tip back   I (1)   He tipped back on his chair and began to read the newspaper. [Leaned backward.] See **tilt back.**

tip over   **1.** I (5)   The vase tipped over and the water spilled out on the piano. [It fell over on its side.]   **2.** T (5)   He tipped over the floor lamp, which fell with a crash. [Caused it to fall over.]

Tip II   To give a tip, a gratuity, a bit of information.

tip off   **1.** T (2)   Informal. One of the neighbors had tipped off the police as to the gangster's hide-out. [Gave them the information about it.]   **2.** *tip-off* N. (2)   The gangsters threatened to kill the man who had given the police the tip-off.

Tire   To reduce or exhaust the strength of; make tired, weary.

tire out   **1.** T (8)   That 300 mile drive over the hot desert tired me out completely. [Exhausted me.]   **2.** *tired-out* A. (8)   We were all tired out after the 10 hour drive. [Exhausted, weary.] See **wear out 5.**

Toe   To stand or walk with the toes in a specified position.

toe in   **1.** I (1)   Athletics. The coach trained his runners to toe in as they practiced for the walking race. [Walk with the toes turned in.]   **2.** T (1)   Automobiles. At the service station I had the mechanic toe the front wheels in a bit. [Align the wheels so that the tires would ride on the inner edge.]

toe out   **1.** I (1)   Athletics. A runner can make better time by toeing in than by toeing out. [Walking or running with the toes turned out.]   **2.** T (1)   If your front wheels toe out you'd better have the service station adjust them. [Aligned them so that the tires wear evenly.]

Tog Informal. To dress.

   tog out T (9) For the costume party (the masquerade, the show, etc.) he togged himself out in a Nehru jacket and beads. [Dressed, got himself up.] See **get up 7, 8.**

   tog up T (2,4) His wife was togged up in her finest Paris gown. [Dressed elaborately.]

Toll To sound with single strokes, slowly and regularly repeated, as a bell, for solemn occasions.

   toll on I (II 2) The great cathedral bells tolled on for three hours in honor of the dead king. [Continued to sound.]

   toll out T (2,9) The church bells tolled out the glad news of the birth of a prince. [Announced it in public.]

Tone To modify or adjust the tone or general coloring of something; to alter the mental tone or physical strength of something.

   tone down **1.** T (6) Mrs. Jones thought the green on the living room walls was too brilliant. She asked the painter to tone it down a bit. [Make it less brilliant.] **2.** T (6) Ext. His campaign manager advised him to tone down his criticism of his opponent. [Make it less severe.]

   tone in (with) I (5) The soft brown of the carpet tones in with the upholstery of the davenport and armchairs. [Blends; makes a pleasant effect, harmonizes.]

   tone up T (2,5) At the gymnasium he is doing special exercises to tone up his abdominal muscles. [Make them tighter, more firm.] See **harden up.**

Tool I To install machinery designed for performing a particular job.

   tool up I (4,11) The auto manufacturers are tooling up for the production of next year's models. [Equipping their factories with the necessary tools.]

Tool II Informal. To drive or ride in a vehicle, generally with smooth, easy progress. May be used with many of the second elements to indicate the direction of the movement.

   tool along I (3) We tooled along on the freeway with very little traffic to worry about. [Rode easily and comfortably.]

   tool by I (2) The children sat on the roadside bank, watching the cars tooling by. [Moving past.]

Top To bring to a successful conclusion.

   top off **1.** T (10) We topped off a delicious meal with coffee and brandy. [Had them as a finishing touch.] **2.** T (10) Charles suggested that we top off the evening by going to a night club. [End the evening's entertainment in that way.]

Topple To became unstable; fall because of being top-heavy.

   topple off I (2) When he bumped against the table the big lamp toppled off. [Fell from the table.]

   topple over **1.** I (5) During the hurricane our big elm tree toppled over. [Fell to the ground.] **2.** I (5)   She toppled over in a faint when she saw her husband lying in a pool of blood. [Fainted and fell to the floor.]

Toss   To throw, pitch, or fling, especially to throw lightly or carelessly.

toss about   1. T (2)   The heavy waves tossed our little boat about like a feather. [Threw it from side to side.]   **2.** T (2)   The players spent some time tossing the ball about (around) before the game started. [Throwing it to each other.] **3.** T (2)   She couldn't get to sleep. She tossed about most of the night. [Turned from side to side in her bed.]

toss aside   T (1)   He picked up the newspaper, read the war headlines, then tossed it aside in disgust. [Threw it away from him.]

toss in   T (1)   Boxing. He tossed in the towel (the sponge) at the end of the seventh round. [He gave up the fight, admitted defeat.] See **throw in 5**.

toss off   1. T (1)   The workmen stood on the wagon tossing off bundles of hay. [Throwing them lightly to the ground.]   **2.** T (8)   You'll just have time to toss off a letter to Uncle John. [Write quickly and briefly.]   **3.** T (8)   He is the kind of writer who can toss off a poem (a short story, an article, a chapter, etc.) between breakfast and lunch. [Write quickly and easily.]   **4.** T (2,9)   He went to the bar and tossed off a brandy (a shot of whiskey, etc.). [Drank it quickly, with one or two swallows.]

toss up   1. T (1)   He tossed the ball up in the air and hit it with his bat as it came down. [Threw it up lightly.]   **2.** T (1)   They decided who would pay the bill by tossing up a coin. [The loser had to pay the bill.] A coin is tossed in the air. When it falls heads up the man who had called "heads" is the winner. If it falls "tails up" he is the loser.   **3.** T (7,11)   While the coffee was perking she tossed up a salad. [Made it quickly and easily, tossing the elements together.]   **4.** I (1) Slang. He tossed up his cookies. [He vomited.] See **throw up 2**.   **5.** *toss-up* N. (1)   a. A toss of the coin. [John won the toss-up so Bob had to pay. John called "heads" and the coin fell heads up.] b. An even chance. [It's a toss-up which candidate will win the election. Both have equal appeal to the voters.] c. An even choice. [Which do you prefer, cherry pie or peach pie? It's a toss-up. I like them both.]

Tot   To add; make a total.

tot up   T (4)   Henry got out paper and pencil and began totting up the score (the bill, the day's expenses, etc.). [Finding the total by adding figures together.]

Total   To compute; tot up.

total up   T (4)   When he had totaled up all the bills (dividends, assets, contributions, etc.) he was able to plan for the future. [Made a careful accounting of them.]

Touch   To come into or be in contact with, especially with the hand.

touch down   1. I (1)   Our plane touched down at three small airports between Salt Lake City and Seattle. [Landed, stopped.] See **set down 3**.   **2.** *touchdown* N.

(1)   Football. A score made by one team by touching the ball to the ground behind the goal line of the opposing team.

touch off   **1.** T (8)   The little boy touched off a firecracker and it exploded in his hand. [He touched the fuse with a lighted match or live coal.]   **2.** T (8)   The arrest of a drunken driver touched off a riot in the slum area. [Started it as if ignited by a fuse.] See **set off 2.**   **3.** T (8)   The author's description touched off the character of a crooked politician to perfection. [Gave a very clear picture of it.]

touch up   **1.** T (2)   They have experts at the museum whose work is to touch up old paintings. [Clean them, improve their appearance with special techniques.] **2.** T (2)   Alice went to the powder room to touch up her eyebrows (her face, her mascara, etc.). [Improve her make-up.]

Toughen   To make or become tough or tougher.

toughen up   **1.** T (2,12)   The Marine Corps puts its recruits through many hard training programs to toughen them up. [Make them physically and mentally more tough.]   **2.** T (2,4)   The school authorities are planning to toughen up the discipline to control the rowdies. [Make their rules of conduct more severe.]

Trace I   To prove by historical evidence.

trace back   **1.** T (4)   She can trace her family back to Henry the Eighth. [Follow it back through history.]   **2.** I (4)   Her family traces back to Henry the Eighth. [Goes, reaches back in history.]   **3.** T (4)   The writer traced the history of medicine back to the early Egyptians. [Showed the beginning of medicine by going back to that period.]

Trace II   To draw in outline.

trace out   **1.** T (7)   The artist traced out the general design of his picture before starting to apply color. [Indicated the location and proportions of persons and objects with lines.] See **sketch out.**   **2.** T (7)   In his introduction the historian traces out the main currents of political thought in the 18th century. [Makes an outline of them.]

Track   To follow or pursue traces or footprints, or to leave foot prints.

track back   T (3)   The hunting dogs tracked the fox back to his lair. [Followed his traces, trail to his abode.]

track down   **1.** T (4)   The hunters tracked down the wounded bear. [Followed its traces till they found it.]   **2.** T (4)   The sheriff tracked down the killer and began shooting it out with him. [Followed his traces until he found him.] See **hunt down.**   **3.** T (4)   Scholars are always trying to track down the "dark lady" of Shakespeare's sonnets. [Trying to discover who she was.]

track up   T (6)   The children came in out of the rain and tracked up her kitchen floor with their muddy shoes. [Left dirty footmarks on the floor.]

Trade   To exchange, give one thing for another.

trade in   **1.** T (1,5)   They trade in their car every three years. [Give their used car as part payment on the new car they buy.]   **2.** *trade-in* N.   (1,5)   a. Goods given in whole, or usually as part payment on a purchase. [We used our old car as a trade-in for the new one.] b. A business transaction involving a trade-in. [The car dealer agreed to a trade-in.] **3.** *trade-in* **A.** What is the trade-in value of my old washing machine? [How much will you allow me for it on the purchase of a new one?] See **I turn-in 6.**

trade off **1.** T (2) We traded our horse off for a couple of cows. [Exchanged the horse for the cows.] **2.** T (4) The public must decide what conveniences it is willing to trade off for environmental gains. [Give up.]

trade up I (2) We traded up on that deal. [We made a profit.]

Trail I To follow tracks or traces. May be used with most of the second elements to indicate the direction of the movement.

trail back T (3) He took a different route to drive home and we trailed him back. [Followed his car in our car for the return trip.]

trail through T (1) They worked their way to the other edge of the jungle and we trailed them through. [Followed their tracks through the jungle.]

Trail II To hang down or drag along.

May be used with most of the second elements to indicate direction.

trail along I (1,2) They made their way with difficulty out of the crowd and we trailed along after them. [Followed them as if being drawn.]

trail by I (2) We stood by the roadside watching the retreating soldiers trail wearily by. [Then dragged along, discouraged.]

trail down **1.** I (1) The Freedom Marchers trailed down to where their camp was set up for the night. [Down the hill or slope.] **2.** I (1) Spanish moss trailed down from the branches of the live oaks. [It hung down.]

Train To develop or form the habits or activities of animals, plants, or people for some purpose.

train back T (1) The gardener said we should train back the vine (the shrub, etc.) so that it would not crowd the entrance door. [Make it grow away from the door.]

train down I (6) The boxer had trained down from 180 to 160 pounds. [Reduced his weight by exercise and diet.]

train up T (2,12) I have tried to train my children up to be good citizens. [Give them education and good training.] See **bring up 4.**

Tramp To tread or trample underfoot.

tramp down T (1) The gardener tramped down the soil around the newly planted tree. [Stepped on it repeatedly to make it firm.] See **tamp down.**

tramp out T (3) We watched the vineyard workers standing in the huge vats and tramping out the juice of the grapes. [Using their feet to press out the juice.]

Trample To injure or crush by treading heavily.

trample out **1.** T (3) We are always careful to trample out our camp fires before leaving. [Extinguish them by stamping on them.] **2.** T (1) "He is trampling out the vintage where the grapes of wrath are stored." [Destroying the harvested crop of bitterness sown by war. Patriotic song.] See **put down.**

Transfer   To convey from one person or place to another.

transfer back   I (3)   In his junior year he went from Rutgers to Cornell, but he transferred back later. [Returned to Rutgers by getting a transfer permit.]

transfer out   I (4)   Military. He had been with Company C till war was declared but he transferred out (they transferred him out) a month later. [He moved to another company or service.]

transfer over   I (3)   After a year in the Infantry he transferred over to the Air Cavalry. [Made the change to another branch of the service.]

Trap   To catch in a snare or trap, as of animals.

trap out   T (8)   We were looking for beaver (muskrat, mink, etc.) but found that the area was trapped out. [All the animals had been trapped, taken by trappers.]

Treasure   To store as valuable; cherish in the mind.

treasure up   T (3,4)   He was a lonely old man who had treasured up memories of his childhood sweetheart. [Cherished them.]

Trick   To dress, array, or deck, especially in a showy or decorative manner.

trick out   T (9)   For the costume party she had tricked herself out in a Spanish dancer's finery. [Dressed up, got herself up.] See **get up 7, 8.**

Trickle   To flow or fall by drops or in a small gentle stream.

trickle down   **1.** I (1)   He stood under the shower and let the cool water trickle down over his tired body. [Fall gently from the shower head.]   **2.** I (1)   Ext. Old fashioned conservatives say that wealth will trickle down to the laboring class from the moneyed class. [Come down as water trickles down.]   **3.** *trickle-down* A. (1)   The trickle-down theory of economics doesn't please the working classes. See **trickle down 2**.

trickle out   I (2)   We let a small stream of water trickle out of the faucet all night to keep it from freezing. [Flow slowly.]

Trifle   To pass or spend time idly or frivolously.

trifle away   T (6)   They trifled away the hours with singing and dancing. [Spent the time without any serious or constructive activity.] See **idle away**.

Trim   To put into a neat or orderly condition by clipping, paring, pruning; reduce the size of by trimming.

trim back   **1.** T (1)   The lilac bushes are crowding the front door step. You'll have to trim them back. [Clip them back to an earlier position.]   **2.** T (1)   If we don't want to go into debt, we'll have to trim back the budget. [Cut expenses.]

trim down   T (6)   He had gained so much weight that his suits no longer fit him. He had to trim down in order to wear them. [Make himself thinner by exercise and diet.] See **thin down**.

trim off   **1.** T (1,2)   He asked the barber to trim off much of his beard. [Remove it by clipping.]   **2.**   The gardener trimmed off the dead branch. [Cut it off.]

trim up   T (3)   The hedge looks very ragged and uneven. I'll trim it up over the weekend. [Make it look better by trimming.]

Trip I   To step or skip lightly; dance; to stumble or cause to stumble.

May be used with most of the second elements to indicate the direction of the movement.

trip along   I (3)   The child went tripping along with his puppy. [Frolicking with him, skipping as he went.]

trip out   I (4)   The power plant developed a boiler tube leak and tripped out. [The fault caused a safety switch to operate and stopped the machinery.]

trip over   I (1)   The dancers came tripping over the stage in a lively folk dance. [Came toward us skipping and dancing.]

trip up   **1.** T (6)   As he walked into the living room a rug tripped him up. [He caught his foot on the rug and it made him fall.]   **2.** T (6)   Ext. During the debate he tripped up his opponent several times by making him contradict himself. [Upset his argument, proved him to be wrong.]

Trip II   To make a journey or excursion.

May be used with many of the second elements to indicate direction.

trip down   I (1)   We tripped down through the southern states and then headed for California. [Down South from the North.]

trip out   I (1,6)   We'll be tripping out your way some time in the spring. [Out West from the East.]

Truckle   To submit or yield obsequiously or tamely.

truckle under   I (4)   He demanded that we follow his instructions without question. We refused to truckle under. [Give in to his demands.]

True   To make level or square; adjust accurately.

true up   T (2)   The old barn (shed, tool house, etc.) was out of line. We hired the village carpenter to true it up. [Make it stand straight on its foundation.]

Trump I   To devise deceitfully or dishonestly, as an accusation.

trump up   **1.** T (7,9)   The candidate's opposition trumped up charges of graft and favoritism against him. [Brought false charges.]   **2.** *trumped-up* A.   (7,9) Those charges were clearly trumped-up. [False, made up.] See **make up.**

Trump II   Bridge. To play a trump in taking a trick.

trump in   I (4)   West led the three of spades and South trumped in with a small heart. [Took the trick with a trump, since he was out of spades.]

trump out   T (8)   South was able to establish a cross ruff and trumped out his losing clubs. [Led losing clubs from his hand and trumped them in dummy.]

Truss   To make fast with skewers, thread or the like; tie or secure the body closely or tightly.

truss up   **1.** T (4,11)   The big Thanksgiving turkey was all beautifully trussed up and ready for the oven. [The wings and legs were fastened close to the body, and the skin sewed together at the openings.]   **2.** T (4,6)   The robbers had trussed up the store owner and pushed him under the counter. [Tied his arms and legs and put a gag in his mouth.]

Try   To make an attempt; examine or test.

try on   T (I 3)   He tried on five or six suits before he found one that he liked. [Put them on in order to judge the appearance and fit of them.]

try out   **1.** T (9)   Don't ever buy a car (bicycle, motor bike, etc.) without trying it out. [Taking it out for a drive, a ride in order to test it.]   **2.** *try out (for)* I (7)   Henry says he is going to try out for the glee club (the football team, the orchestra, etc.). [Take a test, enter a competition to determine his ability, his qualifications for it.]   **3.** *try-out* N.   (3)   A trial or test to ascertain one's fitness for some purpose. [The glee club try-outs will be held tonight.]

try over   T (7)   She played the passage badly the first time, but the judges let her try it over. [Attempt to play it well a second time.]

Tuck   To fold together or put into a snug hiding place.

tuck away   T (5)   Informal. My hungry son tucked away a big meal then lay down on the floor and slept for an hour. [Ate it, put it in his stomach.]

tuck in   **1.** T (1)   When we yelled at the big dog he tucked in his tail and ran off. [Put his tail between his legs.]   **2.** T (1)   Informal. Johnny, you look like a tramp. Tuck in your shirt-tail and brush the hair out of your eyes. [Put your shirt-tail inside your pants.]   **3.** T (1)   She tucked the children in, and kissed them goodnight. [Put them to bed and pulled the covers up around them.]

tuck under   T (2)   The nurse lifted the patient's head and tucked a pillow under. [Under his head.]

tuck up   T (1,11)   Alice tucked up her skirts, got down on her knees, and began to wipe up the kitchen floor. [Fastened them up around her waist.]

Tucker   To weary, to tire, to exhaust.

tucker out   **1.** T (8)   The race to the river and back tuckered him out. [Made him very tired, exhausted.]   **2.** *tuckered-out* A.   (8)   I'm all tuckered out. I think I'll go to bed. [Completely exhausted.]

Tumble   To fall helplessly down, end over end; collapse.

tumble down   **1.** I (1)   The walls of Jericho came tumbling down. [They collapsed, fell to the ground.]   **2.** *tumble-down* A.   (1)   That poor family lives in a tumble-down shack at the edge of town. [A dilapidated little house.] See **III run-down c**.

Tune   To put into condition to function properly, especially to adjust a musical instrument to the proper pitch.

tune down   T (6)   The sound is too loud. Can't you tune it down? [Reduce the volume of the radio or T.V.]

tune in   **1.** I (5,6)   We tuned in just in time to catch the news program. [Adjusted the radio (T.V.) so as to receive the signal (the program, the broadcast) of a certain station.]   **2.** T (5,6)   We were not tuned in to his program. [Our set was not adjusted to receive it.]

tune out   T (4)   Some people always tune out the commercials. [They avoid hearing them by adjusting the set so as not to receive the signal or broadcast.]

tune up   **1.** T (2)   I can't hear the broadcast out in the kitchen. Tune it up a bit.

[Increase the volume of the radio or T.V.] **2.** T (2,12) I left the car at the garage. They will tune up the motor and have it ready for tomorrow. [Put the motor in proper operating order.] **3.** I (2,11) The orchestra began tuning up a quarter of an hour before the program started. [Bringing their instruments to the same pitch in preparation for playing as a unit.] **4.** I (7) Informal. The boys in the back room were tuning up. [Beginning to sing, starting a tune.] **5.** *tune-up* N. (2,4) a. An adjustment to assure proper operation. [The garage mechanic said he would give the motor a good tune-up.] b. A warm-up.

Turn I   To change or cause to change direction, opinion or ownership.

turn about   **1.** I (3) After driving three miles on the wrong road they turned about and went back to the crossroad. [Reversed their direction.] **2.** T (2,3) He picked up the vase and turned it about slowly in his hands, examining its shape and texture. [In circling motion.] **3.** *turn-about* N. (3) a. The act of turning in a different or opposite direction. b. A change of opinion or loyalty. [He had opposed the civil rights legislation at first, but later did a complete turn-about and voted for it.] c. A reciprocal action; doing to someone exactly as he has done to you. [Turn-about is fair play.]

turn across   I (1) Coming to the bridge, they turned across and followed a narrow path along the bank. [Across the bridge.]

turn around   **1.** I (3) We heard a shout behind us and turned around to see who was calling. [Made a complete turn towards the rear.] **2.** I (3) The swimmer reached the end of the pool and turned around. [Reversed his direction.] **3.** T (3) He turned his car around and headed back towards town. [Reversed the direction in which it was headed.] **4.** T (3) Police turned the rioters around with fire hoses. [Caused them to retreat by hitting them with water under high pressure.] **5.** T (3) "Ain't nobody gonna turn me 'round." [Make me change my mind. Negro civil rights protest song.] **6.** *turn-around* N. (3) The total time consumed in a round trip as of a ship or other means of transport. [The turn-around of the Queen Mary was usually 15 days.] b. **turn-about a, b.** c. A place or area allowing sufficient maneuvering room for a vehicle to turn around.

turn aside   **1.** I (1,2) Instead of driving through the business district, we turned aside at the edge of town and followed the boulevard. [Away from the center of town.] **2.** T (1) Several people got up in the meeting to protest the chairman's decision but he turned their objections aside with a joke. [Refused to consider their protest.]

turn away   **1.** I (3) She could not bear to look at the wrecked car, and turned away so as not to see the bodies of the victims. [Turned her head.] **2.** T (2) The cowboys rode to the front of the herd to turn it away from the river bank. [Make it change direction.] **3.** T (2) They're turning them away down at the Capitol Theater. [The show is so popular that there are not enough seats for all those who want to see it.]

turn back   **1.** I (4) The police advised us to turn back on account of the traffic jam in the center of town. [Reverse our direction.] **2.** T (3,4)   After a long, hard battle our troops succeeded in turning back the enemy. [Forcing them to retreat.] **3.** T (4)   Our T.V. set didn't give a good picture so we turned it back and got another model. [Returned it to the store that sold it.] **4.** T (4)   We turned back the clock one hour after arriving in Denver. [Moved the hands back to show a time one hour earlier.] **5.** T (4)   There's no use wishing you were a boy again. You can't turn back the clock. [Go back in time. Relive the past.]

turn down   1. I (1)   We turned down towards the river, to avoid the traffic jam. [Down from higher ground, away from uptown.] **2.** T (3)   Bob asked Mary to marry him, but she turned him down. [She refused his offer.] **3.** T (3)   We turned down an offer of $30,000 for our house. (Refused it.] **4.** *turn-down* A. (1)   That is or may be turned down, folded, or doubled down. [A turn-down collar.]

turn in   1. I (1)   When we reached the Wilson's driveway we turned in, only to find that the house was dark and their car was gone. [Into the driveway.] **2.** I (1)   Informal. It's getting late and I'm very tired. I suggest we turn in. [Go to bed.] **3.** T (1)   The teacher told us to turn in our compositions (homework, essays, lab reports, etc.) at the end of the hour. [Give them to her.] See **hand in**. **4.** T (1)   Our neighbor threatened to turn the boys in for breaking the windshield of his car. [Give their names to the police.] **5.** T (5)   Each year he turns his car in on a new model. [Gives it to the dealer as part payment for a new car.] **6.** *turn-in* A.   (1)   His old car had a turn-in value of $1,200. See **trade in 3**.

turn off   1. I (2)   To get to Ridgewood from the freeway you must turn off at exit 15. [Leave the freeway.] **2.** I (1)   We drove along 5th Street for ten blocks then turned off on Lincoln. [Made a right or left turn off 5th and followed Lincoln.] **3.** *turn-off* N.   (1,2)   a. A small road that branches off from a larger one, especially a ramp or exit leading off from a major highway. [You must take the turn-off at exit 15 to get to Ridgewood.] b. An act of turning off. [We made a turn-off at exit 15.]

turn out   1. I (2,3)   A large crowd turned out for the picnic (the opera, the concert, the meeting, the parade, etc.). [Appeared, attended, was present.] **2.** I (3)   Informal. We had to turn out at 6 a.m. in order to catch the plane at 8. [Get out of bed, get up.] See **turn in 2**. **3.** I (3)   Driving along the narrow country road we had to turn out several times to let the farm trucks go by. [Move to the side of the road and stop, or proceed slowly.] **4.** T (3)   After milking the cows we turn them out to pasture. [Out of the barn or milking shed.] **5.** T (3)   Old fashioned fathers turned their wayward daughters out. [Out of the house and home.] **6.** T (6)   Ballet. Students of ballet must learn to turn the legs out from the hips, with the feet back to back, or heel to heel. **7.** *turn-out* N.   (2,3)   a. The gathering of persons who come to an exhibition, party, parade, etc. [We had a large turn-out at the meeting tonight.] See **turn out 1**. b. A short side track or passage which enables trains, automobiles, etc., to pass one another.

See **turn out 3**. c. Railroads. A track structure composed of a switch, a frog, and closure rails, permitting a train to leave a given track for a branching or parallel track. d. An act of turning out. [The young ballet dancer Irina soon learned to do turn-outs.]

turn over **1.** I (5,6)   His car left the road and turned over several times before coming to a stop. See **roll over.** **2.** T (5)   He turned the rock over and found three big earth-worms. **3.** T (3)   She turned the pages over slowly, searching for the quotation the lecturer had made. [From right to left or left to right.] **4.** T (3)   He decided to turn over a new leaf. [Start living in a better way than he had before.] **5.** T (3)   John found a purse containing a lot of money, and turned it over to the police. [Gave it.] **6.** T (8)   That clothing store turns over its stock of shirts three times a year. [Buys and sells a complete stock.] **7.** T (6)   He was turning over in his mind all the events of the preceding day. [Thinking about them, trying to reach some conclusions about them.] **8.** *turnover* N. (3)   a. An act or result of turning over; upset. b. A change or movement of people as tenants, customers, etc., in, out or through a place. [The restaurant was very popular. It had a big turnover twice daily.] c. The aggregate of worker replacements in a given period, in a given business or industry. [His company had a turnover of three hundred employees in one year.] d. The ratio of the labor turnover to the average number of employees in a given period. [The company had a turnover of ten percent a year.] e. The total amount of business done in a given time. [The company had a turnover of $1,200,000 last year.] f. The rate at which items are sold. [We expect to have a rapid turnover next quarter.] g. The number of times that capital is invested and reinvested in a line of merchandise during a specific period of time. h. The turning over of the capital or stock of goods involved in a particular transaction or course of business. i. The rate of processing, or the amount of material processed in a given period of time, as in manufacturing. j. A change from one position, opinion, belief, etc. to another, especially one contrary to that previously held. [His support of the Republican Party was a complete turnover from his previous political beliefs.] k. A reorganization of a political organization, business, etc., especially one involving a shift or change of personnel. [The new manager ordered a complete turnover in the sales department.] l. A baked pastry with a sweet or savory filling in which the dough is turned over the filling, and the edges sealed to form a semi-circle or triangle. [An apple (peach, apricot) turnover.]

turn up **1.** I (9,10)   Informal. John said he would be there at 8 o'clock but he didn't turn up till 9. [Appear, join the group.] **2.** I (9)   We will be glad to help you no matter what turns up. [Happens, occurs.] **3.** T (1)   She turned up her nose at the idea of eating in that cheap restaurant. [Showed her dislike for it, by that gesture.] **4.** T (1)   Slang. Poor old Jones has turned up his toes. [He has died.]

Turn II   To change condition; adjust or prepare for use.

turn down **1.** T (6) I asked my roommate to please turn down his radio (T.V., lamp, etc.) so I could go to sleep. [Reduce the volume of sound, the intensity of light.] **2.** T (1) She turned down the bed. [Folded the covers back ready for use.]

turn off **1.** T (4) Don't forget to turn off the light (the radio, T.V., water). before you go to bed. [Turn the knob, switch or valve to disconnect the flow of current.] See **put off, shut off, turn out. 2.** T (4) Psychedelic experience. The long walk along the seashore, the cool breezes, and a dip in the ocean turned him off. [Disconnected him from the influence of the drug that had turned him on. Caused him to return to a normal state.] See **turn on 3. 3.** *turn-off* N. (2) a. The finished product of some manufacturing processes, as weaving. b. The quantity of fattened livestock distributed to market. **4.** *turned-off* A. (4) In a state of being disconnected from a source or influence. [The power was turned off all the time we were away.] [The boy was completely turned off by the time he returned from his walk. Recovered from the effect of a drug.]

turn on **1.** T (II 4) He turned on the radio (the T.V.) to listen to the news. [Turned the knob, switch or button to make it start functioning.] **2.** T (II 4) She turned on the light (the gas, the water, etc.) before starting to prepare the meal. [Turned the knob, switch or valve to start the flow of current, water, etc.] **3.** T (II 4) Psychedelic experience. It takes very little pot (marijuana, LSD, etc.) to turn you on. [Put you in a state in which you seem to be connected with an extraordinary power or force.] **4.** *turned-on* A. (II 4) a. When we came home from our vacation we found the power (the water, the gas, etc.) turned on. [Someone had connected them to the source.] 2. Psychedelic experience. After a few inhalations of pot he was really turned-on. [Under the influence of the drug.]

turn out **1.** T (8) Turn out the light before you come to bed. [Extinguish it.] See **II turn off 1. 2.** T (3) Ford Motors turns out more than 2,000 cars and trucks a day. [They produce, manufacture that many.] **3.** T (3) Some writers turn out two or more novels (plays, volumes of verse, etc.) a year. [Produce that many.] **4.** *turn-out* N. (3) a. The quantity of production; output. [Their turn-out of pickup trucks was 200 per day.] b. The manner or style in which a person or thing is equipped. [She came to the costume party in a very unusual turn-out.] See **get-up 7, 8.** c. Equipment; outfit. [The turn-out for the hunting trip was of the most modern type.]

turn under T (5) The gardener was busy turning under the sod (humus, manure) in the corner of the yard where the roses were to be planted. [Spading it, and turning each spadeful upside down.]

turn up **1.** T (1) The gardener turned up the soil around the fruit trees. [Dug it up with his spade and turned it upside down.] **2.** T (17) The prosecuting attorney has turned up some new evidence in the murder case. [Discovered it by investigation.]

Turn III To reach a conclusion; become known.

turn out **1.** I (4) Let me know how your experiment turns out. [What the result will be.] **2.** I (4) I hope everything will turn out all right. [Be satisfactory. Come to a good conclusion.] **3.** I (3) We thought her husband was a doctor, but he turned out to be a lawyer. [We found out that he was a lawyer.] **4.** I (3) As it turned out, he was not the only person invited to the conference. [Happened.] **5.** I (3) If the weather turns out fair, we'll have a picnic. [Becomes, happens to be.] See **fall out.**

Tutor To give private lessons.

  tutor up T (2) Albert had failed the College Entrance Exams three times. His father offered me three hundred dollars to tutor the boy up for a fourth try. [Try to teach him enough to enable him to pass.]

Type To write on a typewriter; typewrite.

  type off T (8) I asked the secretary to type off ten copies of the price list. [Produce them by typing.] See **III run off 2.**

  type out **1.** T (6,9) I want to use two paragraphs from this article in my speech tomorrow. Please type them out for me. [Make a copy of them from the article.] **2.** T (8) There is one sentence in the typed copy of my speech that I don't want to use. Please type it out. [Eliminate it by typing X's over the whole sentence.]

  type over T (7) There are too many mistakes in this letter. You'll have to type it over. [Make another copy.] See **do over 1.**

  type up **1.** T (4,8) I have to spend this evening typing up my notes. [Making a typed copy of hand written notes. Putting them in good order.] **2.** T (7) We don't have a duplicating machine so we'll have to type up as many of the forms as you will need. [Prepare them by typing.]

U

Urge To push or force along; impel with force or vigor.

  urge along T (3) Many thoughtful citizens are doing all they can to urge the civil rights cause along. [Help it to advance, make progress.]

  urge on T (II 1) Mr. Jones was not sure he wanted to run for public office, but we urged him on and he finally decided to run. [Used our influence to persuade him.]

Use To expend, consume, or exhaust by using.

  use over T (7) If the crank-case oil is very dirty it wouldn't be wise to use it over. [Put it back in the crank-case for further use.]

  use up **1.** T (4) We have used up all the soap (sugar, coffee, paper, ink, etc.). We'll have to buy some more. [Exhausted our supply of it.] **2.** T (4) At our meeting last night the chairman used up half of the time talking about things that didn't concern us. [Consumed, spent the time.] **3.** *used-up* A. (6) I feel completely used up after that long hot drive (that bitter argument, those hours of standing, etc.). [Exhausted.] See **wear out 5.**

Usher   To act as an usher; to lead, introduce or show someone or something to a place.

usher in   **1.** T (1)   Friends of the bridegroom were waiting at the church door to usher in the guests. [Take them to their seats.]   **2.** T (1,5)   Ext. The dropping of the bomb at Hiroshima ushered in the Atomic Age. [Led the world to that new period in history.]

usher out   T (2)   The judge ordered the court attendants to usher the disturbers out. [Take them outside the courtroom, by force, if necessary.]

W

Wade   To walk through water, snow, sand, or any other substance that impedes free motion or offers resistance to movement.

May be used with most of the second elements to indicate the direction of the movement.

wade across   I (1)   We came to the river and waded across since there was no bridge. [Across the river.]

wade in   **1.** I (1)   A group of young Negroes went to the segregated bathing beach and waded in, to protest against the ordinance that refused them the right. [Into the sea.]   **2.** *wade-in* N.   (1,7)   The wade-in was successful. The restrictions on Negroes using the beach were abolished. See **wade in 1.**   **3.** I (4)   Ext. After the party was over we all waded in and helped to clean up the house and do the dishes. [Worked energetically and eagerly.]

wade through   I (4)   I found it a long and tedious book, but I finally waded through, in spite of the boring style of the author.

Wait   To continue stationary or inactive in expectation of something.

wait out   T (8)   They told us Senator Smith would not speak till the end of the meeting. We decided not to wait it out, as we had to catch a train. [Stay till the end.]

wait over   I (7)   We missed our plane connection in Denver and had to wait over till 6 a.m. for a flight to Los Angeles. [Over a period of time.]

wait up   **1.** I (1,5)   Informal. Her parents waited up for her until 1 a.m. [They did not go to bed.] See **stay up.**   **2.** I (4)   Wait up for me! I can't walk so fast! [Stop, and let me catch up with you.]

Wake I   To become roused from sleep; to rouse from sleep; awake; awaken. Wake up is tending to replace wake, awake, awaken, in the folk speech.

wake up   **1.** I (12)   When we woke up the sun was shining. [Became awake.]   **2.** T (2,5)   He woke us up at 6 a.m. so we could get an early start. [Awakened us.]   **3.** I (4)   Wake up! It's time for breakfast. [Come awake.]

Wake II To become aware of something, realize what is happening.

    wake up **1.** I (17) We woke up to the fact that he had been kidding us (deceiving us, playing tricks on us). [We became aware of it.] **2.** I (5,10) When the Russians invaded Czechoslovakia it made the whole world wake up and take notice. [Called the world's attention sharply to the aggression.] **3.** T (5,10) The Russian invasion woke us up to the dangers to liberty that the invasion signified. [Made us conscious of them.]

Wall To achieve something by constructing a wall.

    wall about T (1,3) The Illyrian peasants walled their garden plots about to protect them from grazing animals. [Built stone walls around them.]

    wall in **1.** T (3) The Park Authority walled in a play area for young children. [Set off a portion of the park by building a wall.] **2.** T (3) That feeble country was walled in by enemies on every side. [Surrounded closely as if by a wall.] **3.** T (3) Living in a small prairie town, John felt himself walled in by lack of opportunity. [Restricted in his future, his prospects.]

    wall off T (3) The vegetable garden was walled off from the rest of the estate. [Separated from it by a wall.]

    wall up **1.** T (3) The new owner of the house had walled up most of the windows and all but one door, making it look like a prison. [Closed the openings with brick, stone or other material.] **2.** T (3) The police discovered that the murdered man had been walled up in a basement room of the house. [Concealed by a wall of brick, stone or other material.]

Walk To go or travel on foot at a moderate speed; take steps.

May be used with all of the second elements to indicate the direction of the movement.

    walk away (with) **1.** I (2) Marie walked away with first prize in the High School Essay Contest. [She won the contest easily.] **2.** *walk-away* N. (2) Our basketball team won the championship in a walk-away. [They won it easily.]

    walk down **1.** I (1) You have to walk down to reach their little apartment (the pet shop, the restaurant, etc.). [Down from the street level.] **2.** *walk-down* N.A. (1) He rented a little walk-down in Greenwich Village. [A studio, store, living quarters, etc., below the street level.] We found a charming little walk-down restaurant where we had dinner. [One below the street level.]

    walk in **1.** I (1) In many new houses the closets are made large enough for a person to walk in. [Enter on foot.] **2.** *walk-in* N. (1) a. A walk-in refrigerator or cold storage room. b. An easy victory. [Nixon's nomination for the Presidency was a walk-in.) **3.** *walk-in* A. (1) a. Large enough to enter on foot. [My wife insists on having walk-in clothes closets in our new house.] b. Having direct access. Not opening off a hallway or lobby. [A walk-in apartment.] c. Not having or requiring a previous appointment. [A walk-in customer; a walk-in patient; walk-in sales.]

    walk off **1.** I (2) This morning Father walked off without saying goodbye. [He left the house.] **2.** *walk off (with)* I (2) When he left the restaurant he walked off with another man's overcoat. [He was absent-minded and took a coat that was not his.] **3.** I (8) At the County Fair Mrs. Jones walked off with three first prizes for her preserves. [She won them and carried them away proudly.] **4.** I (2) During the riot young teenagers were seen walking off with T.V. sets and tape recorders. [Stealing them in broad daylight.]

walk on 1. I (I 1) His first acting experience was to walk on and stand silent near the king's throne. [Onto the stage.] **2.** I (II 1) As we were strolling along the river a man came up and spoke to Father. Father told us to walk on and he would catch up with us later. [Continue to walk.] **3.** *walk-on* N.A. (1) a. A small part in a play or other entertainment, especially one without speaking lines. [His first role was a walk-on in a production of Hamlet.] b. An entertainer or actor who plays a walk-on role. [He was a walk-on at the first performance of Hamlet.]

walk out 1. I (2,3) At a given signal all the workers put down their tools and walked out. [Out of the shop, the factory, etc.; out on strike.] **2.** *walk-out* N. (2,3) 1. The workers voted to stage a walk-out. [Go out on strike.] See **walk out 1.** 2. A number of the delegates to the convention (members of the party, people at the meeting, etc.) staged a walk-out. [Left the convention (the meeting, etc.) in protest against something.]

walk over 1. T (2) The team was out of practice and their opponents walked all over them. [Beat them easily.] **2.** *walk-over* N. (6) a. Racing. A walking or trotting over the course by a contestant who is the only starter. b. An unopposed or easy victory. [President Johnson's victory in 1964 was a walk-over. He won easily by a landslide.] c. An easy task. [Learning to play canasta is a walk-over for a person who knows how to play bridge.]

walk through 1. T (3) Theater. The director suggested we walk through the play to get the feel of it. [Read the lines without attempting to act them out completely.] **2.** *walk through* N. (3) Theater. a. A rehearsal in which physical action is combined with reading the lines of a play. b. A perfunctory performance of a script. [The director had us do a walk-through as a warm-up for the full rehearsal.] c. A television rehearsal without cameras.

walk up 1. I (1) The elevator is not running. We'll have to walk up. [Go up the stairs on foot.] **2.** *walk-up* N.A. (1) a. An apartment above the ground floor, in a building that has no elevator. [Our apartment is a fourth floor walk-up.] b. A building, especially an apartment house, that has no elevator. [They own a walk-up apartment on Third Avenue.]

Walk II To accomplish something by walking or causing to walk.

May be used with most of the second elements to indicate direction.

walk around T (1,2) When I got to the hospital the male nurse was walking my friend around to give his bad knee a work-out. [Helping him to walk.]

walk away T (6) We walked away the morning with a long stroll along the beach. [Made it pass, spent the morning walking.]

walk back T (3) After dinner we walked our friends back to their hotel which wasn't far away. [Guided them back on foot.]

Want To feel a need for, a desire for something.

May be used with most of the second elements to show the direction in which the subject wishes to move. The verbs to go, to come, to get, to be are understood between "want" and the second element.

want by I (2) Stand back a little. These people want by. [Want to go past us.]

want down I (1) The baby is crying. She wants down. [Wants to get down from the arms of the person holding her.]

want in I (1) Our dog always scratches on the door when he wants in. [Wants to come in the house.]

want off I (1) When you want off, just pull the signal cord and the driver will halt the bus at the next bus stop. [Want to get off the bus.]

want on I (1) Stop the bus. There are still some people who want on. [Want to get on the bus.]

want out I (2) Open the door, please. The cat wants out. [Wants to go outside.]

want up I (1) The baby wants up. [Wants to be up in your arms.]

Ward To defend; protect.

ward off **1.** T (2,3) The B Company succeeded in warding off the attack of the enemy guerilla attack for three hours. [Defending its position, repelling the enemy.] **2.** T (2) She took some aspirin and went to bed hoping she could ward off a cold (the flu, a headache, etc.). [Keep herself free of it.]

Warm To make or become warm; heat or become heated.

warm over **1.** T (7) She wasn't hungry enough to cook a regular meal so she warmed over some of yesterday's stew (soup, casserole, etc.). [Put it on the stove to heat it again.] **2.** *warmed-over* A. (7) My husband doesn't like it when I serve him warmed-over food. [Food cooked the day before.] **3.** (7) The candidates were using warmed-over accusations and arguments from the 1964 election. [They seemed to have no new ideas for their campaign.] See **heat over, warm up.**

warm through T (1) A huge fire in the fireplace soon warmed them through. [Made them feel completely warm.]

warm up **1.** T (3,11) There's still some coffee in the pot from breakfast. I'll warm it up and we'll talk. [Reheat it.] See **warm over. 2.** T (3) We were cold and shivery so our hostess gave us a cup of coffee (some hot tea, a highball, etc.) to warm us up. **3.** T (2) Informal. May I warm it up? [Add some hot coffee, tea, or some alcoholic beverage to what you already have in your cup or glass.] **4.** I (2,11) Athletics. The players were out on the field warming up before the start of the game. [Practicing, doing exercises to loosen their muscles.] **5.** I (2,11) Music. The orchestra (the violinist, etc.) was warming up as the auditorium began to fill. [Practicing, doing exercises, tuning their instruments, etc.] **6.** *warm up (to)* I (4) He is a man it is very difficult to warm up to. [Become friendly with, have warm feelings toward.] **7.** I (2,5) As the speaker warmed up to his subject, the audience sat quietly and listened intently. [Became emotionally stirred by what he was saying. Paid close attention to his remarks.] **8.** *warm-up* N. (2,11) An act or instance of warming up. [The athletes (the orchestra, the dancers) were having a warm-up while the spectators were taking their seats.]

Warn To give notice, advice or counsel to a person or group about possible danger.

   warn away T (2) People were standing too close to the burning building. The firemen had to warn them away. [Advise them to move back.]

   warn off T (2) Guards were stationed at either end of the weakened bridge to warn people off. [Advise them not to go onto the bridge.]

Wash To cleanse by or as if by laving with water; to saturate or dilute with water or other liquid; to carry, bring, remove, or deposit something by or as if by means of water.

   wash away **1.** T (2) The nurse washed away the dirt and dry blood from the wound before applying a bandage. [Removed it with warm water and a cleanser.] **2.** T (2) The flood washed away five houses that stood along the river bank. [Removed them from their foundations and carried them downstream.] **3.** T (2) Ext. Christian theology. The blood of Christ washes away the sins of those who believe on Him. [Removes them. Takes away the responsibility of the faithful for their sins.]

   wash down **1.** T (1,5) We spent the morning washing down the car (the kitchen walls, etc.). [Cleaning it thoroughly by removing the accumulated dirt with water and a cleanser.] **2.** T (1) Ext. He washed down his lunch with a bottle of Burgundy. [Drank a lot of wine while eating, to help the food go down.] **3.** T (1) Our boat was washed down the river by the spring flood. [The high water loosed it from its moorings and carried it along.] **4.** *wash-down* N. (1,5) I'll have to give the car a wash-down before starting on our trip. [Give it a good cleaning.]

   wash off **1.** T (1,2) Mother told the boys to wash off the mud and sand from their feet before coming into the house. [Rinse their feet.] **2.** T (1,2) She washed off the kitchen table after carving up the chickens. [Removed the blood stains and soiled spots from the table top.] **3.** T (7) In panning for gold, the prospector washes off his pay dirt. [He uses swirling water to carry away the gravel while the gold sinks to the bottom of the pan.] **4.** *wash-off* N. (7) I think I'll give the car a wash-off before we start. [A quick washing, not as thorough as a wash-down.]

   wash out **1.** T (1) She washed out the stains on her napkins in lukewarm water, before they had time to set. [Removed them by washing.] **2.** I (9) The stains wash out easily if they don't have time to dry. [They come out with washing.] **3.** T (9) After doing up the dishes she washed out the tea towels. [Gave them a washing to remove soil and stains.] **4.** T (9) A flash flood had washed out two bridges, a railroad embankment and a section of the highway. [It demolished them and swept them away.] **5.** I,T (4) Slang. Poor John! He washed out of college (was washed out of college) in the last quarter of his Senior year. [He failed, was dismissed from college.] **6.** T (6) During the storm many of the boats along the beach were washed out to sea. [Driven out to sea by the action of wind and water.] **7.** *wash-out* n. (5,7) a. A washing out especially of an embankment, or roadway, by heavy rain or a flash flood. [Last night's storm caused a wash-out on the Union Pacific line east of town.] b. Damage caused or a hole left by the surging water. [There was a wash-out where the bridge should have been.] c. Informal. An utter failure. [John was a wash-out when it came to chemistry. He failed it badly.] [His latest play proved to be a wash-out. It "flopped", was not a success.] **8.** *washed-out* a. (1,8) 1. Her clothes all have a washed-out appearance. [They look faded, as though all the color had been removed by washing.] b. Informal. Poor Marie! She looks all washed-out. [Weary, exhausted, pale, lifeless.]

wash up **1.** I (2,11) Children! Dinner's ready! It's time to wash up. [Wash your face and hands.] **2.** I (2,8) You go in and read your newspaper. I'll wash up. [Wash the dishes, pots, and pans after a meal.] **3.** I (2,8) We always hire a woman to wash up after a party. [Do all the cleaning necessary to put the dining room and kitchen in good order.] **4.** T (1) During the hurricane dozens of boats were washed up on the beach. [Driven there by the action of the sea water.] **5.** *wash-up* N. (3,7) a. The act of washing up. [We have plenty of time for a thorough wash-up before sitting down to dinner.] b. A place where one can wash up. [Their new house has a wash-up close to the tennis court.] **6.** *washed-up* A. (6) Informal. Without a future. [Having failed to win this election, he is all washed-up as a politician.]

Watch To be alert, on the lookout; be careful or cautious.

watch out **1.** I (1,2) Watch out! There's a car coming. [Be careful! Watch your step! Don't step in front of the car!] **2.** *watch out (for)* I (1,9) On the freeways you have to watch out for reckless drivers (drunken drivers, speeders, etc.). [Be on the alert for danger from other cars.] **3.** I (9) Grandmother watched out for the baby while its parents went in swimming. [Took care of it.] **4.** I (9) The court appointed a guardian to watch out for the interests of the orphaned children. [Manage their business affairs. Arrange for their housing and welfare.] **5.** I (10) When you go shopping watch out for some bargains in bedding. [Keep your eyes open. Try to find some good buys.] **6.** *watch-out* N. (1,9) The act of looking out for or anticipating something. [Be on the watch-out for thieves (shoplifters, trickery, embezzlers, etc.).] [The police kept a watch-out for concealed weapons in the crowd.] See **look-out.**

Water To moisten or dilute with or as if with water.

water down **1.** T (6)   The army cook watered down the soup when he was told there would be fifty extra men to feed. [Diluted it by adding water.]   **2.** T (6) Old New England grocers used to water down their vinegar to increase their profits. [Adulterate it with water.]   **3.** T (1)   The town watered down the dirt road. [Sprinkled it to reduce the dust.] See **wet down.**   **4.** T (6)   The House of Representatives watered down the Civil Rights bill that the Senate had passed. [Made it weaker, by adding something to it. Reduced the strong language of the bill.]   **5.** *watered-down* A.   (6) a. Weakened. [The final bill was only a watered-down version of the original.] b. Diluted. [The bar-man served us watered-down Martinis. Cocktails diluted with water.]

Wean   To detach or alienate the affections or loyalty of a person to some other person, cause or belief.

wean away **1.** T (2,3)   His girlfriend tried to wean him away from his close family ties. [Get him to center his affections on her rather than on his family.] **2.** T (2,3)   The McCarthy campaign weaned many young radicals away from the Democratic Party regulars. [Caused them to withdraw their support.]

Wear   To impair or diminish by use. To become impaired; deteriorate from hard use.

wear away **1.** T (2,4)   The tramping of many feet had worn away the steps at the entrance to the cathedral. [Eroded them by constant friction.]   **2.** I (2,4) The paint on the floor had worn away near the doorways. [Disappeared through much usage.]   **3.** I (4,6)   The hours of his imprisonment wore away in dull, monotonous routine. [The time passed slowly in a cheerless way.]

wear down **1.** T (1,2)   The old man had worn his teeth down to the gums from biting on his pipe. [Reduced their size.]   **2.** T (2)   Giving birth to and caring for ten children had worn her down till she was completely exhausted, and only a shadow of her former self. [Made her tired and very thin.]   **3.** I (2,6)   The heels of her shoes had worn down. She had to have them repaired. [They had become reduced in size through use.]   **4.** *worn-down* A.   (6)   She was in a terribly worn-down condition as a result of her last operation.

wear off **1.** T (1,9)   Time and the elements had worn off the inscription on the monument. [Caused it to disappear.]   **2.** I (1,10)   The effects of the drug (the alcohol, the fright, the emotional disturbance, etc.) had worn off after a good night's sleep. [They had disappeared.]

wear on **1.** I (II 1)   As time wore on she began to forget the tragedy. [The memory of it diminished with time.]   **2.** T (II 1)   As the day wore on, it got colder. [The wind freshened as the hours passed.]

wear out **1.** T (8)   Johnny has already worn out two pairs of shoes this winter. [Worn them till they are no longer of use.]   **2.** I (8)   His last pair of shoes wore out in two months. [They became unusable in that length of time.]   **3.** T (8) Ext. Mary wore her mother out with her complaints about not having enough clothes. [Made her mother feel weary, irritated, nervous.]   **4.** T (9)   Don't stay so long at the Smith's that you will wear out your welcome. [Cause your hosts to be weary, tired of you, irritated by you.] **5.** *worn-out* A. (7) a. Worn or used until no longer serviceable. [Father had on a pair of worn-out slippers.] b. Physically or nervously exhausted. [I'm completely worn out after that argument with the children about homework.] See **do in 2, do up 5, drag out 5, pooped out, tired out, used up.**

Weed To root out or remove weeds; get rid of something superfluous or harmful.

weed out 1. T (9) The gardener spent the morning weeding out the thistles, wild lettuce and purslane from the garden. [Removing them by pulling or digging.] **2.** T (1,4) After this rain it will be a good time to weed out the onion patch (the flower beds, etc.). [Cull the weeds from them.] **3.** T (1,4) Recently the club's membership committee was given the job of weeding out the undesirable members and sending them notice that they were being dropped. [Removing them from the list of members.]

Weigh I To measure, separate, or apportion a certain quantity of something according to weight.

weigh in 1. T (4,11) Boxing, wrestling. The medical examiner weighed the two contestants in at 9 a.m. [He determined their respective weights in preparation for the bout that was to follow.] **2.** I (4) Gonzalez weighed in at 170 pounds; Robinson at 178. [That was their registered weight.] **3.** I (5) Racing. The jockey must weigh in after each race. [Be weighed with his saddle and the weights the horse must carry.] **4.** *weigh-in* N. (4,6) Sports. An act or instance of weighing in at the start of a contest. [After the weigh-in the fighters posed for photographs.]

weigh out T (9) The grocer weighed out five pounds of sugar for Mrs. Jones. [Took it from a container and put it on the scales for weighing.]

Weigh II To press or exert pressure as by a heavy weight.

weigh down 1. T (1) The boxes of heavy dishes in the trunk weighed the car down. [Made the springs sag down.] **2.** T (2,6) Marion was weighed down by all the family cares and the fear of losing her health. [She was sad, despondent, weary.]

Welcome To greet cordially; receive with courtesy or pleasure.

May be used with most of the second elements to indicate the location or direction of the action.

welcome back 1. T (3) The Nelsons returned last week from a trip around the world. We welcomed them back with a big party. [Expressed our pleasure at their return.] **2.** T (4) After a long, cold winter it is a joy to welcome back the robins. [Great them as heralds of returning spring.]

welcome in T (4) At the banquet the speaker gave a little toast to welcome in the new members of the club. [Express pleasure at having them as members.]

Well To rise, spring, or gush to the surface.

well out I (3) A cool, clear spring welled out from under the cliff. [Came flowing.]

well up 1. I (1) When the cap was removed from the metal casing a flood of petroleum came welling up. [Up from below the earth.] **2.** I (1) The tears welled up in her eyes as she saw her son receive his degree. [They began to flow.] **3.** I (1,4) Profound emotion welled up in our hearts as we watched the parade of the returned heroes. [It arose, seemed to flow.]

Wet To make something wet by moistening with a liquid such as water.

wet down T (1) The roadworkers wet down the newly graded road to keep the dust under control. [Sprinkled it with water.] See **water down.**

wet through **1.** I (1) My jacket has wet through. I'll take it off and put on my sweater. [The rain has penetrated the whole jacket.] **2.** T (1) We were caught in a downpour that wet us through (through and through). [Penetrated all our clothing.]

Wheel I To turn on an axis; revolve.

wheel about/around **1.** I (3) When he heard a shout he wheeled about (around) to see who was calling. [He spun around.] **2.** I (3) The planets wheel around the sun. [Revolve around it.]

Wheel II To move on wheels, roll.

May be used with all of the second elements to indicate direction.

wheel along I (3) We were wheeling along at sixty-five miles an hour when a tire blew out. [Moving smoothly and briskly.]

While To cause time to pass, especially in some easy or pleasant manner.

while away T (4,6) Waiting for the concert to begin we whiled away the time in pleasant conversation. [Spent the time.]

Whip To strike with or as if with a slender and flexible implement, as a last; to prepare hurriedly.

whip down T (1) When the dogs started jumping up on the wagon the driver whipped them down. [Used a whip to force them down.]

whip in **1.** T (6) Hunting. A professional or honorary member of a hunt staff has the duty of preventing the hounds from wandering away from the pack. He whips them in. [Drives them back to the pack by cracking his whip at them.] **2.** *whipper-in* N. (6) The whipper-in at a fox hunt assists the huntsman with the hounds.

whip off T (1,9) The reporter returned to his hotel and whipped off a report on the street riots. [Wrote it quickly.] See **dash off 2**.

whip up **1.** T (2,5) When the coachman saw the bandits riding towards him he whipped up his horses. [Struck them with his whip to make them go faster.] **2.** T (2,5) Richard is traveling about the state trying to whip up interest in and enthusiasm for the proposed liquor law. [He is trying to arouse the voters, get them to take an interest in it.] See **stir up**. **3.** T (2,4) Hitler and Goebbels were the sort of speakers who could whip up a crowd to a frenzy. [Stir them to an unreasoning emotional state.] **4.** T (7,11) Aunt Jane is in the kitchen whipping up a cake. [Preparing the ingredients hurriedly, partly by whipping them together.] **5.** T (7,11) The young people are whipping up a little entertainment (a show, a skit, a picnic, a dance, etc.) for their weekend guests. [Preparing it quickly, informally.]

Whip II   To move or go quickly or suddenly.

May be used with most of the second elements to indicate the direction of the movement.

whip around   I (3)   The man walking in front of us suddenly whipped around and began shooting angrily. [Turned sharply around facing us.]

whip back   I (3)   We dashed out to the suburbs and then whipped back in time for the boxing match. [Back into town at a fast rate.]

whip out   **1.** T (1)   As the sheriff approached him the bandit suddenly whipped out a pistol and began firing. [Drew it quickly from his holster, shirt, pocket, etc.]   **2.** T (1)   One of the young mobsters whipped out a switch blade knife and attacked a policeman. [Drew it suddenly from his pocket.]

whip through   I (3)   Theater. We just have time to whip through Scene 2 before the curtain goes up. [Hold a quick rehearsal of part of the play.]

Whistle   To make a shrill sound by forcing the breath through the puckered lips; summon by or as if by such a sound.

whistle up   **1.** T (7)   Whistle up the dogs. [Call them by whistling.]   **2.** T (7)   Poor Bob! I doubt that he'll ever whistle up enough courage to ask Susie to marry him. [Summon it as if by whistling.]

Whoop   To utter a loud cry or shout in expressing enthusiasm or excitement.

whoop out   T (9)   The crowd in the football stadium whooped out their anger at the decision of the umpire. [Yelled angrily.]

whoop (it) up   **1.** T (5)   Informal. The publicity agents began whooping it up for the circus in the spring. [Making noisy publicity.]   **2.** T (5,6)   Slang. The boys in the back room (of the saloon) were whooping it up. [Being very noisy, laughing, singing, rough-housing.]

Whoosh   To move swiftly with a gushing or hissing noise.

May be used with many of the second elements to indicate direction.

whoosh by   I (2)   Our motel room faced on the freeway. We heard the cars whooshing by all night. [Passing with a rushing sound.]

Widen   To make or become wide or wider.

widen out   **1.** I (10)   The narrow valley widens out into a flat plain with prosperous looking farms. [It broadens.]   **2.** I (10)   A bell usually widens out at the base. [Becomes wider.]

Wilt   To become limp and drooping, as a fading flower.

wilt down   I (1,2)   Because of the 100° heat, the flowers in the garden, so tall and fresh in the morning, had wilted down. [Were bending over, or lying flat on the ground.]

Win   To gain a victory; gain the support of someone.

win back   T (5)   Gambling. He lost $200 during the first two hours of play, but won it back before the evening was over. [Regained the $200.]

win out   **1.** I (4)   There were three other proposals at the meeting, but his own finally won out. [Defeated the other proposals.]   **2.** I (9)   You think that your chances of success are very poor, but if you follow my advice I'm sure you'll win out. [Have success.]

win over   T (3)   Nelson at first was opposed to our plan but we won him over with our arguments. [Brought him to our point of view.] See **bring around.**

win through   I (4)   His life had been a long series of misfortunes, but he won through with the help of a wonderful wife. [Succeeded in making a satisfactory life.]

Wind I   To move in a circuitous course, bending, turning in different directions. May be used with most of the second elements to indicate the direction of the movement.

wind around   I (2)   The road wound around through the forest and finally came out near a village. [Here and there.]

wind back   I (3)   The river cut a channel to the eastern edge of the canyon then wound back to the western side. [Returned towards its original location.]

wind down   I (1)   From the top of the hill a steep path wound down to the valley floor. [Down the hill.]

Wind II   To come to a stop or conclusion; bring to an end.

wind up   **1.** I (13)   We lost our way due to several wrong turns on the country roads, and finally wound up in Cheshire. [Arrived there after changing directions several times.] See **end up 1, land up.**   **2.** I (16)   We had a hard time deciding who to vote for in the election, but wound up voting for Adams. [Finally made the decision after much debate and hesitation.]   **3.** T (13)   We wound up the meeting by voting to adjourn until November. [Finished it, did the actions necessary to bring it to an end.]   **4.** T (4)   Mr. White wound up his campaign for the presidency with a speech in Philadelphia. [Ended it.]   **5.** T (4)   After being transferred to Chicago Mr. Black wound up his affairs in San Diego and left on September 1st. [Sold or disposed of his interests in San Diego. Closed them out.]   **6.** I (16)   If you're not careful you'll wind up in prison. [If you continue to violate laws (commit crimes, misbehave, etc.) they will put you in prison.]   **7.** *wind-up* N.   (3,8)   a. The process of concluding an action or activity [They planned to have the wind-up of the campaign in Philadelphia.] b. The end or close. [We were late for the meeting. We came in at the wind-up.]

Wind II   To twist or roll with a spiral motion; cause to tighten by or as if by turning a key.

wind off   T (1,2)   She wound off enough yarn from the ball to make a pair of mittens for the baby. [Removed it by a winding motion.]

wind up   **1.** T (3,8)   He saved all the string from the packages and wound it up into a ball. [Made it compact, tight, by winding.]   **2.** T (2,4)   Don't forget to wind up the clock before you go to bed. [Make the spring tight, tense, by turning the key.]   **3.** I (4,11)   Baseball. As the pitcher was winding up, the man on second base tried to steal third base. [Making a circling motion with his arm, preparatory to pitching the ball.] **4.** *wind-up* N. (4,11) Baseball. A preparatory arm motion prior to delivering a pitch. [Pitcher Gonzalez has an unusual wind-up.] **5.** *wound up* A. (2,6) In a state of great tension or excitement. [He was so wound up after the debate that he had trouble getting to sleep.

Winter To spend or pass the winter.

winter over I (3) The snapdragons wintered over very well this year. We'll have early bloom. [They survived the cold, the freezing.]

Wipe To remove by rubbing.

wipe off **1.** T (7) Mary used a dish towel to wipe off the table. [Remove dirt, crumbs, etc., by wiping.] **2.** T (7) He wiped off his forehead with his handkerchief. [Removed the sweat by mopping it off.] **3.** T (7) The tough drill sergeant told the new recruit to wipe that smile off his face. [Remove it as if by wiping his face.]

wipe out: **1.** T (6) The teacher wiped out what she had written on the blackboard. [Used an eraser, sponge, or cloth to remove the words from the board.] **2.** T (9) A series of earthquakes wiped out ten villages in Eastern Iran. [Destroyed them completely.] **3.** T (9) Modern medicine has succeeded in wiping out tuberculosis in many parts of the world. [Eliminating it.] **4.** T (4,9) The Wall Street crash wiped out many stock-market gamblers. [Ruined them financially.] **5.** T (8) The Marines wiped out three machine-gun nests with hand grenades. [Destroyed them, killing the machine gunners.]

wipe up **1.** T (1) Mary wiped up the milk the baby had spilled on the floor. [Removed it by using a cloth or sponge to soak it up.] **2.** T (4,5) Ext. Our basketball team wiped up the floor with the Boston team. [Defeated them by a large score.]

Wire I To fasten or bind with wire.

wire back T (2) He opened the gate to the corral and wired it back so it wouldn't swing shut. [Fastened it back against the fence with wire.]

wire on T (I 1) The hinges of the trunk were broken so he had to wire the lid on. [Secure it to the trunk with wire.]

wire up T (3,4) Before leaving their summer cabin for the winter he wired up all the openings to keep out animals and intruders. [Covered the openings with wire mesh.]

Wire II To send a message by telegraph. See **telegraph**.

wire back I (3) Father told James to wire back as soon as he reached the university. [Send a telegram home.]

wire in T (1) The editor told the reporter to wire in any new developments in the murder case. [Send his report to the office by wire.]

Wise Slang. To make or become aware of or knowledgeable about a situation or attitude of which one has been ignorant.

wise up **1.** I (4) He suddenly wised up to the fact that they had been joking.

[Realized, became aware of the fact.] **2.** T (12) His wife is going out with another man. Someone should wise him up. [Tell him about it.]

Wither   To lose the freshness of youth, as from age.

    wither away **1.** I (4) Though only fifty years old, her beauty was fast withering away. [Disappearing as she grew older.] **2.** I (4) Ext. Marxist doctrine claims that under Communism the state will gradually wither away. [Disappear as a way of organizing society.]

Wolf   To devour voraciously as would a wolf.

    wolf down T (1) Slang. The hungry boys wolfed down their sandwiches and asked for more. [Ate them greedily.] See **hog down.**

Work I   To bring about, accomplish something by work, effort.

    work away I (6) When we found Robert out in the garage he was working away on the car engine. [Occupied busily with his work.]

    work in **1.** T (2) She put some ointment on his sore shoulder and worked it in with gentle rubbing. [Made it penetrate the skin.] **2.** T (4) The doctor was very busy but said he could work me in at three o'clock. [Give me an appointment for that time.] **3.** T (4) Mrs. Jones urged us to see the Nureyev Swan Lake when we were in New York. We said we'd try to work it in. [Find a place on our schedule for it.]

    work off **1.** T (2,5) He worked off ten pounds by doing push-ups and jogging two miles every morning. [Reduced his weight by that much exercise.] **2.** T (2,5) John worked off his anger by chopping wood. [Made his angry feelings disappear.] **3.** T (2,8) The farmers worked off their taxes by doing work on the roads. [Avoided having to pay taxes in money.]

    work out **1.** T (7) The students worked out their math problems at the blackboard. [Solved their problems.] **2.** T (7) At the Summit Meeting in Paris the diplomats were working out an agreement on nuclear weapons. [Making an effort to find one.] **3.** T (7) I asked the travel agent to work out a schedule for a round the world trip. [Do the research necessary to arrange the trip.] **4.** T (9) Albert worked out his debt to Mr. Adams by painting his house. [Paid the debt by working.] **5.** T (9) The mine was abandoned when it had been worked out. [Exhausted of all the ore.] **6.** T (7) He worked out a plan for rebuilding the slum areas of Cleveland. [Produced, devised a plan.] **7.** I (9) I hope his plan for rebuilding the slum areas works out. [Is successful.] **8.** I (9) I'm sure everything will work out all right. [Will turn out to be a success, have a good result.] **9.** I (10) Sports. The boxers (wrestlers, track men, etc.) were working out at the gym. [Doing practice exercises, etc., to put themselves in good physical condition.] **10.** *worked-out* A. (7) a. Fully exploited; exhausted. [In the next valley we ran across a worked-out gold mine.] b. Physically or mentally exhausted. [I'm all worked out. I can do no more.] **11.** *work-out* N. (10) a. Athletics. A trial or practice session as in running, boxing, football. [The team had a work-out yesterday afternoon.] b. A training session or rehearsal.

[The debate team (the cast of the play, etc.) had a work-out last night.] c. Physical
exercise. [He goes to the gym for a work-out twice a week.]

work over   **1.** T (2)   Slang. The gangsters threatened to work him over if he
didn't tell them where the money was hidden. [Beat him, torture him, use force
on him.]   **2.** *working-over* N.   (2)   After giving him a good working-over they
threw him out of the car and left him to die. See **work over 1**.

work up   **1.** T (2,11)   I'm trying to work up enough energy to spade the garden
today. [Get enough strength, get into the mood for hard work.]   **2.** T (9)   He
worked up a sweat by running around the block three times. [Made himself
perspire freely.]   **3.** T (2,5)   Hitler's speeches to the multitudes worked up the
passions and enthusiasm of his hearers so that they would shout their approval of
his policies. [He aroused their emotions, stirred them up.]   **4.** T (7,11)   The
young radicals worked up a scheme for taking over the Liberal Party. [Prepared,
elaborated it.]   **5.** T (2,11)   Alice is working up her typing in preparation for
her new secretarial job. [Practicing, perfecting it.]   **6.** *worked-up* A. (2,6)
Emotionally aroused; upset. [Mother is all worked-up over the irresponsible way
the girls are behaving.]

Work II   To go or cause to go by sustained effort, usually against an obstacle, or in
difficult circumstances.

May be used with all the second elements to indicate the direction of the movement.
Often used with "one's way". See **fight one's way**.

work (one's way) along   I (3)   He worked along (his way along) through the
underbrush till he came to the river bank. [Made progress slowly, against ob-
stacles.]

work (one's way) around   I (2,3)   The scout, crawling on his stomach, worked
around (his way around) to where he could observe the enemy camp. [Made
progress slowly, with effort.]

work (one's way) back   I (3)   After counting the number of the enemy troops he
worked back (his way back) to his unit.

work (one's way) in   I (1)   Climbing to the second floor of the house he worked in
(his way in) through a small window. [Into the house.]

work (one's way) through   I (4)   If Charles wants to go to college he'll have to
work his way through. [Earn enough money to pay his college expenses.]

work (one's way) up   I (2,12)   Jones worked his way up from office boy to president
of the company. [Worked steadily and efficiently and was promoted to higher
rank from time to time.]

Worm I   To move or act like a worm; creep, crawl, or advance slowly or stealthily.
Usually with "one's way". See **fight one's way**.

May be used with many of the second elements.

worm (one's way) back   I (4)   He had been discharged from his job, but he wormed his way back into the good graces of the boss and was rehired. [Used promises,
flattery, etc., to regain the favor of the boss.]

worm (one's way) in   I (6)   We really didn't want him in our club, but he succeeded in worming his way in. [Probably by flattering and cajoling some of the members.]

worm (one's way) up   I (2)   He wormed his way up through the ranks and was eventually made a Captain. [Used flattery and devious means to gain advancement.]

Worm II   To get a result by persistent, insidious efforts.

worm out   T (3)   It took him a long time to worm the secret out of her. [Persuade her to tell him the secret.]

Worry   To progress or succeed by constant effort in the presence of difficulties.

worry along   I (3)   She worried along for years without telling anyone about her husband's fatal illness. [Felt anxious but kept it to herself.]

worry through   I (4)   In spite of all his financial difficulties he managed to worry through, and end up with enough to keep the family going. [Reach a stage where the worries ended.] See **get by.**

Wrap   To enclose or envelop by winding or folding.

wrap around: **1.** T (3)   It's the type of robe which just wraps around without buttoning or pinning. [Around the body.]   **2.** *wrap-around* A.   (3)   a. Made with a full-length opening that overlaps to fit the body. [I like the convenience of a wrap-around robe.] b. Curved to fit a contour. [The car has a wrap-around windshield.]

wrap up   **1.** T (7)   Mother was busy wrapping up the Christmas presents and putting name tags on them. [Doing them up in special Christmas paper.] See **bag up.**   **2.** T (3,11)   She wrapped up the children warmly before letting them out to play in the snow. [Put warm clothing on them and fastened it securely.] See **bundle up.**   **3.** T (8)   Informal. Let's wrap up the meeting (the job, etc.) and go home. [Finish it. Put everything in good order.]   **4.** T (4,8)   Sports. The Dodgers wrapped up the game in the ninth inning. [Made enough points to claim the victory.]   **5.** *wrap-up* N.   (4,8)   A report, especially a final report summarizing the highlights of a presentation which has just been given. [The newscaster gave a wrap-up of the evening news.] [Will you please give us a wrap-up of the arguments made by each speaker in the debate?]   **6.** *wrapped up (in)* A.   (4)   Our son is all wrapped up in his work (his girlfriend, his ski lessons, etc.). [He is involved, giving all his attention to it.]

Write   To communicate by or as if by putting words on paper; form or record with a series of inscribed characters.

write back   I (3)   I wrote him a letter asking him to come next week, and he wrote back that it was impossible. [Answered my letter.]

write down   **1.** T (7)   She wrote down the address and phone number of the man who called. [Down on a pad or in a notebook.]   **2.** T (7)   You can write me down for $50.00. [Put my name on your list as one who will give $50.00.] See

put down. 3. I (2) His critics accuse him of writing down to his public. [Using simple language as to people of inferior intelligence.]

write in 1. I (1) One of our subscribers has written in to complain about one of our editorials. [Into the newspaper office.] **2.** T (1) On the ballot there is a space where you can write in the name of a candidate you prefer, whose name is not on the ballot. **3.** *write-in* N.A. (1) a. Written onto the ballot by the voter. [A write-in vote, a write-in candidate.] b. A candidate or vote for a candidate not listed on the printed ballot. [Write-ins may swing the election.]

write off 1. T (4) The company wrote off the $1200 owed them by the soldier who had been killed in action. [Canceled the account as uncollectable.] **2.** T (4) The new equipment in the factory was written off in three years. [It was amortized. It had been paid for.] **3.** T (2) The campaign manager wrote off the attempts of the candidate to win the South. [Considered them to be of no value towards winning the election.] **4.** *write-off* N. (4) a. A cancellation from the accounts as a loss. b. An uncollectable account. c. A reduction in book value, depreciation.

write out 1. T (9) He wrote out his speech in long hand and gave it to the typist. [Put it into writing.] **2.** T (9) I'm not sure I can remember your instructions in detail. Please write them out for me. [Write them in full form; state them completely.] **3.** T (8) Mason's novel is not as good as his earlier ones. He seems to have written himself out. [Written so much that he no longer is able to produce good writing.]

write up 1. T (4,8) John is busy writing up a report (his notes, the lecture, etc.). [Putting it in writing, with all the details.] **2.** T (2) He spent the weekend writing up his diary (expense account, travels, etc.). [Bringing them up to date; adding the latest facts.] **3.** T (8,11) The new reporter was given the job of writing up the Democratic Convention. [Preparing an account for publication.] **4.** T (4,5) Henry did a good job of writing up the achievements of the City Commission. [Presenting a favorable picture of their activities.] **5.** T (2) Accounting. To make an excessive valuation of assets, etc. **6.** *write-up* N. (4,9) a. A written description or review, favorable or unfavorable, as in a newspaper or magazine. [The movie got a good write-up in *Life*.] [The play had a terrible write-up in the *Times*.] b. Accounting. An increase in the book value of a corporation which is not warranted by the true assets of the corporation.

Y

Yell To shout or scream loudly.

May be used with most of the second elements to indicate the direction of the action.

yell around T (2) Informal. Don't go yelling around that you didn't get a chance to express your ideas. [Complain in a loud voice.]

yell back   T (5)   I yelled to him to come down out of the tree and he yelled back that he was safe. [Back to me.]

Yellow   To become yellow.

yellow off   I (9)   The strawberry plants look sick. They're yellowing off. [Losing their green color, perhaps from chlorosis.]

Yoke   To join or couple by means of a yoke.

yoke up   1. T (3,11)   The peasant yoked up a team of oxen to his plow and started the day's work. [Placed the yoke on their necks and fastened it to the plow.]   **2.** I (3)   Informal. I wouldn't yoke up with a person like that if I were you. [Become involved, closely tied to him.]

Z

Zero   To bring a missile into exact aim for a target.

zero in   1. I (5)   The rocket launchers zeroed in on the ammunition dump. [Aimed their missile so that it would strike the dump.]   **2.** I (5)   The fighter planes zeroed in and sprayed the enemy outpost with machine gun fire. [Flew their planes into position for successful strafing of the outpost.]   **3.** I (5)   Ext. The next speaker zeroed in on the misstatements (the errors, the arguments, etc.) of the opposing speaker. [Aimed his verbal fire at them. Struck at them.]

Zig-zag   To proceed on a course consisting of a series of short sharp turns in alternating directions.

May be used with many of the second elements to indicate direction.

zig-zag across   I (1)   Football. The quarter-back caught the ball on the right side of the field and zig-zagged across for a gain of five yards. [To the other side of the field in a series of dodges to left and right.]

zig-zag down   I (1)   Skiing. In the slalom race the skiers zig-zag down through a series of poles or gates. [Make alternate sharp turns between the poles as they come down.]

Zip I   To move or convey with speed and energy.

May be used with most of the second elements to indicate the direction of the action.

zip along   I (3)   They zipped along at 85 miles per hour in their little sports car. [Moved easily at high speed.]

zip back   T (3)   I'll zip you back to the hotel in ten minutes time. [Drive you there speedily.]

zip through   I (4)   The examination wasn't very long or hard. We zipped through in forty minutes. [Finished it easily.]

Zip II   To add vitality or zest to.

zip up   1. T (2,5)   You could zip up that salad by using a bit more garlic. [Make it more tasty, flavorsome.]   **2.** T (2,5)   The second act of the play was rather dull.

The director had to make many changes to zip up the action. [Make it move faster, give it more life.]

Zip III   To fasten or unfasten with a zipper.

   zip in   T (1)   As soon as the scuba diver put on his suit I zipped him in. [Pulled the zippers that closed the openings.]

   zip out   T (1)   John, will you please zip me out? I can't reach the zipper. [Pull the zipper down so I can get out of my dress.]

   zip up   **1.** T (1,3)   He zipped up his windbreaker before climbing into the plane. [Pulled the zipper up to close the jacket tight.]   **2.** T (3)   She asked her husband to zip her up. [Pull up the zipper on the back of her dress.] See **button up.**

Zoom   To move quickly or suddenly with a loud humming or buzzing sound, as insects or motor driven vehicles.

May be used with all the second elements to indicate the direction of the movement.

   zoom around   I (2)   A big bumble-bee was zooming around inside the car and we had to stop to drive it out. [Making a loud buzz as it flew about.]

   zoom by   I (2)   We stood up and waved as the racing cars zoomed by. [Buzzed past us.]

   zoom over   I (1,3)   Five planes zoomed over in V formation. [Flew above our heads with a loud humming noise.]